JAYAPRAKASH NARAYAN
SELECTED WORKS
Volume Two (1936 – 1939)

Jayaprakash Narayan

SELECTED WORKS

Volume Two (1936-1939)

Edited by

BIMAL PRASAD

Issued under the auspices of

Nehru Memorial Museum & Library

MANOHAR
2026

First published 2001
Reprinted 2021, 2022, 2023, 2026

ISBN 978-81-7304-353-6 (Series)

ISBN 978-81-7304-387-1 (Vol. II)

Published by
Ajay Kumar Jain *for*
Manohar Publishers & Distributors
4753/23 Ansari Road, Daryaganj
New Delhi 110 002

Printed at
Replika Press Pvt. Ltd.

CONTENTS

ILLUSTRATIONS

FOREWORD

It gives me great pleasure to place before the readers the second volume of *Jayaprakash Narayan: Selected Works* covering the years 1936-9. These were crucial years in the history of India's struggle for freedom as well as the growth of the socialist movement. J.P. played an important role in both. His was the main role in not only organising the Congress Socialist Party but also in formulating its ideology and programmes. This volume brings to light important policy matters of the party, and J.P.'s own views on various issues like the provincial elections of 1937, the formation of ministries in the provinces, the Congress and mass contact, the Kisan movement, the Tripuri Congress and presidential election thereof, and the relations between the C.S.P. and the Communists. The most important window to J.P.'s mind is provided by his well-known work, *Why Socialism?* which is not easily available now. The volume, thus, should go a long way in adding to the source material for understanding the history of India between 1936 and 1939 and especially the nature of the socialist ideology in the 1930s in the context of the freedom struggle.

Nehru Memorial Museum & Library O.P. KEJARIWAL
New Delhi
26 March 2001

ACKNOWLEDGEMENTS

It is a pleasure to put on record my appreciation of the help rendered by all my colleagues in the preparation of this volume. As in the case of the previous volume, Dr. O.P. Kejariwal, Director, Nehru Memorial Museum & Library, took keen interest in the early completion of this volume and was always ready with whatever help and cooperation were required in this regard. I am most grateful to him for his support.

The late Dr. Hari Dev Sharma closely worked with me on this volume till his retirement from NMML in July 1999. He was a tower of strength and I could safely rely on him for any advice or help I required. It is a matter of regret that he did not live to see the present volume, as also the first volume, in print before he passed away in August 2000.

Shri A.K. Awasthi and Shri S.L. Manchanda, who also left the project shortly after Dr. Sharma's retirement, helped in the collection of material for this volume and I am grateful to them for this. Smt. Sangita Mallik, who had left even earlier, continued to help and I am thankful to her for this. I am also thankful to Dr. (Smt.) Maya Gupta, Shri S.S.A. Abidi and Shri V.D. Lakhanpal, who remain formally associated with the project, for their valuable contribution.

Last, but not least, I may mention the contributions made by Km. Deepa Bhatnagar, Dr. (Km.) Amrit Varsha Gandhi, Smt. Usha Gururaj and Smt. Usha Ali in not merely arranging the material, but also preparing biographical notes. My thanks are due to all of them. While all have helped sincerely and to the best of their abilities, I would like to especially mention Km. Deepa Bhatnagar's contribution. She has been of great help to me in coordinating the work on this volume as editor and in seeing it through the press.

I am also thankful to Shri Deshraj, Administrative Officer, NMML, for his cooperation as and when required. Km. Deepa Sharma made her contribution by preparing the typescript and I am thankful to her for this. I must also thank Shri Anand Bhushan Sharma for his willingness to help whenever required, even though not formally associated with the project.

BIMAL PRASAD

INTRODUCTION

This volume begins with *Why Socialism?* authored by J.P. and published in early January 1936, and includes his other writings, statements, speeches and letters up to the eve of the outbreak of the Second World War in the first week of September 1939. Ever since the formation of the Congress Socialist Party in 1934 J.P. had been carrying on the major responsibility for its organisation. With the publication of *Why Socialism?*, noted alike for clarity of thought and forceful expression, he emerged also as its leading theoretician. Here he seeks to explain the theory of socialism, its applicability to Indian conditions, the programme of the Congress Socialist Party, the deficiencies of other systems of thought, particularly Gandhism, considered by many as an alternative to socialism, and the political strategy to be followed by the C.S.P. in furtherance of its objectives in the context of the ongoing struggle for freedom.

This treatise on socialism makes it clear that although J.P. had decided to keep away from the Communist Party of India, which was functioning under the guidance of the Comintern, dominated by the Communist Party of the Soviet Union, and joined his colleagues and friends in founding another party, his faith in Marxism, acquired during student days in the U.S.A. in the late 1920s, remained intact. Thus in the first chapter entitled 'The Foundation of Socialism', he asserts that there is 'only one type, one theory of socialism—Marxism'. Though he recognises that there are differences between various groups of socialists on the question of methods and tactics, he emphasises that till then only communists had vindicated their theory of tactics by their 'great and remarkable success in Russia'. This is followed by an elucidation of socialism on the basis of a typically Marxist approach. Socialism, J.P. points out, is a system of social reconstruction and not a code of personal conduct. It cannot be established by a group of idealists without power. On the other hand, a socialist party in power can establish socialism provided it has sufficient power of coercion or sufficient popular support to deal with resistance by vested interests. The root cause of inequality in wealth lies in the fact that the gifts of nature as well as instruments of production have been privately appropriated by certain individuals for their own benefit. The way to end inequality, therefore, is to abolish all private ownership of the means of production and to replace it by the ownership of the entire society.

In the next chapter entitled 'What the Congress Socialist Party Stands

For', J.P. strongly refutes the contention of the opponents of socialism that it cannot be established in India because its traditions are different from those of the European countries, where socialism had originated. In this connection he asserts that if there is a socialist party in power, it can build up socialism in any part of the world and proceeds to show how the C.S.P., if it got a chance, planned to usher in socialism in India and explains its programme, in the drawing of which he himself had had a major role to play. The main items of this programme were: transfer of all power to the producing masses; development of the economic life of the country to be planned and controlled by the State; socialisation of key and principal industries, banks, insurance and public utilities, with a view to the progressive socialisation of all the means of production, distribution and exchange; State monopoly of foreign trade; organisation of cooperatives for production, distribution and credit in the unsocialised sector of the economy; elimination of princes and landlords, and all other classes of exploiters without compensation; redistribution of land to peasants; encouragement and promotion of cooperative and collective farming by the State; liquidation of debts owed by peasants and workers; recognition of the right to work or maintenance by the State; 'to everyone according to his needs from everyone according to his capacity' to be the basis ultimately of distribution and production of economic goods; adult franchise on a functional basis; no support to or discrimination between different religions by the State; no recognition of any distinction based on caste or community; and no discrimination between the sexes.

The elaboration of these measures follows the usual Marxist pattern but there are a few points which show J.P.'s capacity for independent thinking even in his Marxist days as also a certain measure of continuity in his approach to some important aspects of development. Thus while advocating the introduction of cooperative and collective farming on the Soviet pattern, he visualises the village and not, like the Soviet Union, a large cluster of villages with huge collective farms, as an unit of agricultural production. The villagisation of land, according to him, is expected to correspond to the situation in the village communes of ancient India. There would, of course, be a significant difference: the socialist village, instead of being a closed economic unit as in ancient times, would be part of a larger cooperative unit. J.P. also takes care to emphasise that the transition to cooperative and collective farming is to be slow and gradual and not pushed forward at a break-neck speed as was done in the Soviet Union. Again, unlike in the Soviet Union, this transition is to be brought about not by coercion, but only by encouragement and promotion, through propaganda, demonstration, subsidy and preferential taxation. Nor are the Soviet techniques of agricultural production to be copied blindly. Thus because of its large population and shortage of land, India would need fewer labour-saving devices than had been the case in the Soviet Union, with its small population and vast tracts of land. While the traditional plough might not be retained, there would be no need, at any rate till industrial development had absorbed the surplus rural population, for many tractors and mechanical reapers and binders. J.P. is also highly critical of the modern city and describes it as a terrible place of habitation for most of its dwellers. Under socialism, he emphasises, cities would be planned and too much concentration at one place avoided by defusing industry, there being geographical planning as well as statistical. On the other hand, the village too can become an unit of industrial production. Thus we come to the concept of the agro-industrial, urbo-rural village, in its embryonic form, which J.P. developed in greater detail in his later years and which remained a key element in his thinking till the end of his life.

Although this divergence from the Soviet pattern of planning illustrates, to some extent, the impact of Gandhi's thinking, according to which the village was to occupy a key place in India's development, J.P. was not conscious of it at that stage and did not mention Gandhi anywhere while expounding his views on socialist approach to India's development. On the contrary, in the third chapter of his book, devoted to a critique of the supposed alternatives to socialism, he presents a most trenchant criticism of Gandhism, describing it as a compound of 'timid economic analysis, good intentions and ineffective moralising'. While admitting that Gandhism is a well-intentioned doctrine, he points out that it is 'a dangerous doctrine'. For it 'hushes up real issues and sets out to remove the evils of society by pious wishes. It thus deceives the masses and encourages the upper classes to continue their domination'.

In the fourth and last chapter entitled 'Methods and Techniques', J.P. answers the criticism that to lay stress on socialism was premature and divisive until independence was achieved. For so long as foreign rule continued, the need of the hour was for all politically conscious persons in the country to maintain national unity and build up resistance against that rule. J.P.'s view was that the term national unity was a misnomer, as all elements of the nation were not interested in the struggle for freedom. The upper classes were being protected and promoted by the imperialist power. They were not likely to have a genuine interest in the struggle against that power and would be prone to making compromises with it. Only the masses, who did not owe any obligation to the imperialist power and could be made to see in it the protector and promoter of their exploitation, could have real interest in the anti-imperialist struggle and would not be prone to making compromises with it. The need of the hour, therefore, was to organise the masses—both the peasants and the labourers—and make them politically conscious. This could best be done by fostering their class organisations and instilling political consciousness among them. This was the main task before the socialists. They also believed that the Congress could be turned into a real mass organisation by keeping it away from any compromise with imperialism and suitably modifying its objectives—bringing into focus not only the struggle against imperialism but also the struggle against all types of exploitation, including exploitation by Indian landlords and capitalists. It would also be necessary to suitably amend the Congress Constitution, making possible the representation in it of class organisations of peasants and workers. It was in the hope of bringing about such a transformation in the Congress and turning it into a powerful fighting machine against imperialism that the socialists had decided to work, not in isolation, but as part of the bigger organisation.

II

The rest of the items (nos. 2 to 87) included in this volume contain J.P.'s statements, articles, circulars, letters and speeches relating to the organisation of the C.S.P., and its chief concerns as elucidated in the last chapter of *Why Socialism?* The primary concern of the C.S.P. was to radicalise the Congress and help develop it into a real anti-imperialist organisation. Item 2, being the General Secretary's report for 1935, gives a fairly detailed account of the work carried out by the C.S.P. in this respect during that year. J.P., along with other leaders of the C.S.P., strove to keep the Congress leadership away from the path of constitutionalism. In this they had the support of no less a person than Jawaharlal Nehru, Congress President (1936-8), but in spite of their pleas the Congress decided to assume office and form ministries in 1937 in provinces where they were in a majority. Some of the items included here show J.P. arguing, with reason as well as passion, against the move of office acceptance. Several other items show J.P.'s unhappiness with the performance of the Congress ministries. He was particularly upset by the Government's repression of some of the agitations launched by the Kisan Sabha in Bihar with which he was closely associated. Some of the items included here show J.P. protesting most vigorously against such repression. Work among the peasants, who also constituted the mainstay of the Congress in Bihar, landed the party in severe conflict with the Congress leadership, headed by Rajendra Prasad, particularly because of quarrels between the Congress workers of the old school and the cadres of the C.S.P. in connection with elections to various Congress Committees. J.P. personally intervened in some of these quarrels and sent strong letters of protest to Prasad against the latter's decisions. Sometimes because of involvement with the peasant movement and criticism of some of Prasad's decisions he had to face strong personal attacks from the editor of the *Searchlight*, a prominent pro-Congress English daily published from Patna. J.P.'s equally strong rejoinders, full of biting sarcasm about the supposedly Gandhian tactics of the old Congress leadership, make interesting reading.

In April 1936 when Nehru became President of the Congress, at Gandhi's suggestion he nominated J.P., along with his two colleagues of the C.S.P., Narendra Deva and Achyut Patwardhan, as members of the Congress Working Committee. This was high honour for J.P., then not yet 34, but he had to resign after a few months as he was not then a member of the All India Congress Committee, an essential requirement for being on the Working Committee. Even so his stature kept on rising and at the Tripuri Session of the Congress (1939) he was asked to move the main resolution of the session called 'The National Demand' dealing with the stand of the Congress (Nehru had moved it in the Subjects Committee). J.P.'s speech on that occasion, delivered in Hindi and presented here in English translation, shows precision as well as clarity and sums up very well the general Congress position vis-a-vis the British at that time.

The chief interest at Tripuri, however, centered on the crisis of leadership triggered by Subhas Chandra Bose's election as President, for a second term, defeating Pattabhi Sitaramayya, the nominee of Gandhi and supported by most of the old leaders of the Congress, including almost all members of the Working Committee, who had resigned from it in the midst of the election campaign in protest against Bose's remarks showing lack of confidence in them. Bose's victory was generally regarded as the victory of the radical wing of the Congress. The old leaders retaliated through the Pant Resolution, so called because it was moved at the Tripuri Session by Govind Ballabh Pant, at that time heading the Congress Ministry in U.P., expressing continued faith in Gandhi's leadership and asking the new Congress President to form the Working Committee according to Gandhi's wishes. At the time of the election many delegates who voted were not aware of the attitude of Gandhi (who had ceased to be a member of the Congress in 1934) and they had seen it primarily as a contest between Bose and Sitaramayya. By the time the Tripuri Congress was held, however, Gandhi's deep involvement in the issue had become clear through his own statement that Pattabhi's defeat was his own as he had been mainly responsible for Pattabhi's candidature. So there was a change in the situation and many felt worried about the prospect of the Congress losing Gandhi's leadership. The Pant Resolution had been moved keeping this in mind. Even so the division on that resolution was expected to be quite close and the attitude of the delegates owing allegiance to the C.S.P. became quite important. J.P., along with other leaders of the C.S.P., had sided with Bose in the election but refused to take it as a contest between the right wing and left wing in the Congress, taking the stand that the Congress must maintain its position as the united front of all persons and groups interested in fighting for India's freedom. When the old leaders resigned from the Working Committee in the midst of the election campaign (Nehru resigning separately) he deplored their action, but also criticised Bose for his statement showing lack of confidence in the old members. At Tripuri he moved an amendment to the Pant Resolution in a bid to soften the blow to Bose and his followers. Even though that amendment was defeated, instead of taking a stand against that resolution, as was generally expected by his followers and admirers, he announced his and his group's neutrality on it—facilitating its passage. The adoption of the Pant Resolution by the Tripuri Congress in due course led to Bose's resignation from the presidentship of the Congress and his expulsion from all elective positions in the Congress for the next three years. J.P. justified his party's position of neutrality, for which he had been mainly responsible, on the ground that Gandhi's continued cooperation with the leadership was at that stage of great value to the Congress and nothing should be done to create a hurdle in its way. The matter remained a subject of controversy in political circles and in the press for quite some time and remains of historical interest even now. A number of items included in this volume will be helpful in understanding J.P.'s role in it.

Another bunch of documents included here will be found useful in understanding the history of relations between the C.S.P. and the Communist Party. As already mentioned, even though not considering it fit to join the Communist Party primarily because of its working under foreign guidance and keeping away from the nationalist movement led by Gandhi, and deciding to form a party of their own, the leaders of the C.S.P., particularly J.P. and Narendra Deva, continued to adhere to Marxism. Similarly they also ardently looked forward to all the Marxists in India coming together to work for socialism. This led them to open the doors of the C.S.P. to the members of the Communist Party which was not allowed to function legally at that time. Many communists took advantage of this oppurtunity for legal functioning and became members of the C.S.P. However, they also continued their underground functioning, separately, as a group. In 1937 the C.S.P. got hold of a statement issued by the Communist Party in which the latter described the former as a party of left unity, but not as a Marxist party. This marked the beginning of developments which finally culminated in the expulsion of the communists from the C.S.P. in 1940. Up to 1939, the C.S.P. leadership held its hand, largely at the instance of J.P. but its relations with the communists went on deteriorating. J.P.'s address on socialist unity at the Lahore Conference of the C.S.P. (1938) as well as the resolution on this subject moved by him there, both included in this volume, throw light on the early phase of the C.S.P.'s troubles with the communists.

The 21 Appendices follow the pattern set in Volume I. They contain documents of two types: (a) those which include J.P. as one of the authors and (b) those to which J.P. reacted at some length and his observations have been included in the volume. While all of them, it is hoped, will help the readers in understanding the working of J.P.'s mind during the years covered by this volume, the texts of Meerut Thesis and Faizpur Thesis adopted respectively by the second and third annual conferences of the C.S.P. held at Meerut (January 1936) and Faizpur (December 1936) and given in Appendices 1 and 2 should be especially useful in understanding the ideology of the C.S.P. in its early years as well as J.P.'s own ideological moorings at that time. Needless to add, J.P. had played a leading role in drafting them.

1. Why Socialism? 1936[1]

FOREWORD

This book[2] is not intended to explain socialist theory. It has been written with a view to elucidate certain problems arising out of the present stage of the national movement and the problem of its future direction. The growth of the Congress Socialist Party has created a thought-ferment within the ranks of the Congress and has brought issues of fundamental importance to the fore. A conflict of ideologies, a juxtaposition of programmes, demands clear-cut decisions. It is to help Congressmen, especially the Congress worker, to make these decisions, that this little attempt has been made. It is addressed primarily to the Congress worker.

I am aware of the many shortcomings of this book. The requirement of presenting rather technical ideas in an easily intelligible form, has led me to over-simplification. Many of the statements in the book have to be refined, qualified and hedged in to answer to strict accuracy. But I thought it to be more desirable to convey the central truth in a direct manner than to confuse the reader with a lot of intricate thought-chopping. As it is, I am afraid I have not been able to avoid technical language and express myself as simply as I should have liked to. While in preparation, I discussed certain passages in the book with some Congress friends; so I am only too well aware of my failure in this direction.

On the other hand, the book will probably appear annoyingly elementary to the *pandits* of Socialism. There is such a gulf between the thinking of the socialist and the average Congress worker, that what is a truism to the one has to be arrived at by the other through an arduous process of reasoning. It is natural, therefore, that what is written for the one, should appear elementary to the other. I, however, invite my socialist friends to offer their criticisms, so that the problems I have tried to discuss might be further elucidated by collective discussion.

A few words regarding the arrangement of the book—I have tried in Chapter 1 to lay bare the essential foundation of Socialism. I have noticed that in discussions on Socialism, there is always a tendency to get lost in details and ignore its central point—the elimination of private ownership of means of production in favour of social ownership.

[1] Jayaprakash Narayan, *Why Socialism?* Benares, n.d., but published in January 1936.

[2] All the footnotes here formed part of *Why Socialism?* We have not made any additions.

In Chapter 2, I have tried, in the light of the basic theory of Socialism, to explain the items of the Programme of the Congress Socialist Party.

Chapter 3 seeks to analyse certain alternatives that have been suggested to Socialism in India. Particular attention has been given to Gandhiji's ideas and to Dr. Bhagavan Das' ancient scientific Socialism.

In Chapter 4, I have attempted to discuss tactics of the anti-imperialist movement and their relation to Socialism and our Party. I have left out a number of rather important questions concerning the last, because of their rather technical nature. They are of little importance to the general reader or even the Congress worker. They concern largely members of the Party itself and so are best discussed in the Party's own manifestoes and theses.

Finally, I wish to offer my grateful thanks to Mr. Sri Prakasa, who, in a busy life, was good enough to see through the proofs of the book and help me with a number of valuable suggestions.

Jayaprakash Narayan

CHAPTER 1

THE FOUNDATION OF SOCIALISM

> *"I am persuaded that till property is taken away there can be no equitable or just distribution of things, nor can the world be happily governed."*
>
> THOMAS MORE

It is often remarked, and not always by the uninformed, that there are so many types of Socialism that it is difficult to tell what is meant by the term.

It is true that there have been, historically, different schools of Socialism and mutually conflicting socialist parties. But, I think it would not be wrong to say that in recent years, especially owing to the impact of the World Crisis and the rise of Fascism, there has been a growing unity in socialist thought; and today more than ever before it is possible to say that there is only one type, one theory of Socialism—Marxism.

It should be remembered, moreover, that the greater part of the differences between various groups of socialists was, and is, based not on the nature and definition of Socialism, but on the method and tactics of changing the present capitalist society into a socialist one. So far only communists have vindicated their theory of tactics by their great and remarkable success in Russia. The proponents of the other methods are today everywhere in the trough of failure.

I am not concerned here with questions of tactics. My object is simply to explain the basic principle of Socialism, the domain of which is too extensive to be covered in a short chapter of a book of this nature. I shall be satisfied if I am able to impress on the reader's mind, just the principle on which, as a foundation, the edifice of Socialism must be raised.

II

The first thing to remember about Socialism is that it is a system of social reconstruction. It is not a code of personal conduct; it is not something which you and I can practise. Nor is it a hot-house growth. When we speak of applying Socialism to India, we mean the reorganization of the whole economic and social life of the country: its farms, factories, schools, theatres. No doubt, it is possible to run the life of a single village or the business of a single factory on socialist lines. But, that would not be Socialism. The picture cast by a prism on the laboratory wall has seven colours, but it is not the rainbow of the skies.

It follows, therefore, that those who desire to construct a socialist society should have the power and the requisite sanction behind them to do so. No group of idealists can build up Socialism unless it has power in its hands.

What is meant by power? If one looks at the world of today, one finds that the instrument through which groups, parties, individuals attempt to enforce their plans, their schemes, over the Community, the Nation, is the *State*. Whether it is a constitutionalist party, like the Labour Party of England, a revolutionary party, like the Bolshevik Party of Russia, a fascist party like that of Hitler in Germany, it seeks in every case to *capture the State*. When the State is in your hands, you can legislate, you can use the whole magnificent apparatus of propaganda and education that modern science has made available; you can enforce your will. And, if there is resistance, you can use the coercive arm of the State—the police and the army—to crush it. Behind every piece of legislation lies the State's power to persuade and, ultimately, to coerce.

No party in the world of today can build up Socialism unless it has the machinery of the State in its hands: whether it has come to acquire it through the will of the electorate or by a *coup d'etat* is irrelevant to our discussion just now.

As a corollary to this, we can state another proposition: A party in power, i.e. in possession of the State, can always establish Socialism, provided it has either of two things: sufficient powers of coercion to put down resistance or sufficient popular support to be able to deal with opposition. Both in the end mean the same thing. The coercive powers of a socialist State, if they exist at all, are bound to be derived from popular support—the "unpopular" support, that is, the support of the classes of property, being rather thrown on the opposite side.

I have said that a party in possession of the State and with the means to keep itself there, can, if it so desired, create a socialist heaven on the Earth. What must it exactly do to begin doing this? Must it haul up all the "exploiters" and pot-bellied capitalists and have them shot? Must Pandit Jawaharlal, supposing he became the Premier or President of Socialist India, line up the Taluqdars of the U.P. and have them blown up to bits? Must he seize the treasures of the Rajas and the Mahajans and distribute them to the people—equally, of course? Must he turn over the Tata Iron works, for instance, to the workers employed there, and leave them to make as good or bad a business of it as they please? Must he split up all the land in the country, divide the total acreage by the total population, and hand over a little plot to each individual? Will that be Socialism?

No. Socialism is something more sensible, more scientific, more civilized than all that.

What, then, must Pandit Jawaharlal do?

We can find the answer to this question, if we take a look at the society we live in—here and abroad.

The first thing that strikes us is the strange and painful fact of inequalities—inequality of rank, of culture, of opportunity: a most disconcertingly unequal distribution of the good things of life. Poverty, hunger, filth, disease, ignorance—for the overwhelming many. Comfort, luxury, culture, position, power—for the select few. In *our* country as much as anywhere else; perhaps more here than elsewhere. Where, indeed, will you find such contrasts of wealth and poverty, of despotism and degradation as in unhappy India?

This fact of inequalities, with all its brood of social consequences, is the central problem of our society. It is to the solution of this problem that have been directed the best efforts of the best of men in all ages, in our age more than in any other. Charity, philanthropy, utopias, appeals to the more fortunate to be kind to the less fortunate, denunciation of the rich and exaltation of poverty, curtailment of wants—these have been the common reactions to this evil of inequalities.

The socialist's reaction is very different from these. His approach to this problem is like that of the physician to disease. He seeks to discover the root cause of the malady. He does not take the fact of inequalities for granted and then proceed to level them up. He endeavours rather to tackle the problem at the source so as to check the very *growth* of inequalities.

III

In tracing the source of this evil, the socialist first of all encounters the biologist. He is told that human beings are not born equal, as the democrat loves to repeat, but very much unequal. From birth we are said to differ in innate capacity—both in quantity and quality. This of course is true and undeniable. Even a behaviourist will have no difficulty in admitting the biologist's claim.

But let us see how this fact of biological inequalities affects the socialists' examination of social inequalities. He admits that the normal bell-shaped curve of probabilities applies as much to human abilities as to any other phenomenon. In society there is at one end a small group of geniuses and at the other an equally small group of half-wits and idiots, while in the centre is the vast majority of humanity with more or less equal capabilities.

These biological differences appear in numerous social forms. We get, for example, inequalities in learning and achievements in the arts and sciences. Then, we have inequalities of rank, of wealth, of power, of opportunity. Now, the socialists' protest never was against the fact that

Tagores and Ramans exist in society. If anything, he is glad that they do exist. He regrets, however, that hundreds of potential Tagores and Ramans go unknown to the grave owing to the fact that they are denied opportunities for self-development. The evil of inequalities was never said to lie, either by socialists or others, in the fact that only a few are gifted by Nature to become great poets and scientists. The socialists' plea is that the evil lies in the inequalities of the second set enumerated above, viz., inequalities of rank, wealth, etc. In our modern world, where property has become a universal social sanction, it is the unequal distribution of property that is the core of the social problem.

Wherefore, then, this unequal distribution of wealth? It may be suggested that here too biology does the trick. The clever ones among us make better businessmen and therefore grow richer than the others. Supposing we grant this for the moment; does it explain the wealth of those who came to acquire it by inheritance? In the case of inherited wealth, it is obvious, of course, that biological qualities play no part at all. The idiotic heir of a millionaire would just as well inherit the millions of his ancestor as he would if he were a genius. Here it is obvious that it is merely the existence of a social standard, custom, that is responsible for the fortunes of heirs. Change that custom, and millions of people who are wealthy today would suddenly grow poor.

But let us take the case of those who have made their own fortunes. Have they not done so because of their superior ability?

That to be a successful businessman a certain type and degree of ability is required, cannot be denied. But, would it not be rather strange that divine dispensation should have ordained that only one type of human ability should be productive of wealth, while all others should acquire wealth only at the will of the wealthy? A great mathematician may be the greatest of his time but his researches, while they bring him immortality perhaps, do not in themselves mean wealth for him. Has not his genius even as much value as that of an ordinary businessman who makes money by following certain set rules of the game? A scientist, no matter how clever, does not make any money from his laboratory, unless, of course, he turns a businessman. The businessman's laboratory alone seems to be productive of wealth.

IV

Let us see what this laboratory is and how wealth is created and accumulated.

In the world we have men on one side and Nature on the other. All wealth is in the womb of Nature. Man must work upon Nature in order to appropriate from it what he wants. All things of use which he does appropriate constitute his wealth. Thus, the source of wealth is Nature and the agency which creates it, is human labour. This is the rock bottom of all economics.

How does wealth accumulate? It is obvious that if men appropriated from Nature just as much as was required for their bare existence, nothing would be left for accumulation. The amount of wealth that man can extract from Nature depends upon his productive power, i.e. the nature of his tools and his methods of work. *For accumulation to be physically possible, therefore, the productive powers of man should be so advanced that he may be able to produce more than he needs for his subsistence.* This is the fundamental basis of accumulation. When the arts of hunting, fishing, planting have advanced enough to yield more than is necessary for the lowest existence, accumulation becomes *possible.*

Now, in a society in which the arts of production have advanced beyond the subsistence level, each member would be *able* to accumulate a certain amount of wealth, *provided* he was free to work for himself, owned his own tools, had free access to Nature and was able to keep all he produced for himself. The maximum rate of accumulation would depend upon the difference between maximum individual production and minimum individual consumption. It might very well happen that some families instead of consuming the minimum used up all they produced. These will not be able to accumulate any thing. They, however, will not starve, because we have assumed that the stage of production has not only reached but passed the subsistence level.

In this society there may also be some others who are exceptionally intelligent. They may naturally produce a little more than the rest and, if they are thrifty too, they might save comparatively more. On the other hand, people of inferior intelligence might save very little or nothing at all. But, in every case, in such a society, every able-bodied person would be able to accumulate wealth or, at least, support himself, if, to repeat the provisos stated above, he is free to work for himself, own his tools, has free access to Nature and is the master of all that he produces.

Let us turn from this hypothetical society to our own. We find that the methods of production—both agricultural and industrial—are so advanced that a man can easily produce much more than he can consume, even at the present standard of living, which is naturally higher than the primitive stage of our hypothetical society. The Indian cultivator, in spite of his comparatively old-fashioned methods and tools, can produce much more than is necessary for him to live on. Yet, we find that millions of our people do not get even a square meal a day. At the same time we also find that there are many people who have not only got their wants satisfied, but who are also enjoying a high degree of comfort. How have these conditions of dire want on one side and ease and luxury on the other been created?

Let us take the case of the poor first. Considering the advanced productive powers of our present society, it should have been possible for every Indian not only to support himself but also to accumulate something. But, as a matter of fact, most Indians are not supporting themselves. Why? Because, the provisos which were mentioned above have nearly all disappeared. *The people do not all work for themselves; they have no longer free access to Nature; in many cases they are not the masters of their tools; they are not able to keep all they produce for themselves.* How all this has come about would be too long a story to tell. That the fact is true, all of us can see.

The poverty of our people, then, is due to the fact that the means of production, i.e. tools, materials, land, etc., are no longer in their hands. They have to pay for most of them, and the more they pay for them the less their own share of the produce and the greater their poverty. A large proportion of them has not even the means to pay for them: there is nothing that they can do except to sell their labour to others. If the means of production were freely available to each individual, there would be no poverty, unless the population rose to such an extent that at the present stage of the productive powers the means of production were unable to produce sufficient wealth to meet the needs of the people. This certainly is not the case in India yet, in spite of its large population.

Now, let us take the case of the rich. How is it that some have come to acquire thousands and lakhs of times as much wealth as the poor? An individual, no matter how clever, cannot possibly produce, at any stage of productivity, thousand of times more than others who are using the same means of production. The great riches of the rich are not obviously of their own production. It is impossible for such disproportion in the productivity of men, living in the same society, to exist. We have pointed out above that there is no other way of creating wealth except by working upon Nature, and that the only way of accumulating wealth is by producing more than one consumes. The limits to production are set by the stage of development the arts of production have reached in society. This is true even in the complicated societies of the West, where production is so mechanized. There we find, as we do here too though not to the same extent, that the means of production, particularly of industrial production, have developed so much that they cannot be used any more by individuals working independently. But, this in no way invalidates my argument. If all the people participating in production took their share of what they produced, the situation would still be the same as in our hypothetical society. Each member of society would accumulate a fair amount of wealth and there would be no poverty nor concentration of too much wealth in a few hands.

How then, have the great fortunes of present society been made? It may be urged that they are the result of patient saving by industrious people. The answer is that thrift and industry have not been known to travel for generations in the same family line, nor in themselves have they been found to result in excessive wealth. None of the fortunes of today, especially those founded on industry, has a hoary ancestry. The secret of wealth does not lie in the peculiar talents or blood of the wealthy.

Our analysis of the process of accumulation furnishes the secret. Suppose that in a society in which production has passed the subsistence level, an individual manages to employ, say, ten other individuals to work for him and pays them only what they require for their subsistence and keeps the surplus for himself. That individual would be accumulating wealth ten times as fast as others who are working for themselves; and he would soon become a very wealthy man. It should be obvious that the volume of his private wealth would increase with the number of individuals he employs.

Suppose again that in the same society another individual came somehow to establish a monopoly over Nature, say, land. By virtue of that monopoly he does not allow anyone to work upon that land, i.e. to cultivate it, unless a share of the produce is vouchsafed for him. He too will begin to grow richer than the rest, and his riches will grow in proportion to the land he "owns" and the tribute he exacts from those who till his land. Likewise with other natural resources.

This is the true secret of the inequality of wealth and the true meaning of *exploitation.*

The question may be asked here, why should any individual work for any one else and be thus cheated out of part of his produce when he could easily work for himself and keep the whole of it to himself? A full treatment of this question will involve a survey of the entire social and political history of mankind. Briefly, the answer is that there is no reason why any one should do it and that, as a matter of fact, in history no one has done it except under compulsion.

In all human societies where the open frontier existed so that any one could clear the jungle and cultivate his own plot, no one worked for another, except for mutual benefit. The gifts of Nature, however, were the first to become the monopoly of the few. This monopoly in the earliest days was based on sheer and naked force. A group of people arose practically everywhere who established an exclusive ownership over Nature, particularly over land, and subjugated others to slavery, serfdom, or to the status of just "free" rent-payers.

In industry, as long as the latter remained at a level where independent individual production was possible, industrial exploitation and, therefore differences in industrial incomes, were slow to arise. As, however, production advanced and cities grew, slaves or even individual craftsmen were made to work together for a master, thus creating inequalities in industrial incomes also. The real and rapid growth of industrial fortunes dates, however, from the time steam power (the Industrial Revolution) came into being, making possible a much larger employment, i.e. *exploitation*, of workers.

It may be urged that there are in society classes of men who neither employ nor receive rent or any other tribute, but who nevertheless are quite rich—richer in some cases than the men of the other two classes. For instance, there are traders, speculators, bankers, etc. These neither produce wealth themselves nor do they directly exploit the labour of others engaged in producing wealth. Whatever may be the immediate source of the wealth of these classes, this much at least should be clear that it too must come somehow from the total wealth created in the Community.

Wealth, as we showed, is created by labour and except that portion of it which goes to the producers, it becomes the property of the employing and exploiting classes. But these classes naturally cannot use themselves all the things that their workers have created. These must be sold and other things bought. Thus, traders and speculators come into being and because goods must be sold in order to enable the manufacturers to buy materials for further manufacture and sale, the latter yield, both as buyers and sellers, some part of the surplus wealth that has fallen into their hands to the traders and speculators. Likewise with bankers. They are said to earn interest on the money they lend. But the interest is created in the process of manufacture and is paid out of the same fund of surplus wealth. Profits, interests, middlemen's commissions,—all these come from the same common fund: the fund created by the surplus wealth appropriated by manufacturers and those who possess a monopoly in the means of production. Money in itself cannot make money, nor can any sort of financial and commercial manipulation do so. The whole game of capitalist business consists in the attempt of the various parts of it to appropriate as large a share of the surplus wealth as possible. Herein lies the secret of all capitalist competition and all the subtle and complicated business practices that are so laboriously taught in the universities!

To repeat, for it will bear repetition, it is the wealth that accumulates in the hands of those who own the means of production, by virtue of their exploitation of others' labour, that constitutes the general fund from which, as a result of the working of the economic organization, other groups draw their share. It is wrong to believe that these "middlemen" in any manner "create" wealth. Their "money-making" merely means diverting as great a share of the total accumulated wealth as possible in their own direction. Even the professions, lawyers, physicians, etc., fill their ladles from this same common bowl, though in their case, part of their share comes from that portion of the total wealth also that goes to the actual producers—the workers, peasants, etc.

To sum up. The root cause of inequalities of wealth lies in the fact that the gifts of Nature, which yield wealth to men, and the instruments of production, have come to be privately owned by people for their own benefit. This leads to economic exploitation, i.e. the withholding from the workers of all that they produce except what they need to live on at a given standard of living. This takes place either directly, as when labourers are employed to produce goods for the manufacturer, or indirectly, as when men rent land, or any other natural resource, for their livelihood.

The earliest manner in which these sources and instruments (collectively termed "means" in socialist writings) of production passed into private hands was through force. This is termed "primitive accumulation". The surplus wealth thus accumulated in the hands of those who were able to use force went on multiplying through the ages through the institution of slavery and indentured labour, till the loot from India and the inventions of certain German-Englishmen combined to usher in the Industrial Revolution. This became *par excellence* the age of exploitation, because it made the employment of unheard of masses of labourers in single manufactures possible.

Such being the causes of the present inequalities of wealth, it should not be difficult to imagine what form the socialist solution of this problem would take.

V

Theoretically speaking, two solutions are possible, each if practicable resulting in a just, equitable and happy society. The first solution is so to reconstitute society that every individual may be free to work for himself—he may either cultivate his own land (without the payment of any tribute to anyone) or work with his own tools in his workshop. No one may be allowed to possess larger means of production than he can possibly make use of with his own hands.

It should be clear that in order to change the existing order into the one described above, very drastic changes will have to be made and great restrictions will have to be imposed. For such a society to work smoothly, a degree of social control and discipline would be required which one does not associate with societies whose economic organization is so primitive. Such a society, moreover, cannot have railways and telegraphs—in fact, nothing but the most primitive forms of transport and communication. From a military standpoint such a society, exposed to the rapacity of highly industrialized countries, would be extremely weak and an easy prey to them. From the point of view of standard of living, the people, especially in India where there is such a large population, would have to live on an extremely low level, for *per capita* productivity would be very low.

In short, even if it were possible to adopt this solution as an escape from our present ills, it would be extremely inadvisable to do so for innumerable reasons.

It is not, however, possible to adopt this solution. Nothing short of a dictatorship would be required to carry it through. Such a drastic transformation of society, involving the destruction of all vested interests, would not be otherwise possible. For such a dictatorship of the small producer there is no social basis in society.

The socialist solution, as it ought to be clear from our analysis of the process of accumulation of wealth, is to *abolish private ownership of the means of production* and to *establish over them the ownership of the whole community.*

The abolition of private and establishment of social ownership over the means of production means the eradication of economic exploitation, the ending of economic inequalities; in other words, the removal of the basic curse of present society. The source of accumulation of wealth in private hands is the exploitation of labour, as we saw above. With social ownership established, people no longer work for others. They work for themselves, not individually but collectively; and what they produce is not for the profit of the manufacturer, but for their own consumption. Social ownership means that all wealth is held in common and shared equitably, the basis of distribution being, initially, the amount and character of work done and, finally, the needs of the individual; only that part of the produce being withheld from distribution which is necessary for defence and administration, for schools and hospitals, for economic development, and for other common purposes.

Here, then, is the basic principle of Socialism—socialization of the means of production. Any attempt at socialist reconstruction of society must start with the abolition of the private ownership of the means of production.

For a young State launching upon Socialism, it may not be possible to accomplish this at one stroke. However, if it is to succeed in its purpose, it must effect this change immediately in all those spheres of large-scale production which dominate the economic life of the country and hold the key positions.

In developed communities, side by side with the means of production, rise also means of exchange and distribution—banks, commercial institutions, transport, etc. The latter issue out of and support the former. Their purpose is to keep the wheels of production turning. Socialization of the former therefore must also be accompanied by socialization of the latter.

We are now perhaps in a position to say what Pandit Jawaharlal would do, if he came to power.

I shall try to show in the next chapter how the Congress Socialist Party proposes to apply these principles to India and what its concrete proposals are.

CHAPTER 2

WHAT THE CONGRESS SOCIALIST PARTY STANDS FOR

"If an indigenous government took the place of the foreign government and kept all the vested interests intact, that would not even be the shadow of freedom."
JAWAHARLAL NEHRU

The objects of the Congress Socialist Party, as laid down in its Constitution, are "the achievement of complete independence, in the sense of separation from the British Empire, and the establishment of a socialist society."

This is direct and simple enough. The Party has two objects: The first is the same as that of the Indian National Congress, except that the Party wishes to make it clear that the complete Independence of India must include separation from the British Empire. The second object of the Party simply means that Independent India must reorganise its economic life on a socialist basis.[1]

Why?

The question at bottom is one of values and ultimate objectives, which once determined, the rest becomes a matter of logical sequence.

If the ultimate objective is to make the masses politically and economically free, to make them prosperous and happy, to free them from all manner of exploitation, to give them unfettered opportunity for development, then, Socialism becomes a goal to which one must irresistibly be drawn. If again, the objective is to take hold of the chaotic and conflicting forces of society and to fashion the latter according to the ideal of utmost social good and to harness all the conscious directives of human intelligence in the service of the commonweal, then, again, Socialism becomes an inescapable destination.

Those who have different aims and objectives need not trouble to read further.

If, then, these be our objectives, as I trust they are, it should take little argument, in view of what has been explained in the last Chapter, to show that Socialism is as definitely "indicated" in India as elsewhere. In India

[1] Compare with these objects the following statement of Pandit Jawaharlal Nehru: "India's immediate goal can therefore only be considered in terms of ending the exploitation of her people. Politically, it must mean independence and the severance of the British connection, which means imperialist domination (our first object—J.P.N.); economically and socially it must mean the ending of all special class privileges and vested interests" (our second object—J.P.N.)—*Whither India*, 1933.

too there is poverty, nay, starvation, on the one hand and wealth and luxury on the other; in India too there is exploitation; the means of production here also are in private hands. That is, the root evil of modern society, namely, economic and social inequality, exists in India too as does its cause: the exploitation of the great many by the very few.

And this is not the result of British rule. It is independent of it and would continue even after it. The ending of the foreign domination would not automatically solve India's problem of poverty; would not put a stop to the exploitation of the vast many; would not, in fact, mean the accomplishment of any of the objectives which we have started with.

II

It is often said that India's conditions are peculiar; that India's traditions are different; that India is industrially a backward country; and that, therefore, Socialism has no applicability here.

If by this it is meant that the basic principles of Socialism have no validity in India, it would be difficult to imagine a greater fallacy.

The laws by which wealth accumulates hold as true in India as elsewhere and the manner in which the accumulation can be stopped is the same here as anywhere else. The peculiarity of Indian conditions may influence and determine the manner and the stages in which the principles of Socialism may be applied here, but never alter those principles. If social ownership of the means of production is essential for stopping exploitation and unequal distribution of wealth in other parts of the world, it is equally essential in India.

As for Indian traditions, as far as I know them, they are not averse to the sharing of life and its privileges. It is said that individualism has always been the dominant feature of Indian civilization and therefore the latter is opposed to Socialism. To put the problem in this manner is not to understand either of the ideals and to get lost in words. Individualism has been the prominent *motif* in our culture only in the sense that perfection of the individual has been its ideal; never in the sense of narrow, self-seeking individualism, which is the *motif* in capitalist society. And, if individual perfection is the goal, the socialist has not the least difficulty in showing that such perfection can come about only by aiming at the utmost common good. Does not Trotsky say somewhere that only in a socialist society can the average of humanity rise to the level of a Plato or a Marx?

Finally, India's industrial backwardness need not discourage us. If anything, this backwardness would be helpful to us because it means a much weaker opposition. As for the practicability of applying Socialism to a region of industrial backwardness, it is enough to remind the reader of what the Russians are doing in some of the most backward parts of the globe. Socialism is being built up as surely in Uzbekistan as in Moscow. If there is a socialist party in power, with the requisite sanction behind it, it can build up Socialism anywhere in the world with the help of modern science.

It is for these reasons that the Party has set for itself the object of establishing a socialist society in India after independence has been won.

III

Now, what is the position of the Indian National Congress with regard to these questions?

It would be wrong to suppose that the Congress is wholly unmindful of the problems we have discussed above and that its objectives do not go beyond national independence. The Congress, in fact, has recognised the twofold problem that faces it, and it has admitted, though grudgingly and vaguely, that the Indian masses must be freed as well from Imperialism as from the indigenous system of exploitation.

In a now little-remembered resolution, the All India Congress Committee only in 1929, declared that:

> In the opinion of this Committee, the great poverty and misery of the Indian people are due not only to foreign exploitation in India but also to the economic structure of society, which the alien rulers support so that their exploitation may continue. In order therefore to remove this poverty and misery and to ameliorate the condition of the Indian masses, it is essential to make revolutionary changes in the present economic and social structure of society and to remove the gross inequalities.
>
> (Bombay, 1929)

Here are revolutionary changes in the economic structure of society demanded. And the reasons for demanding them have been as clearly set out as could be done by a socialist. But, then, where is the rub? Where is our difference with the Congress on this point? The difference arises because the Congress after talking of "revolutionary changes" buries its head in the sand.

I ask Congressmen, who today oppose us and deride us, I ask them in all earnestness, if levying of death duties and a graduated income-tax; nationalization of key industries; reduction of rent; freedom from rent for uneconomic holdings;[2]—if these fall under the daring phrase, "revolutionary changes in the *economic structure of society*"; if these will put an end to that system of exploitation to which the above resolution makes so pointed

[2] *C.f.* The Karachi resolution of the Congress on Fundamental Rights, etc.

a reference? And, yet, this is all that the Karachi Resolution offers by way of basic economic policy.

I may be reminded that the A.I.C.C. is not the Congress. That would be an admirable piece of quibbling, but would hardly answer my question.

But, let us take the Karachi Resolution itself. The preamble to the resolution clearly declares that Swaraj in order to be a real Swaraj for the masses must mean not only the political freedom of the country but also the economic freedom of the masses.

What is economic freedom, pray? Are my friends and leaders who oppose us today prepared to answer this question, and then honestly believe that economic freedom can be secured by passing the puny measures that the Karachi Resolution rather fearfully enumerates?

If all that the Congress understands by economic freedom is death duties and national ownership of key industries, it will be a very fine freedom indeed that it will confer on this unfortunate land! We have known slavery so long that we have forgotten what freedom is!

I do not desire to suggest that at Karachi, the Congress should have outlined a full-grown programme of Socialism. Nor are we insisting that it should do so now. What it must do, however, is to accept such a minimum economic programme as will, when put to practice, free the masses from economic exploitation and transfer full political and economic power into their hands.

It is such a programme that the Congress Socialist Party is advocating.

The present programme of the Congress falls far short of these ideals. It might ameliorate the condition of the masses to a certain extent, but it will neither rid them of exploitation nor put them in power. Far from effecting revolutionary changes in it, as the A.I.C.C. contemplated at Bombay, it leaves the economic structure of society intact. It leaves capitalists, landlords and princes on the one side and workers, tenants and subjects on the other. It leaves the means of production in the hands of private individuals, except in the sphere of key industries. The entire economic organization, based as it is on the exploitation of the poor and middle classes, is preserved. This is not economic freedom. The preamble and substance of the Karachi Resolution are at wide variance with each other. What we are endeavouring to do is to remove this variance and bring them close together. When the Congress professes the economic freedom of the masses, let it distinctly state what that freedom means.

The Congress may be unprepared for the acceptance of such a minimum programme as we advocate; it may require time to grow to the proper ideological stature. But it is one thing to say that we are not ready for any further definition of our goal—which of course may be disputed—and quite another, as latterly repeated *ad nauseum*, that Socialism is moonshine; that it is unsuited to the Indian climate; that Indian socialists are merely adventuring in the realm of theory; that they are only quoting a rusty old German Jew who called himself Karl Heinrich Marx; and the rest of the drivel.

If Congressmen persist in repeating this nonsense, they must tell the people what *they* mean by economic freedom, by freedom of the masses from the native system of exploitation from which they are said to suffer as much as from British imperialism, and which is as much the cause of their poverty and misery as the latter.

IV

As far as we socialists are concerned—and on this are agreed not only Congress Socialists, but all those in India who hold socialist or communist views—economic freedom means only one thing to us—*Socialism*. Without Socialism, economic freedom would be a sham, moonshine, humbug.

What, then, does the Congress Socialist Party propose? What must the Swaraj Government do in addition to nationalising key industries in order to realize the economic freedom of the masses; in order to rid them of exploitation, injustice, suffering, poverty, ignorance?

The measures that are necessary, in the opinion of the Party to achieve this, are clearly set forth in the *Objectives* section of the *Programme* of the All India Congress Socialist Party.

Here they are:

1. Transfer of all power to the producing masses.
2. Development of the economic life of the country to be planned and controlled by the State.
3. Socialization of key and principal industries (e.g., Steel, Cotton, Jute, Railways, Shipping, Plantations, Mines), Banks, Insurance and Public Utilities, with a view to the progressive socialization of all the instruments of production, distribution and exchange.
4. State monopoly of foreign trade.
5. Organization of co-operatives for production, distribution and credit in the unsocialized sector of economic life.
6. Elimination of princes and landlords and all other classes of exploiters without compensation.
7. Redistribution of land to peasants.
8. Encouragement and promotion of co-operative and collective farming by the State.
9. Liquidation of debts owing by peasants and workers.

10. Recognition of the right to work or maintenance by the State.
11. "To every one according to his needs and from every one according to his capacity" to be the basis ultimately of distribution and production of economic goods.
12. Adult franchise on a functional basis.
13. No support to or discrimination between religions by the State and no recognition of any distinction based on caste or community.
14. No discrimination between the sexes by the State.
15. Repudiation of the so-called Public Debt of India.

There are fifteen measures as we see. They look forbidding; appear to be too drastic; too extreme; too foreign sounding. They are, in fact, simple enough, reasonable enough, just and practicable enough. And as for their foreign sound—well, they sound no more foreign than the Constituent Assembly, the Legislative Council, the Tariff Board, the siren of the cotton mills or the hooting of the latest Cadillac (shall we say?).

They are all intended to establish the rather simple principle that we discussed in Chapter I of the abolition of private ownership of functional property, which, as we saw, was the real villain of the piece—the source of all our evils, or most of them. They are further intended to establish the most eminently reasonable of principles of social life—social planning.

V

Of the fifteen measures proposed by the Party, I shall deal only with Nos. 1, 2, 3, 4, 5, 6, 7, 8, 10, 11 and 12. The remaining are self-explanatory.

(1) Transfer of all Power to the Producing Masses

The cornerstone of the whole scheme is the transference of all power, political as well as economic, to the producing masses, i.e. to those engaged in producing goods or rendering services either by hand or by brain. If all power goes into the hands of those who work, it follows that those who do not work shall have no power.

The principle involved here is a basic one. Hitherto, in all the known forms of social organization, sovereign power has always rested not with the labouring masses, who in every society preponderated in numbers, but with the possessing classes. Before the rise of modern democracy, this was obvious in all the political systems that preceded it. The State was openly in the hands of the ruling class; it was an instrument of class oppression. It was so even in the so-called Greek Democracies in which a small group of citizens ruled over and oppressed a much larger number of slaves who worked for them.

It was with the appearance of the ballot-box and the party system of government that the fiction of democracy came into being. These two institutions were supposed to have conferred power on the whole people, equally on the humblest and the highest. But the economic order which weighs the scales too heavily on the side of the propertied interests, makes of this democracy a mockery. The rich have their great resources, their huge election funds, their great newspapers, their schools and colleges. And the poor? Well, they can have their dole, or jolly well starve. The right to exercise the vote in these conditions means little to the workers.

And even this sham democracy, this mockery, turns against the poor workers when, in spite of all odds they seem strong enough to disturb the scales of the economic order ever so little in their favour. The cry of revolution and "reds" goes up and what looked like democracy disappears like a mist. The ballot-box is withdrawn from the reach of the workers, party-government is thrown over on to the scrap-heap. Fascism is enthroned. The scales of the economic order are more firmly adjusted in the interests of the masters.

On such a background we inscribe the words: "All power to the masses".

We might be told that we are talking through our hats. The thing is just not possible.

We firmly declare that it is. We do so, because we know the secret of power—economic domination. When those who toil become masters of the economic order, the thing is not only possible, but natural. If we were to content ourselves merely with this one item, without the proposals which follow, we would no doubt have been guilty not only of talking through our hats but also of perpetrating a fraud.

VI

(2) Development of the Economic Life of the Country to be Planned and Controlled by the State

One of the greatest contributions of Socialism to humanity lies in the fact that it brings social progress under man's conscious control and direction. So far, with individualism and selfishness holding the centre of the stage, society has progressed blindly. A clash of purposes and interests has been the chief lever in its evolution. There has been no planning, no social purpose for which we have consciously and corporately striven. "Each for himself" is a pattern of social behaviour with which we are all so familiar.

It is in the sphere of community of purpose and corporate endeavour that Socialism holds the noblest prospects for the future of mankind; and it is collective planning of the future that so unquestionably establishes its superiority over the present disordered social "order". In releasing hidden springs of initiative and creativity, in making it possible for humanity to mould its growth, Socialism opens a new page in history—new alike from the viewpoint of material progress as from that of moral and intellectual advance. A social will takes the place of the individual will.

What this may mean to men—to masses of men and women—may best be seen by turning to Russia, where a faith and a spirit seem to have been awakened for which neither the sky nor the sea, the wind nor river, remains unconquerable. To think that only a few years back this country was one of darkest despair and most oriental lethargy!

An essential part of any scheme of planned social progress must be a planned economy. The economic organization of a country is the key to its entire life. Therefore, control over the economic organization and its conscious direction in the interests of the commonweal are a basic requirement.

What is economic planning? For a detailed answer we must carefully study the great Russian experiment in socialist planning. Various prejudices have been implanted in the public mind with regard to it, ranging from such remarks as "it is bureaucratic and corrupt", "it has killed initiative" etc., etc., to such emphatic declarations as "it has totally failed".

It will take me too far away from my subject to consider these prejudices. It would be sufficient to observe that while every national and international effort at solving the present crisis of capitalism has abjectly failed, Russia alone has kept her head high, has made steady progress in production and in raising the standard of living. In a period of extensive unemployment, Russia alone is a country where there is a shortage of hands.

The essentials of economic planning are that production, distribution and saving (in the form of State investments) are properly adjusted and that all three march along a road carefully laid out in advance in accordance with the resources, equipment and needs of the people. The fundamental requirement is that there should be no private economic interests, separate from the social interest, between which a clash might develop.

As Grinko has pointed out at the very beginning of his authoritative work on the Five Years Plan, it is incorrect to think that planning is carried out by a group of statisticians sitting in a central place and dictating to the entire economic system. Planning, in reality, is a *process* in which every unit of production, i.e. every factory and collective farm; and every unit of distribution, i.e. every co-operative and State store, take part. The men at the top co-ordinate, fit things together, guide and direct. Indeed, Russia seems most anxious to avoid centralization of economic control. The country has already been divided into autonomous geographical units of production with administrative freedom and full creative initiative.

A common prejudice regarding planned economy is that under it every individual would be dictated to as to the articles he should wear and eat and the manner in which he should live. This, as a matter of fact, is true rather of capitalism than of planned life under Socialism. The forces, however, that determine these things for us under capitalism are the chaotic uncontrolled laws of capitalist economy. Under Socialism not only are these chaotic laws converted into *purposive and determined ends* but also is the individual taken into confidence through his factory, farm or co-operative as to his views of national needs and his own requirements.

In this connection the following excerpt from a recent article of Louis Fischer's on "the Russian Consumer", should prove interesting and enlightening:

Today's *Izvestia* reports as follows: "The flower kiosks and stores of Moscow have commenced to sell roses and peonies at low prices. These flowers are delivered in Moscow by aeroplane from the gardens of the Green Trust in Essentuki, Rostov-on-Don and Yalta. Each day about 5,000 roses and 2,000 peonies are brought to Moscow in this manner." Essentuki, Rostov and Yalta are approximately thirty-six hours by train from Moscow.

During the last few weeks, owing to Moscow's unusually late and cold spring, strawberries, too, are being transported to the city by aeroplanes from points south.

The first cars for the new Moscow subway were made with hard seats. But they were never used. The authorities gave strict instructions that all cars be leather-upholstered. Now, after their trying experiences in the overcrowded surface trolleys, Moscovites would be only too happy to travel by the fast under-ground, even if its cars had no seats at all and even if the stations were not exquisitely decorated with marble columns, coffered ceilings, and modern lighting effects. Why did the Government go to the expense and trouble of introducing exceptional comforts and beauty?

Stalin, according to the Communist daily *Pravda*, has demanded that all factory directors "give the Soviet consumer goods of the highest possible quality, and in any case, goods that are not worse than those shipped abroad." The Red Press insists on "beautiful Soviet goods that please the eye."

In the Soviet Union, there is no competition, either fair or unfair, between manufacturers. Moreover, the shortage which still prevails in some branches and the rapidly rising demand are a guarantee that everything produced is easily sold. No Bolshevik director need be concerned about his market. Eager purses await his output.

In such circumstances, there is no compulsion upon Soviet retail business to go out of its way to supply the best goods or to attract trade with special displays, improved salesmanship methods and home deliveries as it has recently been doing. After all, the State could reason that citizens can live without roses, that they can wait for strawberries until the middle of the summer, that they will carry their packages themselves, that they will wear cotton if they cannot get silk or wool... . The Government has a political monopoly of industrial production and retail distribution. What it does not sell is not available anywhere else. Yet the Kremlin's greatest emphasis today is on quality and variety, and on the beautifying of daily life through the introduction of comforts and luxuries for the greatest number.

"This is the answer", says Louis Fischer, "to an old argument against planned economy and government ownership which has recently been renewed in England and America." The argument, as I have stated, is that every individual would be dictated to as regards every detail of his life. "Everybody would wear brown suits, and eat liver on Thursdays and beans on Fridays." "Soviet experience and practice", Fischer asserts "completely explode this theory". He goes on to say:

Bolshevik factories produce heel-less boots for Georgians, fur boots for Siberian hunters, high-heeled tinted chrome leather slippers for the metropolitan "flapper", light kaftans for the Turkomans, turbans for the Uzbeks, skull caps for the Tartars, felt hats for the stylish city beaux, etc., etc. Each plant has its own artists who turn out different designs for textiles and cloth. As time goes on assortments grow, and the press calls incessantly for richer variety. The Government maintains woman's dressmaking and men's cloth establishments which fill individual orders. One can give free rein to one's imagination as long as one's purse keeps pace with it.

I have seen exhibition arranged by large trusts which display all the articles they make and ask visitors to fill in a card with their preferences. The goods are then manufactured in quantities corresponding to the votes each received. This, to be sure, may be perhaps not the best of all possible methods, but it certainly suggests that the Soviet producer wants his customer's likes and dislikes to affect the character of output.

The *Pravda* recently explained the Bolshevik attitude towards this question. "What is it all for?" the paper asks. Why all these Soviet efforts to improve conditions, build more factories, register technological progress, produce beautiful high-quality goods? "For the sake of the people" it replies. "For the sake of the producers, the Soviet consumer, for the sake of our nation. No matter what product a plant makes, be it a lathe or a shoe, a turbine or a nail, it must always think of the human being, of our Soviet citizens, of the millions of excellent builders of Socialism who will use these articles."

When goods are manufactured for use rather than for profit and when every producer is a consumer and every consumer is a producer, it is only natural that the producer should be interested in creating the best commodities for himself, the consumer. The reason why planned economy, far from eliminating choice, emphasises choice, is that in the U.S.S.R. there is no divorce between production and consumption. The Russians, therefore, can no more have over-production than they can have under-consumption. And the State's first concern is the gratification of the wishes of the gainfully employed. The gainfully employed are the State, in fact. The State plants the strawberries, the State constructs the aeroplane, and the

State or the gainfully employed eat the strawberries. The more strawberries, the more peonies, the softer the seats in the subway, the finer his wife's shoes, the more eagerly and loyally does the worker produce at his bench. The State provides for people so that they may provide for it, that is, for themselves. (*New Statesman and Nation*, July 20, 1935)

I have said above that a fundamental requirement for planning is that there should be no private interests separate from and opposable to the social or common interest. But, I may be asked, are not countries like the U.S.A., Germany and Italy made up wholly of private interests and, yet, are they not planning their economic life?

It is true that the capitalist countries are also taking the road to planning. Owing to the economic crisis that has now continued for six years, in spite of all attempts to liquidate it, it was made clear even to the capitalist class that the old, unrestricted, chaotic capitalist system had grave shortcomings which caused the breakdown of the entire capitalist machinery of production, finance and trade. Therefore, attempts were made to regulate the working of the machinery by certain breaks and gears—starting from the "codes" of Roosevelt to the industrial "corporations" of Fascism.

The general failure of all these attempts, some of which, as, for instance, the fascist attempt in Italy, have had a sufficiently long life, only emphasizes my contention that planning is possible only after private interests have been got out of the way. When Roosevelt ushered in his N.R.A. and A.A.A., there was an outburst of enthusiasm. That enthusiasm has touched the depths of despond now, and the very men—the flower of the American universities—who acclaimed Roosevelt as a saviour, have turned into bitter cynics, if not active opponents. The last embers of hope in the N.R.A. have cooled down.

The failure of capitalist planning, as against the success of socialist planning, is due to the grave difference between the two. The purpose of capitalist planning is not to refashion and run the economic machine in the interest of the whole of society, but to ensure that the stream of profits should flow uninterrupted into the pockets of the capitalists. But profits which are the life-blood of capitalism are also its chief malady. As long as profits are sought, no recovery is possible. The symptoms of the disease will keep reappearing. At the same time if profits are eliminated, capitalism dies. Thus there is a vicious circle drawn from which Socialism alone offers an escape.

VII

(3) Socialization of Key and Principal Industries, etc.

This is the foundation stone of the whole scheme. This State of the masses must be based on the abolition of the rule of the classes over the economic sphere. The economic freedom of the masses must mean the ending of economic exploitation engendered by private ownership of functional property. Socialist planning must start first with destroying vested interests.

The ultimate object as stated in this section is the socialization, that is, bringing under social ownership and control, of all the means of production, distribution and exchange. This means that finally all factories and workshops, all raw materials, all trading, all banking and financing will pass into the hands of the Community. There will be no private ownership at all in these spheres.

This does not mean that a man may not have personal property, i.e. property which is of only personal use to him and is not put to the creation of more property.

Dr. Sherwood Eddy describing the aim of the Russian Communists, who have by no means reached the ultimate goal, writes:

> The aim of the Communists was to confiscate all unearned wealth and all functional property. A man might have his personal property, such as a house, clothing, objects of art, a bicycle, an automobile, a radio, a bank account, and government bonds. He might save his money, though there was now little incentive or opportunity to do so. All the privileges or security for himself and family for which he had once saved or hoarded were now socially provided for all who worked.

Thus, while the ultimate objective is the socialization of life itself, there are certain necessary measures which the Party urges, must be enforced to start with. Not only the key industries, but also all the principal industries (cotton and jute while not being key industries, are certainly the principal industries of India); not only industries but banks, all transport, plantations, mines, public utilities, insurance; in fact, all the important economic institutions and activities which dominate social life, must be brought under social control.

Let us see what exactly would happen by taking one industry. Take cotton. A decree would be issued announcing that the eighty odd mills of Bombay (let us take Bombay alone for illustration) have become the property of the Indian people. A Cotton Industries Department would be set up to run the factories in conjunction with the representatives of the workers in the industry and in accordance with the National Economic Plan. The Department would decide in accordance with that Plan, how much cotton should be bought and what manner and quantity of cotton goods should be manufactured, in order to fulfil the needs of the Community within its existing resources.

Distribution of the manufactured goods might be rationed—that is, it may be fixed that each person is to buy only so much—if the supply is too little. Or the goods might be put on the market at fixed prices, if there is enough of them.

Rationing may seem to be an oppression to some, but only to those who have money to buy as much as they want. It would not seem harsh to those who have even less than a loincloth to cover their body with, to those thousands of Indian families which have just one whole *sari* in common, between a number of women, so that only one of them goes out at a time, the rest keeping indoors, clad in rags and in less than rags.

What of the workers of the mills that have been socialized? The workers, from wage slaves, would become, along with the rest of the Community, the masters of the factories in which till now they slaved and sweated. Their representatives, their unions, will have a decisive hand in running the mills. Their wages will rise. Better houses will be built for them. Shorter hours of work. Schools for their children. Maternity houses. Parks, museums, libraries. The workers would be transplanted into a new world—a world of freedom, of initiative, of power, of opportunities for cultural advancement.

And what of the owners? The owners, in a society of workers, would have to become workers too. They will have opportunities to work and to serve the Community, perhaps as managers and experts—if they had the ability.

No compensation would be paid to the owners, and for very good reasons. A society which aims at social equality cannot start by creating inequalities of wealth. A society which starts with the thesis that ownership of functional property has meant exploitation, that profits are surplus-value, cannot be expected to recognise the claims of individuals who have owned such property in respect of the socialization of that property. A system that is declared to be unjust cannot be tacitly approved of by the payment of compensation. Furthermore, the owners most probably would have enough resources laid by in the shape of personal property not to require any more. What need will they have for more wealth if they, like the others, are fully provided for, i.e. if they work? Owners in fact, with any noble instincts in them, will throw in their lot with the new dispensation and join in building the new and greater society.

All this, of course, would be different if the owners tried to be "funny". If they tried to resist the new decrees; to sabotage the new undertaking; to plot against the new society;—things would indeed go wrong with them. They, in the eyes of the Law, would be the enemies of the people and would be so dealt with. Feeling against them in that case might run very high indeed—because of the revolutionary tension; the instability of the new system; the anxiety to save the newly launched ship from tempests.

What will happen to the owners, therefore, is largely dependent on how the owners will behave.

What has been said of the cotton industry would be true of the others too.

There will be planning and building up everywhere, organised production, ordered and equitable distribution.

VIII

(4) State Monopoly of Foreign Trade

State monopoly of foreign trade is an essential element of economic planning. In plain terms it simply means that the Community decides what it must import and export. If the question is left to private tradesmen, not the needs of the Community but private profit would determine exports and imports, in which case we may witness the strange spectacle of wheat being exported when there is famine in the land, or cotton being imported when the home producer is unable to market his produce.

Economic planning would be very difficult, almost impossible, with foreign trade in the hands of profiteers. It would be difficult in that case to control currency and prices, production and consumption and to follow successfully any plan of industrial or agricultural development. The plan would be dislocated at every place.

Apart from these difficulties, private foreign trade would make it possible for the enemies of the Nation, either within or without, to sabotage its economic schemes and activities.

Foreign trade, in fact, affects national life so vitally that even under Capitalism it nowhere exists in an unrestricted, uncontrolled form. The historic Free Trade country—Great Britain—had also recently to renounce the system of unrestricted foreign trade.

IX

(5) Organization of Co-operatives for Production, Distribution and credit in the Unsocialized sector of Economic Life

The necessity of this measure arises from the fact that the entire economic life cannot be socialized all at once. Only the big concerns can be brought under social ownership at first. That would leave a number of small concerns and businesses still running on individualistic lines. It is to deal with this situation that this measure has been suggested. It aims at replacing this individualistic small business with co-operative concerns.

For instance, let us take the case of small consumers' shops. The State cannot, in the early stages, be expected to open stores in every little community. And yet the individualistic concerns must not be allowed to continue. While they might not do harm, they would, fundamentally, be enemies of Socialism. Therefore, it is suggested that Co-operative Consumers' Stores should be developed which should take the place of the private ones. If the private shopkeepers join the Co-operatives, well and good; otherwise they must be driven out of business by competition. A well organized Co-operative on account of its superior resources, would always be able to beat small business, particularly when it had the State behind it.

X

(6) Elimination of Princes and Landlords and All Other Classes of Exploiters Without Compensation

If our aim is to create a society free from every kind of exploitation and social injustice, a society in which there is no rank or privilege, this measure is but in the nature of a corollary.

The princes, relics of feudal India, are anachronisms in the modern world. They are maintained and protected by Imperialism for its own purposes; otherwise they would long have been swept away by the modern forces of society.

The princes of India are today the greatest despots in the world. Nowhere else is so much authority and power vested in such irresponsible hands. Great as is the injustice resulting from this, our plea for the abolition of the rule of the princes does not rest on it.

It is the system itself that we challenge and not its excesses. A good prince remains a prince, a good landlord remains a landlord, a good mill-owner is still a millowner. And as long as the social relationships inherent in these terms last, exploitation and injustice last, no matter how well-meaning the human units in those relationships are.

This is a viewpoint which should be fully grasped for a correct understanding of our case.

The existence of even constitutional princes in a Free India would be meaningless, an unnecessary burden, a perpetual obstacle, to the growth of democracy. The masses, society as a whole, would gain nothing by their retention and lose much.

Much the same can be said of the landlords. Landlordism was never a feature of Hindu polity. In the "Hindu" period of Indian history, the tiller of the soil paid a fixed share of his produce direct to the king or his agents. There were no middlemen.

It is, indeed, an irony that when we talk of abolishing the Zamindaris, we are accused of copying Bolshevik methods and of forgetting the traditions of our great civilization!

The system of landlordism is wholly unproductive except of indolence and irresponsibility. It is a source of loss to both the State and the people. A class of middlemen, performing no social function, appropriates a share of the produce, which rightfully belongs to the cultivator.

Mr. M.L. Darling, who cannot be suspected of Socialism, thus writes of the Punjab landlord:

> Taking the province as a whole, it may be said that the landlord is even a greater burden upon society than the moneylender. The moneylender is doubtless an evil, but till he can be replaced, he is a necessary evil. On the other hand, the landlord is too often a parasite living on his tenants, wasting his substance and corrupting his neighbourhood.

Apart from its excesses, the system in itself is an outrage on society. Land is a primary means of production and is the chief source of living in India. Its private ownership not only leads to exploitation and unequal distribution of wealth, but, in the peculiar conditions of India, also to progressive impoverishment and bankruptcy of the majority of India's population.

Where would be the sense of maintaining such a monstrous economic institution, even if its excesses of tyranny and oppression were removed? What would the masses gain by it? How would society profit by it?

As for compensation, much the same argument applies to compensating these classes as was advanced in the case of capitalists.

XI

(7) Redistribution of Land to Peasants

Common ownership being our goal, it would appear rather strange that we should think of redistributing land to peasants. This necessity arises from the fact that common ownership and cultivation of land would be slow to develop and therefore we will have to begin with peasant proprietorship.

At present there is grave inequality in the size of holdings. While some holdings are of hundreds of acres, others do not even approach an acre. We, therefore, propose to redistribute the land so as to remove these grave inequalities.

XII

(8) Encouragement and Promotion of Co-operative and Collective Farming by the State

With this item we approach one of the most difficult and baffling problems that would face any socialist government, much more so the Indian socialist government. Let us carefully consider the matter.

India is a predominantly agricultural country. It is argued, therefore, that it can have little to do with Socialism. We have already shown above that under present world conditions and with the productive resources of society developed as they are today, it is possible to build up Socialism anywhere, no matter how backward the place may be. If there is a party in power in India desirous of establishing Socialism in the country, the fact of its being predominantly agricultural will not be an impediment. It will lower the pace of socialist reconstruction, but nothing beyond that.

The real question is not the possibility of establishing Socialism; but, whether Indian agriculture, the Indian peasant, the Indian nation, will gain by Socialism. And to this question our answer is emphatic. There is not the least doubt in our mind that Socialism alone can save Indian agriculture from ruin and bankruptcy; can alone make the peasant prosperous and progressive; can alone make the nation strong and powerful.

The malady of Indian agriculture has gone so far that nothing but a drastic transformation can save it. Briefly, it suffers from the following diseases: vested interests in land which not only exploit the actual tiller of the soil but also make him an indifferent and inefficient cultivator; disproportionately high taxation; an unbearable burden of debt that is fast approaching the breaking point; sub-division of land into utterly uneconomic holdings; low productivity; unsatisfactory methods of marketing; bad credit facilities; lack of balance between industry and agriculture, town and village.

Any of these is a big enough problem to be tackled, but when all of them have to be faced, as they must be, in order to realise a synthetic and comprehensive solution, no possible measure of reform can cope with the situation.

The only solution is to clear away all the vested interests that lead in any manner whatever to the exploitation of the tiller of the soil; liquidate all agrarian debts; pool the holdings and establish co-operative and collective farming, State and co-operative credit and marketing systems and co-operative subsidiary industries.

It should not be supposed that these are "destructive" ideas. They will mean the destruction of nothing but that system of exploitation which is inherent in the relationship of tenant and landlord. For the rest, they are wholly constructive, requiring nothing except State guidance, encouragement and propaganda.

Professor Radhakamal Mukherji, in his Agra Extension Lecture, is reported to have admitted that no improvement was possible in Indian agriculture "unless the Indian village was converted from a collection of small isolated holdings to a single co-operative farm, and agriculture was treated as a collective service". An admission which fully bears out our plea.

Those who get frightened at the mere idea of co-operative and collective enterprise, particularly when applied to the field of agriculture, might suggest that a better alternative would be to create solvent and efficient peasant proprietors, each with an indivisible economic holding, and cultivating his land independently.

Our answer is that, if this is actually done, it too will involve changes no less drastic than those required by us, and at the same time the result will be infinitely inferior—from the point of view of both the peasant and the nation.

From the peasant's point of view, because an independent peasant runs greater risks and is at a greater disadvantage as producer, seller, buyer and borrower than the peasant who is a member of a co-operative farm. At the same time, he gets none of the facilities and amenities that a large co-operative enterprise must offer its members. Culturally and ethically he is bound to be a much less developed individual, speaking in terms of averages, than one who has shed his narrow individualism and identified himself with the Community.

Considered from the nation's point of view, our case is stronger still. And it should be remembered that the peasant too is a part—the greater part in India—of the nation.

While speaking of the necessity of Socialism in India, I pointed out above that we required Socialism here, as elsewhere, not only to free the people from exploitation, but also to enable ourselves to plan and carry out a conscious development of the country's economic and social life. A planned development would be a much greater necessity in India than elsewhere, because life here has been so completely disorganized as a result of imperialistic exploitation.

But with individualistic agriculture, no planning would be possible. Consider the prospect of planning production and distribution in a country where the raw material and the food-stuffs are all grown on little individual holdings. Is the thing possible? What crops must be raised and how much of each?—are questions which the Community must decide if it wants to decide what manufactured goods it must have; what factories it must build; what food it must consume; what materials it must export in order to import the goods it needs.

This is not possible unless agriculture is organized in larger units than an individual holding. With each village becoming a unit for agricultural production and with each unit working in unison with the others, working as a part of an organized economy, this could be made possible. Of course, the State, by preferential taxation, may stimulate or curtail the production of given crops even under individualistic agriculture, and thus establish some control over agricultural production, as they did in the early days in Russia. But this would not take the State very far on the road to planning.

Then, again, consider long-time planning. Say, it is desired within a period of years to double the agricultural production of India. Could this be done if agriculture continued to be on an individualistic basis? Of course, one could educate the farmer in improved methods of cultivation and so on; but that alone would not be sufficient. There are limits to agricultural production when the land is subdivided into little plots individually cultivated.

Take again the problem of establishing a balance between agriculture and industry. There can be no solution of the agricultural problem, unless this balance has been established. But this, again, requires co-operative effort and planning, and here again individualistic farming would prove a stumbling-block.

If we look at the problem from the point of view of psychology, we shall find that Socialism in agriculture, i.e. co-operative and collective farming, is essential for the success of any attempt to recast Indian life on a socialist basis. I have often been asked: why can we not organize our industry on a socialist basis and leave agriculture on the present individualistic one? Our answer is that the existence of the two standards—individualism on the one hand and Socialism on the other—would create such maladjustments and friction that the whole hybrid system would be paralysed. Socialism can never go with millions of peasants, owning their own patches of land, cultivating them for their own profit—narrow, selfish peasants. In the same Community, a part, the smaller part in India and most other countries, cannot live and work in a corporate manner, while the remaining, and larger part, remains wedded to individualism—with all its waste product of social friction and frustration.

If Socialism has to be built up in the country, corporate life and standards must also grow up in the village along with their growth in the cities.

Thus, look at the problem from whichever side you please, the application of socialist principles to Indian agriculture is inescapable.

What exactly, then, is socialist agriculture, what is co-operative and collective farming?

We all know something about the old Indian village commune. It is true that this was neither the most ancient nor the most common form of agricultural organization known in India. It finds no mention in the *Manu-*

smriti. However, it is indisputable that there were long periods of Indian history and long tracts of Indian territory in which a form of village existed—whatever its origin—in which common tenure of land and sometimes also common tillage, were recognized and practised. In Madras such villages existed till the other day.

The socialist aim follows in spirit the lines of the old system—except that the socialist village instead of being a closed circle, a closed economic unit, would be an actively co-operating unit in a larger economic system.

In Russia, where alone in our day Socialism is being built up and where alone a serious attempt has been made, with remarkable success, to socialize agriculture—an agriculture, mind you, no less primitive, no less hide-bound by tradition and dominated no less by an ignorant, indolent, narrowly-selfish peasantry—two types of socialized agriculture, rather three, have grown up.

The first form, a lower one when considered from socialist standards, that we witness, is simply co-operative farming. Under this system, individual holdings remain (though much equalized by the redistribution of the land of the landlords and the capitalist farmers); the old agricultural instruments, horses, etc., remain individual property; but for the purposes of cultivation, the holdings are pooled together and the crop is raised and harvested with joint labour. The produce is distributed according to the size of the holding and the amount of labour put in, after costs have been accounted for.

This is the first lesson in social living. It promotes a community of spirit and by materially increasing the output, it becomes an incentive to the individualistic peasant to take more kindly to community of life and work.

The next step from this is the collective farm. Here no individual holdings remain and the basis of distribution is only the amount of labour put in and, in some unusual cases, unusual needs. But even in the collective village, individual ownership of tools may yet remain, and pigs and cattle and horses may yet be the property of individuals. While an immense growth in communal living has taken place, yet much of life is lived apart.

So we see as the third stage, the "communes" rise, where there is the utmost possible common living.

Commenting on this achievement of socialist enterprise in the U.S.S.R., which he calls a revolution in agriculture, Dr. Sherwood Eddy writes in his latest book:[3]

> The Soviet Union is now in the midst of the greatest revolution ever known in agriculture. Backward agriculture and the dislocation of the relation between city and the country has been a perennial problem since the decay of the Roman Empire.

[3] *Russia To-day: What Can We Learn From It?*

For four and a quarter years the Soviets tried not only to transform a primitive agricultural country into a modern industrial state, but to collectivize, mechanize and socialize its agriculture among a hundred million peasants scattered over one-sixth of the surface of the habitable world. That, of course, was impossible, but that "impossible" was almost accomplished, and the back of the rural problem was actually broken. The Soviets have fought their "battle" of the "Marne" with the peasants—and won. Russia will never retreat from collectivization.

Until two years ago there was the menace of twenty million individualistic, potentially capitalistic, land-hungry peasants, who had a deep antipathy toward Socialism and might some day defeat or overthrow their Union of Soviet Socialist Republics. After the industrial workers, the peasants will now become the most socialized class. Whatever its overhasty and faulty execution, this will probably yet become one of the great achievements of history.

This is the achievement of Socialism in Russia. What about India? Is there anything in this system of socialistic agriculture that is impracticable here? If the Russians have achieved the impossible, why we too cannot do it? There is no reason to suppose that the Indian peasant is any more averse to common endeavour and the sharing of life than the Russian. What else is the significance in the modern sense of

सहनाववतु सहनौभुनक्तु सहवीर्यंकरवावहै ।
तेजस्विनावधीतमस्तु मा विद्विषावहै ।।

Let us be slow instead of hasty as the Russians. Let us use no coercion. Nor does the Party advocate forcible socialization of agriculture, as it does with industry. *Encouragement and promotion* of co-operative and collective farming is the phrase used—encouragement and promotion through education, propaganda, demonstration, subsidy, preferential taxation.

We might use fewer labour-saving agricultural machinery in view of our population and the shortage of land as compared with the virgin expanses of Russia's territory. This does not mean that we shall retain the present inefficient plough, but perhaps we may not require, at least till industrial development absorbs the surplus rural population, many tractors and mechanical reapers and binders. We shall electrify the village and give it radio and easy transport, yes. But we might be slow in mechanizing agriculture. We are criticised as being mere imitators of the West. But we are not out to imitate. We only wish to learn.

Let us make fewer mistakes than the Russians, if we are wise enough to avoid them. Remember, it is easy to be wise after the event. Russians were themselves the first to realize their mistakes; and they never set out deliberately to make them. When with test-tubes mistakes cannot be avoided, much less can they be avoided when you are experimenting with millions of men and one-sixth of the globe's surface.

Let not the Russians' mistakes blind us to their great achievements, to the lessons they are teaching. Let wise parlour philosophers grin over them and shake their sceptic little heads. For us, who have to do things, who have a task before us, it is the great principle of a new life which the Russians are so boldly practising that alone is of value.

There is a certain type of confused and often interested person who goes about the country saying that the socialists will take away the land from the peasants. We socialists do not have an island across the seas where we shall transport all the land that we shall "confiscate" from the peasants. The lands will be where they are and the peasants will have them and cultivate them. The question only is *how* the peasants shall cultivate their land so that society may benefit most—the peasants themselves more than anyone else.

The only plea that we put forth is that social good rather than the good of a small number of individuals should be our goal. And I think, I have been able to show that if the land is tilled in common—better still, if it is owned in common too—a great boon would be conferred on India's entire rural population. The village would be transformed from its present mean position to one of prosperity and culture, unknown in any age of Indian history.

Before leaving this topic, I wish to take up a problem which is closely allied to it. Among Congressmen there is a large section which is devoutly attached to the village and all it stands for. This section, owing to a misunderstanding, feels called upon to take the offensive against the socialists who, it is known, stand for machinery; and therefore, so it is thought, for the exploitation of the village, for the disruption of its beautiful self-sufficient economy (which is non-existent now) and for the growth of parasitic cities.

Let me first of all freely admit all that these friends have to say against the modern cities. These monsters of human habitation—their crowding, their nerve-racking traffic, their insanitation, their ugliness, their slums—rightly make us revolt against them and compel us to look upon them as a menace, as a danger, as enemies of good and sensible living. The city for most of its dwellers is a terrible place of habitation. It has its theatres and resorts of amusement; but these are more like anodynes for tired nerves and fatigued bodies than things of joy and beauty, from which the soul may draw sustenance, or, if you prefer a modern phrase, which may develop and recreate man's personality.

Further, the modern cities have grown on the exploitation of the people—not, however, of the village people alone, but also of the city workers. The conditions of this exploitation bring about an unnatural hostility between city and village, in which the latter invariably gets the worse deal. While art, knowledge, luxury, comfort, are concentrated in the cities, the villages remain neglected, undeveloped—terrible contrasts to the cities which they help to create.

While all this is true, it is wrong to imagine that under Socialism this abnormal growth of the social body would be retained or encouraged. Socialism, if anything, is a technic of social engineering which has as its aim the harmonious and well-balanced growth of the whole of society. Neither the socialist village, nor the socialist city, will bear any resemblance to its present prototype. The contrasts, the inner conflicts, would not only not be perpetuated but systematically fought and eradicated.

It is true that the socialist hugs machinery. But to him machinery is not an instrument of exploitation, not stakes and stocks to which to tie the human body and torture it. Machines to us mean friends of labour—things that relieve human toil; increase its productivity; conquer the wind and the sea for us.

The assumption that machinery will inevitably create monstrosities of cities and rural unemployment by disrupting village economy, is wrong. Machines if used for private benefit by a handful of people who own them, will undoubtedly produce these and worse results. But that society as a whole making use of these efficient and powerful instruments of production for the good of the entire population, will also encounter these same results, is too absurd a proposition to be accepted.

Under Socialism the cities will be planned and concentration avoided, because industry will be diffused. There will be geographical planning as well as statistical. On the other hand the villages will be transformed from little clusters of houses—cut off from the world, tucked away into the recesses of the Earth—to progressive communities, connected with the rest of the world with electric railways, telephones, radios, roads, buses. The village too will become an industrial unit of production like the city. It will have its self-government, its schools, its recreation centre, its museum.

I cannot do better than quote in this connection a fine description of the socialist village and city, which M. Illin has given in his remarkably written *Moscow Has A Plan:*

How was the old city built?

In the centre a fortress, a Kremlin, an inner citadel.

Around this centre a ring of markets, shops and stores grew up. And when they began to build factories, a third ring of the city appeared—the factory district. Among these shops, markets and factories they erected buildings—the better ones in the heart of the city—and the poor ones in the outskirts. A new city will not be built thus. Its centre will be, not a fortress, or a market, but a factory or an electric power station.

About each large electric power station, about each large factory or union of factories, a city will spring up.

Not the grey walls of a fortress with stone teeth and look-out towers, but a green wall of parks will separate the heart of the city—the factory—from the residential sections. This green wall will protect the city from the smoke and soot of factory chimneys.

And the blocks will be different.

From the central square, like the rays of the sun, avenues and boulevards will radiate in all directions. Buildings will not stand in a row like soldiers, all facing one way. Each dwelling will turn toward the sun in order to get as much of its light as possible. While house-communes, schools, libraries, hospitals, will be surrounded with flower-beds. At every entrance you will be greeted by green giants, oaks, pines, lime trees.

Happy singing of birds and the calm, sustained, refreshing voice of trees, instead of the present clang and rumble and roar, will be heard in the streets of the city.

There will be none of those incessant bustle and scramble which now shatter the nerves of all of us city dwellers.

Institutions will be situated far from dwellings. People must live in quiet and peaceful places.

There will be less traffic in the streets and no such colossal cities as we now have. *A city of one hundred thousand inhabitants will be considered too large* (my italics).

Every future city will be a worker's village (mark this word, village—J.P.N.) near a factory. And factories and unions of factories will not all be brought together in one centre as at present; they will be distributed throughout the entire country according to a rational plan. Our raw materials are found, not in one place either, but in a thousand places.

This is the way a city will be built. But how about the village?

There will be no village (my italics). Bread and meat and milk will be secured from factories in govfarms (government farms—J.P.N.) and colfarms (collective farms—J.P.N.). Around each of these agricultural factories will be constructed—food, flour, conserve, meat, refrigeration. All of these will constitute a single union of factories, but agricultural rather than industrial. And around each of these unions a city will rise, an agricultural city. This means that the difference between city and village, between peasant and workman, will disappear. Even the words *peasant* and *labourer* will pass away.

Only the word *worker* will remain.

This will happen after we construct socialism. But already during these five years we shall build about two hundred socialist cities, thousands of house-communes. Already the difference between city and village is being effaced.

Socialism is no longer a myth, a figment of the mind. We ourselves are building it.

A superb vision! And so practicable, so much within the reach of your arm. This is the great thing about socialist visions—they are translatable into fact.

If the problem of city and village has to be solved at all, it is on some such basis that it can be done and not by running away from the city or from the village.

XIII

(10) *Recognition of the Right of Work or Maintenance by the State*

In the capitalist State or in the ones preceding it, there was no security of work and therefore of life. As long as virgin land existed, no security for able-bodied persons was needed. But when land became scarce and could not be secured—nor could employment be found—one had either to starve or rob and plunder. If one did the latter and was caught, one was brought to justice; but if one starved to death—well, God blessed his soul.

This insecurity of employment has become a greater scourge in our days than it ever was. Industrialism has created a propertyless class of workers, who can live only by selling their labour. At the same time, no provision has been made to find employment for them. Each is expected to shift for himself. It was only after industrial crises made a scandal of unemployment, and labour became too militant, that the modern States made provision for unemployment insurance.

In India, the paralysis of both industry and agriculture under Imperialism has resulted in the acutest imaginable form of unemployment.

Under Socialism, this state of affairs would be intolerable. In fact, no just and sensible social order can look with equanimity upon the starvation of millions of its members. Provision for employment or maintenance for every adult member, is the least that can be expected from any reasonable organization of society. This would be one of the first concerns of a Socialist Government in India, and one of the first guarantees it must give the people.

XIV

(11) *"To everyone according to his need and from everyone according to his capacity", etc.*

This is the ultimate ideal of Socialism. It means simply this, that when Socialism is fully developed everyone would put forth his best effort in the service of the Community—in working for it in factories, farms, schools, laboratories, theatres—and would take whatever he needed from the things that were available. Of course if he made, say, bolts and nuts, it is not suggested that he would take as many of them as he wanted. He would have no use for bolts and nuts and there would be no private market in which he could sell them. What he would take according to his needs would be consumption goods—clothes, food, books. There would be no money, no wages, no distinction in incomes.

Let us keep in mind that such would be the ultimate state of society. It presupposes a condition of plenty—that enough of everything of use is available for everyone. Till this condition is reached some restriction on consumption would be necessary, either by the direct method of rationing or the indirect method of wages.

Doubts will be raised about the practicability of the principle stated here, even in the case of plenty. The problem is one of social psychology and common sense and should not be at all difficult in practice. Let us first remember that a new type of human character would have been created, that selfishness would be looked down upon as a crime and vice rolled in one. In Soviet Russia grain-stealers from collective farms are liable to be shot: such is the sanctity of social property.

On the background of this new psychological outlook, let us consider the practicability of the principle. The suggestion is made that if people were free to take as much as they pleased, they would take advantage of such freedom. But let us consider the nature of the society they would be living in. There would be full security of life and work: provision for old age, sickness, child-birth, etc. The individual would have nothing to worry about except making himself a good man and doing his job well. Things would not be bought or sold in that Community—they would merely be manufactured and distributed. Smuggling of goods across the frontier would be well-nigh impossible, except of jewellery and such other trinkets: that much of jewellery or trinkets would be available in a socialist society is doubtful! In a society like this, what motive could the individual have to hoard things? He could get what he needed, whenever he wanted. They would be *his* things, they would not disappear the next day. Social standards and a sense of complete security would eliminate the hoarding instinct.

Till such a development of society has taken place, there would be restriction of consumption, as I have said above. There would be money and wages and some difference in incomes. Wages are a system of apportioning consuming power. If production increases, wages would rise proportionately to socialist saving, i.e. investment in production goods and expenditure on the provision of social amenities. Differences in wages would continue—within much narrower limits than at present—only as a concession to our present moral standards and the great differences in skill that exist today.

XV

(12) Adult Franchise on a Functional Basis

This means that representation instead of being on a territorial basis would be on the basis of occupations. Representatives are supposed to represent interests; but interests within a given country are not distributed territorially but functionally, occupationally. Therefore functional representation means truer representation.

This item, it may be added, is meant to meet only the problems of the transition period. In time, occupations, though still diversified, would acquire a unity and solidarity, a community of interest and purpose, which would make such discriminatory representation meaningless. In fact, the State itself in its modern sense would wither away with the full development of Socialism and a classless society. Representation in that stage would not be to political assemblies of the State but to Boards of industry, education, and so on. Representative Government would be entirely revolutionized.

XVI

These are the measures which we propose. They are far-reaching measures requiring, courage, ability, faith: virtues, surely not wanting in the new youth of India.

If we dream of creating a great India, it is only these measures that can enable us to realize our dream. If we want to wipe off poverty, injustice, filth, indolence, ignorance from the face of this great country, we can do so only by adopting these bold measures.

If we are told that we are asking for the Moon, I shall firmly reply that we are doing nothing of the sort. If complete Independence is not as far as the Moon, *these* measures are certainly not farther.

It is said that Socialism is not applicable to India. Which of these measures, I ask, is inapplicable to our country, if the will to apply them be present? If Indian capitalism is weak, that, instead of being a hindrance to us in our task of building up Socialism, should only facilitate it. The backwardness of India did not prevent the British from building railroads, telegraphs, banks, mills, warehouses. These instead of being a boon, as in themselves they ought to be, turned out to be a scourge simply because they were not built for our good. The backwardness of Turkestan has not prevented the Russians from building up Socialism there.

As I have said repeatedly, if we mean to do it, under modern world conditions, with science and its inventions, it is possible to build up Socialism anywhere.

Shall we have the power to do so in India?

If we acquire sufficient power, as we hope to, to achieve complete Independence, we shall have power to do almost anything in this country. There is no power or party in India stronger than imperialism, and if we humble the latter there will be no one to challenge our will. The princes and the landlords, who may seem rather formidable today, propped up by British force, would wither away at our first touch. The capitalists, perhaps a little stronger, would also be powerless to check us.

CHAPTER 3

ALTERNATIVES

"Something about 'humanity', as the thing has been recently labelled, something about the 'realization' of this humanity or rather—monstrosity; a little about property..., some moans about the proletariat, the organization of labour, miserable associations for the improvement of the lower classes of the people, all combined with boundless ignorance of political economy and actual society—that is the whole story, which, moreover, theoretical impartiality, the 'absolute calm of thought', drains of its last drop of blood, its last energy and elasticity."

FRIEDRICH ENGELS

Are there any alternatives to Socialism?

We are told that there are. There are Gandhism, the Village Industries Association, the old Hindu system found in *Manu-smriti* and other ancient treatises on social organization.

India would be an exception indeed if its soil too did not produce a crop of alternatives to this all-challenging idea. Even in Europe, the birthplace of modern Socialism, these alternatives have not yet lost their vogue. Mr. H.G. Wells has just preached his "Clissoldism" as a rational and decent alternative to the "class-struggle dogma", to the world-leader of the present socialist movement—Joseph Stalin.

It is interesting to note that all these alternatives bear a pronounced family resemblance. What Gandhiji says today was said by Church divines and philosophers of the old order in Europe at the dawn of the Industrial Revolution. Comte said long ago what Wells is now trying to persuade the world to accept.

The resemblance boils down to certain common features. There is found in all of them a conscious attempt to run away from strife and struggle and the sudden upsetting of the *status quo*; and, therefore, a tendency to compose the serious differences and maladjustments—which are universally admitted—through common understanding and goodwill. The method suggested is invariably the betterment of human nature through education and the placing of individuals of high moral and intellectual qualities in positions of authority and power.

II

We have been accused of attempting to import a foreign system into India, which has its own peculiar problems and solutions thereof.

I wish to make it clear that we have no desire to disregard either the peculiar problems of India or its historic cultural background. It would indeed be utterly un-Marxian to do so. We have, in fact, examined to the best of our ability the so-called "Indian" solutions; and we are satisfied that *under present conditions* they cannot take the place of Socialism. This is no reflection on the genius of the social philosophers of ancient India. Unfortunately for them Indian Society has changed so drastically, its problems have been transformed so radically, that their ideas hardly bear any relation to present facts. There are certain broad principles which hold good in all ages and climes. But broad principles are of little value when concrete means are sought for the removal of concrete evils. And it is here—not in their conception of general social and individual good—that the old systems and their new reflections break down completely.

The old principles were laid down when civilization was much simpler than at present. Neither industry nor agriculture had developed far enough to make it possible for men to exploit the labour of others to any considerable extent. All production was on a small individual scale. Population was low and nature kind and bountiful. It was possible for any able-bodied man to clear the jungle and settle down with his family on the reclaimed land.

From this it is a far cry to our present agrarian and industrial problems. Landlordism is an un-Indian institution, mills and factories are also new to the country. New likewise are all the problems that have been created by the imperialist domination. The basic economic problem of our society—the problem of the exploitation of the many by the few—which arises, as I have shown in Chapter 1, from the monopoly of land and other instruments of production—did not exist in its present universal form at the time of Manu, nor, quite naturally, did any solution of it.

This problem, which we find has no relation with India's ancient past, has, on the other hand, a basic unity with the problems of the modern world. In China, Japan, England, France, Germany, the United States of America, the vast majority of people has to face essentially the same problem. The development of the powers of production, in other words, the invention of steam and electric power, has given birth to, and reared, the most extensive and thorough system of human exploitation ever known—the system of capitalist production and distribution.

Socialism, which is an inevitable reaction to this system, is, therefore, not bound by national frontiers. Its home is as much in England as in Japan, as much in Germany as in China, in the United States of America as in

India. Wherever conditions of capitalist exploitation exist, Socialism is bound to raise its head. If capitalism has become a world system, Socialism too will spread to the four corners of the globe. India can be, and, as events are showing, is no exception.

The existence of feudalistic relics in India modifies its problem to some extent, but it does not change its essential nature. The balance of power between the various sections of the exploited masses would be somewhat different here, and their transition to Socialism slower—otherwise their *goal* as well as their initial task of *overthrowing* the system of capitalist-*cum*-feudal exploitation and rule, would remain essentially the same as in the developed capitalist countries.

It is for those who accuse us of imitating the West, to produce a truly Indian solution of the problems that face us. But though there has been a good deal of talk about India's peculiarities and its unique recipes for its ills, no one seems to have taken the trouble of formulating them in intelligible language—with perhaps only one honourable exception.

As far as I am aware, Dr. Bhagavan Das is the only one among the leaders of the country, who has given serious thought to this problem, and laid before the public what he considers are Indian solutions of Indian problems. To us what is of greater value and importance than the solutions that the learned Doctor advocates, is his bold insistence on the view that the nature of Swaraj is a subject of paramount importance and calls for urgent and earnest inquiry and discussion. But apart from the socialists, the Doctor stands almost alone in holding this view.

As far as most other lovers of Indian culture are concerned, their task is finished after they have tarred us with the brush of "foreignism" and prated some nonsense about the folly of troubling about matters that concern the remote future. "Let us win Swaraj first" they say. One wonders if they see the inconsistency of their position when they attack and oppose Socialism. By that action they make it clear that whatever "ism" they might accept after they have won Swaraj, they would, at least, be opposed to Socialism. Apart from being a breach of the neutrality they assume, this gives a clear indication of their sympathies.

Before proceeding to consider some of the alternatives, I should like to point out the curious fact that these Indian culture enthusiasts, when they are faced with Socialism, fail to show the least interest in the Manu-ite solutions presented to them by Dr. Bhagavan Das. The fate of the Das-Das Swaraj Scheme is well known. And now his *Ancient* vs. *Modern Scientific Socialism* has fallen again, it seems, on deaf ears.

To take a concrete instance. It will be recalled that at the time of the last Assembly elections, the learned Doctor had pointed out that according to Indian traditions it was for the people to seek out their leader and ask him to legislate for them and not for "candidates" for leadership to go running about begging the people for their "votes". At that time it was not noticed that the lovers of Indian tradition welcomed Dr. Das' suggestion with any visible enthusiasm. I suspect, on the other hand, that he was looked upon by most of these gentlemen as a mere Manu-crank.

The greater part of this talk of "Indianism" is, to my mind, insincere—a mere cloak for reaction and conservatism. If the leaders of the country (with one or two exceptions) sat down today to forge out a Constitution for India, I have not the least doubt that, in spite of all this condemnation of Socialism as un-Indian, that Constitution would be an utter imitation of the democratic constitutions of the West.

III

This brings me to the first alternative that I wish to examine.

Political Democracy is not an alternative to Socialism. I wish, however, to examine it here because to a very large section of political workers in the country it represents the only conceivable form of Swaraj.

In the days of Bentham and Godwin it was believed that if the franchise were extended to every adult, the "people" would become so powerful that they would wipe off all the injustices and evils of society. Gradually the franchise *was* extended till the dream of the old radicals was realised. But the millennium refused to arrive. The injustices remained, the evils were obdurate. Apparently something was wrong.

What was wrong was soon discovered. Socialists had long been asking for not merely formal changes in political institutions, but also basic changes in the economic structure of society. They pointed out that political power lay not so much in the right to cast votes as in the control of the economic life of the country. Non-socialists, however, had pinned their faith to the powers of the ballot-box. But when that box failed to deliver the goods, the cry of "failure of democracy" went up everywhere. And today there is hardly a progressive political thinker in the West who has not come to advocate economic together with political democracy. There are differences of opinion as to how and in what measure to acquire that democracy but no longer does any one believe that political democracy alone will suffice.

What is the position in India? Unfortunately here we are yet in the days of Bentham and Godwin. The Liberals and the majority of the older Congressmen, have no brighter vision for their country than full Representative Government.

I have again and again been faced with the naive question: would not the masses, if every adult had a vote, capture the political machinery and run it in their own interest? The answer is most emphatically in the negative. The masses, better educated politically than in India, have nowhere done so. While democracy has conferred on them equality of status in a formal, legal sense, it has not enabled them anywhere to free themselves from exploitation, hunger, unemployment, slavery.

The United States of America is the richest country in the world and the birthplace of republicanism. It has had the democratic system of government for a century and a half. Yet today there are fifteen million able-bodied men and women there, with families to support, who cannot even find ordinary means of livelihood. Is it not strange that such a state of affairs should exist in a country that has had, for so long, a government which is proudly said to be "of the people for the people and by the people". Strange that the people should have governed themselves to starvation!

What then is wrong with political democracy? Briefly, that its machinery is such that in a society where great differences in wealth and social status exist, the classes which are economically dominant easily capture and enslave it. In fact, historically considered, the growth of modern democracy was coeval with the growth of capitalism. Democracy was an instrument in the hands of the rising bourgeoisie to fight feudal privilege and power. Thus, the forces that gave birth to democracy themselves tied it to the chariot wheels of capitalism. The democratic State became a tool whereby the rule of the bourgeoisie was established and maintained. Thus, behind the fiction of the People's Sovereignty stalks naked class rule. The experience of every democratic country of the West proves this beyond the shadow of a doubt.

An experiment with pure political democracy in India would yield no better results—indeed, it might have worse consequences. The democratic Indian State might become a worse tool in the hands of the upper classes for grinding the faces of the poor and exploited. There is nothing that one knows about these classes in India that encourages one to hold out a more cheery prospect. It is common knowledge that the British millowner is a better employer than the Indian. The exploits of the Indian landlords and bankers are well known. The princes have no peers in the line of tyranny and oppression.

What will become of the "people" when these classes come to power?

IV

It might be urged that we cannot jump the stages of social evolution, that we must pass through the capitalist-democratic experience of Europe before we can take the next step to Socialism. Soviet Russia and China give the lie to this argument. It is true that full Socialism cannot be established in a country till it is fully industrialized. An industrially backward country like India will naturally take some time to be fully industrialized; and therefore it cannot be immediately converted into a socialist country. There can be no doubt regarding this. What is not equally clear to us is, why this industrialization and general economic development must be under the tutelage of capitalism? When the forces of Socialism have appeared, when they have proved so successful in precisely this very task in one-sixth of the globe, when capitalism is in decay and instead of developing the powers of production is curtailing them, there should be no reason why any intelligent person should deliberately want to hand over the masses to their exploiters merely so that the latter may economically develop the nation. The growing and steady economic success of Socialist Russia amidst general capitalist chaos and paralysis, has already demonstrated the superiority of socialist forces in the task of building up the productive forces of society.

There is another important consideration. If the capitalist class in India succeeds—it cannot, but assuming so for argument's sake—in carrying through the Indian National Revolution under its leadership, then, undoubtedly, it would be in a position to establish its own rule over the country (in alliance with the landed interests) either under the cover of democracy, or openly as a fascist regime. In that case the people would have to go through a second revolution in order to win their emancipation.

If, on the other hand, it is the masses—the workers, peasants and impoverished urban middle classes—that overthrow imperialism, it would be criminal for any one to suggest that after having captured power they should hand it over to the capitalists. A capitalist phase in that event, would mean a deliberate and fatal sacrifice of the interests of the masses. The only reasonable course would be for the masses to establish their own rule under the leadership of their most revolutionary and conscious section—the working class—and march towards Socialism.

V

Gandhiji has never directly and comprehensively dealt with the nature of society under Swaraj; therefore it cannot be said that he has any consistent alternative to Socialism. However, he has made statements on various occasions and some of his economic views can be garnered from his writings. These, if not to Gandhiji himself, to his followers undoubtedly, appear as providing an adequate alternative to Socialism. "Gandhism is true Socialism for India", is a remark which one hears not infrequently. It is for this reason that I propose to examine those views of Gandhiji that are germane to my subject.

Before doing so, let me repeat the problem we have set before us. We are interested in *permanently destroying the basis of economic exploitation and inequality*. I have shown that the socialist solution is to abolish private ownership of means of production. Let us see how Gandhiji proposes to solve the problem.

One of the most explicit statements of Gandhiji's views on the issues raised by us, is found in the interview that he gave to some Zamindars of the U.P. at Cawnpore last year. An authentic version of the interview was published by Sjt. Mahadev Desai.

In order to enable the reader to follow my criticisms, I am giving below the whole of the interview, except a short para at the end which is not relevant to our discussion:

Question 1: The Karachi Congress passed a resolution laying down the fundamental rights of the people; and since it recognized private property, nationalist Zamindars have supported the Congress. But a new socialist party in the Congress threatens the extinction of private property. How would it affect the Congress policy? Don't you think that this will precipitate class war? Will you prevent it?

Answer: The Karachi resolution can be altered only by the open session of the next Congress; but let me assure you that *I shall be no party to dispossessing the propertied classes of their private property without just cause. My objective is to reach your hearts and convert you so that you may hold all your private property in trust for your tenants and use it primarily for their welfare* (my italics). I am aware of the fact that within the ranks of the Congress, a new party called the Socialist Party is coming into being, and I cannot say what would happen if that party succeeds in carrying the Congress with it. But I am quite clear that if a strictly honest and unchallengable referendum of our millions were to be taken, they would not vote for a wholesale expropriation of the propertied classes. I am working for the co-operation and co-ordination of capital and labour and of the landlord and tenant. It is open to you to join the Congress as much as it is open to the poorest by paying a fee of annas four and subscribing to the Congress creed. But I must utter a note of warning. I have always told the millowners that they are not exclusive owners of the mills and workmen are equal sharers in the ownership. In the same way I would tell you that the ownership of your land belongs as much to the Ryots as to you; and you may not squander your gains in luxurious or extravagant living, but must use them for the well-being of the Ryots. Once you make your Ryots experience a sense of kinship with you and a sense of security that their interests as members of a family will never suffer at your hands, you may be sure that there cannot be a clash between you and them and no class war. A class war is foreign to the essential genius of India which is capable of evolving communism broadbased on the fundamental rights of all on equal justice. The Ramarajya of my dream, ensures the rights alike of the prince and the pauper.

You may be sure that I shall throw the whole weight of my influence in preventing a class war. I do not know what I am going to do after the termination of my self-imposed restriction on August 3; but I shall try my best to avoid going back to prison. But it is difficult to predict anything with certainty in a situation of which I am unaware today. But supposing that there is an attempt unjustly to deprive you of your property you will find me fighting on your side.

Question 2: We propose to support the Congress in the next Assembly elections. But we have our misgivings about the policy they will adopt in the Assembly. Could you persuade the Parliamentary Board to dispel our fears?

Answer: I invite you to discuss this thing with the members of the Parliamentary Board. I know, however, that no member will talk of expropriation or extinction of private property. They will certainly insist on a radical reform in your relations with the Ryots, but that should be no new thing to you. Even Sir Malcolm Hailey and Lord Irwin appealed to you to realize and live up to the spirit of the times. If you will only do this, you may be sure that we shall be able to evolve an indigenous Socialism of the purest type. The Socialism and the Communism of the West are based on certain conceptions which are fundamentally different from ours. One of such conceptions is their belief in the essential selfishness of human nature. I do not subscribe to it for I know that the essential difference between man and brute is that the former can respond to the call of the spirit in him, can rise superior to the passions that he owes in common with the brute and, therefore, is superior to the selfishness and violence which belong to the brute nature and not to the immortal spirit of man. That is the fundamental conception of Hinduism which has years of penance and austerity at the back of the discovery of this truth. That is why, whilst we have had saints who have worn out their bodies and laid down their lives in order to explore the secrets of the soul, we have had none as in the West, who have laid down their lives in exploring the remotest or highest regions of the earth. Our Socialism or Communism should, therefore, be based on non-violence, and on the harmonious co-operation of labour and capital, the landlord and tenant.

There is nothing in the Congress creed or policy that need frighten you. All your fears and misgivings, permit me to tell you, are those of a guilty conscience. Wipe out the injustices that you may have been consciously or unconsciously guilty of and shed all fear of the Congress and Congressmen. Once you turn a new leaf in the relations between the Zamindars and the Ryots, you will find us on our side jealously guarding your private rights and property. When I say "us", I have Pandit Jawaharlal also in mind for I am sure that on this essential principle of non-violence there is no difference between us. He does indeed talk of the nationalization of property, but it need not frighten you. The nation cannot own property excepting by vesting it in individuals. It simply insures its just and equitable use and prevents all possible misuse; and I do not think you can have any possible objection to holding your property for the benefit of the Ryots. The Ryots have themselves no greater ambition than to live in peace and freedom, and they will never grudge your possession of property provided you use it for them.

(*Leader*, August 3, 1934)

Before launching upon a criticism of this curious philosophy, it would be profitable to consider if the views of Gandhiji are uniquely Indian. He speaks of "indigenous Socialism"; the "essential genius" of India; the "fundamental conception of Hinduism". Western Socialism is based, according to him, on conceptions that are fundamentally opposed to those of Hinduism. He implies, naturally, that his "indigenous" Socialism, is much better suited to India than our foreign variety. It is important, therefore, to examine this claim to autochthonism.

As a matter of fact, there is nothing new or peculiarly Indian in what Gandhiji says. A large number of Western writers have expressed themselves in a more or less similar strain. The arguments vary in their emphasis but their core remains much the same. Class struggle is silly; capital and labour are interdependent and necessary for each other; revolution is wasteful; a synthesis of the contending forces of society is a higher ideal than revolution; enlightened control of profits, wages and prices; the theory of trusteeship—these are the commonest ideas of the West preached by smug bourgeois professors, thinkers and churchmen.

I mentioned above Mr. H.G. Wells sermonising to Stalin about "Clissoldism". Any one may read that famous interview and discover for himself the essential kinship, behind the superficial difference of language, between Wells' views of class struggle and those of Gandhiji. The whole burden of Wells' talk was that class war is nonsense and that the evils of capitalism can be removed by harmonising and reconciling the interests that are opposed to one another today. What was needed was the right type of leadership. Gandhiji wants to convert the capitalists. So does Mr. Wells.

Mr. Ramsay MacDonald too, in his socialist days, was against class war. Says he:

> The socialist, therefore, looks with some misgivings upon some recent developments in the conflicts between capital and labour. They are contrary to his spirit; he believes they are both immoral and uneconomic and will lead to disaster. It is only when the worker by brain or by hand does his best for his society that he will create in society that sympathy and support without which the Labour movement will never attain its goal.

And again:

> Both capital and labour have to serve communal ends, and the great task before all who understand the true significance of present-day conflicts, is to discover how this synthesis of function can be brought about. (*Socialism: Critical and Constructive*)

Apparently England too had an "indigenous Socialism". Unfortunately for all indigenous varieties, this particular commodity has ended in the most approved form of Toryism.

Much has been made of the idea of trusteeship as being truly Indian and natural to the country's spirit of non-violence. William Godwin writes in his *Political Justice*:

> The doctrine of the injustice of accumulated property has been the foundation of all religious morality. The object of this morality has been, to excite men by individual virtue to repair this injustice. The most energetic teachers of religion have been irresistibly led to assert the precise truth upon this interesting subject. They have taught the rich that *they hold their wealth only as a trust*; (my italics) that they are strictly accountable for every atom of their expenditure; that they are merely administrators, and by no means proprietors in chief.[1]

Here a century and a half ago, the same idea was put so neatly in its historical perspective. In face of this statement, the claim of India to this doctrine can be very slender indeed.

The struggle between revolution and reform is as old as human misery. Gandhiji's views are essentially what in socialist history is known as reformism. Its language is Indian but its substance is international. The chief interest of reformism lies in maintaining the established order of society. Only it sees the forces of disruption, and, sensing danger, wishes to neutralize and quieten them. It therefore advocates the administration of palliatives. All that Gandhiji tells the landlord and the capitalist, is that they should *improve* their relations with their tenants and labourers. All will be well then—no dreaded class-war, no discontent, no revolts and upsettings. Reformism is interested not in securing social justice, but in covering up the ugly fissures of society.

To turn now to Gandhiji's interview. He says: "The Ramarajya of my dream ensures the rights alike of the prince and the pauper." This is the keynote to the entire social philosophy of Mahatma Gandhi. Even in his dream Ramarajya, the pauper remains along with the prince! No doubt, Gandhiji wishes to ensure the pauper's rights, though what those rights will be he does not tell us, nor what the wretched pauper will do with them. But the interesting—almost breath-taking—fact is that in even Gandhiji's *dream* Ramarajya there will be paupers.

A Ramarajya of paupers and princes! Why not? How else will the noble

[1]Godwin's comment on this teaching is very interesting: "The defect of this system is that they rather excite us to palliate our injustice than to forsake it". And again: "If religion had spoken out, and told us it was just that all men should receive the supply of their wants, we should presently have been led to suspect that a gratuitous distribution to be made by the rich was a very indirect and ineffectual way of arriving at this object. The experience of all ages has taught us, that this system is productive only of a very precarious supply. The principal object which it seems to propose, is to place this supply in the disposal of a few, enabling them to make a show of generosity with what is not truly their own, and to purchase the gratitude of the poor by the payment of a debt. It is a system of clemency and charity instead of a system of justice. It fills the rich with unreasonable pride by the spurious denominations with which it decorates their acts; and the poor with servility, by leading them to regard the slender comforts they obtain, not as their incontrovertible due, but as the good pleasure and grace of their opulent neighbours."

souls get an opportunity to practise deeds of high-minded philanthropy and thus prove the Hindu conception of human nature!

Why paupers should remain at all in society—the central question of Socialism—does not even occur to Gandhiji. It cannot, because the existence of paupers is essential for the working out of Gandhian ethics.

Here is the real difference between Socialism and Gandhism—not in the "materialism" of the one and the "spiritualism" of the other. Those, as commonly used, are meaningless words. The starting point of Socialism is the inquiry into the causes of economic inequality; into the origin of princes, landlords, capitalists and paupers; into the secrets of human exploitation. When at the end of the inquiry, the socialist arrives at the root cause, he removes it. The remedy is applied at the source of the social evil.

Gandhism, on the other hand, does not even stop at these questions. It does not occur to it to ask why only a few are in the position of princes, landlords, and capitalists, while the remaining many are paupers or only just a little better than paupers. It accepts the established order with its high and low classes. Its only concern is to improve the conduct of the higher classes towards the lower. Not daring to ask where the landlord's and the capitalist's wealth comes from, it asks them in its compassion, to act as trustees of the poor and to use their wealth for the welfare of the latter.

To a socialist, this philosophy amounts to deception—self-deception and deception of the exploited peoples. According to us, the wealth of the landlord and the capitalist comes from the labour of the Ryots and workers, and is, therefore, in the famous phrase of Proudhon, *theft*. To condone this theft, to let it go unquestioned, nay, to sanctify it, is a deceptive philosophy—no matter how unconsciously so.

Not only are the higher classes guilty of theft; they are guilty also of violence. They are guilty of this because the theft of the people's produce is maintained and preserved under the threat of violence. But for the law—class law be it noted—and the organized forces of violence behind it, the workers and the Ryots would capture tomorrow the lands and factories. As Pandit Jawaharlal writes: "It is well to realize that those who belong to the favoured and possessing classes retain these positions by methods of coercion alone." (See "Some criticisms considered" in his *Recent Essays and Writings*.)

By not questioning the right of the prince, landlord and capitalist to continue their functions, Gandhiji has signified his tacit approval of this large-scale, organized theft and violence. Nay, the approval is not tacit; it is open and avowed. He has told the landlords that he would resist any attempt to deprive them of their property; and a little earlier he had told the Ahmedabad Mill-owners that it was their moral right to make the money they were making.

Gandhiji now tells the upper classes that they must hold their property in trust for their tenants, labourers, etc.; now that they are equal sharers in their property with the latter; again that they should hold their property for the benefit of their poor; yet again that they should treat the latter as members of their family. This is Gandhiji's indigenous Socialism of the purest type—the harmonious co-operation between labour and capital, landlord and tenant.

Let us first note the indefiniteness and self-contradiction of all this. The landlord, for instance, is a trustee. What part of his wealth must he hold as a trust. The whole or a portion of it? If a portion, what and who determines the portion? If again, his tenants are equal sharers in his wealth, what exactly is meant by an equal share? Does it mean that half of the property belongs to the landlord and half to the tenants? Or does it mean that the landlord and his tenants taken together are each an equal partner? How can a sharer remain a trustee? What is the meaning of 'members of a family'? Is it that the tenants are free to use the palaces of the taluqdars and commission their limousines to drive to the city? What again is the meaning of harmonious co-operation? Who will bring about this co-operation?

These are questions not to be lightly brushed aside. There are others and weightier ones.

Why is the tenant or the labourer an equal owner with his master? What proof has Gandhiji for his assertions?

If it is said that the tenants and labourers are equal owners of their master's property because they are its producers, then, why should they not keep for themselves what they produce? Why should they be asked to hand it over to others who will then act as their trustees? Is it just to enable the latter to play the pious philanthropist?

We may consider the same question from the other end: *why* should the upper classes act as trustees? They can very well assert, as in fact they do, that their wealth is wholly theirs, earned by their brains and capital, and that no one has any claim to it.

If the property that is in the hands of the wealthy is not theirs, no one has any justification in encouraging them to keep it and on top of it to make a show of charity. If, on the other hand, it is theirs, earned rightfully by them, no one has any cause to ask them to give it away to others. If the poor starve, let them; it is not the fault of the wealthy.

Thus we find Gandhism to be in a serious bog of timid economic analysis, good intentions and ineffective moralising.

There are only two alternatives: either to prove that the wealth of the wealthy is unjustly acquired and then to demand their expropriation; or to admit that it is rightfully theirs; and then to keep mum in all decency, instead of trotting out pious wishes so that the poor may not feel that they are to be neglected.

The problem is not one of morality or ethics. It is a problem of scientific analysis of property and the method of its production and distribution. This problem should be boldly faced instead of being covered up under a slush of sentimentality. Karl Marx did the greatest service to humanity when he undertook the analysis of capitalist property and proved that it was based on the exploitation of labour. Bourgeois professors have not yet forgiven Marx for proving scientifically what was previously asserted only in fits of moral indignation. That is why we have so many "refutations" of his labour theory of value.

If one shirked this analysis, one lost the right to ask anybody to part with his wealth, except in charity.

How is this theory of trusteeship to be worked out in practice? How does Gandhiji propose to convert the upper classes into trustees of the lower? By appealing to their sense of morality, by reaching their hearts. "My objective is to reach your hearts and convert you", he told the UP landlords, "so that you may hold all your private property in trust for your tenants and use it primarily for their welfare."

I wonder if this too is taken as a peculiarly Indian solution. It is, indeed, a method that is common to all great religious teachers. How much success the previous teachers had—including Jesus Christ—is a fact of history. Now Gandhiji comes along wielding his wand, claiming to perform the old magic.

I do not know if the seven Zamindars who had the benefit of Gandhiji's teaching at Cawnpore, as they also had previously of that of Lord Halifax (Irwin) and Sir Malcolm Hailey, are now acting as the trustees of their tenants. I am aware, however, that Gandhiji's views have found ready and welcome acceptance among the upper classes and that there are some amongst them who are their most eloquent defenders. This is natural enough. For the acceptance of this philosophy costs them nothing except perhaps an occasional donation to a public cause, the amount of which they soon recover either by virtue of the publicity gained or by a business manoeuvre. At the same time, the philosophy strengthens their position a great deal by giving it a moral sanction.

Gandhiji says in his interview that he has "always told the millowners that they are not exclusive owners of the mills and workmen are equal sharers in the ownership". He does not tell us however—and this is the real question—if he has achieved any success in this direction. Gandhiji has been associated with the Labour Union of Ahmedabad and is one of its builders. Can he, or any one else, say that in the struggle between the Union and the millowners, a change of heart has been noticed? Is it not only the fear of the strength of the Union, the risk of a general strike, the odium of turning down the compromises of a man of Mahatmaji's influence, that lead the millowners to come to terms with Labour? And have those terms ever meant a real sacrifice for the capitalists, made willingly for the good of their workers? There is all the difference in the world between a compromise on hours and wages and the theory of trusteeship and family kinship.

If during his lifetime, Gandhiji has not succeeded in reaching the hearts of the upper classes, how does he expect that this will be done after he is removed from the arena of the world? A great teacher has never been succeeded by an equal. "Followers" have always been known to be petty people, chopping texts and quarelling over interpretations. Does Gandhiji believe that he is leaving behind him a band of people who will carry his mission of conversion to fruition? If not, what other agency has he in mind that will ensure its success?

Whatever agency it is, it should be evident that it must have two virtues: it must be effective and self-procreating. Hearts must be changed—not of isolated individuals, but of whole classes. And the "changed hearts" must be handed down from generation to generation. But the acquired virtues of the heart are not necessarily inherited. A good father not infrequently begets an unworthy heir. Therefore, an agency of such permanence is needed as will make it possible for each generation of capitalists and landlords to be inculcated with the spirit of trusteeship.

It is necessary to point out that this conversion will have to be carried on in an environment to which the very idea of trusteeship is foreign—an environment of individualism, of private profit; an environment, furthermore, in which, if a "trustee" reverts to type there is no punishment, either automatic, as resulting from the laws of his society, or imposed deliberately by some outside agency. If anything, the deserter will find that as far as his own interests go, they are served much better than when he was playing at trusteeship.

Is it possible that an agency that will succeed in this stupendous task of conversion can be created? Dr. Bhagavan Das suggests a school of Yoga. A great leader may succeed in founding such a school, but that it will bear any fruits, it is difficult to believe.[2]

The question is not one of human nature. When the socialist denies the

[2]I may be reminded here of the Brahmins of ancient India. But what was the function of the Brahmins? Briefly, to protect and strengthen, by moral and religious sanction, the established order. No amount of intellectual heterodoxy was disagreeable to the Brahmins if the social order was left undisturbed. Every movement of social reform found the power of the Brahmins arrayed against it. It is a mistake to imagine that the Brahmin was engaged in mitigating social differences. If anything, he strengthened and buttressed them. True, he preached charity; but charity has ever been known to be the ally of vested interests.

I should point out that I am speaking here only of the Brahmins as a class and not of individual revolutionary Brahmin leaders.

practicability of the change-of-heart philosophy, he does it for no lack of faith in human nature. Gandhiji has misunderstood "Western" Socialism entirely when he says that it is based on the essential selfishness of human nature. Nothing can be further from the truth. Had socialists taken such a low view of human nature, they would never have dared to proclaim as their ideal, a society based on the pursuit of common welfare. Has it not been the most persistent argument against Socialism that it assumes an impossible refinement of man's nature?[3]

Quite contrary to what Gandhiji thinks, the socialist has un unlimited faith in human nature and it is one of the major items of his constructive programme to remould it. Russia, of whose crude methods so much nonsense has been written, has already achieved a remarkable success in this direction. I shall quote the testimony of an impartial observer like Sherwood Eddy:

> In Russia where motives are anticipated ends, the very bigness of the end modifies all ordinary pursuits and methods. Immediate needs can be controlled in the light of long time values. Actually where private property in land and all means of production has practically ceased to exist, and where it is virtually impossible to make a private fortune, *human service is taking the place of private profit upon such a scale that it is something new under the Sun.*

And again:

> Humanitarian and higher ethical ends are increasingly utilised as incentives in Soviet·Russia. Their *faith in human nature* and especially in the common man that he will respond favourably to a favourable environment is validating itself in results. (my italics)

The socialist's denial of the philosophy of change-of-heart does not spring from his lack of faith in human nature, but from his understanding of human psychology—the relation between behaviour and environment. He believes that it is the social environment which shapes human behaviour. A capitalist exploits labour not because he is vicious, but because that is what the particular society in which he lives wants him to do. If he attempted to do anything else, he would be pushed aside and others would take his place.

The socialist, therefore, believes that if the behaviour of whole groups and classes has to be changed, a change should be effected in the social organization itself. For instance, if the capitalist class has to be prevented

[3]Only the other day at the Bombay Suburban Conference, Mr. Bhulabhai Desai repeated the age-worn argument. "This was not the occasion", he continued, "to evaluate Socialism and Communism as the basic structure of society; but it had to be admitted that in the ultimate analysis, Socialism and Communism, to be a stable basis of society, could come into existence only with a radical change in human nature, and in particular the tendency of the human mind to put forth the best so that the gain might be appropriated by him; and the instinct was to be supplanted by a new, when man would put forward the best, in order that society might gain its result". (Report of the *Hindustan Times*)

from exploiting labour, the organization of society must be so altered as to make that exploitation *impossible*. That is why Sherwood Eddy in the above citation prefaces his remark about human service taking the place of private profit in Russia by the words: "actually where private property in land and all means of production has practically *ceased to exist*, and where it is virtually *impossible* to make a private fortune" (my italics). Human nature responds not to the so-called spirit that is said to be in all of us, but to the environment. It will respond favourably to a favourable environment, as it is doing according to Eddy in Soviet Russia.

When the environment encourages, nay, demands, as a matter of fulfilment of its laws, the exploitation of man by man, it is too much to expect that moral precept will do more than touch the heart of a stray individual or so. It cannot transform society.

The socialist wants, therefore, first to change the social environment and acquire full power over the State in order to be in possession of the means of propaganda and education. He creates the predisposing environment and then uses systematic methods of education. How does he change the environment? By organizing the exploited and oppressed for the overthrow of the established order and the seizure of power. Then he proceeds to build a new society on the new foundations.

There remain a number of minor points in the interview to be considered. It would serve no purpose, and would only detract attention from the central problem, to deal with all of them. Some, however, may be considered with profit.

Gandhiji says: "But I am quite clear that if a strictly honest and unchallengable referendum of our millions were to be taken they would not vote for a wholesale expropriation of the propertied classes". Supposing that were so, what value will that opinion have for a social scientist, for one who is trying to get a scientific understanding of present society and preparing a scheme for such a social organization from which the present evils would be permanently banished. What value would he attach to the opinion of backward, ignorant, oppressed masses? Does not Gandhiji know that till the other day large sections of the British working class were voting Conservative? In America the workers still vote in overwhelming proportions for the candidates of the Republican and Democratic Parties (which are patently controlled by the upper classes) rather than for Norman Thomas (Socialist) or Wm. Z. Foster (Communist). Should we on that account accept the opinion of these workers as representing what is in their best interests?

Are there not hundreds of thousands of untouchables in India who would consider it a sacrilege to touch the food of a Brahmin even when invited to do so? Are there not women in Bihar and the U.P. who would denounce the anti-*purdah* movements as immoral?

What the masses vote or do not vote for is not important—their opinion depends wholly on the extent to which they have been made conscious of their rights and potentialities. All the problems of society would have disappeared immediately if the masses really knew what was good for them.

In Russia there was a group of intellectuals known as the 'Economists' who also believed that the workers were already conscious of what they wanted; and therefore the task of leadership was only to help them in the realization of those desires without attempting to add anything to them or to put them in a scientific shape. Lenin wrote a smashing criticism of their view, which he termed "tailism" (following at the tail end), in a famous pamphlet, *What is to be done*. In that pamphlet Lenin made it clear that it was the task of the revolutionary intellectual to develop a programme for the masses and lead them to its realization. Socialism was a product not of the working class but of "individual members of the bourgeois intelligentsia" who addressed themselves to the problems created by capitalism and brought a clear head and a sincere heart to their task. In Lenin's own words:

> The history of all countries testifies to the fact that by its own efforts the working class can only evolve a trade unionist consciousness—that is, the conviction that it is necessary to coalesce into unions in order to fight the employees, to demand of the Government laws in favour of labour, etc. *The doctrine of Socialism grew up out of the philosophical, historical, economic theories that were elaborated by educated members of the propertied classes, by the intelligentsia.*

Referendum is a poor and untrustworthy tool in the hands of the social architect.

> Once you turn a new leaf in the relations between the Zamindars and the Ryots, you will find us on our side jealously guarding your private rights and property. When I say 'us', I have Pandit Jawaharlal also in mind, for I am sure that on this essential principle of non-violence there is no difference between us. He does indeed talk of nationalization of property, but it need not frighten you. The nation cannot own property excepting by vesting it in individuals. It simply insures its just and equitable use and prevents all possible misuse and I do not think you can have any possible objection to holding your property for the benefit of the Ryots.

I confess that in recent years I have read few things that have caused me so much surprise as this statement. Such a curious mix-up of ideas and issues it has rarely been my luck to come across. It is not my purpose to offer any explanation on behalf of Pandit Jawaharlal. I have no doubt that when he is free he will make his position clear to Gandhiji and the Zamindars. I must, however, point out that when Gandhiji made this statement, *Whither India* and the other writings connected with it had already appeared, so I cannot see how anybody who had read them could have made these remarks about their author.

Gandhiji assumes that, because there is agreement between Jawaharlal and him on non-violence, the latter would jealously guard the private rights and properties of the Zamindars. In "Some Criticisms Considered", Pandit Jawaharlal made it clear while discussing non-violence that for him the method was of secondary importance. "However important the method may be I entirely fail to understand how it can take the place of the objective. It is essential to have the objective and know the direction before a single step can be taken". As for the method itself, i.e. non-violence, he makes it clear that he has accepted it only as a weapon in the struggle against imperialism. There too he does not consider it to be infallible. "But I have made it clear on many occasions that non-violence is no infallible creed with me and although I greatly prefer it to violence I prefer freedom with violence to subjection with non-violence".[4] In the relation in which Gandhiji is using the term, i.e. a method for adjustment of group interests within the nation after Swaraj, it seems to me that Jawaharlal leaves no doubt that he will not hesitate to use the coercive arm of the State.

> The question of violence or non-violence may arise, and indeed is bound to arise, in another form after the conquest of the State power. There may be attempts to upset the new form of Government by reactionary groups. Will 'G' (one of the critics of *Whither India*—J.P.N.) advise the new Government to use the resources of the State to coerce these elements into submission or does he think that the religious and philanthropic argument should be used to convert them? Then again the new Government may pass laws which, carrying out the will of the great majority of the people, seek to de-vest privileged groups. Will 'G' then advise these groups to submit to the majority opinion or to resist; and if the latter, how should their resistance be met?[5]

Whatever may be 'G's' answer, Jawaharlal's seems to be obvious.

In face of such statements—and the *Recent Essays and Writings* is full of them—what warrant Gandhiji had to bracket Jawaharlal with himself in this matter it is difficult to understand.

It is Gandhiji's remarks about nationalization, however, that take the prize. Jawaharlal talks of nationalization but no one need be frightened; the nation cannot own property without vesting it in individuals. Is it possible that Gandhiji really believes in this arrant nonsense? Even the veriest tyro in modern economics knows what nationalization means. Will Gandhiji tell us in whom is the ownership of the State Railways vested? Who owns the nationalized mines, banks and factories of Soviet Russia?

Gandhiji seems to confuse property which is for individual consumption with property which is used for producing property of the former kind. If Gandhiji means that the nation cannot own houses, clothes, cycles, gramophones, tables, chairs, except through individual ownership, no one will quarrel with him. Nationalization of property did never mean

[4]*Recent Essays and Writings*, p. 33.
[5]op. cit., pp. 35-6.

that individuals will not have their own houses, clothes, etc.

When the socialist talks of nationalization of property, he means functional property, viz., land, mines, factories. Not only is there no difficulty about the nation owning such property but to vest their ownership in individuals is unjust, unreasonable and unscientific. They are large institutions with which are bound up the interests of the whole community; and so the community must own them.

That will mean that servants of the Community will work these institutions, as they are doing in Soviet Russia; and their proceeds would be shared by the whole community according to some agreed scheme.

In the interview that we have just considered, Gandhiji defined his indigenous Socialism as co-ordination and co-operation between capital and labour, landlord and tenant. There is also another type of Gandhian "Socialism"—though it did not find a mention in the interview. It has for its central doctrine the idea that we should eschew machinery, and in its place develop cottage industries. The arguments against machinery are varied, the chief of which are that it leads to violence and exploitation and creates unemployment, particularly in a country with such a large population as India.

The criticism that machinery means violence and exploitation is not so much a criticism of machinery itself, as that of the system which uses machinery for private profit, i.e. of capitalism. Some people believe that machinery makes capitalism inevitable. Soviet Russia clearly disproves this. There we find a social order rising literally on the foundations of machinery and yet being as free from exploitation as any society of idyllic fancy. There is violence indeed in Soviet Russia, but it is not engendered by the new economic order. It is revolutionary violence—political violence, if you please—made necessary by the task of destroying the old order of privilege, exploitation and violence.[6]

The argument about unemployment is a persistent fallacy in this country. It needs, therefore, to be examined in some detail.

It is commonly believed by those who are opposed to machinery that it causes unemployment. "If we installed a machine," they argue, "which does the work of ten labourers, it would displace that many people from employment." It does that, no doubt, but it is forgotten that at the same time it does much more—it creates new employments, new demands, new standards of living.

[6]For a detailed treatment of this question see the author's article on "Professor Kumarappa's thesis of Centralization vs. Decentralization" in *India and Socialism* to be published shortly. [Editor's Note: This was published as a pamphlet entitled *Socialism versus the A.I.V.I.A.* (1935). See *Jayaprakash Narayan: Selected Works* (hereinafter referred to as *JSPW*), Volume One, pp. 125-40. As far as is known to the Editor no book under the title 'India and Socialism' by J.P. was ever published.]

Let us take a country like the United States of America. When the Thirteen Colonies rebelled and won their independence, the level of production was very low and so was their population. Now, according to the above hypothesis, as the country began to be mechanized, unemployment should have grown in a corresponding proportion. Nothing of the sort actually happened. It may be urged that foreign markets and imperialism kept the American workers employed at home. But this too was not true in fact. Till the war, the export of American manufactures was next to nothing. Even during the period of the post-war boom, I believe, not more than ten per cent of the total American manufactures was exported. The reason why there was no unemployment in the U.S.A., on the scale that should have been expected on the hypothesis of the anti-machinist, was that, for various causes, the standard of living of the American workers and farmers went on ascending, as compared with other capitalist countries. That made it possible for most of the American manufactures to be consumed at home.

This is not to say that there was no unemployment in the U.S.A. Unemployment there was indeed, but it was periodic and was not due to mechanization and in proportion to it. Its cause was different which I shall consider below. What the American experience does show is that *if the purchasing power of the people goes on rising proportionately to production, no amount of mechanization will produce unemployment, unless production has crossed the saturation point of human needs*—a very distant point at present.

Let us take another country. Soviet Russia believes in machinery more than the Americans ever did. The Russians are mechanizing both industry and agriculture at a pace that has staggered every one. Yet, from all accounts, Russia is the only country where there is no unemployment at a time when in the rest of the civilized world it has become the foremost social problem. How will the anti-machinists explain this?

The answer will be found in the origins of unemployment under capitalism. What do we find there? We find that production has been curtailed ruthlessly; factories are lying idle; credit is frozen; warehouses are glutted. At the same time we find people who are in dire need of all the things that are locked up in warehouses or are wantonly destroyed by the State and the capitalists. On the one hand, there is said to be over-production; on the other, an appalling under-consumption.

Can there be anything more contradictory of each other than this? Yet it is one of the most persistent characteristics of capitalism. It is clear that in a world where the vast majority of people lives in dire need there can be no over-production. All that can be produced today, and a thousand times more, can be consumed without any difficulty. But, then, where is the rub? The rub is in the fact that the poverty of the people, their lack of purchasing power, does not allow them to buy the goods that are lying idle or being dumped into the sea or thrown into the bonfire. The purchasing power of the great majority of the people in capitalist countries comes from the wages they receive; and the latter are kept down as low as possible by the capitalists so that their profits may be the highest possible. Thus a vicious circle is drawn. The capitalist goes on manufacturing goods so that by selling them he may draw his profit, at the same time he restricts the consuming power of the community by his policy of wages. Naturally, there is maladjustment between production and consumption; and he periodically finds that he has produced "too much". Then he restricts production and throws his workers out of employment.

Now, it should be clear that if goods were produced for consumption and not for the profit of a few, all that was produced would be consumed. There would be no limit to the purchasing power of the people except the supply of goods itself, because "wages" would represent under those conditions the sum total of consumption goods produced. Over-production would arise only when the needs of the community have been satisfied, and these, as I have already indicated, are almost insatiable. Restriction of production and demechanization would not be necessary till that point has been reached.

In India that point will take a very long time indeed to reach. Imagine a well-kept upper middle-class household: a smart house with a neat little garden; furniture; rugs and carpets; electricity; a radio-set; perhaps a Chevrolet; a modest library; music; wholesome and nourishing food; good clothes; enough leisure for recreation, reading and writing. Now, consider that you have to raise the standard of the poorest Indian home to this level. Will you kindly compute how many times our productive resources must be multiplied to make that possible in the course of, let us say, fifty years?

To run away from machinery, to take shelter in small industries, is again a symptom of the disease we considered above—the fear of facing the issue. The examination of present society must be avoided to avoid inconvenient conclusions. It is less troublesome to take recourse to sentimentality and idyllic fancies. Therefore, instead of tracing the real offender, the guilt is readily fastened on poor inoffensive objects of steel and mortar, which, in reality, are a blessing for mankind.

So much for the theoretical position of the anti-machinist. His position from the point of view of practice is still worse. The fact that machinery slowly displaced handicrafts all over the world must have had good reasons for it. The reasons, in fact, were excellent, viz., that machinery makes a higher return of profits possible and holds all the points of vantage in the game of economic competition with small-scale production.

These reasons still hold good. Those who have capital to invest cannot eschew machinery. On the other hand, handicrafts have no chance against modern industry. We see in India too that, in spite of the blighting influences of imperialism, there is a steady progress in machine production. As soon as the imperialist obstruction is out of the way, there will be an absolute fever of mechanization, though, I should add parenthetically that under capitalism the prospects of mechanization or industrialization are very limited in India. Just consider the Sugar Rush. The Government made a gesture of goodwill to the Indian capitalist and created an opportunity for him to pile up huge profits by levying a sugar tariff. At once mills went up literally like mushrooms. No amount of counter-propaganda in favour of hand-made *gur* could have stopped that avalanche.

How, in face of these economic tendencies, is the gospel of small industries to spread? There is no enlightenment from the quarter to which one naturally turns for an answer. There is only a mouthful of sentimentality.

As I pointed out in Chapter 1, unless dictatorial methods are used, it would neither be possible to demechanize present production nor prevent its future mechanization. In existing society it is not possible for the small producer to acquire such dictatorial powers. His is not a key position as that of the capitalist on the one hand and the worker on the other. He is not even in the position of the peasant, who in the conditions of India has a unique importance. If, however, there are idealists who imagine that they would succeed in this task, I shall only ask them if it is common sense deliberately to destroy the productive powers of society when only a better control over them would yield all the moral and material values they dream of creating?

To conclude. Gandhism may be a well-intentioned doctrine. I personally think it is. But even with the best of intentions, it is, I must admit—it gives me no pleasure to do so—a dangerous doctrine. It is dangerous because it hushes up real issues and sets out to remove the evils of society by pious wishes. It thus deceives the masses and encourages the upper classes to continue their domination.

VI

There is perhaps no Indian scholar today who is more competent to interpret ancient India to us than Doctor Bhagavan Das. It was natural, therefore, that I should have turned with avidity to his ancient Scientific Socialism.[7]

The greater part of the Doctor's book is taken up with criticisms of Marxism, Russia, Fascism, etc. It is not my purpose here to reply to these. Much of his criticism follows the liberal bourgeois line. With some of it, communists will heartily agree. No communist has ever claimed that a faultless society has been created in Russia or that mistakes have not been committed.

[7]See his *Ancient vs. Modern Scientific Socialism*, Theosophical Publishing House, Madras.

The Doctor, in my humble opinion, has misunderstood some of the basic ideas of Marxism, viz., the materialist interpretation of history, the theory of the State, the classless society. To give just one instance: Commenting upon Lenin's remark that talents are not born by the hundred, he says "Why, on the 'materialist interpretation of history', is talent born only by the ten (scarcely even that) and not by the hundred? Why are there 'exceptional individuals'?" It is surprising that the Doctor did not go on to ask why, if the materialistic interpretation of history is correct, are the Himalayas taller than the Vindhyas. And, yet, differences in the talents of men have as little to do with historical materialism as the difference in the height of these mountains. Just as it was possible for physical forces to produce the latter difference so it was possible for them to produce the former. Why there are exceptional individuals, is a question which biology can answer and not history—no matter which interpretation of history one accepts. Matter in its infinite combinations produces the peach and the dogberry, the tulip and the dandelion; in the same manner it produces an Einstein and an Ivan the Fool.

In the same context the Doctor goes on to ask: "Is *self*-sacrifice materialist, rationalist, or is it mystical, theosophical?" It is a pity that the adjective 'materialist' should have given rise to so much misunderstanding. The misunderstanding is due to two different uses of the word—one popular, the other philosophical. Marxian critical literature is strewn with remarks to the effect that historical materialism denies that man possesses finer, spiritual, idealistic qualities of nature; that it asserts that "mankind progresses only on its belly", as Malinowski puts it; and so on. Historical materialism does nothing of the sort, however. That there is a type of human behaviour which involves self-sacrifice, self-denial, service and suffering, the Marxist is not so blind as to deny. The wonder is that critics take him to be so devoid of sight as not to see what is a common phenomenon. But what the Marxist does say is that when a man is behaving in a self-sacrificing manner, in a manner that would be termed spiritual, mystical, theosophical, he is doing so, like others, because of given *bio-social*[8] *influences*. Human behaviour according to the Marxist (as to the modern behaviourists) is a compound of biological (nervous, muscular, glandular structure) and social (home, education, association, etc.) influences. Merely because, in current language, a certain type of behaviour has been named spiritual, it does not mean that it is independent of these two influences—which in the scientific sense of the term are "material". When we speak of "spiritual" behaviour, we do no more than describe a certain type of human conduct. The term is descriptive and not explanatory. To a Marxist, spiritual behaviour too, like

[8] I am indebted to my professor, Dr. Albert Weiss, for these categories. See his *A Theoretical Basis of Human Behaviour*.

all other behaviour, has a material (in the sense of not non-material) explanation—concretely, a bio-social explanation.

We could examine many other criticisms made by the learned Doctor. But that would take us too far away from the main enquiry. We must return to his ancient Socialism.

It is a matter of satisfaction that the problem as formulated by Dr. Das is such that a socialist will find himself in substantial agreement with it. He puts it in these terms:

It is necessary to work out a fresh *Technique*, a modified old or a wholly new *Scheme of Social Organization*, a scheme of administration of all the affairs of the *individual* as well as the *collective* human life. This Technique must be such as would make it *possible* for the Golden Rule to become objectively and actually operative, as would make Universal Brotherhood *practicable*, would make it *feasible* to change Society, under the existing industrial, mechanical and urban conditions (assuming, as we must, that they cannot be wholly abolished so as to leave behind only pastoral, agricultural and rural ones) from its present basis of grossly iniquitous and excessively individualist capitalism, and the subservient militarism and imperialism, to the basis of a really *equitable* (not any impossible *equal* or *exactly similar*) *sharing*, by all and each, in the world's work as well as the world's good things, its necessaries, comforts, luxuries and enjoyments. (p. 6)

What is the technique that will do all this? We read:

Manu has given us such a technique in his permanent (and not merely five-year or ten-year or twenty-five-year) Plan of the Individual Life and the Social Life in combination, for the whole of the Human Race. In that Plan are included the fundamental Principles of Planned Education, Planned Family-Life, Planned Economy, Planned Defence-Sanitation-Judication, and Planned Religion-Recreation-Art. (pp. 6-7)

The ancient Indian Scheme of Social Organization endeavours,

we read further,

to effect just the desiderated compromise between unlimited competition and enforced co-operation, egoism and altruism, individualism and socialism, all-liberty and no-liberty, only private enterprise and only state-management, too little government and too much government, King Log and King Stork. *It does this by means of the definition and the partition of the rights and duties of each individual, as an Individual in the successive stages of life* (*Ashrama-dharma*), *and as an adult Member of Society, a Social, during the stage of the Family-life as Householder* (*Varna-dharma*) [my italics]. The rights and duties, work and enjoyment (of appropriate rewards), are so partitioned that genuine *equitability* is achieved, (or even equality, *sama-ta*, but more in *psychological* and *spiritual* sense than in the *economic* sense of the Communist).[9] (pp. 31-2)

[9]No communist claims that he will establish economic *equality*. The communist ideal is rather the fulfilment of needs: "from each according to his capacity, to each according to his needs".

The scheme is further elaborated as below:

It follows from the traditional Indian principles that there should be four main 'guilds' or 'trusts' or 'artels' or 'corporations' or 'organizations' or 'trade-unions' in each state; one, of the learned professions; another, of the executive professions; a third, of the wealth-making-and-managing professions; a fourth of the labouring profession. Provision is also made by those principles for co-ordinating the activities of all four and unifying the whole state under a supreme Legislature composed of elected functional representatives of all four, with special *ethical* and intellectual qualifications, and a supreme Executive head *subordinate* to the Legislature. This co-ordination is made in such a manner that the wisdom of the first shall principally make the laws and guide the defensive valour and the law-enforcing compulsive power of the *second*, so that the work of the *third* for supplying all the needs of all may prosper, and the *fourth* may be kept happy and enabled to help all. (p. 69)

Here is the kernel of Dr. Das' ancient Socialism.[10] He pictures a society, well-ordered, balanced, rational and happy. His scheme is simple enough: the division of society into four, functionally correlated, professions in the manner of Manu, viz., the learned, executive, wealth-making-and-managing and labouring professions. The duties, obligations, rights and privileges of these groups are to be defined. The supreme legislative power is to be vested in the learned profession.

Two criticisms immediately come to one's mind. Firstly, is not this division arbitrary and somewhat out of date? It will be difficult always to maintain a distinction between the learned and executive professions. The higher executive positions, in a modern and rational society, are likely to be filled up by men of the learned profession. On the other hand, the lower executive offices may be grouped together with the labouring professions. The wealth-making profession is likely to disappear and its functions to be merged into those of the executive and labouring professions. As a matter

[10]There are various points of detail which the Doctor gives concerning the economic and political features of his scheme. For instance, he elaborates a scale for the distribution of wealth in the following manner: the minimum wage for unskilled labour (in regions such as the U.P.), Rs. 10 per month; the maximum for skilled labour, ten times as much; for the learned professions, twenty-five times; for the executive, hundred times; for the wealth-making, five hundred to one thousand times. He further suggests a very much simplified schedule of taxation, with its incidence varying with the different professions. He also advocates social control of interest and profit. He says: "The Ancient Socialism suggests that rates of interest and proportions of profits to investments should be fixed also between lower and higher limits, and that trade in certain 'necessaries' should be so restricted and supervised, and prices of them so fixed, as to make 'cornering' and 'speculation' in them, to the distress of the general public, impossible."

In the political sphere he suggests a hierarchy of legislative bodies beginning with the *gram panchayat* and ending with a supreme legislature. The primary body is to be elected directly while all the higher bodies are to be elected indirectly much as is done in Soviet Russia. The Doctor prescribes various qualifications for membership of these bodies, particularly of the supreme legislature.

of fact, it is a mistake to call the class of merchants, industrialists, bankers, etc., a wealth-making class. Wealth, as I have shown above, is really made by the labouring classes. The so-called wealth-making-and-managing class 'makes' no wealth in reality and even manages it only in such a manner as to draw as large a profit for itself as possible. In any reasonable society, this wealth-making class is bound to merge in the administrative and executive profession.

The Doctor's division seems to be far from perfect. It is obvious, however, that any society, much more so the complicated societies of the present, must be divided into various, more or less distinct, occupations. What is not equally obvious, and this is the other and more important criticism, is: how merely a division of society into four or any number of professions can solve the problem which faces present society and which is the starting point of Dr. Das' ancient Socialism—the problem of exploitation and gross economic inequality.

First of all, it should be pointed out that no society is divided artificially, i.e. according to *a priori* theories of social thinkers. Social division is an organic process of society. Marx showed that its *primary* source lay in the manner in which men earned their livelihood. It is quite possible that at a given state of civilization and, in order to fortify that particular civilization, the existing social divisions, that have sprung up naturally, are systematized, codified and intellectualized. Manu, or the intellectual efforts whose consummation he personifies, perhaps, represented just such an attempt at codification.

It seems to me that, by placing a scheme of social division before us, as a solution of the problems of modern society, Dr. Bhagavan Das has placed the cart before the horse. He rightly finds fault with the present divisions of society. But in trying to replace them by another, may be an ideal, division he has begged the whole question. Before suggesting an alternative scheme he should have paused to consider *why present society is so divided.* The present divisions, either in India or abroad, have not been superimposed from the outside: they have grown up *naturally* from their respective social soils. If we would have a different sort of division, we must prepare the necessary soil.

Here lies the superiority of the socialist's method. He points out that as long as the means of livelihood and of production of goods are in private hands, there is bound to be exploitation and the present unjust division of society into master and slave, rich and poor, powerful and weak. If we leave the first untouched, the latter is bound to appear—no matter in what disguise. If the basis of the economic organization is set right, the rest, including social division, would automatically right itself.

I recognise that the learned Doctor may not accept this principle. He might say that it is possible to impose on society, from without, a scheme of social organization so that it transforms, in time, even its very basis. That is, he might suggest a cure not from the roots upwards but from the branches downwards. Theoretically, it is possible to conceive of such a course of treatment. But I doubt whether the patient will feel the least relieved.

It is true that the Doctor does not content himself only with the division of society into professions; he apportions at the same time, duties, obligations, etc., to them. This may be thought to solve the problem. But apportioning duties is the least part of the job. The greater part is, firstly, to *put* people into the various divisions and, secondly, to *make them conform* to the codes prescribed for them. It is on this rock, I am afraid, that the Doctor's ship splits.

Let us examine the question a little more closely. We have on one side a society that is divided into classes of exploiters and exploited, rich and poor, strong and weak, master and servant. The class of masters is very small, while the underdogs run into millions. We find furthermore that this iniquitous society, is maintained with violence and coercion. The state in all its panoply of power—its legal apparatus, its police and army—stands guard to protect and nourish this injustice.

On the other side, we have Dr. Bhagavan Das with a plan to literally churn up this whole society—to redistribute wealth, power, privilege, duties and occupations. How does the Doctor propose to carry out his plan? A scheme, which does not suit the ruling class in society—and the Doctor's is eminently unsuited to it—has only two chances of success: either it must find proponents strong enough to impose it on society, or it must somehow persuade the entrenched interests to accept it. No scheme, hallowed even though it may be with such a name as Manu, can succeed unless it does one of these two things.

I have indicated above that the socialist relies for the fulfilment of his scheme on finding in the exploited classes of society, particularly in the working class, proponents of the required strength and outlook. He relies, in other words, on the forces of class struggle in society, and endeavours to organize the oppressed and exploited for the destruction of the present basis of society and the creation of a new one, whereupon he will build the new society.

Dr. Das, however, like Mahatma Gandhi, relies entirely on the method of persuasion. He has elaborated a scheme for this purpose, which he has linked up with the revered name: Manu. He writes:

> The only means seems to be to create a permanent 'class' of persons, from whom primarily good and wise legislators and secondarily trustworthy rulers could be drawn, and who could have sufficient honoured recognition amidst and influence

over the general public to be *able to check effectively* the aberrations of persons in official authority... Manu founds his Technique of Social Organization, and builds the whole superstructure thereof, expressly upon such a class of Brahmans, 'missionaries of Brahma' (by *Karma* and not by *Janma*). (pp. 151-2)

We read again:

If the system of Ashramas is revived properly, and persons begin to retire, as a rule, soon after completing their fiftieth year, from the life of 'the household' and competitive bread-winning, among any people, then that people will automatically begin to have a sufficient number of persons in the third stage of life, *vanasth*, who would be sages worthy of all trust and reverence fitted to make good laws, and able to guide and control the Executive by their moral force and influence. (pp. 152-3)

Further on:

The men and women, all over the world, who are devoted to the worship of the Divinity of Wisdom, Science, Learning, and are engaged in that noblest of all vocations, the vocation of teaching, of implanting right knowledge and developing righteous character and building up strong body in the younger generation, have only to add to their achievement and their work, their *vidya*, their *ilm*, the virtue of *tapasya*, *zohd*, resolute public spirit and philanthropy, and the holiness of asceticism and its inseparable will-power, its moral force, its spiritual all-subduing energy. As soon as they do so, the disease of the world would be cured—in a single day; the devils of greed, pride, lust, vice, would all be exorcised at once, and would take flight in fear and trembling from the hearts of the rulers, who would then become true public servants; .... (pp. 153-4)

It is refreshing to look at the inspired vision of the learned Doctor. But is not the onlooker likely to comment that there is a deep shadow of unreality over the whole thing? In a world where the universities turn out job-hungry youths, where society is governed by self and class-interest, where the State is a conscious instrument of class rule, where senility is yoked to self-seeking with the aid of monkey-glands, the vision of Dr. Das seems too unreal and foreign indeed.

However, to continue the description of Dr. Das' scheme. In order to produce the type of leaders he has described, he suggests a school of occult studies. Writing in his book under the caption, "Wanted—A Real School of Yoga" he says:

Persons who have the needed ethical, intellectual, physical, superphysical qualifications, who are real practical yogis along any of the recognised lines of the 'right-hand' path should be sought for and invited to Lodges of the T.S. (Theosophical Society—J.P.N.) or the E.S. (Eastern School of the T.S.—J.P.N.), on their own conditions, as far as possible, to act as guides to the others; moral, mental, and physical qualifications and tests may be prescribed for those who seek guidance and are prepared to run risks; one of the qualifications may perhaps be freedom from family ties or at least dependents; scientific methods should be adopted for demonstration and experiment; faith should not be asked for if proof cannot be given. If such a school of occult studies succeeds in producing the right kind of *alumni*, missionaries of the supreme spirit in heart and mind, even though they may not have succeeded in developing any superphysical faculties. . . , then indeed the world would be set on the right path of peace, progress, prosperity, material and spiritual happiness, by their moral and spiritual influence and their active labours for the good of mankind. (pp. 155-6)

Dr. Das suggests a "school of yoga" as an alternative to class struggle. Mr. H.G. Wells offered Stalin the P.E.N. Club as his alternative. These are two thought processes in two distant parts of the world; and yet they are impelled by identical social forces: the desire of the middle classes to reform the world, in accordance with middle class aspirations, without endangering their social and economic position.

However, to return to the school of Yoga. In my humble opinion, the very assumption on which the idea of this school is based is wrong. Dr. Das obviously thinks that the world is in this terrible mess because it lacks men of the type which he has called "missionaries of Brahma"; or, conversely, that the disease of the world would be cured—even in a single day—if such men were somehow created in sufficient numbers. This assumption, to my mind, again puts the cart before the horse. It is more correct to say that there are no "missionaries of Brahma" in the present world because it is dominated by capitalism and imperialism than to say that it is because there are no "missionaries of Brahma" that the world is dominated by these iniquitous systems. The present capitalist society has set its own standards and produces and values a different type of man. Its heroes are Fords and Monds; Lindbergs and Hansens, Hoares and Hitlers, Hindenburgs, even Einsteins—but not missionaries of Brahma. The latter are not likely to arise as long as capitalism is in existence.

It is different with "missionaries of Socialism", Capitalism itself produces them. The class struggle that is set up in capitalist society is just the soil in which Socialism takes root and grows. A glance at present society will show adequate proofs of this. The socialists—in using this term I am not excluding communists—constitute the largest political party in the world in opposition to the established order. I shall not hazard an estimate of the number of missionaries of Brahma, engaged in social planning. It is true that in India the number of socialists is very small. But here the forces that create Socialism are themselves of very recent origin. There is no doubt that in India too the socialists will constitute by far the largest group of those who have any conception of social reconstruction.

But let us suppose that the Lodges of the TS or such other occult bodies do succeed in creating enough missionaries of Brahma. What guarantee is there that they will be effective? Will they be able, for instance, to re-divide society; to redistribute wealth, power, occupations? It requires an immeasurable faith in occultism to answer the question in the affirmative.

In conclusion I might add that it takes one's breath away to consider the serenity with which this scheme has been conceived. Here is our world, crumbling, tearing, madly rushing on to ruin; here are millions starving, tortured, unemployed; here are rapacious capitalism and imperialism forging new tools of oppression and exploitation, piling up armaments, eating up colonies, gambling away with the lives of millions—and here is this philosopher, calmly thinking of a school of Yoga!

VII

No one having the least understanding of the forces that are at work in the modern world will for a moment think of Fascism as an alternative to Socialism. Fascism is, in fact, just the opposite of Socialism—its most relentless enemy.

Fascism represents the period of capitalist decay—the period in which capitalism attempts to sustain itself *at any cost.* The economic crisis which it has to face as a result of its own chaotic laws and the political danger it has to meet on account of the rising strength of the working class have driven it to overthrow democracy, which so far served as a convenient tool but does not give it the concentrated and unchallenged power that it now requires, and to deliberately destroy the culture that it had built up in the days of its effulgence. To the ruling class Fascism may be an alternative to Socialism—even though a temporary and effective one—but to those who are seeking means to serve the masses and to establish a Swaraj for them, as I assume the self-sacrificing Congress worker is doing, Fascism must ever remain the most dangerous enemy, to be given no quarter whatever.

The opposition of Fascism to the interests of the masses is so clear that I would not have troubled to consider it here, had it not been for the reason that certain prominent Congressmen have spoken approvingly of it and have even talked of a synthesis of Fascism and Socialism! To speak of such a synthesis is not only absurd but also most dangerous. Certain superficial "similarities", between Fascism and Socialism, such as "dictatorship", have encouraged this idea of synthesis. The "similarities" are very deceptive, however. The rule of industrialists and bankers under the cover of fascist dictatorship is very different from the rule of the workers and peasants. The former exists solely for the purpose of exploiting the workers and peasants whereas the latter exists for the destruction of that exploitation. There can be no manner of comparison between the two.

When we look at Fascism and Socialism we must not confine our view to their outward forms but must penetrate within and look at their foundations. The foundation of Fascism is capitalist greed and exploitation, the foundation of Socialism is the emancipation of the masses from that greed and exploitation. One is the enemy of the other. There can be no synthesis of the two.

I would be going too far away from my subject-matter if I were to launch upon a detailed analysis of Fascism. It is enough to have sounded a warning. I should like, however, to make a suggestion to those who are interested in following the matter further. A number of valuable works are available on the subject; but I know of no abler analysis of Fascism than that made by R. Palme Dutt in his *Fascism and Social Revolution*. Mr. Dutt is perhaps the ablest Marxist writing in the English language, and his *Fascism*, to my mind, is as important a study of the present disintegrating phase of capitalism as Lenin's *Imperialism* was of the phase that culminated in the Great War. The book will undoubtedly have a niche close to that of *Imperialism* in the temple of Marxism.

CHAPTER 4

METHODS AND TECHNIQUES

"The time of surprise attacks and revolutions, carried through by small conscious minorities at the head of unconscious masses, is past. When it is a question of a complete transformation of the social organization, the masses themselves must also be in it, must themselves already have grasped what is at stake, what they are going in for.... The history of the last fifty years has taught us that. But, in order that the masses may understand what is to be done, long persistent work is required, and it is just this work which we are now pursuing, and with a success which drives the enemy to despair."

FRIEDRICH ENGELS

The *Hindustan Times* delivered itself of the following homily the other day:

It is the incubus of foreign domination that is petrifying all progress, and stunting our national life. Let the nation once get rid of it and then the socialists will have enough time and opportunity to preach their doctrines, if the public are prepared to listen to them. It is not patriotism to divide the country in the face of common peril.

The *Hindustan Times* is the voice of Indian capital and is therefore fully entitled to teach us patriotism. National patriotism has been the peculiar weakness of capitalists. In fact, the very rise of nations was coeval with the origin of capitalism. The period of capitalist ascendency has been *par excellence* a period of nationalism. The cry of "the nation in danger" has been the strongest bulwark of capitalism. The 1931 British General Election was a classic example of this.

I have shown in the previous chapters that Socialism is the only and inescapable solution of the problems of present society. I have also shown that before we can undertake a socialist reconstruction of society we must have full power over the State. It is possible to argue from this, as in fact it is argued, that it is purposeless to talk of Socialism till we have won Swaraj. Nay, there are people, like the editor of the *Hindustan Times*, who do not consider it only purposeless but also positively mischievous. In their view, the struggle for Swaraj demands national unity, and Socialism is a doctrine which destroys that unity. Therefore a socialist agitation at this stage will weaken the national forces—so they think. This feeling is so widespread that it deserves to be carefully examined.

II

What is national unity? What is a nation? What is nationalism?

Let us compare two notable events of our national history: 1857 and 1885.[1] There were only twenty-eight years that separated those two events. Yet they wrought an incredible change in "national" outlook. 1857 witnessed an open and armed struggle for sovereign power; 1885 an act of humble petitioning.

From a struggle for sovereign power to a prayer for a Royal Commission marks a great change. Yet, the latter has been called "the beginning of the formulation of India's demands".

If, however, both 1857 and 1885 represented national[2] movements, it is obvious that nationalism means different things at different times. The difference lies not only in its objectives but in its human content as well. In 1857 feudal chiefs and their soldiers were the "nationalists"; in 1885, seventy-two gentlemen extracted from the middle classes, including the cadre of retired government servants.

These facts throw a flood of light on the problem of nationalism and national unity. Neither the feudal chiefs who fought in 1857 nor the *baboos* who founded the Congress in 1885, comprised the whole nation and stood for all the classes and groups within it. It would have been comic for the peasants in 1885 to have "united" with the *baboos* in demanding "seats" in the councils and more jobs for the English-educated! (Perhaps it is not quite obvious even now that it is only slightly less comic today to expect the peasants to unite, again with the *baboos*, in fighting for an undefined Swaraj and a mysterious thing called the Motherland.)

Thus we see that a "nation" does not in reality mean the whole nation, nor does nationalism comprise the interests of all the classes and groups within it. At different times different classes constitute the "nation" and give expression to nationalism. What class or group would play this role at a given time depends upon the circumstances of history and the structure of society. It may often happen that the so-called national interest of the moment is actually against the real interests of the majority of the people. When the cry of "the nation in danger" was raised in the General Election of 1931 in Great Britain, the purpose in reality was to stampede the people into voting for the perpetuation of British capitalism, standing as it did for

[1] 1857 was the year of the so-called "Sepoy Mutiny" and 1885 was the birth-year of the Indian National Congress.

[2] I have said above that nationalism in its modern sense is a recent development and grew with the nation-states of capitalism. Psychological equivalents of the nation, however, in the sense of political institutions being made the centre of the loyalties of masses of men, have always existed in history. Such were the loyalties of men to their kings and the devotion of the Greek to his city. I am using the word nationalism in this broad sense here.

their exploitation and economic bondage. To talk, therefore, of the nation as something undivided and whole, is to become victim to class propaganda.

The Indian nation is made up of princes, industrialists, bankers, merchants, peasants, labourers, etc. Nationalism does not mean the same thing to all these classes. The freedom of one of them is not the same as the freedom of the other. Nor is the manner in which they would fight for freedom, the same for all.

Let us take the princes. Their freedom means complete sovereignty which can be won only on the battlefield. But which of the princes, since 1857, is in a position to go to war for his sovereignty? It is clear that the princes must permanently remain vassals of British imperialism. This naturally ranges them against the "national" movement in so far as it opposes that imperialism. Here is the first breach in national unity.

The landlords of India, as is well known, are largely the creation of British imperialism. The bigger landlords have always solidly stood with imperialism and have been its strongest props in the countryside. Nationalism has no meaning to these people—except jobs in the higher services; and if any political power is to be given to Indians on account of nationalist forces gathering strength, then the balance of such power. They themselves are not interested in opposing or even agitating against imperialism. Their entry into politics is merely to ensure that their interests do not suffer on account of any power being "transferred" to Indian hands. No one with the least political understanding or experience can talk of unity with the landlords. Here is the second breach in national unity.

Let us take the industrialists next. Nationalism to them means complete freedom to exploit the country's resources (of men and materials) and to build up their fortunes, or, as it is euphemistically put, to develop the country. To do this they require a great deal of control over the State—leading ultimately to complete control. They would, no doubt, prefer complete control at once; but, since that is too risky to secure, they would be satisfied with gradual concessions of such control, i.e. with "reforms".

The Indian industrial class has grown up under the aegis of imperialism and is completely at its mercy economically and politically. It has no other foreign support, as the Irish bourgeoisie had in the U.S.A. In India itself its growth has not resulted in such benefits to the people, nor has it so made its influence felt on the economic or cultural life of the country, as to arouse and gather enthusiasm and support for itself. The result is the inability of this class to oppose imperialism. At best it can put pressure on it. But even this pressure it is unable to exert as a class. The only manner in which it can bring pressure to be exerted on imperialism is by inducing and surreptitiously helping other classes, with lesser stakes, to do so. This help, too, it will withdraw if the objective of the pressure is any other than to vest power in

Jayaprakash Narayan

J.P. with wife, Prabhavati Devi

J.P. with M.R. Masani

J.P. with Yusuf Meherally and Subhas Chandra Bose

J.P. with Swami Sahajanand Saraswati and other Kisan leaders

J.P. with members of the National Executive of the C.S.P. From left to right: Yusuf Meherally, Achyut Patwardhan, Rammnohar Lohia, S. Sajjed Zaheer, Asoka Mehta, Dinkar Mehta, Narendra Deva, S.M. Joshi, Kamaladevi Chattopadhyay, Mubarak Saghar, J.P., M.R. Masani, and S.S. Batlivala.

its hands. In other words, the industrialists are nationalists only in so far as nationalism aims at a bourgeois State. Nationalism will have no interest for them if its objective is any other than what is demanded by the interests of their class.

Thus we see, firstly, that the Indian industrialists are unable themselves to oppose imperialism; secondly, that they would be satisfied with facilities for economic development; and thirdly, they would support nationalism only when it aims at placing them in the seat of power. Here is the third breach in national unity.

Let us take the peasants now. India is a land of peasants. If Indian nationalism has any meaning, it should mean the freedom of the peasants. What is that freedom? Above all, it is freedom from exploitation, irrespective of whether that exploitation is carried on by a brown or a white skin. It is, further, the opportunity to shape the nation's economic and political policies in accordance with their own interests. In short, it is a peasant *raj*.

As for method of struggle, peasants have always known only one method—direct action. Such action, however, is as dangerous for the foreign oppressor as for the native. It is necessary, therefore, that in the interest of the latter, the peasants do not become conscious of their economic and political destiny. In other words, "national" unity breaks up as soon as the peasantry becomes conscious. Here is another breach in unity.

Likewise with the workers. The workers' freedom means freedom from wage-slavery by social ownership of means of production. Like the peasants, the workers' weapon too is direct action. And they too must not become class conscious, so that national unity may be maintained. A class-conscious working class means the break-up of national unity. Here is a further breach.

The above analysis has shown that there is no such thing as national unity which the socialists are trying to destroy. Nationalism does not mean the same thing to all the classes within the nation—it is not so simply expressed as the overthrow of the foreign incubus. Some classes in their very nature are *for* that incubus. Of those that are against, some are incapable of opposing it, and those that are in a position to do so, have fundamental interests directly opposed to those of the first.

The analysis shows, further, that the national unity of which the *Hindustan Times* speaks, means in reality that the lower classes—the masses—should fight imperialism not to secure their own freedom from exploitation but to enthrone the bourgeoisie and the landed magnates, who themselves do not participate in that fight, in the place of the imperial power. This unity can be maintained only at the cost of mass consciousness.

I grant that it is debatable whether this is not in the interests of the masses themselves. We shall take up this question in the next section. Here let us clearly understand what this magical, but highly deceptive, phrase, "national unity", really means.

III

I said above that it was debatable whether it was not in the interests of the masses themselves to remain unconscious, for the present, of their rights and destiny; and to fight imperialism merely to replace it with the vested interests of the country. It is so only if one believes that the united front of the masses and the bourgeoisie (including the landed interests) would lead to a surer and speedier defeat of imperialism. "In that case", it may be asked, "would not the defeat of imperialism be in itself of sufficient value to the masses to justify their having fought for the establishment of bourgeois democracy? After that they could have a second revolution if they so desired."

This point of view is typical of the mental attitude of the average Congress worker. It, therefore, deserves a careful examination.

Socialist though I am, I have not the least hesitation in saying that, were the consummation above envisaged possible, I should work for it willingly, though I should like to ensure at the same time that the second revolution followed the first as quickly as possible. The defeat of imperialism on such a broad sector as India, would have been of sufficient value to induce me work out that policy. But as circumstances obtain, it turns out to be a sterile policy—leading not to the defeat of imperialism but to a series of weak-kneed compromises with it.

These circumstances, briefly, are that the Indian bourgeoisie is not in a position to play a revolutionary role. I wrote in the last section, of its close ties with and dependence upon imperialism. This dependence and these ties completely destroy its revolutionary character and prevent it from becoming anti-imperialist. A section of it is, indeed, so dependent upon imperialism that, far from opposing, it wishes to perpetuate it. This is the section which performs the task of the middleman of imperialism. The other section which would like to be rid of imperialism—the industrial bourgeoisie—is too afraid to oppose it directly. As for the landlords, I have already indicated their relationship with imperialism and their consequent pro-imperialist role.

This position of the Indian bourgeoisie makes any united front of the masses with it absolutely barren. Firstly, because the alliance on the side of the bourgeoisie means very little. It is able to contribute very little to the struggle—even though the latter is merely demonstrative. Let us take an example of its ineffectiveness. The most important part of the programme of the last two civil disobedience movements—particularly of the last one—was economic boycott. This is a programme which in its very nature can be carried out best by the bourgeoisie itself. But, owing to its precarious position, the Indian bourgeoisie was unable to take it up. On the other hand, thousands of those, who had entered into an alliance, even though unconscious, with it to fight for a bourgeois Swaraj, had to court imprisonment by picketing its doors. Such a situation is not conducive to confidence in the bourgeoisie. The latter cannot be justified in asking others to fight a battle, none of the risks of which it is prepared to take, and of the spoils of which it claims an undivided share. Had the bourgeoisie courageously declared a telling and spectacular boycott of British interests during the last movement, it would still have commanded, in spite of us socialists, the confidence of the national forces; and the fears of disunity which are haunting so many minds would not have arisen at all. The failure of the Indian bourgeoisie to play a revolutionary role has struck the first blow to national unity, i.e. to the united front of the masses and the bourgeoisie.

I do not suggest that the average Congress worker has thought out the whole question in this manner. But he has certainly been severely disillusioned and made to wonder if a change of front had not become necessary.

The Indian bourgeoisie has proved un-revolutionary, i.e. failed to develop a vigorous anti-imperialist movement under its leadership, not only because it failed to participate in the struggle. For such a movement to develop, it is also necessary that the masses are drawn into it in large numbers, that is, it must be made a mass movement. This too the bourgeoisie has failed to do. A mass movement under bourgeois leadership is not a unique thing. It has unfortunately been a frequent historical occurrence. It is not possible, however, to create a mass movement in India under present conditions merely on the strength of appeals to national sentiment and acts of social service. In a country like modern Germany or Great Britain, where bourgeois rule has elevated national sentiment to holy heights, an appeal to it can do miracles. But in India where such sentiments have never prevailed and are not found in the masses (on account of there never having been a bourgeois order here), it has little appeal or other utility. It may arouse, as it has done, educated young men, but the latter alone cannot make a revolution.

Social service, likewise, falls flat. At best, its approach is individual and only very indirectly political. It therefore takes long to produce political results even in individuals. I know Congress workers, who love "solid" work, attach a great deal of importance to social service activity—in the shape of medical relief, educational work, *harijan* and *khadi* work, etc. This may appear to be solid work when there is no other programme, but it is an extremely ineffective programme for drawing out the masses in their millions into the political arena. The hypothesis behind such an approach is that, if a sufficiently large number of individuals are converted, a revolution would be created. Converted individuals are required; but only for the cadre of revolutionary workers. Revolution itself requires participation of classes, moved by class motives, hopes and fears. Has the Indian bourgeoisie a programme so to move the masses?

How has the bourgeoisie brought the masses under their banner elsewhere? Firstly, by inspiring confidence in itself by entering the thick of the fight. (I have already dealt with this point.) Secondly, by placing alluring slogans and programmes before the masses, which, while not touching its own interests, appear sufficiently attractive to the latter. Thirdly, by its ability and willingness to finance the whole movement.

The Indian bourgeoisie has failed to place any attractive programme before the masses. To attract, it must show that it has more to give than imperialism. But its economic position does not make it possible for it to do so. Under world capitalist conditions, if the Indian bourgeoisie has to prosper, it must do so only by intense exploitation of the Indian masses—by paying as low and selling as dear as possible. As far as the industrial workers are concerned, it has absolutely nothing to offer. Even in the sphere of agriculture, it cannot afford to follow a progressive policy. It must get its raw materials cheap. Today, in Bihar and the U.P., there is an open war between the newly opened Indian sugar mills and the cane-cultivators. And, ironically enough, the Provincial governments have become the arbitrators. Such a situation cannot conduce to the growth of a bond of community of interest, even though only as against the foreign power, between the masses and the bourgeoisie. One wonders if in such a situation the talk of unity does not appear ridiculous to those who indulge in it.

The bourgeoisie would like to give the peasantry some relief in the matter of rent and taxation. But here too, its relationship with the landed interests, on the one hand, and its reluctance to take recourse to direct action against imperialism, on the other, prevents it from going beyond half-hearted promises. These promises naturally are not convincing. Firstly, they do not go far enough; secondly, they do not touch the majority of the Indian peasants who have uneconomic holdings and therefore cannot bear any taxation; thirdly, the present share of the bourgeoisie in the exploitation of the peasantry, to which I drew attention above, gives rise to grave suspicions. Unity requires mutual trust, and it would be too platonic to insist that it must be based on future intentions rather than on present conduct.

As for the third, the bourgeoisie, because of the limitations and inhibitions I have described above, has followed an ungenerous and step-motherly policy. A revolutionary bourgeoisie would have flooded the national movement with its money. It has not been the case in India. Take even such an innocuous programme of the national movement as *swadeshi*. Any one would have thought that here was a programme after the bourgeoisie's own heart. A really "national" bourgeoisie would have made the country ring with the cry of *swadeshi*. Tons of money would have been poured into *swadeshi* propaganda. But whereas the British bourgeoisie, in spite of its immense reserves, has been carrying on a vigorous "Buy British" propaganda in its own country, the Indian capitalists have left it to sentimental young men to sing the praises of *swadeshi*.

This two-fold limitation of the Indian bourgeoisie—its inability to join the anti-imperialist movement and its failure to attract the masses under its banner, that is, with slogans that do not strike at its foundations—means that unity with it in the anti-imperialist struggle can end only in limiting, checking and thwarting the struggle itself. If the masses are not attracted to it and the bourgeoisie cannot participate in it, can it be otherwise? This means that the point of view with which we started, namely, that it would be in the interest of the masses themselves to put behind their final class interests and join the bourgeoisie in fighting a common enemy, does not hold good. The policy is proved to be wholly ineffective, leading only to compromises with imperialism. It should be realized further that these compromises can only be at the cost of the masses, because they will always mean agreement between imperialism and the native bourgeoisie as to the manner of exploiting the masses and resources of the country. It would be too naive to believe that a compromise between the upper classes of India and imperialism can have any other objective. This means that the acceptance of the above point of view, means not only frustration of the national movement, in so far as it means complete independence, but also a tragic betrayal of the masses. The betrayal becomes more tragic when one considers that the compromises with imperialism are made possible by the pressure of the masses themselves.

The new Constitution that has been "granted" to India, beautifully brings out this argument. That Constitution represents, as it has been pointed out so often, just such a compromise between imperialism and the upper classes of India for the further exploitation of its masses. And, as it is already history, the Constitution was made possible by the pressure of the latter themselves.

IV

I have tried to show above that there is no such thing as national unity against the foreign "incubus". Those who talk of such unity mean thereby that the masses should fight imperialism in order to secure political and economic power for the upper classes. Such a policy in actual practice, because of the counter-revolutionary character of the upper classes, results in frustration of the independence movement and betrayal of the masses.

The question then is: how can the independence movement be developed? For the satisfaction of those who say that they would have independence first and then think of the nature of Swaraj, let us consider this question without any reference to the interests of the masses. I shall show later that this attitude is essentially wrong and self-delusive. No politics can be above class interests. However, for the moment, let us consider the question of independence from a "detached" point of view, thinking of the masses and the other classes as pawns in the game.

I have shown above that of the various classes in the country, only the masses, in which term I include workers, peasants and the lower middle classes, can fight imperialism, because they are not dependent upon it. Not only are they in a position to fight, but it is they alone who stand for a hundred per cent independence from imperialism. The very life-blood of the latter comes from the exploitation of the former. Imperialism may throw crumbs to the masses to allay their rising discontent, but it would be defeating its very purpose and denying its very inner nature, if it forswore that exploitation. With the other classes in the country it can come to terms by agreements and concessions, but it will sign its death warrant if it agrees to stop the exploitation of the masses, carried on either directly or indirectly through its native agents. This means, as I have already said, that the masses are the only classes in India which are uncompromisingly anti-imperialist. They alone stand for the complete independence of the country. Others either openly ridicule and oppose the idea or only pay lip-service to it. Those classes which flourish under the foreign "incubus", like the highly paid government servants, the titled gentry, the big landlords, "the middlemen" of imperialism, are opposed to the country's independence. Those who find the incubus a serious obstacle to their progress but are not in a position to fight it, like the Indian industrialists, would be satisfied with facilities to exploit the masses as junior partners of imperialism, particularly when the independence struggle threatens to awaken the class consciousness of the former.

So if we agree that the masses only are anti-imperialists and the others are counter-revolutionary, what should be our tactics—even as movers of pawns on the chess-board? Obviously, we should adopt such tactics as would succeed in bringing the masses in opposition to imperialism. How can we do it?

Let us reflect on the pathetic fact that the population of the country is over thirty-five crores and our foreign rulers number a bare two lakhs. How is such a monstrous mathematical proportion maintained? Someone has remarked that even if the thirty-five crores were sheep, it would have taken more than two lakhs of men to tend them and keep them under control! Is this monstrosity possible because we are not nationally conscious? We are not united? We are not educated? What are the foundations of British rule in India?

Years ago I was listening to a speech of an eloquent Indian publicist in the beautiful city of San Francisco. The speaker's presence was as pleasant as his diction. He undoubtedly made a great impression on the audience. At the end of the speech when the last echoes of hearty applause were yet ringing, up rose a small figure from the centre of the hall to ask the speaker a question: "How is it, Sir, that a handful of Britishers hold down 300 millions of Indians?" That simple question seemed suddenly to break the whole spell that the speaker had woven in his two hours' oration. The latter, however, rose with what seemed to me to be an exaggerated air of confidence and replied: "If you gave me just a couple of pistols, I could hold up this entire audience." What he meant, of course, was that a handful of armed men—armed with the most modern weapons of destruction—could easily keep in subjection millions of unarmed people. I am unable to say what impression that answer created on the audience. The latter was made up mostly of the Irish, who naturally did not ask for much logic where the British were concerned. For myself the question and its answer completely destroyed the effect of that undoubtedly beautiful speech. Fourteen years later, British arms seem to me even less the reason of our subjection.

No, we are a subject nation not because we are unarmed. No arms could have enabled two lakhs of men to keep in subjection thirty-five crores of people. Nor is it out disunity—the multiplicity of races, tongues, and creeds—that is the cause of our slavery. Nor is it racial inferiority or any such thing. We must look elsewhere for the foundations of foreign rule.

To do that, we shall have to take a look at certain aspects of social organization and dynamics. Since exploitation became possible in society (because labour began to produce more than what was required to recreate it[3]) it became divided into classes. The division invariably followed a uniform pattern—the dichotomy of society into the exploiting and exploited classes. There were intermediary classes, no doubt, but this dichotomy was always the predominant feature of the social organization. The resultant of this dichotomy was that every class—society was organized around the interests of the ruling class. Its laws, its ideals, its entire civilization were centered round those interests. It should not be understood that such a society was, or is, in a state of stable equilibrium. The exploiting and exploited interests are, as a matter of fact, ever at war—sometimes open, sometimes latent. But we are not immediately concerned with this inner conflict. Let us see what happens when such a society is threatened by an outside force.

It is clear that that force will immediately come into conflict with the ruling class. The superior of the two—and here I am not excluding the personal abilities of the leaders on both sides—will win.

[3]See Chapter 1 for a fuller explanation.

What will be the position of the other classes in this conflict? The intermediary classes will stand by the ruling class because their existence largely depends upon the social organization that it upholds. Of the exploited classes, those will stand by it whose loyalty it has been able to secure with money or the influence of psychological factors created by the prevailing culture. Another incentive for these classes to support the ruling class, may be the fear of the foreigner and the changes that may come with him. At the same time, it is also possible that where the ruling class is too oppressive and the foreigner is expected to be an improvement, the latter may even be welcomed by the exploited classes.

However, the important thing to bear in mind is that the opposition to the foreigner is always led by the class which happens to be at the head of society. And once this class is humbled and the possibility of any opposition even from the remnants of its ruins, has been removed, the other classes lose all chance of expressing their discontent, except sporadically. Till a new class comes into existence with such a position in society as to replace the foreign power, as the ruling power, the discontent of the masses must only end in dissipation.

Let us apply these principles to the Indian situation. When the foreign power appeared on the scene, India was organized on a feudal basis. Naturally the feudal lords opposed it. One by one they were crushed. The masses as a whole do not seem to have taken much interest in this warfare. The frequent dynastic changes, the territorial shiftings, the exhaustion of frequent wars, had probably snapped what psychological bonds might have existed between the feudal chiefs and their subjects.

As the foreign power established itself, the masses began to realize what had happened. Peasants, craftsmen, merchants found themselves ground down with an unaccustomed ferocity. But, with their *rajas* and *nabobs* crushed, they were helpless. The foreign power no doubt had to face spasmodic uprisings, but it had no fear of organized challenge to its rule, as long as the remnants of the feudal order were kept in control. This is what actually happened.

From the beginning of its career, imperialism was conscious of its slender foundations and was anxious to broaden them. It was impossible for it to colonize here. Nor could it order from "home" an adequate army of occupation. It must build its foundations on native soil, with native materials.

At the beginning, it had to destroy certain interests, in order to establish its own. But after that was done, it had no desire to carry on wanton destruction. In fact, it required an ordered and peaceful regime for the new type of imperial exploitation that it represented. So it established law and order, creating thereby an illusion regarding its real intentions. But this was only a part of its policy of stabilization, and is of no particular moment to us just now.

Along with its policy of peaceful government, it set out to create a sort of an inner buffer State between itself and the masses. The cities, which were the seats of feudal power, were in its hands, and it was more or less sure of itself in them. It was the country, the villages, where it needed to lay its foundations. And there it created its most valuable buffer State. Picking up those elements of the upper classes of feudal India which had betrayed their side during its wars of conquest, it created a class of landlords to whom it handed over the millions of the peasantry.

That master-stroke of policy accomplished various results. It provided imperialism with an influential and absolutely reliable ally. It also largely assured the loyalty of the peasantry. The economic position and privileges of the landlords gave them tremendous prestige in the countryside. So their expression of loyalty towards the imperial power naturally found reflection in the vast peasantry. The *sarkar bahadur* came to be respected and feared. Finally, that policy created a shock-absorber between the peasants and imperialism. The discontent of the latter, whenever it came to the surface, turned not so much against the *sarkar bahadur* as against the landlords. Thus landlordism was the first and broadest foundation of British rule in India.

As imperialism progressed, it created other hangers-on—middlemen to do its business, retainers, servants, titled gentry, and so on. These groups and classes formed the upper strata of society and exercised considerable influence over the people in their own spheres. They thus formed a further safeguard for imperialism. In brief, imperialism broadened its basis by creating hangers-on, who formed the upper strata of society. Its rule, thus, was not based on arms but an alliance of class interests. Imperialism did not give rewards to its hangers-on out of its own pockets. They too drew their profits, rents and tributes from the masses, just as imperialism did. It was this illicit understanding to exploit in common, the real producers of the country and its resources, that has been the main bulwark of British rule in the country.

While on the one hand there is this understanding, on the other, there is complete confusion and lack of consciousness. The creation of buffer classes has checked the growth of anti-imperialist feeling in the masses. On the one hand, they have been taught to regard landlords and capitalists as their own kith and kin against whom they should not show any temper; on the other, they find that it is these kith and kin largely who are their immediate exploiters. It is naturally difficult for them to generate feelings of hostility against imperialism, the exploitation of which they do not experience directly, or do so only as one of various other exploitations from which they suffer; and, at the same time, preserve a feeling of friendship and identity of interest with their so-called kith and kin who exploit them no less. Any appeal to the masses to fight imperialism on grounds of exploitation, is bound to leave them unmoved if it makes no reference to those who share—and more immediately—in that exploitation. A consciousness of antagonism towards imperialism cannot grow and leave the latter out of its purview, because the basis of antagonism towards both is the same—realization of the injury done. Those who wish to develop an anti-imperialist consciousness among the masses, must make up their minds about the native system of exploitation—the junior imperialism. They will fail in their purpose, as they have done so far, if they advocate the retention of the latter and the elimination of the former. An anti-imperialist programme for the masses must be based on the slogan of elimination of all exploiters. I had said above that since the masses (peasants, workers and the lower middle class) were the only anti-imperialist elements in the country, our tactics obviously should be to bring them into conflict with imperialism; and I had asked how could that be done. Here is the answer. Freedom from exploitation must be placed in the forefront. Their immediate economic exploitation must be kept before them in its true perspective, as a part of the working of imperialism. They must be helped to develop a vigorous struggle against this exploitation; and the larger struggle against imperialism must be made to grow out of it as a logical consequence. If the fight against imperialism is to mean a fight against exploitation, it must begin at the nearest front. This is the new front to which we must move—the economic front of the masses. How will this front be developed? Who will be its leaders? What will be its programme?

V

The first requirement for the development of this front is the building up of class organizations of the masses, particularly of peasant and labour unions. These unions will organize their struggle against oppression and exploitation; and through that struggle develop in them that anti-imperialist consciousness and solidarity which will lead them finally to defeat imperialism. It is only in this manner that the masses will be brought collectively (and not individually) into conflict with imperialism.

It should be noted, however, that the process envisaged above would not materialize if the class organizations of the masses aimed merely at wringing concessions from the exploiting classes. They must aim not at adjustment with exploitation and oppression, but at complete freedom from them. In other words, they must be revolutionary and not reformist in character. They must aim at development of class consciousness and must be uncompromising organs of class struggle.

This is the "solid" work before us. We must break the spell of national unity; and in the interest of national independence build up these organizations. Looking at the vastness of the country and the numbers of the masses, one would be justified in thinking that this work is solid enough for the most inveterate lover of solid work. It is true that it may not appeal to those who want to do "constructive" work. It is not a constructive programme. I have often been faced with the demand to produce a socialist constructive programme and been advised to demonstrate Socialism on a small scale before glibly talking of class struggle. The constructive programme of Socialism—and its immense reality can be seen by turning to Russia—can begin only after the revolution. Till then our programme consists in constructing one thing—the struggle of the masses. It must therefore be left to the Congress worker to decide if he would prefer to construct Khadi and A.I.V.I.A. centres or the fighting organizations of the masses which I have described above.

I have mentioned peasant and labour unions as the most important of these organizations. Of these two, labour organizations have been in existence for a considerable period of time and have been knit together in an all-India body—the All-India Trades Union Congress. To develop the T.U.C. is one of our urgent tasks.

Peasants' unions have had a rather checkered career. However, they are rapidly developing now all over the country. Their development must be stimulated and integrated. In a peasant country, this is naturally our most important task.

Alongside of these class organizations of the masses, there must also be developed a common political organization for them to carry on the anti-imperialist struggle. The class organizations will enable the workers, peasants, etc., to develop their economic and political struggle separately. We need an organization to integrate their struggle. The former are essential; without them the masses will neither be organized nor made conscious. It is on the basis of their class interests that they will first unite. But that will not be enough. They must combine together in one organization to secure their common ends—economic and political freedom.

Is not the Congress such a common organization?—it may be asked. Yes and no. The Congress certainly is not such an organization, as it is at present. Neither its constitution nor its programme answers the requirements of such an organization. Firstly, it claims to be a national body representing all classes in the country—the bourgeoisie as much as the worker, the landlord as much as the tenant. I have already shown what such a united front means. Where the upper and lower classes are united in one organization, the latter unquestionably stands primarily for the interests of the former. It is deliberate deception or tragic self-delusion to say that the interests of both can be equally represented within the same organization.

So the first thing the Congress must do to become an organization of the masses, is to declare that it does not represent the bourgeoisie; and that it stands as much against them as against imperialism. People believe that that would destroy the "national" character of the Congress. What it would really do, however, is to convert it from a bourgeoisie body into a mass organization. It will mean a sudden leap for the Congress though a fall from its present respectability.

The Congress constitution does not give the Congress Committees any representative character, apart from that of representing individuals, "enrolled" Congressmen by the members of those very committees. This is too artificial a basis for the Congress to be a mass organization. In order that it may become so, it ought to be constituted of representatives of mass organizations. In other words, it should be given a sort of a Soviet constitution from the *bottom* upwards. A District Congress Committee ought to represent the peasant unions, the labour unions and other functional organizations of the anti-imperialist classes in that district. The higher bodies may be indirectly elected or through a combined direct and indirect method. In the transitional period from the present to this constitution, the prevailing practice of individual membership may be retained in combination with the suggested form.

Finally, the present programme of the Congress and its declarations of objectives, do not give it the character of a representative of the masses. Its objective must include, as a minimum, the following points:

1. Complete independence, in the sense of separation from British Imperialism.
2. All political and economic power to the producing masses (including brain workers).
3. Nationalization of all key and large industries, banks, mines, plantations, etc.
4. Abolition of landlordism in all its forms.
5. Land to the tiller of the soil.
6. Liquidation of all debts owed by peasants and workers.

Its programme of work must chiefly consist in the development, through its members, of the class organizations of the masses.

These are the three irreducible minima which the Congress must adopt or follow in order to become a proper anti-imperialist body. Till then it is not such a body.

But I said "Yes and no" to the question above. "Yes" in the sense that while the Congress in its organized form (i.e. taking its constitution and programme in consideration) is not such a body, it contains largely petty bourgeois (including peasant) elements which objectively are anti-imperialist. These elements have to be made conscious in order to become active anti-imperialist.

These changes which I have indicated as necessary before the Congress becomes an anti-imperialist body, are so basic that they do not involve merely a conversion but a disruption also. The anti-imperialist elements must be converted, but it is impossible to convert the bourgeois elements. Even of the former many will continue to cling to the bourgeois programme, if for no other reason, at least, for the sake of preserving "national unity". Therefore, a break with the bourgeois wing, together with its adherents, would be necessary. And the break while it should not be premature, should not be delayed either.

The formation of the Congress Socialist Party shows that a considerable portion of the petty bourgeois elements in the Congress has broken away from the bourgeois ideology. The Party has been criticised for not breaking away from the Congress. On that ground it has been dubbed fascist by certain people. The argument advanced is that by remaining within the Congress, it is strengthening the bourgeois hold over the anti-imperialist elements within the Congress. Nothing can be further removed from reality, however. The very purpose of the Party remaining in the Congress is to weaken by inside propaganda and opposition, that hold; and ripen the anti-imperialist elements for a final break with it. The Party's going out would have meant isolation of the most conscious elements in the Congress from the rank and file; and consequently its continued attachment to the bourgeois programme. This is so obvious that it is strange to find it being questioned. Those who, remaining outside, talk of the Congress rank and file and the anti-imperialist movement, are shirking their responsibility. However it was a pleasure to learn of the remarks made by Mr. R. Palme Dutt at the last Congress of the Communist International. He admitted his mistake in characterizing the Congress Socialist Party as a fascist party and sounded a warning against such facile characterizations. One hopes that this is the beginning of a more correct appreciation of the needs of the situation.

VI

There is only one question remaining to be considered in connection with the anti-imperialist movement. Who will be its leaders? We have seen that there was a stage of feudal leadership. Then came the phase of the national reformist movement under bourgeois leadership. What will be the nature of the future leadership? If the objective of the anti-imperialist movement is complete freedom from exploitation, then it is clear that the class which at the present stage of development of the means of production, can be the centre of an exploitation-less society, must lead. Exploitation at this stage can be removed only by the social ownership of means of production. The class which most consciously can put forward the demand for such ownership, is the working class. The fact that it already produces socially, naturally impels it to make that demand; and it not only makes that demand, but in the construction of the new society, it is going to play the central role. Thus the destiny which the masses have to reach, is most consciously envisaged and strived for by the working class. Therefore it alone must assume the leadership. Its leadership will largely operate through the ideological influence that it will exert on the development of the anti-imperialist movement.

Before concluding, I wish to touch on the attitude of political workers (briefly referred to before) of looking upon themselves as above classes and upon the classes as pawns in the political game which they move. The reality is just the reverse of this. Political workers are not individuals. In spite of slight differences of opinion, such workers can be grouped together in parties. Each one of us thinks that he has formed his opinions independently. Obviously there is something beyond and above individuals that moulds their opinions. This something is social classes. Political workers if classified, will fall into parties; and these will be found to coincide with class or group interests. The seventy-two gentlemen who founded the Congress in 1885 were of one mind. Why? Because they represented more or less identical interests which were finding expression through them.

This is one of the most difficult concepts to drive into people's minds. Every one has his ego, which refuses to admit outside dictation of his views. It is a fact, nevertheless.

We have all been taught to understand political and social movements in terms of personalities. We seldom, if ever, look behind individuals—to those forces of society which push and jog us on, which shape political programmes for us and give us philosophies and religions. Individuals count—some count a great deal—but only as the agents of those forces, as their executors. They are not exactly mannequins; they are themselves parts of those forces, and shape them in their turn.

But no individual, however brilliant, can create a social movement unless the conditions in that society are appropriate for it; in reality, he hardly "creates" it even then. His individuality undoubtedly contributes to its success or failure, but its character and its ideals can be only those prescribed by the existing social conditions. The essence of leadership lies in interpreting those conditions correctly so as to fulfil the process which they have set up. Leadership is essential, but only that leadership succeeds which fulfils the laws of society.

It is for this reason that in the analysis that I have made above of the national movement, the foundations of imperialism, etc. I have talked only in terms of classes and not individuals. Those Congress workers who think that they are taking a detached view of political movements, are falling victim to one of the gravest distortions of bourgeois social science. A "detached" view is not possible in politics, because we do not live in a vacuum, nor are politics brewed in it.

2. General Secretary's Report (1935), 20 January 1936[1]

Comrades,

I crave your permission to place before you my report on the activities of the Party since its inception more than a year ago.

In October 1934 a Conference of representatives of thirteen Provincial Congress Socialist parties[2] was held at Bombay. It was at that Conference that the All India Congress Socialist Party was launched with the unanimous consent of the representatives present, the thirteen Provincial parties becoming its affiliated bodies.

Our Party is thus only a year and a quarter old. During this brief period, it has made steady progress. If our resources were larger, we might have done better; but we have no reason to be dissatisfied with the results achieved.

I shall briefly review the work done.

The primary task of the Party is in relation with the Congress, in radicalising it and developing the anti-imperialist elements in it so as to make it a real anti-imperialist organization. The Party has been able to do a considerable amount of work in this direction, though the tightening of the Congress Constitution may not allow the result to appear in its real proportions.

Immediately after its formation, the Party had a unique opportunity for its work in this connection in the Bombay Congress. Members of the Party were able to raise many important issues and give a new lead on them. The work of the Party at the Congress was the first of its kind in Congress history. It was for the first time that an organized group appeared in the Congress with its own political philosophy and a complete alternative programme. This fact made a deep impression on the public and the birth of the Party was accounted on all sides to be a development of fundamental national importance. Not only did Socialism suddenly leap into the foreground of Indian politics, but the basic weakness of the Congress position and the direction of its future development were forcefully brought into relief.

After the Bombay Congress the Party continued this work in the All India Congress Committee and Provincial Committees and Conferences. In several of the latter, such as Utkal, United Provinces, Karnatak, Bengal,

[1] *All India Congress Socialist Party. Constitution, Programme and Resolutions of the First Conference of the Party and Report of the Organising Secretary, 1936.*

[2] The thirteen Provincial Congress Socialist parties, whose representatives met in Bombay at Readymoney Terrace, Worli, 21-2 October 1934, in order to form an All India Congress Socialist Party belonged to Ajmer, Andhra, Bengal, Berar, Bihar, Bombay (City), C.P. (Hindi), Delhi, Gujarat, Kerala, Maharashtra, U.P. and Utkal.

Kerala and Berar, we were successful in getting adopted several or all our resolutions. This indicates the influence of our ideas on the Congress rank and file. Unfortunately, the Provincial Conferences, though they reflect the opinion of the broadest section of Congressmen of the Province, have no constitutional authority at present.

The issues which the Party has tried to raise in the Congress whether in the Congress session, the All India Congress Committee or the Provincial Congress Committees have been the following: the programme of the Congress, its attitude towards the slave Constitution, the danger of an imperialist war involving Great Britain, the State's peoples, the Bengal detenus. The first three are issues of the utmost importance.

With regard to the first, we have pressed consistently for the acceptance of a minimum programme for the peasants and workers and their organization so as to develop their struggle for economic and political emancipation. We have emphasized that not only is political freedom meaningless without economic freedom, but it is even difficult if not impossible to achieve it without the development of the economic struggle of the masses.

With regard to the last two, we were perhaps the only All-India organization to have raised them and given a clear and unequivocal lead regarding them. We declared at the very beginning that the only possible answer to the slave Constitution was to destroy it by bringing its working to a standstill. We have been the most uncompromising opponents of the move of some prominent Congressmen in favour of acceptance of ministerial offices under the new Constitution. We have held that such a policy would destroy the Congress as an organization relying on direct action for the achievement of its goal. It is a pleasure to note in this connection that an influential committee of prominent Congressmen has just been formed under the able presidentship of Sardar Sardul Singh Caveeshar[3] to carry on propaganda against the pro-ministerialist move. Comrade M.R. Masani[4] is one of the Secretaries of that Committee. I need hardly say that the Party will render all possible assistance to the Committee.

The danger of an international war is now much more real than it was in October 1934. This growing danger has completely justified the stand of the Party on this issue and the efforts made by it to bring it to the fore. During the past year and a quarter, the Party held numerous anti-war meetings, Abyssinia meetings, and observed an Anti-War Day throughout the country on Armistice Day. The position taken by the Party has not been the usual pacifist one. Instead of vainly speaking of averting war, the Party has tried to show its inevitability. It has further attempted to show that such

[3] For biographical note on Sardul Singh Caveeshar see *JPSW*, Volume One, p. 159.

[4] For biographical note on M.R. Masani see *JPSW*, Volume One, p. 66.

a war could only be waged for imperialist aggrandisement and has therefore warned the people that they could have nothing to do with such a war and that indeed they should take advantage of it to further the cause of Indian Independence.

If I were reviewing the work of the Congress in the past year, the one thing to which I should point as its outstanding failure would be its lack of appreciation of the international situation and its failure to find any significance for the national movement in the war danger.

The Party was the only group in the Congress, indeed the only political Party in the country, which took up the cause of the Bengal detenus. It observed an All-India Detenu Day and otherwise carried on propaganda for their release. It raised the issue in the Congress and was to a large extent responsible for the creation of the Congress Detenu Fund. Over two thousand rupees were collected for the detenus by the Bombay Party on our Detenu Day. This sum was handed over to the above Fund.

So much for the activities of the Party in the general political sphere. In the development of a mass movement also it has played a notable part—though a year is hardly sufficient to show visible results. We have succeeded in preparing the ground and in building up nuclei for our work.

Organization of peasants and workers is the most important part of the mass movement. Working class organizations have been in existence for some time. These the Party joined, and undertook to build up new ones. Immediately after its formation, the Party entered into an agreement with the All India Trades Union Congress and pledged to make it the central organization of Indian labour. Unions organized by members of the party in different parts of the country, as in Ahmedabad, Calicut, Dhulia and Bombay, have been or will soon be affiliated to the All India Trades Union Congress. Party members have participated in labour strikes in a number of places such as the Ahmedabad textile workers' strike, Calicut tile and textile workers' strike, the British India Steam Navigation Company workers' strike, the Berhampur and Jalgaon textile workers' strike. The Party enjoys considerable influence in the Trade Union movement and both the present President and General Secretary of the All India Trade Union Congress are its members.

From the very beginning of its career the Party has stood for unity in the Trade Union movement. From time to time it has issued appeals for unity and, through consultation, has sought to bring pressure on the organizations concerned in that behalf. Members of the Party who are in the Trade Union Congress have consistently followed a 'Unity Policy'. It is a matter of satisfaction that the possibility of unity has grown steadily in recent months and it seems to be only a matter of time for unity to become a fact. One hopes that structural unity in the trade union movement will only be a prelude to a hitherto unrealized intensification of the struggle of the working class.

Peasant organizations have had a much more chequered career than the Trade Union movement. There have been periods of intense peasant struggle during which spontaneous organizations were built up. But these died away when the struggle ended. Till recently, no concerted attempt was made to organize the peasantry on a proper basis.

The formation of our Party has opened a new chapter in the peasant movement. Our contacts with the peasantry and our ideological stand have made it possible for that movement to be placed on a stable basis. Our Party includes the largest cadre of peasant workers in the country. Already they have been prominent in the formation of several provincial peasant organizations. The Party has also been considering the desirability of co-ordinating the provincial movements into an All-India body. Only three days ago, a meeting of representatives of peasant organizations was held here at which an Organizing Committee was appointed to expedite the formation of such an organization. Two of the three secretaries of the Committee are members of the Party.

Thus the chief spheres of Party activity have been the Congress, and the labour and peasant movements. The year's achievements in these spheres have given us a solid basis for our future work.

In addition to the above, I must mention another notable activity of the Party. It is the publication of the Party organ, the *Congress Socialist* which has already proved to be of invaluable service to the movement. The *Congress Socialist* was first started by the Bengal Party under the able editorship of Dr. R.M. Lohia[5] and was subsequently taken over by the All India Party. The journal had to suspend publication for some months after which it is again appearing, this time from Bombay under the editorship of Comrade Asoka Mehta.[6] Several new attractions have been added to the paper this time and there is no doubt that it is one of the finest weeklies in the country and has already won the admiration of intellectuals of all political shades of thought.

Just a few remarks on the debit side. A party working under serious limitations is bound to make mistakes. These are to be expected and I need not mention them. There is, however, one weakness in the Party which we must take serious note of and remove as early as possible. I refer to the lack of the spirit of solidarity within the Party. Members have not shown the spirit of discipline and loyalty to the Party that socialists are expected to possess for their organization. Many members have shown an indifference enough to have justified their removal from the Party. Many others seemed

[5] For biographical note on Rammanohar Lohia see *JPSW*, Volume One, p. 91.

[6] For biographical note on Asoka Mehta see *JPSW*. Volume One, p. 122.

to be using the Party to further the policies of outside groups and parties. This lack of oneness of purpose and solidarity has been one greatest weakness and it must go if we are to grow. A spirit of loyalty and devotion to the Party and its work must be instilled into every member. For the active member, at least, the Party must become his chief interest in life. I do not think this is possible unless we are more careful and discriminating in the enrolment of new members and stricter in enforcing discipline. I hope the new Executive will frame rules to this end and do all else that is necessary.

Before concluding, I must give you an idea of the foreign work of the Party. While the Party believes that the emancipation of the masses of India can come through their own efforts, it recognises the importance of international events and movements in influencing the course of our political struggle, and the international character of both imperialist and anti-imperialist forces. The Party therefore attaches considerable value to international contacts. It believes, however, that these contacts should not confine themselves almost entirely, as has been the case so far, to individuals and associations evincing a platonic interest in India but must be developed with forces that are themselves struggling against imperialism.

It was with this object in view that the Party appointed two secretaries in London, Mr. V.K. Krishna Menon[7] and Mr. M.R. Masani, to bring about a closer understanding between the working-class and other anti-imperialist movements in great Britain and the struggle of the Indian masses.

A further opportunity for this was given to the Party by the British Socialist League, which invited the Party to send one or two representatives to Great Britain. The Party was glad to be able to send Comrade M.R. Masani in response to the invitation.

Comrade Masani left India in June last year and returned early in November. Of the five months that he was away, he spent three months in Great Britain where he did excellent work for the Party. He was also able in the time left to him to pay a flying visit to Soviet Russia, where he was able to bring about a better understanding of our Party and its work.

In Britain, Comrade Masani addressed about 40 meetings, the audience always being labour or otherwise politically progressive such as Labour M.P.s, miners from the Durham and South Wales coalfields, university students, Christian pacifists, Marxists and Labour Leagues of Youths. Some of these meetings were organized during a lecture tour arranged for him by the University Labour Federation in co-operation with the Socialist League.

[7] V.K. Krishna Menon (1896-1974); born at Calicut; educated at Madras and London; joined Independent Labour Party in England, 1924; Secretary, India League, 1929-47; High Commissioner for India in London, 1947-52; Chairman, Indian Delegation to the General Assembly of the United Nations, 1952-3, and 1954-62; Minister of Defence, 1957-62, Government of India.

I shall quote from Comrade Masani's Report regarding his impressions of these meetings and tours:

From these meetings I got the impression that both the British workers and the university students could be won for Socialist and Anti-Imperialist Policy. At no meeting of working people was there any attempt at defending the policy of Labour Governments in the past or the Labour Party to-day against my criticisms. But ignorance of conditions in India, pre-occupation with bread-and-butter problems at home and the lack of correct leadership conspire to keep from them an appreciation of the need for common action by the British working class with the colonial peoples of the Empire against the common enemy, Imperialism.

Apart from these public meetings, Masani was able to establish contacts with a number of organizations. The first of these which I must mention was the Socialist League. He had talks with the Executive Committee of the League, and its National Council, as well as with its Chairman, Sir Stafford Cripps.[8] At these meetings discussions were held both about our own movement and about what could be done by the League "in promoting a better understanding and closer co-operation between the Socialist movements in India and Britain". The League leaders showed keenness to understand our point of view and "to help in placing before the larger British Labour movement policies which would help us in our struggle against Imperialism".

Masani also had meetings with the Secretary and the International Secretary of the Labour Party. These talks "were frankly unsatisfactory". His next approach to the Labour Party leaders was at the British Conference of the Party. After the main resolutions condemning Mussolini's[9] invasion of Abyssinia and supporting League sanctions against Italy was carried, Masani wrote a letter to the Executive of the Party suggesting a similar resolution of condemnation of the British bombing of the Trans-Frontier villages which was then proceeding on the N.W. Frontier of India. Acting on the suggestion, Professor Laski[10] and others gave notice of a resolution. The Conference, however, adjourned just before the resolution was due to come up for discussion. It was understood that the Executive of the Labour Party had decided not to accept the resolution, in any case.

[8] Stafford Cripps (1889-1952); Solicitor General in Labour Government, 1930-1; British Ambassador to U.S.S.R., 1940-2; deputed to negotiate with Indian leaders, 1942; member of Cabinet Mission to India, 1946; Chancellor of the Exchequer, 1947-50.

[9] Benito Mussolini (1883-1945); organized Fascist Party of Italy, 1919; elected to Parliament, 1921; appointed Prime Minister, 1922; assumed dictatorial powers and established complete control over the government, 1928-9; joined the Second World War on the side of Germany in June 1940; assassinated, April 1945.

[10] Harold J. Laski (1893-1950); British political scientist who influenced Socialist thinking in Britain in the 1930s and 1940s; Chairman of Labour Party, 1945; works include: *A Grammar of Politics, Communism, Liberty in the Modern State, Democracy in Crisis*, and *The American Democracy*.

Other organizations with which Masani established contacts were the I.L.P., the International Bureau for Revolutionary Socialist Unity, the Communist Party of Great Britain, the minority Labour Federation, the Fellowship of Reconciliation and the No More War Movement.

Masani was invited to attend the summer school of the I.L.P. at Letchworth and to address the students on the Indian Socialist movement.

At the same time and place the International Bureau for Revolutionary Socialist Unity was also meeting and Masani attended the gathering as an observer. He was asked to explain the Party's history and its position, which was followed by an interesting discussion of a couple of hours. There were representatives of about ten Left Socialist Parties from the Continental countries at the meeting.

I feel I may legitimately be asked,

says Masani in his Report,

to express an opinion on certain questions as the result of my tour. The first is the question of foreign affiliation of our Party. I was asked several times whether the Party was affiliated to either the Second or Third International or to the International Bureau for Revolutionary Socialist Unity. I explained that our having no International was not due to insularity or any nationalist motive. It seems to me that any affiliation at this stage would be undesirable. The Socialist movement internationally is in a flux. The Second International is hardly a real International. It has little capacity for co-ordinating policies and for giving central direction. On the other hand the Third International is dominated too much by the Communist Party of Russia owing to its numerical and financial strength which is out of all proportion to that of other parties in the International.

The International Bureau of Left Socialist Parties contains only about a dozen parties of the Continent most of which are not bigger than the I.L.P. in England.

The policies these organizations pursue are also undergoing rapid changes. This is particularly true of the Communists and these changes are likely in the not distant future to lead to a merger of the two or three International organizations existing at present. That being the case it seems to me that any question of foreign affiliation does not arise until first there is a United Socialist International.

Stating his conclusions regarding foreign propaganda by the Party, Masani is of the opinion that the present representation of the Party by two Secretaries in London is adequate for the time being. As for foreign propaganda by the Indian National Congress, he is of the opinion that

what is needed is not a branch of the Congress or a London Congress Committee but simply an information bureau which would serve the double purpose of providing information about India and also of obtaining contacts with sympathetic organizations abroad. Such a bureau under the control of permanent officials with a broad international outlook and able to represent the growing anti-Imperialist movement in India, might well be established by the Congress in England, on the Continent and America. These offices should be under the direct control of the Working Committee of the Congress and should not initiate any policies as was done by the branch of the Congress in London which had to be dissolved.

Masani's report concludes by referring to the organizations already doing propaganda in England on behalf of the Indian national movement.

The India League of which Lord (Bertrand) Russell[11] is President, D.R. Grenfell,[12] M.P., Chairman, and V.K. Krishna Menon Secretary, is, he states, the organization which has got the most political contacts and has been able to do more than any other group.

The Indian Conciliation Group with Miss Agatha Harrison[13] as Secretary has also been doing good work. The League Against Imperialism and the Friends of India Society have also in different ways been contributing to the knowledge of the British public on Indian affairs.

Masani states that from all these organizations and various others he received very cordial co-operation in making his visit to England of maximum use.

The Party, I am sure, would like to convey its thanks to these organizations and also to the other organizations mentioned earlier in the report for their assistance to Comrade Masani in his work abroad.

Jayaprakash Narayan
Meerut, 20 January 1936

[11] Bertrand (Arthur William) Russell (1872-1970); eminent British philosopher, mathematician and social activist; awarded Nobel Prize for Literature, 1950; works include: *Principles of Mathematics*, *Education and the Social Order*, *History of Western Philosophy*, and *Autobiography*.

[12] David Rhys Grenfell (1881-1968); member, British Parliament, 1922-59; Secretary for Mines, 1940-2.

[13] Agatha Harrison (1885-1954); Quaker social worker; friend of C.F. Andrews, M.K. Gandhi and Jawaharlal Nehru; Secretary, Indian Conciliation Group, London, 1936.

3. Letter to Kishori Prasanna Singh, 31 January 1936[1]

Benares
31 January 1936

Dear Kishori Babu,[2]
Saprem Namaskar,

Received the sad news[3] while proceeding to Shahabad Kisan Sammelan. I express my heart-felt condolences on your bereavement. I did not have the privilege of knowing Suniti Devi, yet whatever I had heard about her from

[1] *JP Papers* (Nehru Memorial Museum & Library, hereinafter referred to as NMML). Original in Hindi.

[2] For biographical note on Kishori Prasanna Singh see *JPSW*, Volume One, p. 142.

[3] Refers to the demise of Suniti Devi, the wife of Kishori Prasanna Singh. For biographical note on Suniti Devi see *JPSW*, Volume One, p. 183.

friends makes it clear that her demise is not only a personal loss to you, but has also caused a great loss to the political movement of the region.

However, knowing your nature I shall not venture to advise you to be patient and firm at this moment. I know you will quietly bear your pain.

I do not know what happened to the Rajgir Camp. I had been to Patna recently, but nothing could be known. Possibly, Panna Babu[4] might have met you today or yesterday. If he has given you Rs. 50/-, then you yourself go to Rajgir with that money and make appropriate arrangements. Ganga Babu[5] had promised to get a hut constructed for me, but I do not know what happened. Today I am writing to Ganga Babu.

I will go to Patna on the 3rd. Stay there till the 4th. Can I meet you then. Arrange camp for the 10th.

Yours,
Jayaprakash

[4] B.P. Sinha. For biographical note see *JPSW*, Volume One, p. 61.

[5] Ganga Sharan Sinha (1905-87); Secretary, Bihar Socialist Party, 1931-4; Founder-member, Congress Socialist Party, 1934; member, National Executive and Central Parliamentary Board, Praja Socialist Party, 1956-9, its Deputy Chairman, 1956, and Chairman, 1956-9; member, Rajya Sabha, 1956-74; Founder-President, Acharya Narendra Deva Sansthan, Benares.

4. Circular to Secretary, Bihar Congress Socialist Party, 1 February 1936[1]

Kabir Chaura
Benares City, U.P.
1 February 1936

The Secretary,
Bihar C.S.P.

Dear Comrade,

This is merely to inform you that owing to reasons of health I have taken leave from the Party till the Lucknow Congress. The Central Executive has appointed Com. M.R. Masani to officiate for me. Please address all communications to him at Dadabhai Manzil, Congress House, Girgaum, Bombay.

Yours fraternally,
Jayaprakash Narayan
All India Congress Socialist Party
General Secretary

[1] *JP Papers* (NMML). The same circular was sent to all the provincial secretaries of the Congress Socialist Party.

5. Britain versus India: Article in the *Congress Socialist*, 21 and 28 March 1936[1]

What is the situation before us? The imperialist power is attempting to force upon us a device for the further perpetuation of its domination. I need not describe that device to you with all its traps and dangers. It has been fully analysed and it has met with universal condemnation. The Congress has declared that it would rather struggle under the existing order of things than have the new dispensation. The new dispensation will however be upon us in a few months, in spite of our rejection.

The question is what should we do with it?

The first course that suggests itself is to work the constitution for what it is worth. This is the policy that the Liberal Party would adopt, notwithstanding its severe condemnation of the constitution. In doing that the Liberal Party would be acting logically; mind you, I do not say correctly. Logically, because the Liberal Party knows only one method of political work—constitutionalism.

Now, the Congress long ago gave up its belief in constitutionalism and embraced direct action as its basic policy. The respective strengths of the Liberal and Congress parties shows which has been the more fruitful and correct of the two.

Direct action and constitutionalism are incompatible. The Congress cannot truthfully profess its faith in the former, if it agrees to work the constitution. I need not dilate on this point because I think no Congressman will be found to disagree with it. I doubt if even the great ministry—enthusiast, Mr. Satyamurthi,[2] will disagree.

So, if it is agreed that we cannot work the constitution, what must we do? What policy should the Congress accept? Our answer is that where possible, i.e. where the Congress has a majority, we should make its working impossible.

The Congress has decided to reject the new constitution. Does it not follow as a natural corollary that the Congress policy should be to carry out the decision of rejection, by forcing the governor to continue the administration by the exercise of his special powers?

Lest this policy should be considered futile and barren, I quote some very interesting remarks of a British statesman. Captain Wedgewood Benn,[3] writing on the "Outlook on the Indian Reforms" in the *Political Quarterly* for July-September, 1935, hazards some guesses about the policy that the

[1] *Congress Socialist*, 21 March 1936 and 28 March 1936.

[2] For biographical note on S. Satyamurti see *JPSW*, Volume One, p. 92.

[3] For biographical note on Wedgewood Benn see *JPSW*, Volume One, p. 168.

Congress would be likely to follow with regard to what has been termed the Indian Reforms.

He begins by asking: "The most powerful, the best organized and the most important of all Indian national parties is the Congress. What will they do?" He thinks that "in all but a few of the Provincial Assemblies, they (Congress candidates) will secure a victory". Then he goes on to say that, and this is interesting, "the Congress candidates, if elected, will undoubtedly attempt to wreck the constitution".

Discussing the underlying principle of Congress policy he says, "The issues they (Congress members of Legislatures) will present will not be offered as local at all. Everything will be put into the guise of opposition to the hated British domination. *The issue which they wish to keep before the public, that of Britain versus India, will be most clearly presented of course*." I want you to take special note of this, "*if they can force the Governor into the use of autocratic powers which he now possesses in an unprecedented degree*".

This is a most significant statement, coming as it does from such high quarters. Capt. Benn adds, "The technique of the Irish, which has been closely studied in India, will be copied, possibly with success."

Capt. Benn has gone to the root of the problem. If there is any issue which it is the duty of the Congress to keep perpetually before the public, it is that of Britain versus India, as he puts it. And by forcing the Governor to continue his administration without the aid of ministers this issue is kept alive.

To elucidate this point further, as it does not seem to be clear to many of us, it is better to look for a while at a very important aspect of the new constitution, which I am afraid has not been kept before the public eye as prominently as it ought to have been. The new constitution, without transferring any real power to the ministers, creates the fiction of responsible government in the provinces. The British Power withdraws itself into the background keeping all the leading strings in its hands. This means that the issue, Britain versus India, is covered up by this subterfuge. The issue, in fact, is turned into "the people versus the party in office", in other words, one part of the people versus the other part. This, from the British point of view, is a master stroke of political craft. By thus blurring the issue, the British politicians wish to destroy the directness and keenness of the Indian struggle. They further seek to shift the responsibility of carrying on an unpopular administration to the shoulders of Indian ministers, thus hoping to dull the edge of popular resentment against them.

There is a difference between Indian ministers and "members of Government" of the present and the ministers of the new constitution. At present the position is that the foreign power is able to secure the services of individual Indians, who in return for a title and a consideration carry on the administration for the British. Under the new arrangements, ministers will represent parties, which in turn will represent a section of the electorate. For the actions of the ministry, a party, and ultimately a section of the people itself, will be responsible, at least in theory—and not the British Government. What use a clever governor will make of this situation can well be imagined. Of course, it is obvious what will happen. It has often been said that imperialism has attempted through this constitution to strengthen itself in the face of gathering mass discontent by rallying around it the vested interests in the country. These "responsible" ministries would be the constitutional mechanism through which this plan would be put into practice. The vested interests will become a facade behind which imperialism will continue its rule. But I am digressing.

To return to the original point, I was saying that the issue of India versus Britain can most clearly be brought out only by forcing the suspension of the constitution, where this is possible.

This is a course desirable for another reason also. We rejected the J.P.C. Report [Joint Parliamentary Committee Report, 1934]. After that Report has been made a fact in the new constitution, shall we drop our policy of rejection? Remember that the British have always been counting on the constitution being worked. It is with that belief that they went on, most cynically disregarding the counsel even of their Indian friends, with their reactionary measure. The Government members in the Legislative Assembly have often mockingly replied to the Opposition that however much it may howl against the "reforms" everyone would come and work them.

Under these circumstances it is the duty of the Congress Party, wherever in a majority, to defeat the objects of the foreign power and to foil their well-laid plans by showing that the constitution they have laboured so long to perfect is a broken reed and that the Governor must carry on the administration himself. The impression that this will create in India and abroad would be infinitely superior to anything that can be achieved by any other tactics. From the point of view of keeping up the spirit of the Congress, which after all is the thing that matters, there can be no better course to follow.

It is said that there will be no popular enthusiasm for this policy, because it will not enable the Congress Party to throw any crumbs to the people. This is a pathetic plea.

The manner in which the electorate responds depends entirely on the manner in which the issue is presented to it. If we go to it in a defeatist, apologist frame of mind, it is clear we shall fail to inspire confidence. If, on the other hand, our campaign is marked with vigour, our case presented aggressively, the electorate is bound to respond. Suppose that on this constitutional issue a whirlwind propaganda is carried on, raising the one issue of wrecking the constitution, on the ground that it has been thrust on us forcibly and is a mischievous device for our further enslavement. I feel sure that in that case we shall be able to arouse sufficient enthusiasm to be returned every time in a majority. Even if we don't we shall have done excellent political propaganda during the election campaign which will prove its utility when we resort to direct action again. For, all our efforts must lead to that.

There is another important aspect of this policy which makes its acceptance well-nigh imperative by the Congress. In its resolution on the J.P.C. Report the Working Committee declared that "the only satisfactory alternative (to the constitution adumberated in the Report) is a constitution drawn up by a Constituent Assembly".

If the only satisfactory alternative to a constitution devised in Westminster is a constitution drawn up by a Constituent Assembly, is it not our duty to raise the slogan of the Constituent Assembly during the coming election and place it before the electorate as the only alternative, as we have said in our resolution? It may be urged that the Constituent Assembly is a distant prospect and therefore it is mere bluff, as Dr. Pattabhi[4] says, to talk of it as an alternative to any current political measure. Is the Constituent Assembly more distant than independence, and yet have we not "declared" independence from a thousand platforms? Moreover, why, if it is a distant prospect, was it made a slogan at the last Assembly elections? In its resolution from which I have quoted before, the Working Committee expressed pleasure that the "demand for a Constituent Assembly has been endorsed in a clear and unambiguous manner by the country, at the recent general election to the Legislative Assembly". That demand was put forward as an alternative to the J.P.C. scheme which we were asked to reject. Now when that scheme is actually being foisted on us, should it not be our policy to raise the issue of the Constituent Assembly still more vigorously?

But if we do that on the one hand, we must say on the other that, where we can, we shall wreck that constitution by making its working impossible. Just as when the constitution was in the making and we were asked to consider it, rejection and the Constituent Assembly were complementary parts of a whole policy, so now when the constitution is an accomplished fact and we are asked to work it, wrecking and the Constituent Assembly are again the inseparable complements of any self-respecting policy that we may adopt. The slogan of the Constituent Assembly cannot be part of any election programme which contemplates acceptance of offices under the new constitution. Its counterpart can only be the slogan of wrecking.

[4] For biographical note on Pattabhi Sitaramayya see *JPSW*, Volume One, p. 126.

Let us now consider the alternative proposal. I have said before that an objection is raised to this policy on the ground that the electorate would lose interest in it because it would not get any concrete and immediate benefits from it. Suppose that we adopt such a programme of benefits. If we really wanted to give benefits, we would have to remain in office as long as possible, because going out in that case would be a barren policy. At the same time it is well known how much scope for ameliorative measures the constitution provides. In other words, we will have to work the reforms, and will have the satisfaction of finding at the end of the term of our ministries that very little has been done for the people—so little, indeed, that they have become as much dissatisfied with us as with the British. We shall also find that we have succeeded in killing that mentality of fight against the Government which is the soul of the Congress movement and in its place have taught the people to look for loaves and fishes to it. The argument of not being able to do anything for the people if we follow a wrecking policy leads inevitably to constitutionalism. There is no half-way house.

I have considered so far only our tactics in case the Congress has a majority. What should be its policy where it fails to be so successful?

Before taking up that question, let me examine briefly the case of those who are advocating acceptance of offices. First of all, we note that they absolutely overlook all the considerations I have urged. All the underlying principles of our movement, its psychological foundations, our past commitments—all these are given the go-by.

It is interesting to recall in this regard the old policy of the Congress when it decided in 1926 to contest elections: The A.I.C.C. laid it down that "Congressmen in the legislatures shall refuse to accept offices in the gift of the government until, in the opinion of the Congress, a satisfactory response is made by the Government." I wish to draw your attention particularly to the condition for accepting office. The Government must make a satisfactory response. Considering the objectives of the Congress of those days, it was an honourable and self-respecting decision, consistent with the spirit of the times. The present Congress has travelled far away from its old objectives and it no longer looks for a "response" from the British Government. Is it not regretful therefore that Congressmen should advocate acceptance of offices under the present circumstances, and with no qualifications? It might be said that the offices are no longer in the gift of the Government. That would be a very superficial view of the matter. There is no popular sanction behind the constitution. The whole thing is a gift of the Government—withal a most unwelcome gift.

Thus the first thing the ministerialist seeks to do is to destroy a valuable psychological aspect of Congress policy.

What does it offer in return? It is difficult to say, because this point has not been made clear yet. Mr. Satyamurthi and certain others have spoken of benefits and ameliorative measures; of clothing the services in *khadi*; of flying the national flag over government buildings and so on. A rather doubtful fare. The Congress which has stood for large measures cannot forsake them and seek to appeal to the electorate with a programme of petty reforms. If the Congress did so, it will divert the public mind from the basic and fundamental issues and teach the electorate and the people to look to the Government for petty favours. This would mean the diverting of mass energy into fruitless channels and therefore the weakening of the national movement.

At the same time, it is obvious that if the Congress adopts a programme consistent with Congress policy and objective, it will be of such a far-reaching character that no Congress ministry would be allowed to carry it out. A Congress ministry can only be a very short-lived experiment under these conditions, leading us nowhere and greatly damaging some of our basic ideas and principles.

I do not wish to devote more time to this question. However, let me mention a few more dangers and risks that lie hidden in the programme of the ministerialists.

Take the election campaign itself. If it is decided that Congress should accept offices, then every attempt would be made by the Congress Party to secure a majority. This would inevitably lead to compromise with non-Congress groups and the modification of the Congress programme in such a manner as to allow non-Congress and vested interests to join the Congress campaign. It was a genuine surprise to me when I came across a Hindi manifesto of the U.P. Congress Parliamentary Committee, issued over the signature of its assistant secretary during the last Assembly election, setting forth reasons why the landlords of the province must support the Congress candidates. The manifesto, in short, tried to make out that the Congress has always stood for and defended the rights of the landlords. It is interesting to note that the spirit of this manifesto runs wholly counter to another of the same committee, issued in English for the general voter. It is also interesting to recall that in this same province, a few years ago, a resolution was passed by the Provincial Political Conference advocating the elimination of all middlemen between the tiller of the soil and the State.

I have brought up this matter merely to show how the exigencies of winning a majority leads to watering down, vulgarising and distorting of even the present Congress ideals, moderate as they are. I do not for a moment believe that U.P. was an exception in this regard. This sort of thing must have happened everywhere.

So we see that at the very outset of this policy, in the election campaign itself, there is compromise and a drift to the right. Whereas the election campaign should be utilised for raising fundamental issues, for educating the masses, for organizing them, we will be led to make compromises and to give up the more revolutionary slogans and programmes.

Then the dangers after the ministries have been actually formed are not negligible—the dangers, I mean, of demoralization, leading in the end to constitutionalism on the one hand and serious disruption of the Congress ranks on the other.

Now, I shall briefly touch upon the policy the Congress Party should follow where in a minority. The policy of the old Swaraj Party was "one of determined resistance and obstruction to every activity, Governmental or other, that may impede the nation's progress towards Swaraj" coupled with enactment of ameliorative measures. We suggest an improvement upon this. Mere obstruction will not be sufficient. We must also use the legislatures as tribunes for voicing the people's grievances, their rights and demands. The most effective form of legislative activity is one which brings the struggle that is waged outside into the legislative chamber. This means that the Congress must attempt to develop mass activity in the shape of an economic agitation of peasants, workers and other exploited groups, and use the legislature to further that activity.

Without linking up in some such manner legislative work with an agitation outside, the former becomes utterly sterile and ineffective.

I need not dilate on this point any further. The policy in cases where the Congress is in a minority is not difficult to determine. There are also a number of instances in history to guide us in this regard.

In concluding my remarks on the constitutional issue, I should like to state, as a resume of what I have said already, the underlying principle of entire policy in the matter of legislative work. We believe that legislatures have to be used only in order to strengthen and support the revolutionary work outside. For us there is no parliamentary work, as such. I remember Mr. Rajagopalachari[5] saying at Jubbulpore, in his speech on our resolution concerning the work of the Congress Party in the Assembly, that when we go to the legislative chamber we must do what is customarily done there. What he meant to say was that we must work there on approved constitutional lines. According to him, our insistence, for example, on the slogan of the Constituent Assembly having been raised in the Assembly chamber, was misplaced tactics. That was a slogan which had to be raised outside at the proper time.

Our whole conception of legislative activity is opposed to this. We hold that when we go to the legislatures our purpose should be not only to inflict constitutional defeats on the Government, but also to raise fundamental slogans for the purposes of propaganda, to relate the work within to the

[5] For biographical note on C. Rajagopalachari see *JPSW*, Volume One, p. 174.

day-to-day struggle of the masses outside, to expose Imperialism, to obstruct its working. This, of course, means that the Congress while sending its members into the legislature must simultaneously bestir itself in organizing the grievances of the masses outside. A strong labour and peasant movement outside coupled with revolutionary use of legislatures—that is the principle which ought to govern the constitutional policy of any fighting organization like the Congress.

6. Interview to Press on Lucknow Congress, 14 April 1936[1]

The Lucknow Session has largely been a disappointment. The fine start made at Delhi received rude shock at Allahabad and Lucknow has nearly dashed the hopes that were aroused in us.

There is no doubt that Pt. Jawaharlal Nehru's[2] position in the Congress is second only to that of Mahatma Gandhi.[3] Although unanimously elected as President, he failed to get the support of his colleagues on the Working Committee, who almost throughout the session, remained in opposition to him.

The old junta took advantage of the fact that it had the Congress machinery in its hands. I am sure, its success does not reflect its true strength. I have no doubt that the majority of the Congress rank and file and the general public is with Pt. Jawaharlal.

Disappointing though the Lucknow Congress has been it bears the stamp of the personality of its President. Resolutions on war, mass contact, agrarian programme, civil liberties all owe their origin to the President and, if I may point out, to our party. Even in their mutilated form [they represent] a very appreciable advance.

[1] *Bombay Chronicle*, 15 April 1936. Interview at Lucknow.
[2] For biographical note on Jawaharlal Nehru see *JPSW*, Volume One, p. 41.
[3] For biographical note on M.K. Gandhi see *JPSW*, Volume One, p. 41.

7. Issues Before and After Lucknow: Article in the *Congress Socialist*, 23 May 1936[1]

Pandit Jawaharlal has utilised his visit to Bombay to clarify many important issues. The most important of these is the issue of Socialism in the Congress. He has made it clear that while he expressed himself unequivocally in favour of Socialism as the only effective solution of India's economic and social problems, the immediate issue before the Congress was of a political nature

[1] *Congress Socialist*, 23 May 1936.

and it was that of independence and how to achieve it. He pointed out in his numerous speeches in Bombay—one has lost count of them by now—that there was not a single issue raised in the discussions and deliberations of the Lucknow Congress that could be described as socialist. The task before the Congress was that of achieving complete independence from imperialism. The differences that made their appearance in Congress ranks at Lucknow were on questions relating to just this task.

What were the issues at Lucknow?—issues on which there was such a sharp division of opinion? Acceptance of office, proportional representation, Indian States, relation of workers and peasants to the Congress. Anyone can see that these were not issues that had anything to do with Socialism.

It is interesting to consider why, in spite of this plain fact, there has been so much confusion of thought. Why has the bogey of Socialism been raised? It has been because some want to justify their opposition to the Congress and their alliance with imperialism. Others, particularly those in the Congress, have raised it, in order to cover up certain political issues, which are the real issues today, and to create a prejudice in the public mind against those who dare to raise them. At the Lucknow Congress, practically every one who opposed the amendments advocating wrecking of the new Constitution and refusal to form ministries under it, started with some such remarks, "We assure our socialist friends", "We warn our socialist friends". As if acceptance of office had anything to do with Socialism and as if it was socialists alone who were opposed to it. Thus on every issue Socialism was dragged in. If a demand was made to give representation to workers and peasants, that too was Socialism. Even proportional representation, of such political respectability, was somehow linked up with Socialism!

Pandit Jawaharlal has done well to break that link, though it should be pointed out that it is not the first time that he has tried to do so. One hopes, however, that the persistence with which he has tried to clear the issue from such numerous platforms will at last succeed in killing the bogey as far as he is concerned.

But that would still leave our Party to be made the scapegoat. It is desirable therefore to make our position clear in this matter. We too shall not be doing so for the first time, but in view of the confusion that prevails, it is necessary to clear our position once again.

The Party's position in this regard is very clearly stated in its first thesis which was formulated by the Central Executive early in 1935. That thesis states: "The immediate task before us is to develop the national movement into a real anti-imperialist movement." Having defined the task it goes on to say: "Consistent with its task, the Party should take only an anti-imperialist stand on Congress platforms. *We should not in this connection make the mistake of placing a full socialist programme before the Congress.*"

Can anything be clearer than this?

In the Plan of Action of the Party as incorporated in its published Programme the first item reads thus: "Work within the Indian National Congress with a view to develop it *into a real anti-imperialist organization.*" It should be noticed that we do not say: "into a socialist organization".

So much for the theoretical position of the Party. Let us see what has been its practice? Has the Party ever tried to force Socialism on the Congress? Has it ever raised socialist issues from Congress platforms?

The Party has been functioning as a party within the Congress since the time of the Bombay Session.

If the resolutions and amendments that were moved by members of the Party in the various Congress Committees between Bombay and Lucknow are reviewed, it will be seen that we never sought to force Socialism or a socialist programme on the Congress. All the dust and tumult of controversy that were raised at Bombay, Jubbulpore (A.I.C.C.), Madras (A.I.C.C.) and Lucknow were due not to any attempt on our part to persuade the Congress to accept Socialism. All the abuse, the criticism, the ridicule that we have had to put up with, arose because we dared to criticise the Parliamentary Board, the Labour Franchise, to demand that the Congress turn its attention a little towards the international situation and consider the fact of developing danger of war; that it declare its policy clearly on the issue of acceptance of office; that it give representation to organized workers and peasants; that it take an active part in the economic struggle of the masses and in organizing them. These and such other were the issues that were raised before Lucknow, and these are the issues that remain thereafter.

It may appear strange that those who profess Socialism should say that they do not want to raise the issue of Socialism in the Congress. This may look like a ruse, a camouflage. It is neither. Our policy is dictated by the simple consideration that an organization the task of which is to unite all genuinely anti-imperialist classes on one front against imperialism needs not a socialist but a broad anti-imperialist programme. We have no anxiety regarding Socialism. We know that the march towards it is inevitable and that complete freedom from imperialism is the first step towards Socialism.

8. Comment on S. Satyamurti's Speech at the European Association, 28 May 1936[1]

In his anxiety to placate the European big businessmen and win European co-operation, Mr. Satyamurti[2] forgot the responsibility he owed as the

[1] *Leader*, 2 June 1936. Interview to Press at Allahabad. It was also published in slightly shorter form in the *Hindu*, 29 May 1936.

[2] S. Satyamurti in his speech at Coimbatore on 22 May 1936 criticised the Congress policy towards the new reforms.

President of the Tamil Nad Congress Committee. He adumbrated a policy and programme which went directly against the Congress official policy and creed. He is reported to have said that dominion status, if it came in time, might be acceptable. This was a complete travesty of the Congress policy. The council policy enunciated by him had no justification. He desired to get as much good out of the Constitution as possible, while the Congress saw no good in the Constitution and rejected it. One failed to see the difference between Mr. Satyamurti's policy and the policy of those parties desiring to work the constitution.

Certain other responsible Congressmen think that something must be done to check the tendency on the part of some responsible men holding office in the Congress to give utterance to policies repugnant to the Congress creed and the official policy.

9. Circular to Provincial Secretaries, Congress Socialist Party, 4 June 1936[1]

Circular No. 4

60 A, Hughes Road
Bombay, 4 June 1936

To
The Secretary,
Congress Socialist Party

Dear Comrade,
It is now six weeks since the Lucknow Session. Since then the All India Trade Union Congress met at Bombay, but, apart from participation in that Session, very little activity on the part of our members is to be seen. Pandit Jawaharlal Nehru, it is true, is carrying on a whirlwind campaign propagating ideas which he and we have at heart. It is necessary, however, if that campaign is to bear fruit, that our Party should take the fullest advantage of his inspiring leadership and follow up his call with sustained work, both in the way of agitation as well as labour and peasant organization.

Enrolment of Congress Members

In the next three months, in particular there is one form of activity which demands our attention and that is the enrolment of members for the National Congress in our respective provinces and districts. The period for such enrolment closes on 31 August. It should not be necessary to stress the

[1] *JP Papers* (NMML).

importance of such enrolment if our Party is to be strongly represented at the next Session of the Congress. Work in this direction is absolutely essential. This is particularly so in view of the removal of the provision for proportional representation in the election of delegates.

The Mass Contact Resolution of the Lucknow Session should provide a method of approach for us in tackling this problem. Our Party's scheme for functional representation of workers has already been adopted by the T.U.C.[2] Session last month and a similar scheme is being drawn up in consultation with peasant organizations. Till such time, however, as such a scheme is incorporated in the Congress Constitution, and in any case it cannot be earlier than next year, it is essential that we should seek to rally more mass support for ourselves in the Congress by the enrolment of large numbers of industrial workers and peasants along with lower middle-class people as four-anna members in the Congress organization.

Enrolling Workers as Congress Members

The basis for the enrolment of workers as Congress members was laid down by the Labour Committee of the Party last year when it decided that the approach for such enrolment should be not on an individual basis but on a political basis. Our approach to the workers in this matter should be through leaflets and public meetings where an appeal is made to the workers to become members of the Congress in large numbers so that in the Congress elections they might vote for Socialist candidates as against those of the Right Wing and so that they might strengthen us generally in the fight we are putting up for their point of view on all the main political issues of the day. By such an approach not only is any danger of exposing the workers to the influence of reactionary leadership obviated but on the other hand their political consciousness will be raised and they will be mobilized under conscious socialist leadership.

Implementing T.U.C. Decisions

The decisions of the T.U.C. Session will have become known to you through the Press. Unfortunately, the T.U.C. office has not been able to supply us with full copies of all the resolutions passed. So, I cannot forward them to you as I would have liked. Two very gratifying features of the T.U.C. Session were the unanimity with which the resolutions were adopted and the team work put in by Party members. It is now essential that Provincial Executives of our Party should review these decisions and give direction and guidance

[2] Trade Union Congress.

to members of their Party who are doing labour work in the implementing of these resolutions. A large share of the burden of putting these resolutions into effect must naturally fall on the shoulders of the members of our Party, and unless that burden is taken up the success of the Bombay Session will be marred.

One result of the Session and of recent development is the achievement of smoother and friendlier relations with other radical groups in the Labour field. With the wastage of friction and opposition removed, more constructive work in building up the Unions ought to be possible this year.

The Labour Secretary of the Party, Comrade Dinkar Mehta,[3] (Navi Duniya Karyalaya, Gandhi Road, Ahmedabad) asks me to request you to forward to him information on the following points:

1. The names and addresses of members who are active in the Trade Unions and the Provincial Trade Union Committee in your Province.
2. The extent to which the Trade Unions in your province have mass membership.
3. The possibilities of starting new unions for hitherto unorganized sections of Labour.

Student Organization

With the opening of the Colleges and Universities in the course of this month and the next, we are faced with the problem of student organization. Owing to the inevitable pre-occupation with the primary tasks of building up our Party organization and Labour and Peasant organizations, it was not possible for our members last year to take up in any organized fashion work among the students. This year however, the opportunity must not be missed. The students are an important section of the Anti-Imperialist front in this country and we cannot afford to neglect them.

Comrade Yusuf Meherally,[4] one of the Secretaries of our Party, who has had valuable experience of student organization in the past, will place before our members in the columns of the *Congress Socialist* some suggestions for student organization. I would like, however, to mention just a few points to be borne in mind in this task.

The first is that most of the work of forming and developing Students Leagues must be undertaken by the students themselves. Student organizations with "outsiders" as bosses have been brought into existence and have died a natural death over and over again. While the inspiration may

[3] For biographical note on Dinkar Mehta see *JPSW*, Volume One, p. 122.
[4] For biographical note on Yusuf Meherally see *JPSW*, Volume One, p. 156.

no doubt be derived from outside, the main initiative and the building up must be undertaken by the actual students themselves. It will therefore be a salutary thing to provide in the constitutions of Students' Associations or Leagues which may be formed in the near future that only students should be eligible for holding office or serving on the executives of such bodies. It may be provided, however, that a limited number of honorary members who are not students may be elected as advisers by the students themselves.

Closely allied with this point is the one that, while student organizations should undoubtedly participate in the political life of the country, they should be non-party organizations. We should therefore as strongly resist attempts made by our own members to "capture" or control these organizations as we should resist similar attempts made by members of other groups. Party advantage should not be sought to be taken on any side from such organizations. Student Leagues should, while participating in general political activities, agitate on the basis of the demands and needs of the students as a class. This will give the student organizations much greater reality and stability than has been enjoyed or can be enjoyed by "Youth Leagues" which suffer from lack of any functional or other basis of existence.

Elections to Provincial Legislatures

The Executive of our Party will probably be meeting at the end of this month and certain data is needed to enable its deliberations to have the fullest value. One of the things our Executive will have to consider will be the attitude of our Party in the coming campaign in connection with the elections to the new Provincial Legislatures.

In this connection two questions arise. The first is of the programme and the second of candidates. As regards the programme, the Meerut Conference of our Party[5] has formulated one and this will be placed before the All India Congress Committee whenever the matter comes up for decision.

As regards candidates, already a lot of informal canvassing of names is going on and it is necessary that our Party should not be caught napping and find itself faced with an accomplished fact.

The T.U.C. Session at Bombay decided (1) to contest officially seats in the "Special Labour" and Trade Union constituencies created by the Government of India Act; (2) in the case of general (i.e. territorial) constituencies where there is a large working-class vote, Trade Unions in such constituencies should suggest names of such Congressmen as candidates as enjoy the confidence and have the support of organized Labour. It

[5] See Appendix 1 for text of Meerut Thesis of the C.S.P.

will be our Party's task, both locally and on a national scale, to urge the acceptance as candidates of Congressmen recommended by the Trade Unions, whether they are members of our Party or not.

I would request you to send me *before the 25th of June at the latest* information on the following points:

1. What is the machinery set up in your province for electoral and legislative activity by the Provincial Congress Committee and to what extent is the Party represented on it?
2. Who are the Party members who in the opinion of your Executive should be nominated as Congress candidates and for what constituencies?
3. What chances are there of such persons being actually nominated by the Congress organization in your province?
4. Which are the constituencies in your province which have a large working-class vote?
5. Who are likely to be suggested by the Trade Unions in these constituencies as Congress candidates? And which of them are members of the Party?
6. What are the chances of these persons being nominated by the Congress organization and of being successful in the elections?
7. What Trade Union or "Special Labour" constituencies are there in your Province?
8. What names would you suggest of Party members who would be suitable candidates in T.U. or "Special Labour" constituencies to suggest to the Committee set up by the T.U.C. Executive?

Sardar Sardul Singh's Tour

Sardar Sardul Singh Caveeshar, the Chairman of the Anti-Ministry Committee of Congressmen, is prepared to undertake an All India tour in furtherance of the Anti-Ministry agitation. I have to request you to get immediately into touch with him (Chamberlain Road, Lahore) inquiring when he can visit your province and suggesting suitable time and an itinerary to him. It is very essential that our Party should co-operate fully both in regard to Sardar Sardul Singh's tour and with the local Anti-Ministry Committee not functioning actively, every attempt should be made to put life into it and, as far as possible, the tour should be under the auspices of the Anti-Ministry Committee and not of the Party.

Yours fraternally,
Jayaprakash Narayan
General Secretary

10. Statement on Darbhanga District Kisan Conference, 4 June 1936[1]

The Darbhanga District Kisan Conference, at which I had been invited to preside, has revealed to me a new aspect of that system of arrogance and exploitation which is known as landlordism. The conference met at Bithan near Hasanpore Road.[2] Unfortunately, I could not be present on the first day of the conference; so Sjt. Jamuna Karji[3] presided. When I arrived the next morning I learnt from Swami Sahajanandji[4] and Sjt. Karji about the hooligan methods employed by the Darbhanga Raj people to prevent the conference from meeting and to break it up after it met in spite of those methods. First of all, the servants of the Raj carried on a campaign of threat and intimidation in the neighbouring villages, warning the peasants of the dire consequences that would follow if they attended the conference. All sorts of difficulties were put in the way of the organizers. People of Bithan were intimidated into refusing the use of their ground for the conference. When, however, a plot of land was secured, the Raj Amalas [retainers] actually sent men to plough up that land. They were prevented from doing it only by the firmness of the organizers. When at last the conference started, agents of the Raj tried in various ways to obstruct the proceedings. These disturbances continued throughout the address of the president. It was only after Swamiji's fighting speech and the hostile mood of the peasants had become too obvious that they were silenced.

Their failure on the first day did not prevent the agents of the Raj from indulging in hooliganism on the second day again. I was presiding that day and, though I tried to be indulgent to them, they continued to interrupt and disturb the proceedings in the course of which they made many libellous allegations against the Kisan Sabha and the Congress. Their action so excited the audience that there was a universal demand for their being turned out of the meeting. They quietened down after that, but did not stop their mischief. They went out and threatened to let loose the elephants of the Raj on the audience. The elephants did actually run about but without doing any injury. This was too much for the peasants who suddenly stood up and rushed

[1] *Searchlight*, 5 June 1936. Statement to Press at Patna.

[2] The conference was held on 30-1 May 1936.

[3] Jamuna Karjee (1898-1953); participated in the non-cooperation, civil disobedience, and Bihar Kisan movements; was one of the divisional secretaries of the Bihar Provincial Kisan Sabha, 1929, and its President, 1941; member, Bihar Legislative Assembly, 1937-40; Editor of Hindi weeklies, *Lok Sangrah* (Muzaffarpur), 1927-38, and *Hunkar* (Patna), 1944-53; President, Bihar Journalists' Association, 1948; publications include *Krishi Sopan* in three parts.

[4] For biographical note on Swami Sahajanand Saraswati see *JPSW*, Volume One, p. 147.

towards the elephants, shouting angrily at the men of the Raj. At this demonstration, the Raj Amalas stopped their hooliganism, but it was some time before the peasants could be persuaded to return to the meeting. They did so when they found there was no fresh mischief afoot, after which the conference proceeded peacefully amidst great enthusiasm.

That the Zamindars should not be satisfied with subjecting the peasants to all sorts of exactions and extortions, humiliations and indignities but should also dare to attempt to obstruct in this unlawful manner the legitimate attempts of their victims for defending their rights and bettering their miserable condition is a matter which calls not only for the strongest condemnation, but vigorous opposition from all those who stand for the ordinary rights of every individual and for the liberties of the people.

11. Circular to Provincial Secretaries, Congress Socialist Party, 28 July 1936[1]

Circular No. 6

60 A, Hughes Road
Bombay, 28 July 1936

The Secretary,
Congress Socialist Party

Dear Comrade,

In an earlier circular (Circular No. 4)[2] I had requested your Executive to supply certain information in reply to questions in that circular regarding candidates from among the Party members for both General and "Special Labour" seats in the coming elections to the Provincial Legislatures. I regret that no answer has still come from your Party to this inquiry. The All India Executive meets in Bombay on August 21, 1936 and it is absolutely essential that the material which I have asked for should be ready to be placed before it. Kindly therefore let me have answers to that questionnaire by *15th August at the latest*. If your Executive cannot meet before that date for this purpose, then the next best thing will be for you and your fellow office-bearers to answer the questions to the best of your ability.

The organizer (Prem Narayan Bhargava,[3] Literature Palace, Lucknow) of the First All India Students' Conference which meets at Lucknow on

[1] *JP Papers* (NMML).

[2] See item no. 9.

[3] Prem Narayan Bhargava (1912-85); one of the founders of Lucknow University Students' Union; Convener and Chairman, Reception Committee, All India Students' Federation, Lucknow, 1936, and its General Secretary, 1936-8.

August 15 and 16, has asked me to draw your attention to the Conference and to suggest that students of your province should be represented at that Conference in as large numbers as possible. I would suggest that you should get into touch with the local students' organizations or where they do not exist with such student contacts as you may have and to urge upon them the necessity of participating in this Conference.

I am not in full possession of the facts regarding the nature and the composition of this Conference but, obviously when a move of this nature is taking place it is not desirable that students who are members of our Party or who are under our influence should keep away. They must attend the Conference and have their proper share in it.

It does seem to me, however, that the formation of an All India Students' Organization, should it be contemplated as a result of this Conference [would be] premature. Today genuine students' organizations do not exist in most of the provinces and without their existence an All India Organization can only be a paper organization. I would therefore suggest that members of our Party who may be participating in the Conference should place that point of view before the Conference and should see that no definite organization is formed this year but that, if desired, an Organizing Committee should be formed to foster the growth of Provincial Organizations with a view later to bring an All India Organization into existence. This was done at the All India Kisan Conference at Lucknow in April with advantage.

Yours fraternally,
Jayaprakash Narayan
General Secretary

12. Protest against C.I.D. Methods, 3 August 1936[1]

Sometime ago it had come to my notice that a certain officer of the Criminal Investigation Department had approached a Congress friend with a very offensive proposal. It is needless to say that the proposal was not only rejected at once but the Government's hireling was also given a bit of a talking to.

This morning a Bengali gentleman in *dhoti* and *kurta* came to my house. I was standing on the verandah. He came up to me and enquired if I was

[1] *Searchlight*, 5 August 1936. J.P.'s protest was sent to the *Searchlight* on 3 August 1936. It was published as a news item on 5 August 1936.

Jayaprakash Narayan. Then he introduced himself as a personal assistant of a "high government official" in the Political Department. I asked him what did he want from me. He replied that he had a proposal to make to me on behalf of his superior. A proposal to me from the Political Department—such absurdity!

I confess I felt like thrashing the fellow. He went away quite safely all right, but I am sure he will not venture anywhere near me in the future.

My object in writing this letter, Sir, is to protest publicly against these methods of the C.I.D. and to warn the latter of the consequences. After all, even the C.I.D. may have a little decency, if not any intelligence.

The Secret Service in Bihar, Sir, seems to be anything but secret. Its hirelings keep openly prowling about one's residence and cause great annoyance to people in the house. The Service may do what it pleases; no one worries about it. But there is one thing which it may not do—it may not become a public nuisance. The Political Department or whichever Department it is that looks after the C.I.D. should look into the matter and spare us this abominable nuisance. If the King's Government cannot be carried on without resorting to such tactics, it is time those responsible for it cleared away.

As for this morning's incident, I have only this much to say that whoever dares repeat it will do so at his peril.

13. Interview to Press on Resignation from Congress Working Committee, 18 August 1936[1]

I do not want to discuss the matter in the press. But I would like to say that my resignation has no political reason.[2] There is no question of [other] socialist members in the Working Committee resigning. On the other hand it is reasonable to expect the appointment of another socialist in the place vacated by me. I would continue to remain in the Congress and would participate in all its activities and contest the elections to the All India Congress Committee and other bodies within the Congress organization.

[1] Adapted from a report of J.P.'s interview at Allahabad published in the *Hindustan Times*, 19 August 1936.

[2] J.P. was selected by the President of the Congress for the Congress Working Committee at the A.I.C.C. meeting, Lucknow, 16 April 1936. Since he was not a member of the A.I.C.C. he could not continue on the Congress Working Committee.

14. Interview to Press on Congress and Mass Contact, 12 October 1936[1]

Question: What are your views regarding the establishment of contact between Congress and masses?

Jayaprakash Narayan: I cannot exactly say what the Mass Contact Committee will finally decide. I only hope that in the interest of the freedom movement, the Congress would take a forward step in this matter. It is becoming increasingly clear day by day that the basis for day-to-day work among the masses that the Congress has at present is too narrow. The Congress must move closer to the struggle of the millions of the peasants and workers of the country.

Our own proposal in this respect you know. We are pressing the Congress to include in its working programme active participation in the work and development of peasant and labour unions and to give representation in its Committees to the masses thus organized. How much of this the Mass Contact Committee of the A.I.C.C. will accept is more than I can say. I do think, however, that the popularity of this proposal is growing daily.

Q: Is the Faizpur session of the Congress going to finally decide the question of office acceptance?

J.P.: I cannot say if this issue will be decided at Faizpur. We shall certainly press for its decision.

Q: Who will be the president of the next Congress?

J.P.: I know the strain under which Pandit Jawaharlal is working. However, I feel strongly that, in the circumstances we are placed, there is no alternative but to his carrying on for another year. So, I am emphatically for his re-election.

[1] *Searchlight*, 14 October 1936. Interview at Patna.

15. Presidential Address at the Second Bihar Provincial Kisan Conference, Bihpur, 7 November 1936[1]

The very first thought that naturally comes to my mind is about the difficulties and obstacles that you had to face in convening this Conference. Over eighty peasants and Kisan Sabha workers, including the most prominent and tried workers of Bihpur Swaraj Ashram, have been recently arrested. They have been charged with various grave offences, such as preaching non-payment of rent and forcible occupation of attached land.

[1] *Searchlight*, 8 November 1936.

One had not witnessed arrests on such a large scale since the days of the Civil Disobedience movement and it certainly looks like repression. It does strike one as strange that Bihpur should be the only place in the whole province where the peasants have grown so desperate that they are preparing to stake their all in a no-rent campaign. Surely, the meanest official mind could see that such a situation, if it were real, could not have been brought about merely by a handful of agitators. There must be reason why, even if we accept the agitator's role, the peasants of the Grant Estate are so susceptible to such risk-bearing propaganda. Surely, the peasants' plight must really be desperate, and that should have called for enquiry and redress of grievances rather than arrests and repression. Obviously, if the charges of the local authorities are true, then their handling of the situation leads one to only two conclusions: either the authorities are thoroughly incompetent or they have been influenced by the Grant Estate.

The Bihar Kisan Sabha is a well-organized and centrally controlled and directed body. It is impossible that its workers may follow a policy that is opposed to or inconsistent with the central policy of the Sabha. No-rent campaign or forcible occupation of any kind of land is not a part of the present policy of the Sabha. It is impossible, therefore, that any worker of the Sabha should preach this programme in any part of the province. Anyone found doing it would be immediately brought under discipline.

I should add here that neither the Kisan Sabha nor the Bihpur workers are parties that will do anything on the sly. When the Kisan Sabha decides to launch a no-rent campaign, not only the local Magistrate will hear about it, but all the forces of the Government will be invited to the challenge. The present policy pursued in this area, therefore, deserves strong condemnation.

It is a matter of great satisfaction, however, that your difficulties have not daunted you. This Conference itself is a proof of your courage and your determination to carry on. I assure you friends that if you keep up your spirit you will triumph not only over the Grant Estate, but over all the Zamindars no matter how oppressive or powerful they may be. The Zamindari system may take long to go, but the daily pin-pricks, annoyances, the petty *zulum* and mulcting from which you suffer are things which will not last even a couple of years, if you earnestly took to building up your organization.

II

Now let us turn to your more fundamental problems.

You are all Kisans and know your problems and the conditions under which you live much better than I do. I might tell you this much that your condition today is worse than it ever was and is steadily deteriorating. You are bankrupt today and debt-laden and agriculture for most of you has become a losing concern. Your debts continue piling up; the margin of your loss not profit, goes on widening while your obligations are multiplying. Hunger gnaws at you and abject poverty has become your second name.

Have you thought over your poverty and misery? Are you satisfied when you are told that you are victims of the law of Karma? Millions of hungry men and women cannot be satisfied by this preposterous casuistry. You doubtless think over your sorrows and troubles. Let us think it over together.

Let us take the obvious facts. Here you are plodding away on your little plot of land, summer, winter and monsoon. The earth is not too unkind to you. You do harvest a fair crop, if drought or flood has not taken its toll. But then a strange thing happens. You are compelled on pain of punishment to part with the greater part and, in most cases, the whole of your labour's produce. Surely, there must be something radically wrong with society that such a strange and unjust thing should happen. A juster dispensation would have required you to first feed and clothe your children and yourself before allowing anyone to take anything from you. In fact, it would have made laws to prevent anyone from doing so. In the society in which you live, however, the contrary is the fact. Here laws have been made which enable other parties to take away even your last pie, if that be what is pompously termed their legal due. That is, laws have been made for your perpetual starvation. You know this process well because everyday you have to part with your hard-earned penny.

Take a concrete example. According to official figures themselves, every peasant has a burden of debt on which he has to pay on an average Rs. 10 per year. The average rent plus other Zamindari dues and taxes like Chowkidari, etc., come to Rs. 10, following Government figures again. The cost of cultivating an acre of land has been computed at Rs. 10. On the other hand the average holding of a peasant in Bihar is less than an acre. The yield of an acre of land, according to Sir John Hubback,[2] is Rs. 30 in value. So the average peasant makes thirty rupees in a year out of which he pays Rs. 10 to his Mahajan, another ten to his landlord and his servants, and another ten for cost of cultivation. In addition to all this he pays various indirect taxes. He uses salt, sugar, kerosine oil, tobacco. He pays taxes on these. He uses postcards and travels by the railway and is taxed again. There are still other means of his exploitation. The Government by manipulating its exchange and currency policy can, with one stroke of the pen, send down or raise the prices of the agriculturist's products, thus taking away another chunk from his income. Here is a subtle method of

[2] Sir John Austen Hubback (1878-1968); entered the I.C.S. in 1902; served in Bengal, 1909-11; transferred to Bihar and Orissa, 1912; Secretary, Revenue Department, Government of Bihar and Orissa, 1919; Director of Land Records, 1923; member, Governor's Executive Council, Bihar and Orissa, 1935-6; Governor of Orissa, 1936-41.

exploitation. What was done in the old imperialism by loot and pillage and direct extortion is subtly done under our modern imperialism by a stroke of the pen and the hidden device of the indirect tax. It is this subtle machinery which enables imperialism, on the one hand, to exploit ruthlessly and, on the other to pose as benefactors by presenting bulls and talking piously about the peasant's welfare. The peasants should clearly understand this double policy, for therein lies their good. Doubtless, it is a good thing to improve the breed of their cattle. Likewise are other improvements in agriculture desirable. But before everything else, the peasant must be freed from the terrible burdens which oppress him today.

Thus we find that the average peasant is not only bankrupt, but also falling deeper and deeper into debt. This is because all that he produces is taken away from him. Clearly the salvation of the peasants lies in stopping the flow of this drain which will enable them to fulfil their wants before letting a pie go out of their hands.

How can you do this? From what I have said just now, it would appear that you have to fight three parties in order to succeed in your purpose. That is, you have to free yourself from the octopus of the Mahajan, the Zamindar, and the Government. As a matter of fact, the fight against the first two, also, ultimately, resolves into a fight with the last.

No Government in the world has been so neglectful of controlling and regulating the credit system in its country as the Indian Government. In India, the Bihar Government is the greatest offender, and this, in spite of the finding of the Banking Enquiry Committee[3] that Bihar shoulders the heaviest burden of rural indebtedness—the debt on the peasantry alone being 129 crores of rupees. This figure must be much higher today than when it was originally computed. But not a single step has been taken even to relieve the situation, much less solve the problem. So, if you want freedom from the burden of debt, you must, by your organized strength, force Government to wipe off your present debts and arrange for cheap credit and control of usury and the custom of Mahajani. I do not suggest that Mahajans must be destroyed root and branch. But they must be brought under control.

Take next the exploitation of the Zamindars. It is the Government again which is responsible for this.

First of all, the Zamindars are their own creation and they were deliberately allowed to exploit their tenantry so that they may feel grateful and loyal to their creators—the British. Secondly, you know well what the

[3] The Indian Central Banking Enquiry Committee was appointed by the Government on 22 July 1929 under the chairmanship of Bhupendra Nath Mitra. Its recommendations (1931) included the establishment of a Provincial Land Mortgage Corporation and a Provincial Industrial Corporation in each province, a Reserve Bank, and an Indian Exchange Bank to facilitate indigenous banking.

strength of the Zamindars, apart from the Government's forces, is. There is no doubt that if you were to pit yourself only against the Zamindars' own strength and resources, victory would be yours in no time. But what happens is that whenever you try to settle your score with the Zamindars or even resist their oppression, you have to face arrests, and 'lathis' and bullets. So, finally, your economic struggle resolves into a struggle against Government, a struggle for political power.

As far as your direct exploitation by imperialism is concerned, it is obvious that you must directly fight it and capture political power. Then only would you be able to order things to suit to your interests. All this may frighten you. But I am telling this to you so that you may have a clear conception of your task. Till you realise that, you would not have reached to the roots of your problems.

You cannot fight imperialism unless you are thoroughly organized. That will take time. I know that, at this stage, freedom and Swaraj sound distant things to you. That is natural. At present you must organize yourselves to remove you day-to-day grievances. As your movement will grow, you will rise to higher levels of consciousness. And your economic struggle itself will lead you to anti-imperialism.

Let me now touch briefly upon some of your day-to-day problems.

Since we are meeting here, the first thing that comes to my mind is the Lattipur Gogri Bund, recent breaches in which have meant the ruination of no less than a hundred villages. The callousness that the Government, and the Grant Estate particularly, have shown in the matter deserves to be condemned with the utmost force. I hope that you will put up a strong fight and compel the Government to repair the Bund.

Among more general of your immediate problems are the problems of debt, rent, free transfer of land, price of cane and other such things. You must carry on ceaseless campaign for the liquidation of your ruinous debts, at least 50 per cent reduction in your rent charges, the right of free transfer, and fixation of the price of cane at 8 annas per maund. There has been an alarming development lately, which must form part of your agitation. Large numbers of tenants have become landless recently and their number is growing daily. Being deprived of their lands, they are left utterly without any means of livelihood. There are numerous other problems which I need not go into.

III

I have spoken so far of your economic struggle only and exhorted you to organize yourselves into Kisan Sabhas. What about your political struggle? I have said that ultimately you must face imperialism and fight for political power.

Your economic struggle you will conduct through your Kisan Sabhas. If you were the only class in the country that had to fight imperialism, you could conduct that fight also through the Kisan Sabha. But there are other classes also, for instance, workers, middle class men of various professions and occupations. Therefore, there must be a common organization through which the political struggle can be conducted. We have, in the Congress, a body that answers to some extent the needs of such an organization. From the peasants' point of view, there are certain important directions in which we must change the Congress so that it becomes completely identified with us and also acquires requisite strength.

The first improvement that we at present would desire is that the Congress should accept our fundamental and immediate demands. Demands in this connection do not mean points for a petition to some authority. Demands mean the things we stand for and fight for.

It is said that since in Bihar at least 90 per cent of the Congress members are peasants, the Congress is a peasant organization. A factory does not become a workers' organization simply because mostly workers work there. If the Congress is a Kisan body it must accept the Kisan's platform.

Secondly, as peasants, we are interested in finding how much help the Congress renders us in our organization. We must see that the Congress adopts as a part of its programme the organization of Kisan Sabhas.

Thirdly, we must see that the Kisans who go into the Congress as members do so as our representatives. Kisans going there in their individual capacity—no matter how numerous they may be—cannot, unless they are participating in our economic struggle, place or represent our point of view. Kisans for the mere fact of being Kisans do not know what is needed to save them. . . .

IV

A few words regarding a matter which would be the chief subject of talk and activity in the coming months. I mean the coming Assembly elections.

Imperialism has forged a new constitution which means a new chain around our necks. The Congress has decided to wreck this constitution. This is a most important decision and you must help the Congress to do this.

There is, however, a dangerous factor in this election and parliamentary programme. You know that so-called responsible Ministries have been created under the new constitution. Whatever other parties do, you need not bother about, because they are all your enemies. But you should see that the Congress, too, does not get caught in the snare, because that would retard your struggle for political freedom.

People may tell you that unless those who are your well-wishers become

Ministers how will you get your demands fulfilled? This is nonsense. Your demands cannot be fulfilled within the framework of this constitution. Petty measures can be passed, but for that demoralizing task you need not have your men in the Ministries, for that would mean accepting and working of the reforms. Your men and Congressmen have to fight and not become Ministers and hand you loaves and fishes. No ministry dare refuse you loaves and fishes if you are up and doing and your power is growing. So you must raise your voice against the Congress accepting offices.

In this connection, I should also say that the Kisan Sabha has made it clear from the beginning that it would not participate in the elections, i.e. set up candidates on its own ticket. It has declared that it would want the Congress to win. At the same time, it has expressed the hope that the Congress would adopt candidates who stand for the Kisans and would support their demands. I merely want to remind the Congress once again of these things at a time when selection of candidates is in progress.

Finally, I wish to warn you against the evil of casteism entering your movement. Kisans are one, and no matter what their caste, their interests are one. So, do not break your solidarity by being misled by caste and communal parties. Keep in the forefront your common economic interests and build up an unbreakable unity. Victory is yours.

16. Interview to Press after meeting M.N. Roy, 5 December 1936[1]

It was for the first time that I met Mr. M.N. Roy[2] last Thursday at 'Anand Bhawan', Allahabad. Roy for many years was a name to conjure with in Indian Socialist circles. Those were my students days in the U.S.A. Far away, both from India and the Workers' Fatherland, the Union of Socialist Soviet Republics, Roy's name and his activities had their sway. It was at Chicago and Wisconsin that Roy's writings reached us, and the echo of his doings. Some of us were deeply stirred.

[1] *Searchlight*, 6 December 1936, and *Bombay Chronicle*, 7 December 1936. Interview at Patna.

[2] M.N. Roy (1887-1954); earlier name Narendranath Bhattacharya; accused in Howrah Conspiracy Case, 1910; travelled widely in Japan, China, U.S.A., Mexico, Spain, Germany and Russia; founded the Communist Party of Mexico, 1919; presented the decolonization thesis at the Second Congress of the Communist International, 1920; started the *Vanguard of Indian Independence*, a fortnightly, 1922; accused in Kanpur and Meerut Conspiracy cases of 1924 and 1929; expelled from Communist International, 1929; returned to India, 1930; imprisoned, 1931-6; in later years propounded the philosophy of Radical Humanism; author of several books.

In my own progress towards Socialism, Mr. Roy's contribution was next only to that of the Marxian classics. It can be imagined therefore with what feeling I went to meet Mr. Roy. It is true [that] at the back of my mind was also the thought that Mr. Roy later on had serious difficulties with that fountain-head of revolution, the Communist International, which he was forced to leave. That thought raised in me misgivings and I met him with mixed feelings. When we sat down after a warm exchange of greetings he told me I would have to do most of the talking and I did. I was anxious that he should know facts and viewpoints that I represented before he decided upon his course of action. Some press reports about his views had made me wonder. I found, however, that, as usual, [those] reports [contained certain misrepresentations]. I found Mr. Roy to be in a much larger measure of agreement with us than I had reason to expect. The points of difference were not material, at least not now.

As a socialist Mr. Roy naturally lays emphasis upon independence as immediate goal but at the same time he fully realizes the role for the socialist movement and party in independence struggle. He has friendliest feelings for the Congress Socialist Party and will be glad to lend it his co-operation. I discussed with him the future of the party and we again found ourselves to be in full agreement. He was keen on the base of party being broadened and I assured him that we were consciously moving in that direction. I also told him that at our annual conference at Faizpur we shall more definitely and concretely put our anti-Imperialist task in the forefront.

Mr. Roy, while not bed-ridden, is very ill at present. He needs rest most and a thorough overhauling of his system. I hope he will soon recover his health.

17. Presidential Address at the Third Congress Socialist Party Conference, Faizpur, 23 December 1936[1]

It would be trite to say that we are going through very critical times. Yet, I wish its force were widely realized.

I have met colleagues in the Congress who take a different and rather complacent view of things and brush away all talk about critical times by saying that we are inclined to be alarmist and that it was best to concentrate on the immediate work in hand, namely, securing a victory for the Congress at the polls next January and February. There are other colleagues who do not bother even about the immediate task and who, in the midst of tumult

[1] *Bombay Chronicle*, 24 December 1936.

and gathering storm pursue with unruffled serenity their lofty dream of reviving the dead and dying industries of the ancient land.

Frankly, this attitude—not of the man in the street, mind you, but of the active national worker—alarms me. We do not seem to be conscious at all of the headlong speed with which the forces of society are impelling us onwards. We seem to believe that nothing extraordinary has happened in the last six or seven years in this rapidly changing world. We do not seem to be aware that we are passing through a period of intense crisis of Imperialism—a crisis which is disintegrating the old imperialisms, a crisis which is driving the masses the world over into deeper poverty and misery, a crisis which has brought war to our very doors, a crisis which has called up a resurgence of revolutionary activity, a crisis that therefore demands a new technique, new slogans, new forms of struggle.

We do not also realize more clearly that we failed in our previous battles with Imperialism. We take our failure as if we expected it and seem to show no anxiety for ensuring a success in the next struggle.

We seem to rely on time to lift the "depression" which has supposedly fallen over the country. When we shall have another fight which will take us further on our road to Swaraj, then we shall have another respite, then another fight and then yet another, till we reach our goal. This is not a parody, but a description of reality. I have met numberless people who think in this manner. Naturally, they do not feel any responsibility consciously to evolve a higher and more effective form of struggle. A few months spent in jail at periodical intervals is about all that most of us in the Congress conceive our anti-imperialist struggle to be.

II

I venture to suggest that this is a typical middle-class way of looking at things. Struggle for the middle-class is synonymous with what is called self-sacrifice. If this sort of mentality persists, the Congress will find itself completely ineffective.

We must learn to realize that the next fight must be our last. Till we do it there will be little seriousness in our work. Moreover, if we understood more clearly what was happening around us, we could see that it was so. When I tell people that within five years we shall be a free nation, my friends laugh at me. But I do believe that our proportions and our work must be on the basis of an even shorter calculation.

The deepening crisis of Imperialism sets new tasks for us and demands new forms of struggle. Let me make my meaning clear.

The transformation that has taken place in the life of our peasantry in the last six or seven years as a result of the crisis is without parallel. The poverty of the Indian peasant under British rule has been a major premise of our politics. So, we miss the significance of what has happened to him in the past some years.

When the Government allocates a crore of rupees to rural development and when the Viceroy goes around presenting stud bulls, we take it that it is all as a counter-blast to Gandhiji's scheme of village industries. There may be some truth in it, but the real conclusion to which it points is that the peasants' condition is becoming so desperate that even Imperialism sits up and takes notice. Being, however, unable to do anything real in the matter, it tries to woo the peasant by this show of solicitude.

The crisis has suddenly reduced the peasant's income by half and more than half. But his debts went on piling; there was little difference in his rent, revenue, water and other charges; the mill of indirect taxation continues its grinding. The result is that 70 to 80 per cent of the Indian peasantry is bankrupt today and millions have become landless.

What has been the peasant's reaction to all this? He sees that his very existence is in danger. He waited long enough for someone to take up his cause. Being disappointed, he seems to be taking things in his own hands. We hear today more than ever before of peasant conferences, peasant marches and of peasants' demands.

Here was a situation which clearly defined the task of the Congress. Here was a basis for vigorous and militant work among the peasantry, for developing their movement. Instead we have been tinkering with the sanitation and lighting of the villages. Could our programme be more unsuited to the needs of the times?

The real trouble lies in the manner in which we have learnt to approach this problem. We think that British rule is responsible for the plight of the peasantry and it cannot be improved as long as that rule lasts. This, of course, is true. But, then, we conclude from this that we have first to rid ourselves of that rule and then improve the condition of the peasants. Some of us even think that after we win the coming elections and take charge of the Government, we shall try to do something for the peasants. Therefore, no attempt is made in the present to relate the dire needs of the peasants with the struggle for independence—to make that struggle itself a struggle for reduced rents and revenue, freedom from debt, a juster distribution of the burden of taxation, a juster system of tenancy, and so on.

I venture to suggest that this way of thinking is again a typical middle-class way. The peasants themselves cannot think of their present struggle against starvation and penury as being separate from their struggle for independence. Clearly we have not yet learnt to think like the masses, because we are not yet close enough to them.

What is true of the peasantry is also true of the industrial workers and of the middle classes who too are being ground down by the crisis.

III

The first point we have been trying to drive home with regard to our method of struggle and the day-to-day activity of the Congress is that the Congress should identify itself with the struggle of the masses that is developing around their immediate demands and needs and should further intensify it and link it with the larger political struggle. This would lead to a countrywide peasant and labour movement and formation of peasant and labour organizations, all solidly behind the Congress. The entire masses would be roused to activity and the national movement would be raised to unprecedented heights. To put it briefly, the Congress must take hold of the developing mass unrest and forge it into a mighty weapon against Imperialism. This is, as I said, our first basic suggestion to the Congress.

I shall draw your attention to just one other suggestion we have been making. This is in regard to the organization of the Congress. We feel that the Congress as at present organized has too restricted and narrow a basis. It is based at present on the members we enrol. A national organization speaking for the whole nation cannot remain so restricted. It must be able to include the widest possible section of the people.

I am not suggesting that the influence of the Congress is restricted to its primary members alone. That influence undoubtedly covers a much wider range. But organizationally the Congress is based on the members alone—most of whom do not take any interest in its work after once they elect their representatives in twelve months.

This state of affairs cannot make for the organizational strength of the Congress and for its being in a position to mobilize a much larger section of the people than it has been hitherto able to do.

Of course, the membership can be enlarged, but in the very nature of things there is a limit to it. Is there no other way of recruiting larger sections of the masses into it? There is, and we have been constantly demanding it. The All-India Trade Union Congress has asked for it and the various peasant organizations have also done so. What we ask for can be described simply. There are in the country many peasant and labour unions. Their number will undoubtedly grow. Large numbers of peasants and workers are organized in these unions. They are mostly militant bodies fighting for the immediate demands of the workers and peasants, and pledged to independence.

We suggest that a provision be made for giving these organized sections of the masses collective representation in the Congress, thereby broadening the organizational base of the Congress, beyond calculations. I should mention the Chinese Kuomintang which under the leadership of the great Dr. Sun-Yat-Sen[2] was reorganized on a similar basis—the peasant and Trade Unions becoming the vital organs of the Peoples' Party, i.e. the Kuomintang. It is a matter of history now, how the Kuomintang grew in power and spread far and wide to the distant corners of that vast country.

A fear is often expressed that if such a scheme were adopted the Congress would become the cock-pit of the clash of class interests. To believe in this fear is to bury one's head in the sand. If there is clash of interests in the country it cannot be kept out of the Congress and it has not been kept out. Moreover, it is not possible to understand how, if the workers and peasants are brought into the Congress individually, this clash will be avoided.

It is reasonable to expect that, with their preponderance in the Congress, these questions will come to the fore. I have no hesitation in saying that this fear of the masses, particularly of the organized masses, is not worthy of the Congress and goes contrary to its declared intention of moving closer to the masses and identifying itself with them. This is the best that can be said in reply to those who express such fears.

I believe that if the Congress were reorganized on the lines suggested, it will rapidly grow in strength and popularity and would soon be in a position to lead the masses to a last and successful fight against Imperialism.

If we are able to achieve this at Faizpur a new landmark would have been reached in the evolution of our national movement and the year 1936 would be remembered as a turning point in our national history, much as 1924, the year of the reorganization in the history of the Chinese revolutions.

Before leaving this point I should make a mention of the splendid lead Pandit Jawaharlal Nehru has given in this regard. Since he took reigns of the Congress organization he has ceaselessly stressed the necessity of the Congress moving closer to the masses and becoming a joint front of all the anti-Imperialist forces in the country. I hope that during his presidentship he would be able, like Dr. Sun-Yat-Sen, to carry through the reorganization of the Congress and give it new life and vigour.

I shall now touch briefly upon a few problems of more immediate value.

IV

The first issue that comes to my mind is the slave Constitution. Much has been said of this fresh Imperialist device. I need not repeat all that has been said. The whole country has by now come to understand that the Constitution

[2] Sun Yat-sen (1866-1925); leader of the republican revolution in China; first President of the Chinese Republic, 1912; reorganized Kuomintang on basis of his Three Principles—Nationalism, Democracy and Socialism; withdrew to Canton, where he headed the unofficial government, 1921.

is only a new fetter of slavery and as such must be resisted and broken to pieces. The Congress has declared that it will oppose it uncompromisingly and bring it to an end. We welcome that declaration.

The elections are no election at all. They are merely a form of our anti-Imperialist struggle and in them there are two parties only—one, the Indian people, as represented by the Congress, the other, Imperialism. I have no doubt that the people will register their will to freedom at the polls. But winning the elections is only a small part of our task. The slave Constitution cannot be wrecked merely by an electoral victory. It is this fact that is not always being kept in view.

The Congress Election manifesto declared that the only effective way of opposing the Constitution is to mobilize the masses against it. Whatever is done in or through the legislatures should be merely to help organize that mass opposition. This declaration has largely remained on paper. We have seen how in the selection of candidates due regard was not given to this policy, and pacts and alliances were entered into with uncertain parties and persons merely with a view to winning seats.

However that chapter has closed now. The election is still before us and the question of policy to be followed in the legislatures. It is of the utmost importance that the campaign be utilized to mobilize the masses against the Constitution and against Imperialism. It was necessary for this that the Congress make a clear declaration with regard to the pressing demands and needs of the people. It was expected that the provincial Congress Committees would make such declarations regarding agrarian and other problems. It is even now not too late and the Faizpur Congress must give a clear lead on this point. Such a declaration of policy would also serve as a basis for the Congress parties in the legislatures. The latter have little other use than for pressing the demands of the masses.

While I am on this point, I must repeat once again that we feel that it would be wrong for the Congress to accept offices under the new Constitution. It would cause great injury to our cause if the Congress took responsibility even for a day to run this repressive administration. We have emphasized in the past two or three years more than any other party or group the nearness of the war danger. It is time now that our propaganda took a more positive shape.

V

Now I shall close with just a few words about our Party. I am today more convinced than ever before that our Party has a definite role to play in the Congress and the anti-Imperialist movement. It is essential that there should be in the vanguard of the national movement an organized group of people with definite and clear-cut ideas and policies. It has been our policy not to impose Socialism on the Congress. The Congress is an anti-Imperialist organization and its immediate task is to fight Imperialism and defeat it. Our anxiety is to develop this fight. We believe that Socialism finds a way for it. We further believe that Socialism can offer the only solution of the problems of poverty and exploitation which faces the people. Thus, while Socialism is not our immediate objective, it colours and orients it and gives us greater strength to fight for it. The existence of a party of socialists within the Congress gives an organized direction to our movement. It further draws the Congress nearer the masses and makes it a real anti-Imperialist body. The work we have already done stands witness to it.

18. First Things First: Article in the *Congress Socialist*, 26 December 1936[1]

Independence first, then anything else! Do not raise remote issues! Let us put our shoulders to the immediate task! First things first!

These are slogans that have been revived recently. They have received support from quarters which were not expected merely to repeat them as an admonition to the Left of the national movement. However, as slogans they are reasonable enough. The trouble lies in the lesson they are meant to convey. The essence of slogans is in their application to action!

When it is said that we have to win independence first, we heartily agree. But when from that premise we are led to a campaign for removing untouchability, the proposition takes on a different colour. It is then our turn to reply: "Let us win independence first." "Removal of untouchability is a step towards independence" is the rejoinder. Thus the controversy goes on.

What is important, therefore, is to realize that mere repetition of platitudes does not take us very far. It may serve the purpose of covering up issues and confusing action, but it cannot help us in solving the real problem that faces us.

We all want independence first. But having admitted that, it is foolish to pretend that we have no problems to solve, no difference left to face; that the only thing left to do is to "act" and not to "talk", as if, talking or acting were the only alternatives before us. It is a pathetic naivete to believe at this stage of our struggle that merely by repeating that meaningless phrase, "first things first", we will have solved all the problems that face us today. The question now is not whether we want or do not want independence.

[1] *Congress Socialist*, 26 December 1936.

We have passed that stage. It has taken us 50 years to do so! The problem that we face today is the problem of developing and shaping a strong and effective instrument and method for conducting the struggle for independence. That is the question now. It is unity on this question that will mean real strength. And it is the answer to it that we have to seek.

Thousands of Congressmen who have been in the thick of the struggle, who have gone through the fire, are searching their hearts and searching for an answer. They are growing in the belief that the basis of the freedom movement should be widened; its forms and methods of struggle should be re-shaped; its fundamental assumptions should be changed. The whole national movement is going through this process of internal adjustment. Differences, sharp and bitter, are natural. A vast organization like the Congress cannot go through such a reconstruction, cannot be re-born, as it were, without controversy, without a certain amount of internal confusion. Those who do not see any need for a change, those who believe that all is well, naturally look upon this controversy, this questioning, this self-examination as disloyalty, as disruption. They try to damn the whole thing by describing it as "raising of remote issues". The issues raised, as a matter of fact, are not remote but have a living, organic touch with the present.

Independence is not an abstract concept except for a few misguided intellectuals. It is a concrete thing for all the various sections of the people. The masses, it is true, do not conceive it in terms of assemblies and constitutions. Nevertheless, to them it does mean certain very concrete things. If to the peasant, ground down by landlordism, independence means freedom from that system, it cannot be said that abolition of landlordism is to him an issue remote from independence. If the masses take conscious part in the struggle for independence they surely will put their own interpretation upon it. It is significant that even reactionary parties in the country, particularly the Muslim parties—because the Muslim masses are poorer and more exploited—have given place in their programmes to a fair number of radical economic slogans. The platform of the Praja Party in Bengal, of which a retired minister of government is the leader, includes economic items that will scare away many leaders of the Bengal Congress. It is daily becoming clear to people in Bengal that the Congress cannot go deeper into the peasantry of the Province and cannot be identified with it unless it makes its position clear with regard to the Zamindari system and the other vital questions that face it, and takes an active part in its struggle against landlordism and indebtedness. That may scare away a few of the landlord bosses of the Congress, but it will change the whole character of the Congress in Bengal and transform it into a real mass organization. Incidentally it will also go a long way towards solving the Hindu-Muslim question that now distracts political Bengal so tragically.

We have heard a great deal in the past, particularly in the last month, about Socialism and Communism not being the immediate issues. Here again is a slogan about which it is difficult to make up one's mind unless one knows what use is made of it. If by raising this cry it is intended to gag the socialists it is a dangerous and reactionary slogan. It is one thing to say that the achievement of independence is our first and immediate task and quite another to say that independence is the only issue before us. For the greater number of India's millions the real issues are hunger and poverty and heartless oppression and exploitation. Is independence synonymous with freedom from these? Can we tell the masses that independence under any circumstance means bread, employment, freedom from exploitation and oppression? Can we say justly that unless independence takes on this meaning it is a real issue for the people? Hunger and poverty do not need any definition. Independence does. It can become real for the people only when its definition covers their fundamental needs. What is the guarantee that independence will assume this definition? Have Socialism and Communism any part to play in this? If they have, it is foolish to separate them from the issue of independence. Socialism for the masses is not that scientific system which we find in the works of scholars. Socialism to them is identified in a general and broad way with the ending of poverty and exploitation. Therefore it suffuses and colours the struggle of the masses for independence and gives it an orientation. When thousands upon thousands of hungry and oppressed peasants flock to hear Pandit Jawaharlal declare that Socialism is the only solution of the problems of poverty and unemployment, the struggle of independence rises to higher heights because it receives a content which is understood by the millions of the country. The deeper the people sink in poverty and degradation as a result of Imperialist exploitation and the deepening crisis that grips the world, the more will the urge for independence and the urge for economic emancipation draw nearer and enforce each other. Independence cannot be separated from its content. Therefore to put Socialism and independence in water-tight compartments, to deny that any relation exists between them is to weaken the fight for independence itself. No one says that our immediate fight is for Socialism and yet Socialism is the warp and woof of the immediate fight. It colours it, it gives it direction, it provides it with an edge of Idealism. Men must know where they are going before they can take their steps firmly. Men fight and sacrifice their lives not for the first things that they see before their noses but for ultimate ideals and objectives.

It is not only the objective that is coloured by Socialism but also the manner in which we shall strive to arrive at it. As far as the masses are concerned their urge is to fight against the day-to-day oppression which they suffer. For them that struggle and the struggle for independence are the same things. One develops into the other. But there must be direction, they must be guided to the ultimate goal. Who will direct and who will guide? How shall we learn that Imperialism cannot be overthrown by the manufacture of salt or picketing of liquor shops? From experience-our own and of others. Socialism is the embodiment of the revolutionary experience of humanity. It tells us about the springs of mass action and therefore helps us in providing a lead and directing the action. Therefore for all those thousands of active national revolutionaries, Socialism is not only an issue but a live issue. The propagation of Socialism and the organization and consolidation of socialist forces are of the utmost importance to the national movement. The socialist forces must be active participants in that movement. For that, they must organize themselves. They must organize, however, not as a coterie to capture offices in the Congress but as the torch-bearers of the National Revolution. They must become its vanguard—by not emphasizing the superiority of their ideology but by their work and their dynamic lead.

19. Draft Note on Congress Mass Contact Programme[1]

The Congress is an organization of the Indian people working for the independence of the country from Imperialist domination, conceiving that independence to include both political and economic freedom of the masses. It has a widespread organization throughout the country (but excluding almost the entire territory of the Indian States) and wields a very large influence over the masses of the people. Its organization has grown and been extended in course of years and its influence enlarged as a result of its activities—the great national upheavals that it has led in 1919-22 and 1930-4 the day-to-day work that its ever increasing band of workers has done, the local struggles, like the Bardoli movement, that it has conducted, the relief and aid it has rendered in stricken areas and above all by the sacrifice and suffering of tens of thousands of the country's brave sons and daughters who have responded to its call.

The Congress, however, is conscious that its task remains unfinished and that it must be able to mobilize a much more powerful mass movement to achieve its objective. It must extend and strengthen its organization, it must associate itself more fully with the masses so as to be able to mobilize them on a much vaster scale than it has done so far. It was with this objective in view that the Lucknow Congress appointed this Committee to go into the problem and present considered proposals.

[1] *AICC Papers* (NMML). This draft was prepared by J.P. for the consideration of the Mass Contacts Committee appointed by the Lucknow Congress in April 1936 (vide Resolution No. 11). Its other members were Rajendra Prasad and Jairamdas Doulatram.

The problem as conceived by the Committee divides itself into three different, but inter-related parts. The first is extension of the Congress organization and making it more active and alive; the second is to establish a closer association between the masses and the organization of the Congress; the last is to bring the Congress and the organizations of peasants, workers, youths and others, which aim at freedom from Imperialism, closer together so as to make the Congress a joint front of all anti-imperialist elements in the country.

The replies received to the questionnaire show that although the Congress has a network of committees spread over the whole country, it is apparent from the information made available that it is yet far from having an organization covering every village and every quarter of every town and city of the country. The number of members enrolled in 1935 and 1936 classified as rural and urban is given below and it shows that the Congress has on its rolls about . . . per cent of the population only. But it is not to be inferred from this that the members on the rolls are a sufficient indication of the Congress influence. The number of members enrolled depends upon the enthusiasm and diligence of the local workers, on the capacity of the poorer classes of people to pay the annual subscription of 4 annas, on the convenience or otherwise with which the people can be approached and on a number of other considerations. It will be true to say that the number of members can be increased almost without limit if we can command the services of workers who are able to reach vast masses in villages and towns, reduce or abolish the subscription and render the formality of enrolment less elaborate and easier. This contact has also not been uniform in all parts of the country or at all times. Local variations are very great and have been determined by the considerations mentioned above. The reports received by the Committee show that in some provinces even District Committees do not function regularly and in some they are not even properly constituted. In some cases there are not more than a few scores of primary members in a whole district. The variation in the extent and intensity of the contact with the masses has depended upon the problems which have arisen from time to time, upon the reaction of the people to the activities of the Government, upon the intensity of the consciousness of wrong and oppression felt by the people and generally upon what may be called for want of a better expression the political atmosphere in the country. Thus the years 1919 to 1922 and especially 1921 were years of great upheaval and whatever the number of members on the Congress rolls, the contact with the masses of the people was great both in extent and intensity. This followed by a period of comparative lull and quiet which did not fail to be reflected on the Congress organization. A revival occurred again in 1928 with the successful campaign of no-tax in Bardoli which went on intensifying till it ended in the great Civil Disobedience movement of 1930-4. Within this period also quite irrespective of the numbers enrolled as Congress members the enthusiasm and active support of the masses was immense. It must be remembered that during the Civil Disobedience period the Congress organization was declared illegal and committees were not functioning for the most part openly. But the movement was taken up and carried on in many places by new workers thrown up from amongst masses when all the old workers were arrested and imprisoned. Without this support which was spontaneous and almost without any previous preparation it was impossible to continue the movement for any length of time, as most of the workers and leaders especially during the second movement were clapped into prison within a few days of its start in the beginning of 1932.

However, the Committee feels that while there has been variation in the spread and depth of the Congress organization, the extension of the latter is a problem which must be met with in a more systematic manner from the centre. While local conditions will affect the result, a concerted lead and stimulus seems to be urgently called for.

Physical extension of the organization is only one aspect of the problem however. The provincial reports show, and they are unanimous on this point, that most of the lower committees of the Congress, particularly the primary committees and members, are largely inactive and hardly play any part in the determination of Congress policies or in the life of the people of the localities concerned. This makes for the top organizations of the Congress taking all political initiative and for the detachment of the local organs of the Congress from the life of the people. The primary members meet merely to elect their delegates and their executives or office-bearers. The local executives too meet largely to carry out specific programmes of the Congress and are not live organizations responding to the needs and problems of the masses in their areas and influencing their upper committees in arriving at decisions. This is largely the fault of the way the work of the Congress is conducted at present. The provinces unanimously recommend giving more initiative to the local committees and the primary members and suggest various methods of doing so. They also think it necessary that the Congress organizations should take greater part in the daily life of the people, and again various methods have been suggested. In our recommendations we shall make mention of some of these.

As regards the last part of the problem—the relationship of the anti-Imperialist mass organizations with the Congress—there is a sharp difference of opinion. The questionnaire had asked if it was advisable to give representation to these organizations in the Congress committees. Most provinces do not favour this proposal, though it appears from their replies that some of them have misunderstood the suggestion and have taken it to mean that this representation will replace individual enrolment. A few have favoured this proposal.

We feel that systematic attempts should be made in every province for the extension of the Congress organization. Those provinces where the position is weakest should be immediately tackled and a minimum organizational structure built up within a specified period of time. We feel that in every province there must at least be properly functioning district and taluk (or their equivalent) committees. This should be the minimum required. Where this has already been achieved, the organization should be further extended and lower committees built up.

In order to facilitate this work, we suggest an Organizing Committee to be set up by the All India Congress Committee to help and direct the provinces in the matter of organization. This Committee may also take up other problems of organization which we shall mention below.

Along with this Central Organizing Committee there should be set up in every province similar organizing committees, appointed by the P.C.C.s, which shall work under the guidance of and in consultation with the Central Organizing Committee.

The problem of extension of the Congress organization involves the problem of larger enrolment of Congress members. Many provinces have felt that the membership fee of four annas is too large for the mass of our people—particularly the poor peasantry. A reduction in this fee to two or one anna has been suggested. We suggest that this should be reduced to two annas realizable in cash or kind.

The Committee is aware that merely lowering the membership fee will not be enough to swell the ranks of Congress members. There is a widespread tendency today to enrol members merely for the purposes of election and usually no attempts are made to enrol any more members than necessary for a given election.

The Committee feels, however, that this situation results from the fact that primary members have practically no function to perform and the lower committees too are largely inactive. If more activity is developed among them and they begin to play a part in the shaping of Congress policy and the life of the people around them, an incentive would be created for people to enrol as members and to join the committees and strengthen and organize them on a much wider scale. In this the low membership fee will prove a great help.

The Committee at the same time recommends to the P.C.C.s to stimulate enrolment by membership drives, fixing quotas for districts, and otherwise promoting a healthy competition in this matter. The Committee also recommends that apart from door-to-door visits, efforts should be made as a part of the membership campaign to hold public meetings where the meaning of the Congress movement should be explained and people asked to join it and enrol as members on the spot. If this method of enrolment is followed it will remove to a large extent the evil we mentioned above and help to develop mass consciousness.

The provincial reports show that at the present time the lower committees of the Congress are not at all developed. In several provinces these committees do not reach lower than the District Committees. This is not always due to lack of workers or absence of what we have described above as political atmosphere. There is no conscious effort at present in this direction. While emphasis is laid on ever larger enrolment of members, it is not considered necessary or important to organize them in committees and thus develop the lower organs of the Congress. The latter do not find a place in the Congress constitution nor is there any specific function ascribed to them. We feel that if an effort is made to organize these committees and their rights, duties and manner of functioning are carefully defined, their number can be largely multiplied and they may be made vigorous and influencial organs of the Congress.

We propose therefore that the primary members should be organized in small committees in which they may meet face-to-face to discuss and deliberate. In the towns, for instance, Mohalla or ward, or, if possible, even smaller, committees should be formed. In the rural areas the village should be the ideal for the primary committee.

The Central Organizing Committee should study the problem of organization in each province and help the P.C.C.s to extend their organization in this manner. We recommend that rules and procedures that may be made in this connection should keep in view the fundamental consideration that the lower committees have to be given greater initiative and larger share in sharing policy and have to be made to take keen interest in the work of the Congress.

The Committee wishes to emphasize that extension of the Congress organization will be of little use unless the Congress committees are made active and vigorous bodies. As a matter of fact the problem of extension itself is only partly a problem of organization. Largely it is a problem involving policy, programme and work. The problem of activising Congress members and its lower organizations is one of the chief problems before us. As we have already pointed out, the primary members do not meet except perhaps once a year to elect delegates to the Congress, and perhaps committees and office-bearers. Thereafter the entire work of the Congress is carried on by the committees and in many places by the office-bearers. This is not satisfactory and if the primary members have to take direct part in the formation of the Congress policy and programme, they must be given opportunities to take direct part in the discussions during the formative period of policies and programmes. They should be encouraged to meet frequently and at these meetings they would naturally first of all discuss

J.P. with P.C. Joshi

All India Congress Socialist Party

General Secretary:
JAYAPRAKASH NARAYAN

Joint Secretaries:
M. R. MASANI
E. M. S. NAMBOODIRIPAD
DINKAR MEHTA
SAMPURNANAND

Kadam Kuan
Patna
26-3-'37

Dear Bhai,

We are arranging a series of lectures here under the auspices of the Party from April 5 to 13. We want you to inaugurate the series. It will help us financially and make the series successful in every other way too. I hesitate always to ask you to accept such programmes, but in the present case I am rather keen on having you here. If it be not possible for you to come on the 5th you may chose any other date.

Please give the money about which we talked in the train to Minoo for the Congress Socialist.

With love,

yours
Jayaprakash

Facsimile of J.P.'s Letter to Jawaharlal Nehru

Jayaprakash Narayan

All India Congress Socialist Party

General Secretary:
JAYAPRAKASH NARAYAN

Joint Secretaries:
M. R. MASANI
E. M. S. NAMBOODIRIPAD
DINKAR MEHTA
SAMPURNANAND

Kadam Kuan
Patna
13-2-37

Dear Rammanohar,

Your rule continues unbroken, let's see how long. It is impossible to forget one till eternity. By the way, I should have written earlier, the wrapper arrived. Its wonderful.

Heres a small job. We are organising a series of lectures here from the 6th March. The list and the schedule are attached herewith. Will you please tell me which of the subjects you choose and when you would wish to speak. This is urgent, so break that damned silence of yours. I think I shall move a resolution in the Exec. that any member of the Exec. who does not reply to three consecutive letters of the Gen. Secy. should be dropped from the Committee, even if he has topped the polls. So will you wake up?

What did you think of the Political Earthquake?

With love
Yours
JP

Facsimilie of J.P.'s Letter to Rammanohar Lohia

local questions in which they are interested. The local Congress committees should take up such local questions at the instance of these meetings of primary members and if they are unable to tackle them to send them up to the higher and more influential committees for consideration and action. The constitution should provide for questions of general importance to be referred to subordinate committees and to meetings of primary members for consideration and opinion. These questions may relate to particular localities and be referred to primary members of these localities or of general importance and may in that case be referred to primary members of a district or province or the country as a whole. Such references may be made by the All India [Congress] Committee, the Provincial Committee or the District Committee as the case may be. The constitution should provide that certain questions should necessarily be referred for opinion, e.g. questions relating to any big changes in the constitution of the Congress or in any fundamental policy or programme of the Congress.

We make the following further recommendations with regard to primary members and primary and lower committees:

Provision should be made in the constitution for consulting the primary members before decisions on policy are taken by the Provincial or National Congress. For this, draft resolutions should be published well in advance of the conference or meetings in question. In the case of the Annual Session of the National Congress, draft resolutions should be published three months in advance and opinion should be invited of the primary members and of the other committees from the bottom upwards. In addition to the drafts circulated fresh resolutions received should also be forwarded to the A.I.C.C. by the P.C.C.s.

In the case of provincial and other conferences, a similar procedure should be followed, the time to be given for discussion of resolutions being adjusted according to requirement.

The constitution should also provide for important issues to be referred to primary members on a demand being made for it. Such referendums may be limited to members of a locality, the province or the country as a whole, depending upon the nature of the issue.

Meetings of primary members should be held as often as possible. We recommend that they should meet at least once in two months. At these meetings resolutions passed since the last meeting by the higher bodies should be explained and discussed. Members should be encouraged to bring up topics for discussion that may be of local or wider interest. Economic or other problems that may touch the members and the people among whom they live should be particularly discussed. The work done by them or their committees should be reviewed and further plan of work discussed. Report of activities should be periodically placed before the members for their criticism and guidance.

The primary committees should function as much as possible as executive agents of the primary members, from whom all matters of local policy and activity should initiate. Before deciding upon a line of action the primary committees should call meetings of the members and take their opinion. The members themselves should be encouraged to initiate activities and the right of requisitioning meetings should be given to them. As the activity of the Congress among the masses develops, the primary committees may find it necessary to appoint special committees for specific kinds of work. These committees which will directly work among the masses—peasants, workers, youth, etc.,—should be appointed by the primary members instead of by their executives.

Elections to the higher bodies of Congress should be direct. As far as possible the system of proportional representation should be followed in all elections. For the election of delegates to the lower committees we recommend the system of cumulative voting.

Elections should be so arranged that no member is prevented by avoidable inconveniences from participating in them. Constituencies should be made as small as possible for this purpose and where they have to be spread out convenient polling arrangements should be made so that no member may go unrepresented on account of handicaps of distance, etc.

Efforts should be made to see that delegates and representatives elected by the primary members know and represent the views of their constituents. For this it is necessary that candidates explain their views in meetings of primary members and the latter express their opinions on the issues of the day. It is the views thus expressed that should guide the action of the delegates and representatives. Primary members should be given the right to recall any of their delegates or representatives should they find that they were not carrying out the policies they had been charged with or were going against them.

We stress that we cannot have too many meetings under the auspices of the Congress. We particularly stress the necessity of holding regular annual conferences of the various Congress bodies—local, district and provincial.

So far we have approached the problem of activization from the point of view of giving greater initiative to the members and lower committees of Congress. For this various procedures have been suggested. But while procedures will help, they cannot by themselves solve the problem. We therefore turn now to another aspect of the question that of programme of work. Not only the procedure of Congress work but also its content should be such that a closer association with the masses automatically and naturally results from it.

We come now to the second problem: the problem of bringing about a closer association between the masses and the organizations of the Congress.

The Congress has to identify itself more and more with the life of the masses. Whatever the influence the Congress commands among them today has been gained by the service rendered to them by Congress workers. It has been stated by many of the committees that the constructive work of the Congress has to some extent been instrumental in bringing the Congress nearer the masses. The programme has been conceived in a spirit of service and wherever it has been carried out on any extensive scale it has been appreciated by the masses. Similarly, work by Congress to relieve distress caused by flood or famine, disease or pestilence, oppression by landlords, Government petty officials and others, has naturally received its due need of praise and a certain consideration at the hands of masses in the form of attachment. It is also well known that even where the Congress has done no such appreciable service it has commanded respect and confidence on account of the suffering its members have undergone for the larger cause of Swaraj. The Congress must therefore extend its sphere of activity in all directions, making itself serviceable in every way to the masses, taking up every cause which touches them and trying to remedy it. The illiteracy of the masses, poverty, disease and oppression of the weak by the comparatively strong naturally offer opportunities of service and action suited to each locality may be taken in hand.

The Committee feels that such a programme of day-to-day work can be evolved only by the provincial and local committees in accordance with local conditions and needs. It can do no more than give the barest outline of such a programme here.

There is first of all the constructive programme of the Congress. It is true that this programme is in the hands of various autonomous organizations and the Congress committees may not interfere in the working of the latter. But they can do a good deal to help them. The extent and nature of this help will depend on the bond that should be built up between the local branches or units of these organizations and the units of the Congress. An attempt should be made to develop these bonds.

The Committee feels that the peasantry is the backbone of the national movement. The more the struggle for independence identifies itself with the desires and needs of the peasantry, the greater will be its strength. The constructive programme does touch a little the problems that face the peasants. But it leaves untouched innumerable other problems. The harassment and oppression from which our peasants suffer are well known. In many parts of the country they still live under feudal or semi-feudal conditions, where they are subject to innumerable forms of extortion, insult and humiliation. They are crushed under an unbearable load of debt which grows heavier day by day. Most of them work on uneconomic holdings and yet are forced to pay their rents and taxes and interest charges on pain of starvation. Various agencies beginning with the local Government official down to the village Mahajan mulct them, exploit them in a number of ways. Some of these things are done under the cover of the law, but many are illegal acts which happen only because the poor illiterate peasant is helpless and in most cases not even aware of his rights. When he is, he has not the courage to face his despoilers. Sometimes in his desperation he tries to do so but has to pay heavily for it.

We feel that this state of affairs is not only leading the peasantry to utter ruin and degradation but is also a great source of weakness to the national movement. A harassed, oppressed, demoralized peasantry cannot take its just place in the national revolution. The peasantry must be put on its feet, it must be made conscious of its strength and power, it must be organized and welded together. With the strength of the peasantry will grow the strength of the nation and of the fight for freedom.

We are of the opinion that the best method of welding the peasants together so as to make them conscious of their position and to enable them to fight against oppression and exploitation, is to organize them in peasant associations—bodies wholly of the peasants, taking care to define the word "peasant" so as to include the largest possible section of those who live by agriculture—tenants, small peasant proprietors petty landlords, land labourers and others whose subsidiary occupation is tilling of the land.

We suggest this course because we do not think that the Congress committees, in which are also represented other classes and interests, can undertake the work that the peasants' associations will be able to do. Nor would the peasantry be able to develop otherwise that self-reliance and internal strength which alone will save them. Therefore we lay great emphasis on Congress workers undertaking to develop these associations and to take active part in their fight for the peasants' vital day-to-day needs. The Congress committees also should associate themselves with this fight in an ever larger measure.

We are aware that the local committees of the Congress and the peasant unions may mean nearly the same thing. Yet, the two, while working in closest co-operation, must keep their identity apart. The Congress committees will have other programmes to carry out. But the peasant unions will concentrate all attention on the problems of the peasantry alone.

Furthermore, a purely peasant movement will bring to the forefront the demand and desires of the peasantry, and thus shape and influence the national movement itself.

We wish to point to a previous experience of this nature—the experience of the Chinese Kuomintang, Mr. T.C. Woo in his book on the Kuomintang says:

> In tracing the history of the Kuomintang it will be found that it is a consistent and continuous broadening of the basis of the revolution. In the beginning of the history of the Party the main strength of the Party were principally the students and the merchants overseas. The students who were then studying abroad furnished the brain and the Chinese merchants abroad gave the money necessary for the carrying out of the Revolution of 1911. . . . The history of the Party from 1911 to 1927 shows that the Kuomintang under the influence of this bourgeois group and on the narrow basis of the intellectuals and the merchants and other bourgeois elements, has not been able to achieve the work of revolution as envisaged in the principles

of Dr. Sun. At the end of this period came the reorganisation of the Kuomintang and the whole spirit that dominated the work of the organization is the attention that was directed to the broadening of the basis of the Revolution.

The reorganized Congress of the Kuomintang declared,

> China is today still in the age of agricultural economy. Agricultural products form more than 90 per cent of the total national production and peasants form more than 80 per cent of the total population. Therefore the Chinese National Revolution is specially an agrarian Revolution. In order to strengthen the foundation of the Revolution, the Kuomintang must first of all seek the participation of the peasants.

To quote the words of Dr. Sun himself:

> If the Chinese peasants do not come to participate in the Revolution, then we have no basis for it. In the reorganization of the Kuomintang we have added the peasant movement to our programme because we want the peasants to be the foundation of our Revolution. . . . If this foundation is not strengthened, then the Revolution will fail.

Explaining the peasant movement, Mr. Woo writes:

> The essential feature of the movement lies in the organization of the 'peasant union' in every village and district. A peasant union in the village corresponds in a way to the labour union in the city. It represents the poor farmers and the farm labourers. . . . The peasant union as organized under the Kuomintang is in a way the centre of self-government in the village and meets a timely demand of the poor farmers. In each village, in each rural district, and in each province there are the corresponding peasant unions, which together form a unified system, to be controlled and directed by the National Federation of the Peasant Unions.

The rapid development of the peasant movement and therefore of the Kuomintang, of which it was but a part after the adoption of this scheme, was phenomenal. Within a few years the membership of the union leaped up to millions—in Hunan alone it was claimed to be 30 million. It is universally admitted that the progress of the Chinese Revolution would not have been possible but for the re-organization of the Kuomintang. We feel that the time for the reorganization of the Congress on similar lines has also arrived. It has become necessary for the further broadening of the National Revolution.

We are aware that a fear is often expressed that the peasant movement will become a rival to the Congress. That fear is based on a fear of the masses. If the Congress has to move more progressively towards the masses, it has nothing to fear from the peasant movement. It will only draw its strength and inspiration from it. We even make bold to say that the peasant movement will be the foundation of the Congress.

The Committee has received reports of developing peasant movements

The Committee has received reports of developing peasant movements in various provinces, particularly in Bihar and Andhra. There are beginnings in Bengal, the Punjab, Utkal and a few other provinces too. Henceforth it must become the outstanding duty of Congress workers and committees to lend active co-operation to this development and to fight for the vital needs of the peasant masses. But it has to be kept in mind that the peasant movement must be founded, in the words of Dr. Sun Yat-sen, on the interests of the peasants themselves.

The Committee recommend a similar policy with regard to the labour movement and development of labour unions. The working class is one of the most intensely exploited classes in the country. Being propertyless, it is also a consistently revolutionary class. It controls the centres of production and transport and as such holds a key position in the economic order. The strength of an organized working class will be of inestimable value to the national movement. In fact, if that movement is to reach its destiny and end in the liberation of the Indian people from political and economic slavery, the workers must be in the forefront, because they stand most consistently opposed to exploitation. Therefore a close link should be forged between the national and labour movements. For this it is necessary for the Congress to give its active support to the working class in its day-to-day struggle and to its demands. Congress workers and committees should strengthen the existing labour unions and help in creating new ones. It should be kept in mind that, as in the case of the peasant movement, the working class movement must develop on the basis of the workers' interest and not of a programme imposed from the outside.

We do not wish to leave the impression that all that we propose is that the Congress programme should include the development of peasant and labour movements. We emphasize that there should be close link between these and the Congress movements. We suggest that as far as possible attempts should be made to associate the peasant and labour organizations in the political programme of the Congress and evolve a joint plan of action—joint meetings, demonstrations, campaigns, and so on.

Before such a link is established it would be necessary for the Congress to come to a joint platform of agreement with the peasant and labour organizations on a national as well as local basis, which will then serve as the basis for all joint work in the future. The Committee is of opinion that the ground is ready for such joint agreements. It recommends to the A.I.C.C. to take the necessary steps in the matter. As a starting point the Committee suggests the setting up of national and provincial committees appointed by the A.I.C.C. to meet the representatives of the national or local labour and peasant organizations. The results of these consultations should be placed before the respective Congress committees for sanction.

The Committee is aware that while the labour and peasant programme suggested above will bring the Congress into close and intimate touch with the masses, it leaves out a large section of the people untouched—particularly the urban middle class. The labour programme can be worked out only in industrial centres. But that does not mean that the Congress committees in the numerous town and cities where there is no industrial working class should have no programme of day-to-day work. It is difficult to describe this programme in any specific manner. It will depend largely on the resourcefulness of the local Congress committees. There is first the task of building and extending the Congress organization, formation of Mohalla committees, holding of members' meetings, etc. Local committees in addition to carrying out specified programmes should also undertake systematic political propaganda through lectures, study-groups, libraries etc. Committees should study the grievances of employees, shopkeepers, municipal workers, rent-payers etc., and try to get them redressed. In suitable cases attempts should be made to form some organization of these groups. Housing, sanitary and other problems of the city should be studied and agitation carried on for bettering them. Youth movement, training of volunteers and national workers may also be taken up if resources permit. The question of unemployment should be taken up and organizations of the unemployed should be formed. Other local questions of Government and municipal administration and other questions may also provide a basis for work.

In the rural areas too, while the peasant programme would form the predominant part of the Congress programme, the Congress bodies should develop other activities too. Here again the extension of the Congress organization and carrying out specified programmes shall come first. Then would come meetings of primary members for the discussion of Congress policy and resolution. In the rural areas we stress the utility of as many political meetings as possible and arranging such meetings and demonstrations and processions may itself be a programme. Then there are educational activities—opening of libraries, training of village workers and volunteers.

This list can be multiplied, but it will serve little purpose to do so. If the higher committees take greater interest in activizing the lower bodies a large variety of activities should be easily found. Here we have pointed out two lines of activity of fundamental importance and have also suggested various other forms of work.

Before closing this section we should like to point out that it would be a mistake to assume that in order to develop the Congress organization, to increase its strength, to bring it closer to the masses all that is necessary is to suggest new lines of activity, new procedures of work. It is necessary to point these out, and we have tried to do so above. But we must also point out that along with programmes are required men to work them out. The

Congress work is largely carried on by the voluntary labour of patriotic men and women. Our work will not progress unless we are able to attract fresh workers. Some Provincial Committees in their reply to our questionnaire have suggested a paid service—paid not high salaries and allowances but only just maintenance. If we remember the vast number of villages and if we think of having one worker for every ten village the number will come to hundreds and thousands and even the small pittance of Rs. 4 or 5/- per month will require crores. The pecuniary resources of the Congress are not large enough for this, at any rate at present, and it has to depend mostly on voluntary workers who may be part time but who must be maintained to keep the entire organization in a working order. One method which has been tried in some provinces and has worked well at a very cheap cost has been the establishment of ashrams which may be described as centres of Congress activity, maintaining a few workers according to the necessity of work and the supply of resources for their maintenance. In our view these ashrams may be indefinitely multiplied and depend as they will for their maintenance on local support, they will be constantly on their trial and will live only so long as they are capable of rendering useful service.

20. Notes on Faizpur Congress: Article in the *Congress Socialist*, 9 January 1937[1]

Those who were not present at Faizpur and who had little time to read beyond headlines in the newspapers are not likely to have understood the real significance of the Faizpur Congress. The headlines seem to have taught two lessons: first, that the socialists got an all-round thrashing; second, that the Faizpur Congress was a grand success because everybody said so.

That the Faizpur Congress was a notable success cannot be questioned. But it would be a grave error to relate in any manner the meaning of that success with the sub-editors' headlines.

The Faizpur Congress was a success in many ways. First, it was a great success as the first village Congress. The lakhs of peasants who flocked to it gave it a meaning and a content which were new in the history of the Congress. The leaders of the Maharashtra Congress deserve our utmost praise for the courage with which they went on with their bold experiment and our gratitude for showing us a new path to follow.

The real success of the last Congress, however, lies in the definite, and I hope lasting, check that it gave to the forces of the Right. I am not suggesting that the Right was decisively defeated at Faizpur. The Right is still the stronger wing. But Faizpur put an end to its aggression, and I have little

[1] *Congress Socialist*, 9 January 1937.

doubt that henceforth the Left will steadily grow till it comes to dominate the Congress.

This may appear to some as wishful thinking. There are friends who have expressed their disappointment because we did not "put up a strong fight". Fighting there was, of course, but not enough to satisfy those whose only conception of politics is indiscriminate opposition. The fact of the matter is that many of the official resolutions were themselves the products of Left propaganda and leadership. Such were the agrarian, the war, the mass contact—to name only a few—resolutions. Several other resolutions which came from the Working Committee were readily amended in the manner demanded by the Left. The most notable of such was the Convention resolution. Lastly, there was the resolution regarding Hartal on April 1. The Working Committee had turned it down and yet it was carried by an overwhelming majority in the Subjects Committee. There were some notable defeats also, such as that on the office issue. However, the fight on this issue was not a straight one, i.e. between those who were against office and those who were for it, but between the first and all those who were opposed to deciding the issue at Faizpur. I have little doubt that when the straight issue will be fought a few weeks hence, the Left will succeed in convincing the Congress that the only course consistent with its ideals and declarations is to reject offices.

When the Working Committee published its resolution on the proposed Convention some days before the Congress session, I confess, I felt rather apprehensive. The newspapers featured it under steamer headlines of "A National Convention". The thought that we could call anything like a National Convention at the present stage of our struggle and under the aegis of Imperialism seemed too dangerous to be allowed to get currency. Secondly, that even under present conditions it was not the plenary session of the Congress but a smaller and less representative body, and a body removed from the struggle, that was conceived of as a National Convention also seemed to be a dangerous idea.

The amendments that were made in the resolution at Faizpur and the assurances that were given in its connection have removed these dangers to a large extent. It has been made that the Convention can in no manner be conceived as a National Convention or as a step towards it. It has been called merely as a demonstration and so as to ensure that the different provincial Congress parties do not go in different directions but follow a common and mutually understood policy. It has also been made clear that the Convention will not determine any question of policy but only ways and means of carrying out the policy or policies laid down by the Congress and the A.I.C.C. that will meet immediately before the Convention.

Thus shorn of its dangerous attributes, the Convention becomes only a weapon in our struggle against the slave constitution and nothing more. It will concentrate the country's opposition to the constitution as no other single demonstration could do. It will therefore be a most valuable weapon.

I should give a warning, however. There are elements in the Congress who will seek every opportunity to clothe the Convention with those very attributes of which it has been shorn. In that Convention there will be many, unfortunately, who are not tried soldiers of the Congress, who till the other day held titles under Imperialism, who are close to the vested interests in the country. There will be a pull by these forces in a different direction. They would resent the "interference" of the A.I.C.C. and there would be others in the Congress to support them. We must therefore be vigilant.

It was after two years that Gandhiji made his appearance on the Congress rostrum. The President[2] of the Congress had just finished his inspiring address. As Gandhiji climbed up and his small figure came into view, there was a spontaneous sensation of joy and enthusiasm in that vast sea of humanity which was the Faizpur session of the Congress. There were a lakh of people or more to hear him.

Gandhiji had made his first political speech the same day[3] a few hours before. I was not able to hear him then. I therefore followed his speech with utmost concentration. The man who moved India's millions more than any one else in the near past was, it seemed, again taking the field. What was he going to say? Since he left the Congress a great many things had happened. The Congress had slowly but steadily been moving towards new visions and new paths; momentous issues and keen controversies had raged within its camp. Was he going to make a pronouncement on them? With these questions uppermost in the mind I followed every word that fell from his toothless lips. There was the same old self-confidence in him, the same sense of mastery. But as his words rolled on they fell, so it seemed to me—more and more flatly. When he finished there was no cheering, no waves of acclamation breaking through in cries of "Gandhi-ki-Jai".

In his speech Gandhiji sublimely ignored all that had happened in the Congress since he retired from its active work. It seemed as if he had come merely to remind us of his programme and his undiminished faith in it; to tell us that whatever we may say or do, his was the path that led to victory. The new ideas, the new programmes that were coming more and more to the forefront meant nothing to him it seemed. He took no notice of them. He repeated that unless the programmes of khadi, untouchability, village industries, Hindu-Muslim unity were fulfilled, India would not be freed. I do not think his reminder produced any deep impression. As challenge to the Left, if it was a challenge, I must say that it was completely ineffective.

Our success at Faizpur throws upon us a great responsibility. There are, unfortunately people in our ranks who think that criticism is the beginning

[2] Jawaharlal Nehru.

[3] Refers to Gandhi's speech at Exhibition Ground, Faizpur, 27 December 1936.

and end of our activities. We must fight this mentality and put our shoulders to the wheel and carry forward the Congress programme. The first task before us is to make the Hartal on April 1, a resounding success. Onward Comrades!

21. Statement to Press regarding Election Campaign, 13 January 1937[1]

It has been brought to my notice that a member of the Congress Socialist Party spoke recently at an election meeting in support of a non-Congress candidate, who is standing from a constituency, where the Congress has set up its candidate. Lest this incident should create confusion, I wish to make it clear that no member of the Party may oppose a Congress candidate or work for a non-Congress candidate who is opposing the Congress in a general or territorial constituency.

In the case of special constituencies such as Trade Union and unorganized labour constituencies, the members of the Party should support the candidates of the Trade Union Congress or its unions.

[1] *Hindustan Times*, 15 January 1937. Statement issued at Bombay.

22. Appeal to Voters, 15 January 1937[1]

I understand Comrade V.V. Narasimham[2] is contesting the Guntur-cum-Kistna-cum-West Godavari labour seat on behalf of the Congress. Any candidate who seeks the suffrage of the voters in the name of the Congress is entitled to their fullest support. Comrade Narasimham at the same time is a worker himself, and, as such, is eminently fitted to represent a working class constituency. Therefore, I appeal to every voter in the Guntur-cum-Kistna-cum-West Godavari labour constituency to vote for Comrade Narasimham, who stands for freedom and the Working Class!

Jayaprakash Narayan
General Secretary
All India Congress Socialist Party

Patna
15.1.37

[1] *Brahmanand Papers* (NMML).

[2] V.V. Narasimham; belonged to Vijayawada; member, C.S.P., and Madras Legislative Assembly, 1937-46; participated in the individual satyagraha, and imprisoned for nine months, 1940-1.

23. Letter to Rammanohar Lohia, 18 January 1937[1]

Congress Socialist Office
Kadam Kuan
Patna
18 January 1937

Dear Rammanohar,
I wonder what has happened to the alwan [woollen wrapper]. I hope you did not send it to my old address at Kannalal Road. I am not living there now and I think I mentioned this to you before. However, if you have not found another use for it, will you send the wrapper to me at the above address? I am leaving Patna again tonight and expect to be back by the 23rd or so.

Yours,
Jayaprakash

[1] *AICC Papers* (NMML).

24. Appeal to Contribute to the *Congress Socialist*, 22 January 1937[1]

Kadam Kuan
Patna
22 January 1937

Dear Comrade,
The current year will be an year of trial for our Party. Momentous issues are coming before the Congress this year and the responsibility of giving a clear lead on these issues rests more heavily on us today than ever before. Above every thing else, this requires that the Party's mouthpiece and organ, the *Congress Socialist*—should be further strengthened and developed into a powerful instrument of political propaganda.

The Editor alone cannot do this. All the leading members of the Party must come to his aid. I appeal to you particularly to contribute regularly to *Socialist*. The Editor suggests that we should start certain new features which should be taken up by different members of the Party and for which they should be responsible. I invite your suggestions in this connection. Will you take responsibility for some features? I shall be obliged to have your reply soon.

In the meanwhile, please begin writing for the *Socialist*. You have a

[1] *JP Papers* (NMML).

wide range to select from—theoretical articles, topical articles, studies of special subjects, critical notes, literary notes, book reviews, anything!

Please remember that our effectiveness as a Party very largely depends on the influence and popularity of our organ.

The address of the Editor, you know, is 139 Medows Street, Fort, Bombay. Do send him an article today!

Yours fraternally,
Jayaprakash Narayan
General Secretary

25. Appeal to Support the *Congress Socialist*, 25 January 1937[1]

Kadam Kuan
Patna
25 January 1937

Comrade,

It is a matter of great regret that I have to remind you of your responsibility towards the Party organ—*Congress Socialist*. The support and cooperation that it had so far from the Provincial parties and Party members in general has been far from satisfactory.

Congress Socialist has rendered invaluable service to our movement. As that movement grows, it will have to render yet greater service, but its worth and value are entirely dependent on the co-operation of the members of the Party. Our resources are limited and the only resource we can count on is your co-operation. No member of the Party is free from his responsibility towards *Congress Socialist*.

Every active member of the Party must become or get a subscriber.

Every member of the Provincial Executive must secure at least ten subscribers (or ten regular buyers).

Secretaries of the Provincial parties should regularly send reports, provincial letters, etc., for publication. If possible, provincial "editors" should be appointed for preparing these reports and letters and obtaining articles for the *Congress Socialist*.

Selected articles from the *C.S.* should be translated in [to] the language of the province and published in the local journals.

Jayaprakash Narayan
General Secretary
A.I.C.S.P.

[1] *JP Papers* (NMML).

26. Circular to Members of National Executive, Congress Socialist Party, 4 February 1937[1]

Kadam Kuan
Patna
4 February 1937

Dear Comrade,
Immediately after the Elections are over, the Working Committee of the A.I.C.C. will meet. It is necessary that before that a meeting of our Executive is held to review the position and formulate policies for A.I.C.C. and the Convention. Our members in the Working Committee should also accept the advice of the Central Committee.

In view of the fact that the dates and venue of the Working Committee have not been announced, it is not possible for me to fix the time and place of our meeting. I am writing, however, to ask you to be prepared to attend the meeting at short notice—most probably telegraphic—some time during the second half of February.

The most important problem we will have to consider at the meeting will be ways and means of fighting the Constitution. For this it is necessary that you come well posted with facts and details pertaining to the problem as arising and envisaged in your province. It would be desirable for the Provincial Executives to meet and discuss this problem. . . .

Will you see that in your province a meeting of the Central Executive is held for this purpose. If there is time district branches of the party may also meet.

Yours fraternally,
Jayaprakash Narayan

[1] *JP Papers* (NMML).

27. Political Earthquake in Bihar: Article in the *Congress Socialist*, 6 February 1937[1]

Bihar is in the grip of election fever. A province where the Congress has penetrated deep into the villages, the General Election has roused the entire countryside.

Reports of the polling of the past four days show that the Congress is

[1] *Congress Socialist*, 6 February 1937.

sweeping everything before it—big landed magnates who have the cruel audacity to seek the suffrage of those whom they have beaten, badgered and bled white; ministerial candidates who constitute formidable combines of wealth and borrowed power; communalists and weighty frauds.

The sweep of the Congress reminds one of the recent floods that washed away all obstacles before them. On the first day I witnessed polling at two stations. The excitement is indescribable. The entire prospect before the booths was a sea of tricolours in which the ensigns of the rival candidates appeared as insignificant specks of dirt. National cries and slogans drowned everything else. Crowds of voters came marching with banners and songs and the raucous thudding of drums. They came mostly on foot, but there were elephants and horses too with the tricolour flying!

As I watched all this, freedom seemed to rise up from the dust that lay over everything in that unforgettable demonstration. And I wondered how frenzied would the crowd be and how high would run its enthusiasm when it would meet, not in the distant future, to elect its representatives to its first real assembly—the Constituent Assembly!

The Election campaign in Bihar began in right earnest after the visit of the stormy Pandit Nehru. In this province of frequent natural calamities, everything reminds one of the wrathful demonstrations of nature.

If the landslide at the polls reminds us of the great floods, Pandit Jawaharlal's visit inevitably makes us think of the great earthquake. For his visit was a veritable political earthquake. He shook up the whole province as nothing else had done in the recent past. It was as if a giant had come forth who picked up the sleeping province in his hands and gave it a mighty shake-up that brought it to life and consciousness. Wherever he went the populace rose up, as if from the very furrows of the field, to see and hear his message. And his speeches! Simple, they went straight to the hearts of the people; and they opened their eyes. The peasants' common comment was *babuji hamari ankhon ka to parda gir gaya*. The Election had been won!

The response and enthusiasm of the people have been a revelation to us. And such touching faith in the Congress! Simple peasants, they enter the booth as if it were a place of worship, drop their cards in "Gandhiji's" box and joining their hands devoutly make their salutation. Thousands come trekking from distant homes without inducements, defying threat and coercion, and shouting *Swatantra bharat ki jai* to vote for the Congress.

The Congress is their hope—it will relieve them of their distress. This march of the hungry peasant to the polling booth is a prelude to the march to the battlefield.

Apart from far-reaching political results the election is producing two interesting and no less far-reaching, social results. Bihar lives under two masters: the British power and the great landlords. The biggest landlords in the country live in Bihar. In respect of these "lords" the social status of the tenants, no matter of what caste or community or of what economic or other circumstance, is such as could exist only in a country of slaves. There are landlords whose wealthiest tenants may not sit down in their presence and may not come with their shoes on. There are prescribed forms of salutation. And the terror to which the tenantry is subjected! The tenants are so many cattle at whom the lord may not even deign to cast a look.

Now, the same lord, if he is a candidate—and fortunately some of the most oppressive are in the ring—goes from door to door begging for votes, promising redress and relief, fraternizing and rubbing shoulders with his cattle. The result is bridging of the social distance that separated master and slave.

The slave is coming to his own. The vote is making him a man. The terror falls off from his heart like a veil. He looks at the world with a new sense of self-respect and dignity. And, if the master is defeated, as in most cases he will be, he shall cease henceforth to be anything but a landlord entitled to little more than the rent of his land. This in Bihar will be an important social change.

The other important social result is in the sphere of the Hindu social organization. Our Hindu society is organized on the basis of caste which today is nothing more but a division of human beings into a hierarchy of social positions. The election has come as a powerful challenge to this scheme of things. Such challenge had so far come from social reformers. The so-called lower castes themselves were more or less quiescent. The election has roused them. They see that upper-caste men, who after all are a handful compared with them, are taking all the plums and are doing so largely with their own votes. Why should they allow this? Why can they not have the plums for themselves? Ideas of social equality are rising and spreading fast—*ideas that promise to batter down this monstrous structure of Hindu society which has been the dream of reformers to abolish.*

At present it is the opportunists and self-seekers who are trying to exploit the growth of this feeling. But it has nevertheless set the whole Hindu society in ferment and started a process of democratization in it that augurs a deep-going social revolution in India.

I feel I shall not be taking too much advantage of your readers' indulgence if I mentioned a conversation I had the other day with a casual co-traveller. A railway compartment is a fairly representative slice of real life. And the classes in the railway trains correspond roughly to the classes in society. The Inter Class corresponds to my mind to the lower middle class in the

Great Society outside. I happened to be among the lower middle class on this particular occasion. There was a bright looking young Muslim, who looked like a recent graduate. I was attracted to him and picked up a conversation with him. His brightness was not only physical, but apparently he had a very keen mind also.

He had the "good fortune", as he himself put it, to hear Pandit Jawaharlal at one of his great meetings and he was full of him. Jawaharlal was the only leader. He could lead the Muslims and Hindus alike. The Congress was the only organization which was selfless and which worked for the good of the people. The rest were all self-seekers. He himself had worked for the Independent Muslim Party, but was disgusted with it. He described it as *andhon mein kana raja* (among the blind the one-eyed is the king). He did not think much of his Party, but it was the best of the lot! Which, of course, is true. The other two parties are worse still. The United Muslim Party of which the present minister, Mr. Aziz,[2] is the leader, is an openly pro-Government Party; while the other, the Ahrar Party, is rank communalist, with Moulana Shafi Daudi[3] as its leader. Mr. Jinnah[4] cut no ice in my province, somehow.

The Independent Muslim Party comes nearest to the nationalist position. But only in words. Its candidates are mostly reactionaries, pro-imperialist and communalist. In one constituency it is even fighting the Congress Muslim candidate! And these were the main grievances of my Muslim fellow-traveller against his Party. He regretted that the Congress did not enter the Muslim constituencies more boldly and put in more candidates.

My friends have told me that in the villages Muslim peasants often asked them who the Congress candidate was and for whom they should vote and they felt disappointed when they were informed that Congress was not in contest. I think not fighting the Muslim seats will go down as one of the major mistakes of the Congress in the election campaign.

Every shield has "the other side". Universal response to the Congress at the polls is one side, and the brighter side of the shield. The other side is the

[2] Syed Abdul Aziz (1885-1949); Bar-at-Law; member, Bihar Legislative Council, 1927-36; Minister of Education, Bihar and Orissa Government, 1933-6; President, Bihar Provincial Muslim League, 1938-40; Chairman, Reception Committee, All India Muslim League, Patna, 1938; Judicial and Ecclesiastical Member, Nizam's Government, Hyderabad, 1940-4.

[3] Maulvi Muhammad Shafee Daoodi (1863-1949); Secretary, Bihar Khilafat Committee; President, Bihar P.C.C., 1921; member, Indian Legislative Assembly, 1923-9, re-elected in 1934; formed Ahrar Party in Bihar, 1937.

[4] M.A. Jinnah (1876-1948); President, All India Muslim League, 1916, 1920, and 1934-47; champion of Muslim separatism and creator of Pakistan; Governor-General of Pakistan, 1947-8.

failure to make full use of the campaign. The tendency in most constituencies has been to make the election a matter of personal success. Idea and principles were thrust into the background. Groups of workers here and there, mostly socialists, but some others also, such as the workers of the Kisan Sabha, were bravely counteracting this tendency, and in several areas very successfully. It was Pandit Jawaharlal's visit that revolutionized the campaign generally and a new tone was given to it which is being kept up to an extent.

It is to be regretted that the provincial leaders have not given any lead yet to turn the election campaign to some permanent good to the Congress organization. Attempts, however, are being made to save the machinery that has sprung up to meet the needs of the election and preserve the forces that have been created. The credit for this too must go to the socialist workers. Their popular idea in this connection seems to be to build ashrams or workers' camps in every thana and to raise a corps of volunteers from out of the election workers and agents.

The other night as I was returning from an election meeting perched on a rustic *ekka* I happened to pass by a smithy. Suddenly, I heard the cry *Swatantra Bharat ki-jai* followed by the age-old cry *Raja Ramchandra ki-jai.*

Apparently a group of workers was listening to a recitation of *Ramayana* which is periodically punctuated by the most popular of popular cries, "Raja Ramchandra etc.". *But the thought that a national cry had gained such respectability and popularity as to be coupled with this religious and deeply devout cry gripped my mind. It signified nothing short of a great mental revolution among the people. The Revolution has almost matured, I thought.*

28. Letter to Rammanohar Lohia, 13 February 1937[1]

Kadam Kuan
Patna
13 February 1937

Dear Rammanohar,

Your rule continues unbroken, let's see how long. It is impossible to forget one till eternity. By the way, I should have written earlier, the wrapper arrived. It's wonderful.

Here's a small job. We are organizing a series of Lectures here from the 6th March. The list and the schedule are attached herewith. Will you please tell me which of the subjects you choose and when would you wish to

[1] *AICC Papers* (NMML).

speak. This is urgent, so break that damned silence of yours. I think I shall move a resolution in the Exec[utive] that any member of the Exec[utive] who does not reply to three consecutive letters of the Gen[eral] Sec[retary] should be dropped from the Committee, even if he has topped the polls. So will you wake up?

What did you think of the 'Political Earthquake'?

With love,

Yours,
J.P.

List of topics for lectures:

1. Development of Socialist Thought culminating in Marx and Lenin.
2. Society and its Evolution. The Interpretation of History: classes and the class struggle.
3. Development of Capitalism and Imperialism.
4. Fascism and the Decay of Capitalism.
5. Soviet Russia.
6. The Modern World—War & Revolution.
7. Imperialism in India.
8. The Anti-Imperialist Struggle in India.
9. Liberty, Culture, Religion under Socialism.
10. The Middle Classes and Socialism.
11. Socialism and India—cultural, economic, political and social prospects.

29. Appeal to Observe Hartal, 13 February 1937[1]

Immediately after the elections we shall have to prepare for the Hartal of April 1. The Party inasmuch as it sponsored the Hartal resolution in the last Congress, bears the primary responsibility towards making the Hartal a resounding success. Party members must take the initiative in the Congress Committees and outside them in preparing for the Hartal.

The Hartal should be complete and militant. It should include closing of shops, factories, schools and colleges, local transport, municipal establishments, etc. In the villages Hartal not being a practical programme—except to the extent of closing of local bazars—attempts should be made to organize processions which should converge on local government offices and outposts. In the cities too in addition to the Hartal there should be demonstrations, including meetings, processions, burning of effigies. In the provincial capitals the processions should converge on the Legislatures.

[1] *Congress Socialist*, 13 February 1937.

30. Interview to Press on Elections in Bengal and Differences with M.N. Roy, 17 February 1937[1]

Question: What are your views about the implications of the last general elections in Bengal?

Jayaprakash Narayan: The most important task before the Bengal Congress as revealed by the election results is to approach the peasantry with a bold economic programme. The greatest weakness of the Bengal Congress is the lack of hold over the Muslim masses of this province which are playing into the hands of the communalists at present. Only an agrarian programme and work among the peasantry will give the Congress this hold which will make it not only the strongest but the only mass organization in the province. I do not think this is a difficult task for Congressmen in general.

Q: Is there going to be a rapprochement between the Congress Socialists and Mr. M.N. Roy?

J.P.: There are differences between our party and Mr. M.N. Roy, but in spite of these differences, there is a keen desire on both sides to work together and co-operate fully in futherance of the anti-Imperialist movement. As to the differences, it is difficult to say what will ultimately happen. But I hope they would be gradually resolved and we may be able to work as if we belonged to the same organization or one party. On my part there would be a constant attempt to minimize differences and to keep the points of agreement in the forefront.

[1] *Bombay Chronicle*, 20 February 1937. Interview at Calcutta.

31. Interview to Press on Acceptance of Ministerial Offices, 22 February 1937[1]

I have seen report of rumours that the Congress Socialists in the United Provinces are agreeable to join the Congress Ministry if it is formed. I am amazed at these reports. The policy of the Congress Socialist Party has always been one of uncompromising opposition to the idea of acceptance of Ministerial office under the new charter of slavery. That policy still continues and I cannot conceive any deviation from it.

I have not the least doubt therefore that these rumours are baseless. Even if the Congress comes to a wrong decision and decides to form Ministries there cannot be any question of any member of the Congress Socialist Party joining them.

[1] *Bombay Chronicle*, 23 February 1937. Interview at Patna.

32. Amendment to Resolution on Office Acceptance at A.I.C.C. Meeting, Delhi, 17 March 1937[1]

The Socialist amendment suggested the deletion of the last para of the resolution[2] and substitution of the following: "the A.I.C.C. is of opinion that the acceptance of Ministerial offices by Congressmen is inconsistent with the policy adumbrated above and would weaken the struggle for national independence. The A.I.C.C. deprecates the idea that the Congress Ministers can, within the framework of the Government of India Act, secure any appreciable amelioration in the condition of the exploited and oppressed section of the people or any substantial political or economic concessions for them. On the other hand the acceptance of responsibility without the transfer of any real power will make the Congress Ministers a party to repression and exploitation which is implicit in the imperialist regime and will thus discredit the Congress in the eyes of the people. The A.I.C.C., therefore, decides against acceptance of Ministerial offices by Congressmen".

[1] *Hindu*, 18 March 1937. The amendment was lost by 135 votes to 78.
[2] See Appendix 3 for A.I.C.C. Resolution on Office Acceptance.

33. Speech while Moving the Amendment to Resolution on Office Acceptance at A.I.C.C. Meeting, Delhi, 17 March 1937[1]

The question of office acceptance has been discussed for a long time, but nothing that has happened or been said has changed my mind. My conviction is that acceptance of office will be a blunder. It is clear that there are two mentalities within the Congress: one the reformist and the other the revolutionary. On the one hand we have been professing to wreck the constitution and, on the other, we are declaring that we shall accept Ministries. I cannot understand how these two things can be reconciled. Again, the Working Committee resolution first says that deadlocks are inevitable and later that we should have an assurance from the Government that special powers will not be used. If such an assurance is obtained, then deadlocks will not be so very inevitable. It is no use saying that we shall make whatever use we can of the constitution and through it prepare for the final struggle. That is a reversal of policy. If we are going to work the

[1] Adapted from a report of the speech published in the *Hindu*, and the *Hindustan Times*, 18 March 1937.

constitution, let us do so without imposing conditions. These conditions are derogatory to self-respect. We can acquire strength only by wrecking the constitution and carrying on the struggle.

34. Letter to Jawaharlal Nehru, 26 March 1937[1]

Kadam Kuan
Patna
26 March 1937

Dear Bhai,
We are arranging a series of lectures here under the auspices of the Party from April 5 to 13. We want you to inaugurate the series. It will help us financially and make the series successful in every other way too. I hesitate always to ask you to accept such programmes, but in the present case I am rather keen on having you here. If it be not possible for you to come on the 5th you may choose any other date.

Please give the money about which we talked in the train to Minoo [Masani] for the *Congress Socialist*.

With love,

Yours,
Jayaprakash

[1] *AICC Papers* (NMML).

35. Interview to Press on Formation of Ministries, 30 March 1937[1]

I rejoice at this new and healthy turn of events.[2] Not only has it removed the strain whereunder we, who had to adjust ourselves to the decision

[1] *Bombay Chronicle*, 31 March 1937. Interview at Patna.

[2] The A.I.C.C. at its meeting at Delhi, 17-18 March 1937, resolved to authorize and permit the acceptance of office in provinces where the Congress was in a majority provided the leader of the Congress party in the legislature was satisfied and able to state publicly that the Governor will not use his special powers of interference or set aside the advice of ministers in regard to constitutional activities. Following the refusal of the Governors to give assurances, Congress leaders declined to form ministries in their respective provinces. This was the 'new and healthy turn of events' to which J.P. refers here.

of the A.I.C.C. in the interest of the Congress solidarity, were labouring, but it has rescued the Congress from what appeared to us as a disastrous policy.

If the assurance that has been asked for were forthcoming, Congress would have been placed in a position of working the despised Constitution that, to us, was a policy inconsistent with our self-respect and fundamentally opposed to the Congress policy of uncompromising opposition to and combating the Act. It is a great piece of luck for the Congress to have escaped that.

At the same time, I am afraid, I cannot share in the satisfaction of some deriving from the fact that the hollowness of the Autonomy has been exposed. We had never required this drama to convince us of the wretchedness of the Constitution and of the unreality of transfer of power.

I don't think Congress was ever in doubt about its Ministers [who] were always understood to be in a position of Governors' helpless prisoners. The Constitution is conceived in a spirit of Imperialist domination and the only spirit in which we could approach it, was one of uncompromising opposition. I am glad, after a brief [talk] . . . of experimental cooperation Congress has come back to that path. If that has united us, I say it has been all to the good.

To my mind, the outstanding advantage of the position wherein the Congress finds itself is the complete unity that has been brought about within its ranks on this issue. Thus united we can march in solid phalanx to batter down the new wall of slavery that the Constitution has built around us.

Finally, I should like to point out one weakness in our position which must be set right immediately. Activities of the Congress in the last few months has unfortunately background of acceptance of office. Today, we are faced with the opposite situation and we are to an extent unprepared. We must take this up in the shortest possible time.

Today, our work, more than ever before, is outside the Legislature. We must bend all energies to perfecting and extending the Congress machinery, in bringing it ever nearer to the masses, in organizing the masses for their daily struggle for bread, in mobilizing the youth of the country. Sooner we apply ourselves to these tasks, speedier will the end of this Act be and with [it] of British power in the country. Let us make the Congress an irresistible force.

36. Circular to Provincial Secretaries, Congress Socialist Party, 31 March 1937[1]

Circular Letter No. 4

Patna
31 March 1937

To Provincial Secretaries

The fight that the Party put up at the A.I.C.C. meeting in Delhi[2] is known to all members. From both the debating point of view and the big vote in favour of the Party's amendment, our stand in the A.I.C.C. was very successful and won the admiration of all present.

Following on the decision for acceptance of ministerial offices, the Party had to consider its position. This it did, and a statement was issued to the Press by the Executive Committee (vide *Congress Socialist*, 27th March, 1937).[3]

The decision of the A.I.C.C. opened up the question of the policy to be followed by members of the Party who were elected to the Legislatures as Congress candidates.

The Committee decided that it was not necessary at this stage for these comrades to resign their seats in the Legislatures. On the other hand the Committee also decided that members of the Party who might be offered ministerial office should not accept it. There was no objection, however, to accepting the Presidentship of an Assembly or Council.

The question of whether the two socialist members on the Working Committee should resign was also raised. After deep deliberation the Committee decided that Comrades Narendra Deva[4] and Achyut Patwardhan[5] should not be allowed to take such a step. It will be remembered that these comrades were given an opportunity to dissociate themselves from the Working Committee's Resolution in the A.I.C.C.

[1] *JP Papers* (NMML).

[2] Refers to the A.I.C.C. meeting at Delhi on 18 March 1937 where the Congress Socialists had strongly opposed the resolution on office acceptance.

[3] See Appendix 4 for statement of National Executive of the C.S.P. on acceptance of offices by the Congress.

[4] For biographical note on Acharya Narendra Deva see *JPSW*, Volume One, p. 61.

[5] Achyut Patwardhan (1905-92); Founder-member, C.S.P, 1934, and member of its National Executive, 1934-8; member, Congress Working Committee, 1936-8; offered individual satyagraha and imprisoned, 1940-1; participated in the Quit India movement, 1942; remained underground, 1942-6; retired from politics, 1950; wrote *Ideologies and the Perspective of Social Change in India*, and co-author with Asoka Mehta of *The Communal Triangle in India*.

Anti-Constitution Rally

The Anti-Constitution Rally organized by the Party at Delhi on 16th March was a great success. There was a huge audience of about five thousand. Representatives of the Anti-Ministry Committee of Congressmen, the All India Trade Union Congress, the All India Kisan Committee, the All India Students' Federation and the Bengal Labour Party joined members of the Party in support of the resolutions placed before the Rally.

It was from all points of view a very successful demonstration.

Meeting of Party Members

A meeting of Party members present in Delhi was arranged on 20th March. It was fairly well-attended. Certain organizational and ideological issues were raised by members present and the General Secretary, who presided, explained the Party's position with regard to them. The discussion proved to be very successful and removed many misunderstandings.

Party Reorganization

The Executive Committee of the Party took several decisions affecting the organization of the Party.

Among these were the dissolution of the Nagpur Provincial C.S.P. and the suspension of the present Executive and membership of the Delhi Provincial C.S.P., both the Parties having failed to function at all satisfactorily. In the case of the latter, Comrades Satyavati[6] and Farid Ansari[7] were authorized, in consultation with the General Secretary, to enrol fresh members and to reconstitute the Party.

May Day

The Committee resolved that in addition to the usual meetings, May Day (1st May) should be observed this year as a Flag Day *in aid of the funds of the* C.S.P. The nature of the emblem to be sold on that day was left to the

[6] Satyavati (1907-45); granddaughter of Swami Shraddhanand; married Balbhadra Vidyalankar, 1923; engaged in social work among mill workers at Jiyajee Rao Cotton Mills, Gwalior, and later at Birla Mills, Delhi; one of the founders of Naujawan Bharat Sabha in Delhi; participated in the salt satyagraha, 1930; jailed, 1930-1, 1932-4; member, National Executive of C.S.P., 1937-8, Delhi P.C.C., and A.I.C.C.; Chairperson, Reception Committee of C.S.P. Conference, Meerut, 1936; took part in the individual satyagraha and jailed, 1940-1; detained during the Quit India movement, 1942-4.

[7] For biographical note on Faridul Haq Ansari see *JPSW*, Volume One, p. 156.

discretion of Provincial Parties. It was decided that 25 per cent of the net receipts should be remitted by Provincial Parties to the A.I.C.S.P.

Study Camp

I referred in an earlier circular to the idea of holding an all India Study Camp[8] this year. Comrade Meherally who is in charge of the arrangements complains that he is not getting the co-operation of the Provincial Parties. I draw your attention to it and request you to send him immediately the names of those Party members from your Province who are desirous of joining the camp or whom you have selected for the purpose. There should be no further delay in this.

The Camp will be at Almora (U.P.) in the second half of May and will last two weeks (probably from 15th May to 31st May). Those who desire to join may do so for either one or both weeks. The cost for board and lodging will be very low—Re 1/- per day.

I suggest that Provincial Parties should contribute towards meeting the train fare of those members who they feel should attend the Camp but cannot afford to do so.

Those desiring to join the Camp should immediately get into touch with Comrade Yusuf Meherally (Bombay View, Forjett Street, Bombay 7). Party Secretaries are requested to see that all members are informed about the Camp. The Camp can only be organized if it is known in advance how many are coming. It will not be possible to accept last minute entrants.

Widening the Basis of the Party

There is some misunderstanding among Party members as to the meaning of the Faizpur Thesis[9] when it speaks of widening the base of the Party. Some comrades imagine that the Thesis opens the door to mass enrolment of members. It is therefore necessary to state clearly what the Thesis really means.

The conditions for mass enrolment of members of a socialist party do not yet exist in India. Any party in India whose members are enrolled in this manner will at best be a popular party representing an urge for national freedom. A socialist party must enrol its members from those with whom it has come into contact *in the course of its work* and who are themselves

[8] The Study Camp was held from 15 to 31 May 1937 at 'Shail Ashram', the bungalow of R.S. Pandit, Khali Estate, 9 miles from Almora. Yusuf Meherally was the convener of the Camp. Lectures were delivered by Rammanohar Lohia, Asoka Mehta, M.R. Masani, M.L. Dantwala, Yusuf Meherally and Ranchhod Patel.

[9] See Appendix 2 for text of Faizpur Thesis of the C.S.P.

active elements. As the Thesis itself says, we have to enlarge our membership "so as to include a wider section of *Congress workers and conscious elements active in the labour, peasant and other movements*". Thus we do not recruit our members from the masses generally, but chiefly from amongst those who are working among the masses. This again does not mean that whoever is working in the Congress or the labour or other movements has a right to enter our Party; only such of these may do so as have come in touch with the Party and have come to accept its objects, programme and line of work. Any Party secretary or member who attempts to enlarge the membership of the Party with the aid of receipt books will do incalculable harm to the Party. Our membership must grow as a result of Party activity rather than of membership drives and campaigns. The Faizpur Thesis did no more than point out the lack of uniformity in the development of the Party in the various provinces and the desirability of having a larger membership than what we have had hitherto. That did not mean that members had to be enrolled *en masse*. Our Party is a Marxist Party and its membership must therefore be restrictive.

Fraction Work in the Party

I drew your attention in my first circular to lack of solidarity and homogeneity in our Party. It is a matter of regret that this fault has grown more serious since then. The Executive reviewed the position in this regard throughout the country and adopted the following resolution:

> The Committee feels that fraction work is being carried on in the Party at the instance of certain elements both in the '*Roy Group*' and the '*Red Group*' and reaffirms its policy of combating such factionalism on both sides, if necessary by resort to disciplinary action.

The Executive defined fraction work in the following manner:

> Fraction work includes:
>
> (a) Such activities as are designed to create a compact group or groups hostile to the Party leadership with a view to capture or to break up the Party finally. (Organization of differing opinions with genuine aim of revising Party policies is permitted).
>
> (b) Libelling of the Party, either among members or others, and such expression of opinions and commission of acts as bring the Party into discredit.
>
> (c) Consistent and repeated attacks on members of the Party or a section of Party leadership in order to throw doubt on their *bona fides* and thus isolate them.

In order to check this factionalism the Executive decided:

> (1) That the rule barring admission of members of both groups, *except by special*

permission of the Central Executive, be strictly enforced. (I may point out here that though this rule is expressly laid down and published in the Blue Book, it has not been followed so far by the Provincial Parties at all.)

(2) The Secretaries (of the A.I.C.S.P.) should scrutinize provincial lists and report to the Executive the names of persons who were ineligible but who were *admitted to membership in breach of the rule*. Provincial Secretaries should prepare a list of such members and forward it to the General Secretary by hand or some other safe method.

(3) Provincial Executives should be asked to exercise vigilance and are hereby authorized to take disciplinary action against any member who, there is evidence to show, is doing fraction work in the Party.

These are important and far-reaching decisions and should receive your immediate attention.

The Party in the Trade Union Movement

The Executive reviewed the position of the Party in the T.U.C. In this it had the benefit of the views of certain prominent T.U. members of the Party who were in Delhi to attend the Convention or the Executive of the A.I.T.U.C. The Committee felt that the position was far from satisfactory. After a full discussion the following conclusions were reached:

The Party should have a more clearly defined labour policy and within the T.U.C. it must stand as a homogeneous group. For this it is necessary that Party members should function as a disciplined group carrying out Party decisions. The Party Executive should meet and lay down policy, if possible in consultation with the T.U. fraction of the Party, before T.U. meetings. In the absence of an Executive meeting, the Party fraction should meet and take decisions.

It was also decided that a more definite T.U. policy be formulated and placed before the next Executive.

A Left Bloc within the Congress

Enquiries have been made as to the policy to be followed with regard to formation of what is termed a 'left bloc' in the Congress. The Executive discussed this question and decided that it would be inadvisable to give an organizational shape to any such bloc. Blocs form within the Congress on specific questions and are large or small depending upon the nature of the question. Any attempt to circumscribe this process by forming an organization with a definite constitution and programme would only retard this process and the growth of the left movement.

Last Circulars

Finally I wish to say that many Provincial Secretaries have not sent yet the information I had asked for in my first circular regarding organizational matters. If you have not already sent this information, will you please do so at your earliest convenience?

The Congress Socialist

I should also like to know what definite steps you have taken to secure subscribers for the *Congress Socialist.* You will recall that I had recommended that every member of the Provincial Executive should enrol at least ten subscribers. I have got subscription forms printed and bound in books of ten forms each. Please let me know how many books you require. You will not require these books if you have already been supplied with them by the Bombay office.

Yours fraternally,
Jayaprakash Narayan
General Secretary

37. Reply to the Royists, 9 August 1937[1]

When the Congress Socialist Party was formed in 1934, the Roy group offered neither opposition to it nor any vital criticism. At the Bombay Conference of the Party, their whole anxiety was concentrated on putting the Constituent Assembly in the forefront of the Party's programme; and as the founders of the Party were one with them on this issue, this was readily done.

For a considerable period of time, many members of the Roy group took a prominent part in the activities of the Party and held leading positions in it. In course of time every known member of the group, with rare exceptions, was absorbed into the Party. Thus the Party was able to fulfil a substantial part of its task of bringing about socialist unity in the country.

During this period there was only one instance in which the Royists expressed their difference with the Party line; and that was in connection with the Party's task within the Congress. This task as described in the Plan

[1] *Brahmanand Papers* (NMML). The above statement was drafted by J.P. and adopted by the National Executive of the C.S.P. at its meeting at Patna on 9 August 1937.

of action was to secure the acceptance by the Congress of "the object and programme of the Party" although in practice only anti-Imperialist issues were raised by us. Leading members of the Party soon realized the need for a change on this point. Royist criticism played a part in strengthening this view. Accordingly the National Executive adopted a thesis in which it made clear that the task of the Party was not to convert the Congress into a socialist body but into a more consistent and real anti-Imperialist organization. This thesis was subsequently endorsed by the Meerut Conference [1936] of the Party. This instance illustrates the internal democracy that has always existed in the Party and also demonstrates how it was possible through a democratic process to influence its decisions and policies.

It is necessary to mention here that some time before the Meerut Conference an alleged Royist circular was discovered in which members of the group were exhorted to attempt to liquidate the C.S.P. This circular was subsequently repudiated by the chief spokesmen of the group who assured the Party that it was a spurious document and did not represent the policy of the group, which was definitely to develop and strengthen the C.S.P. members of that group assured the Party of their loyalty and their readiness to tow its line.

This was the position till the time Mr. Roy was released.[2] The Roy group had been partially absorbed into the Party.

After Mr. Roy's release, the General Secretary met him at Allahabad [1936] and discussed the Party in all its aspects. At the end of the discussion Mr. Roy categorically stated that he agreed with all that we had done—though he was sceptical about our relations with the Red group—and wanted himself to be considered as one of us. He even discussed his joining the Party.

During the course of the discussion, Mr. Roy had raised two points of criticism: (1) whether it was desirable for a socialist party to exist openly within the Congress; (2) whether an open socialist party was not likely to degenerate in India into a reformist party. On both these points the Party's position was explained to him and the impression gathered by the General Secretary was that it satisfied him.

After Mr. Roy went to Bombay he issued certain statements and made certain remarks in his speeches which appeared as veiled attacks on the C.S.P. But when the General Secretary saw him at Bombay after the Faizpur Congress [1936] and drew his attention to the misunderstanding created by his remarks, he said that he stood by every word that he had said at Allahabad. When questioned specifically about the conduct of the Royist members of the Party, he gave a definite assurance that they would loyally carry out the

[2] M.N. Roy was released on 20 November 1936.

Party's policies. It is also necessary to recall here that at the Faizpur Conference [1936] of the Party the Royist delegates had voted unanimously for the Faizpur Thesis, which described the nature and task of the Party. It is also necessary to remember that this was done with Mr. Roy's implicit concurrence for he was present all through at Faizpur and was in constant touch with all that was happening at the Conference.

In view of such a background, it was with a great shock that the Executive learnt at Delhi that Mr. Roy had gathered his camp followers and issued instructions to disrupt and break up the C.S.P. and that a scheme had been evolved for the purpose. The scheme was that the Royists were to resign from the Party in such a spectacular and public manner and at such suitable intervals as to give the impression that the C.S.P. was gradually breaking up. This scheme has already been put into practice as the public knows, though the process has not yet ended as there are still a few Royists left in the Party. As a matter of fact, Mr. Roy's agents have even now been found to be attempting to secure admission into the Party of such members who would later on resign at their call. No doubt, in course of time, we shall hear of some more resignations and read more statements.

Apart from these stage-managed resignations, Mr. Roy has also been carrying on a crusade against the Party through his weekly, *Independent India*,[3] and through his speeches and statements.

The reasons for the attitude taken up by Mr. Roy towards the Party are best known to him. The withdrawal of the Royists from the Party will not do it any harm, for their members were small and they had practically no influence over the Congress. However, Mr. Roy will be held responsible for one major consequence; the disruption of the process of Left unity which the Party had initiated and successfully carried out so far. At the time Mr. Roy launched his secretly hatched offensive against the Party, it had come to be considered as the only focal point of socialist unity and the only effective Left leadership. By trying to destroy this focal point Mr. Roy is proving himself an enemy of the Left and of the radical forces in the country.

The C.S.P. contains the most conscious elements in the national movement. Most of its active members are active Congress workers and hold responsible positions in the Congress. It constitutes the only link between the working class and the national movement. It has already made its impress on the course of that movement. It is the first socialist party of India exercising such considerable influence over the Congress and the peasant and labour organizations. To attempt to disrupt such a party, notwithstanding that such an attempt must fail, is a great disservice to the cause of the masses and a blow to both the national and socialist movements.

[3] *Independent India*, an English weekly started in Bombay in 1937 by M.N. Roy who was also its Editor. It was renamed *Radical Humanist* in 1949.

This attempt becomes still the more reprehensible when it is recalled that the C.S.P. has always been a democratically functioning body; it has never tried to be a coterie or caucus. It willingly admitted Royists into it and established friendly relations with the Red group. Its policies were democratically settled.

Mr. Roy has not only set himself up against the C.S.P. but has gone further and repudiated practically every programme and slogan of the Left nationalists: his approval of office-acceptance, his opposition to collective representation, his discouragement of the peasant movement, and his description of the Zamindari evil as a remote problem. In short, Mr. Roy is endeavouring not only to discredit the leadership of the Left, but to disrupt the Left movement itself. In recent months, nothing has proved a stronger weapon in the hands of the Right than the unfortunate statements of Mr. Roy.

Mr. Roy in his statements has made all manner of criticisms and has often descended to personal attacks. Two of these, however, judging from their constant repetition and the emphasis laid on them, seem to be important from Mr. Roy's point of view.

Mr. Roy says that there should be no socialist party within the Congress. This he sometimes implies to say that there should be no party within the Congress. What Mr. Roy really means is that there should be only secret parties and caucuses, preferably turning around select individuals and not open parties. For, what Mr. Roy is really attempting to do is to organize a secret party that will work within the Congress under his leadership. Our fault is that we do not deign to hide our identity and sail under false colours, but rather take the Congress and the public into confidence and carry on our work openly and above-board. It is for the public to judge if this is not a more straightforward method of work and one which is more suited to the genius of the Congress and of our people.

Mr. Roy's arguments against the existence of a socialist party within the Congress may be considered at some length. He says in brief that Socialism is not the issue of the moment; that the label of Socialism will stand in the way of the radicalization of the Congress; that socialist leadership of the national movement is a fantastic idea; that by remaining within the Congress, a socialist party will suffer a great deal on account of the discipline of the larger body. At the same time, he does not deny that propaganda for Socialism is necessary.

That Socialism is not the issue of the moment might mean various things. It might mean that there should be no talk of Socialism and no socialist propaganda. Obviously Mr. Roy does not mean that.

In fact Mr. Roy says that socialist propaganda is essential. If that is so, can it not be done better by an openly functioning socialist party? Can it be denied that in little over three years the C.S.P. has done more to popularize Socialism that any other party or individual had done before? If socialist propaganda be necessary, there cannot be a better way of doing it than through a party like the C.S.P.

Then, in what other sense is Socialism not the issue if socialist propaganda is necessary? It is not an issue in the sense that the immediate task is the overthrow of imperialism and not establishment of Socialism. This is an obvious and patent fact and has indeed been an axiomatic thought with us, as it must be with all Marxists. The question is, what follows from this? Does it mean that Socialism and socialist technique and science and socialists have as such no definite role to play in the overthrow of Imperialism and the establishment of Swaraj? Mr. Roy may believe that they have no such role. But we as Marxists are convinced that socialists and more particularly a socialist party—for it is ridiculous to imagine that socialists can conceive of political action in terms of individual action—have a decisive role to play in the national movement. And it can play that role only when it is intimately connected with that movement. The whole conscious directive of the movement must emanate from such a party. Thus while Socialism is not the immediate objective, a socialist party is an immediate necessity and has an immediate task to perform. The question again is whether this task is to be performed by an openly functioning Congress Socialist Party or a secret caucus under the dominance of Mr. Roy? It is obvious that the existence of the C.S.P. clashes with the ambitions of Mr. Roy and Marxism is strained to provide him with specious ideological justifications.

As for the label of Socialism creating a bias in the minds of nationalists and therefore standing in the way of radicalization of the Congress, the argument is as groundless as any other. The label of socialist can attach to a person as much by virtue of his being a member of a socialist party as by his expressing socialist views or by his describing himself as a socialist. The label 'socialist' attaches as much to Pandit Jawaharlal as to Acharya Narendra Deva. If one is to avoid the label, it follows that in public he must not speak of Socialism. Can a genuine socialist do that? Even Mr. Roy takes care to declare on every occasion that he is a communist. Does not therefore a label get attached to him? We believe that it is not by hiding our identity but by proclaiming it and at the same time by popularizing Socialism that we shall serve our cause. The work of the C.S.P. has produced an universal impression today that socialism is synonymous with freedom from exploitation and hunger. The socialist label, far from being offensive, has become synonymous with "friend of the poor and downtrodden".

As for the other criticism, Mr. Roy says that an open socialist party in India must become a reformist party. Mr. Roy forgets, first of all, that there is no suitable soil in India for reformism. Reformism can grow only when the ruling class is in a position to make major concessions to the masses. In India the condition of the masses is such and the conditions of Imperialist exploitation are such that they do not leave much room for reformism. That does not mean that reformism is impossible in India. There are reformist organizations here too. But no political party in touch with the masses and with their struggle for freedom can thrive on reformism.

The C.S.P. is an open party. Does it follow that only for that reason it will become reformist? The Congress is an open organization. Is it therefore reformist? The C.S.P. is the vanguard of the nationalist Left. Is it possible for it to maintain that position and go reformist? The C.S.P. has shown in the past that it will not curb its activities for the sake of avoiding the law. It is ceaselessly engaged in preparing the masses for direct action. There is no reason why the opportunities for open work should be given up, and as experience has shown, these opportunities are quite considerable. It is romanticism to preach that all socialist work in the country will be done underground.

Mr. Roy sometimes says that since the C.S.P. is "within" the Congress it is bound by its discipline and it is not good for a socialist party to suffer from that limitation. There are several flaws in this argument. First of all, his conception of being "within" the Congress is incorrect. The C.S.P. is an independent political party and has no connection as such with the Congress. All its members, however, are Congressmen and are bound by its discipline. This is the only limitation the Party suffers from and in the present situation it is an inescapable and even desirable limitation.

That is a limitation from which Mr. Roy, no matter to what independent organization he belongs to, becomes subject to Congress discipline once he enters it and begins to take part in its activities. The limitations from which the C.S.P. suffers are necessary in the present stage of our struggle and are wholesome both for the national and socialist movements.

38. Speech at the Kisan Bandobast (Land Settlement) Conference, Amritsar, 30 September 1937[1]

It must be evident to anybody who visits the Punjab even for a short time that the people of this province were not lacking in courage or patriotism. In respect of self-sacrifice and suffering, Punjab will rank with the foremost provinces in India. Yet, it was a matter of surprise that the mass movement in this province was so backward.

It is high time now that the people of this province realized that their interests and problems cannot be divided on a communal basis. All

[1] *Tribune*, 1 October 1937.

agriculturists, for instance, irrespective of whether they are Hindus, Muslim or Sikhs, have identical interests and identical problems. Those people who divide them on a communal basis are traitors to their real interests. They divide you, so that they may continue to exploit and rule over you, for the communal leaders belong to the exploiting classes.

In short, you must once for all realize that communal divisions and quarrels are the road to ruin for you, and are the invention of your exploiters and enemies. Your interests are divided on class, rather than on communal basis. Therefore, the first thing that you have to do is to develop and strengthen your class organization irrespective of communal considerations. Form your Kisan Committees, join them in your lakhs and fight for your demands.

But, friends do not go away with the impression that you will achieve your object and your conditions will improve to the extent you desire only by your forming Kisan Committees and fighting for your demands. You have to fight for political freedom and power. Therefore, along with your Kisan Committees you must also form Congress Committees. You must join and strengthen the Congress.

Now, in a few words I would like to tell you that you should remember that the object of the Congress is to achieve complete independence for India. Even complete independence will not solve your problems. Along with political freedom we must also fight for economic freedom. We must from today take care that the Swaraj that we shall achieve will be our Swaraj, that is, Swaraj of the peasants and workers of India.

39. Extract of Letter to Jawaharlal Nehru [before 7 October 1937][1]

.... From Wardha I had gone for a few hours to Nagpur. There Dwarkaprasad Misra[2] and P.Y. Deshpande[3] showed me a scheme of Local Self-government reform which impressed me very much. In the districts the District Magistrate and Superintendent of Police are still immensely powerful. They

[1] *Linlithgow Collection*, Mss. Eur. F.125/113, India Office Library and Records. Cited in a letter from Hyde Gowan (Governor of C.P. and Berar) to Linlithgow (Viceroy of India), 7 October 1937.

[2] Dwarka Prasad Mishra (1901-88); participated in the national movement and jailed; member, Indian Legislative Assembly, 1927-30; started *Lokmat*, a Hindi daily, 1930, and *Sarathi*, a Hindi weekly, 1942; Minister for Local Self-Government, C.P. and Berar, 1937-9; Home Minister, Madhya Pradesh, 1946-50; resigned from the Congress, 1951; joined the Socialist Party, 1952; rejoined the Congress, 1955; Vice-Chancellor, Saugar University, 1956-62; Chief Minister, Madhya Pradesh, 1963-7; publications include *Krishnayana*, and *Living an Era* (2 vols.).

[3] For biographical note on P.Y. Deshpande see *JPSW*, Volume One, p. 98.

are the steel frame of the foreign power. That frame must be broken, and local administration brought under proper [popular] control. The Central Provinces scheme follows mainly the British country [county] system. In it the President of the District Board is the highest authority for the district and the District Magistrate is his Chief Secretary.

[J.P.]

40. Statement to Press on Impressions of Andhra Visit, 24 October 1937[1]

I have spent nearly a week in Andhra Desa and expect to come back soon for a longer tour. I have chiefly been concerned in this tour with organizational affairs of the Andhra Congress Socialist Party. I am going away full of hope in the future of the Party in the Province.

There are some members of the Party who, due to certain differences, had ceased to take active interest in the Party. I am glad to say that they have promised fullest co-operation. Due to their differences, these members had so far been indifferent to enrolment of Party members. Therefore, at their request, I have allowed them two weeks' time for enrolment. I have authorized Mr. Annapurnaih[2] to organize the next conference of the Andhra Party in co-operation with the Reception Committee.

[1] *Hindu*, 27 October 1937.

[2] M. Annapurnaih (1898-1953); journalist; first Editor of the *Congress*, a Telegu weekly started in 1921; jailed several times for participating in the national movement; associated with the Forward Bloc and youth movement in Andhra.

41. Lecture on the 'Future of the National Movement in India', 26 October 1937[1]

Nationalism was not one and the same thing for all countries and for all times. It had different meanings in different countries and in different times. Taking the present, for instance, the concept of Nationalism in India was not the same as in America and England. Nationalism in England meant the defence of the present capitalistic order of society in which peasants and workers had no place. The last World War was fought by England not

[1] Adapted from a report of the lecture at Albert Hall, Calcutta, published in the *Amrita Bazar Patrika*, 27 October 1937.

for the toiling masses but for the big capitalists and financiers. If anybody was profited by this war it was the British financiers and not the working classes who mainly were the cannon-fodder in the last War. The same was the case with America and other capitalistic states. In these countries Nationalism meant the defence of the upper classes at the cost of the upper classes of society. Italian Nationalism meant the defence of Fascism which was another name for all that was undemocratic. Suppression of freedom of speech, suppression of freedom of thought, suppression of civil liberties, suppression of all that was considered sacred in an ordered society. German Nationalism meant defence of the Fascist Fatherland. Nationalism in Russia meant defence of the Soviet Fatherland. So Nationalism was not one and the same thing in all countries.

As for India, the national movement began in this country in 1885, i.e. in the year in which the Indian National Congress was founded. Seventy-two gentlemen started the National Congress at Poona which directed the national movement. It began with the expression of loyalty to the British Throne and in the old days it demanded of the Government of the country things like holding of the I.C.S. examination in India, which at that time used to be held exclusively in England. But with the change of time, the ideal and objective of national movement also changed and before the Lahore Congress in 1929, its whole political aspiration centred on the attainment of Dominion Status for India. At the Lahore Congress, Indian Nationalism took one more forward step and now it stood for complete Independence.

Such was our national demoralization that it took fifty years for us to realize that we wanted to be free; we wanted to be independent. However, it showed one thing, and it was this that the evolution of Nationalism went on also in this country with the inevitable march of time.

Now the question is whether India would have her desideratum, if she won independence. Would that bring real Swaraj to the country? Would that solve all her problems, the problem of poverty, the problem of exploitation and unemployment which were the real driving forces of her Nationalism? It might bring Swaraj to the Princes, to the Capitalists but not to the teeming millions of her children. The Congress stands for all, for masses as well as for classes. So Nationalism as sponsored by the Congress cannot bring Swaraj to the masses. There lies the difference between the Congress and the Congress Socialist Party. The latter wants the development of the national movement on economic basis. In its conception the national movement should give primacy to the masses. This can alone bring real Swaraj to the people and for the people, evolving an order of society which will be run in the interest of the people at large and not in the interest of a blessed few.

42. Proposed Amendment to A.I.C.C. Resolution, 29 October 1937[1]

Sir

I wish to move the following amendment to the Resolution on Ratification of the Working Committee's decision:

Add at the end of the Resolution:

"In view, however, of the experience of the working out of the policy so decided on, the A.I.C.C. feels that the need has arisen to consider the results of that decision.

In this connection, the Committee while welcoming the steps taken by Congress Cabinets in the direction of the release of political prisoners and detenus, notes with regret that there are still several political prisoners in provinces where Congress Cabinets exist and that in some cases steps have not yet been taken to repeal repressive laws, even those which authorize detention without trial.

The Committee also regrets the fact that certain Congress Cabinets have chosen to take action under such repressive provisions of law as Section 124-A of the Indian Penal Code and Section 144 of the Criminal Procedure Code.

The A.I.C.C. calls for the complete implementation of the Congress Election Manifesto in this connection by the immediate and unconditional release of all political prisoners, the withdrawal of prosecutions for political activities and the taking of immediate steps for the repeal of all repressive laws.

The Committee is of opinion that if the objects of strengthening the national movement and wrecking the Constitution for which the policy of office acceptance was adopted are to be achieved, there must be no further delay in the taking of steps to carry out the election programme of the Congress not only with regard to civil liberties but also to the agrarian and other problems."

Jayaprakash Narayan

[1] *AICC Papers* (NMML). J.P. wanted to move these paragraphs as amendment to the resolution on ratification of the Congress Working Committee's decision permitting acceptance of offices by Congressmen at the A.I.C.C. meeting at Calcutta on 29 October 1937. The amendment was, however, ruled out of order by Jawaharlal Nehru who was presiding over the A.I.C.C. meeting. See Appendix 5 for text of the Working Committee's resolution on office acceptance.

43. Speech at Public Meeting, Guntur, 13 November 1937[1]

The Congress has, no doubt, adopted a comprehensive programme, but it has stopped with declaring that it stands for Purna Swaraj. The Socialists' conception of Purna Swaraj is a Swaraj achieved on an economic foundation. Congressmen today, if Swaraj was to come tomorrow, would prefer to establish it copying the British or American Constitution. But Socialists would insist on a constitution following the principles of the Soviet system, which has succeeded in solving serious economic problems, such as unemployment.

The present programme of the Congress is inadequate. There should be widening of the scope of its activities. The Congress should accept the programme of organizing the peasants and workers and develop their strength to achieve political and economic freedom. The Congress Ministries have begun to forget the purpose for which they had accepted offices. They seem to think that Swaraj can be achieved through working the constitution. This is a very dangerous tendency.

There are many people who say that we should not say anything in criticism of the Congress Ministers' acts. But if we want our Government to succeed, it is necessary that there should be criticism. It must be courteous, of course. After all, our Ministers are human beings, apt to commit mistakes. It is our duty to point out those mistakes. In your own province there are certain things happening which are contrary to the declared policy of the Congress.

One important item of our programme is the restoration of civil liberty. This the Ministry has not achieved. There are still police reporters here. I think the first thing you should do is to agitate for the discontinuation of this practice. I am told that there are a number of Congress workers who are even now being followed by the police.

I am not quite sure how long these Congress Ministries will last. I have a feeling that they will not last very long. It is up to us, therefore, to utilize this occasion and strengthen ourselves in every possible way.

One thing I would like being done is to amend the Local Self-Government Act so as to vest in the local bodies autonomous powers concerning the whole district. I would rather submit to a corrupt Local Board Administration, which I can ultimately hope to rectify, than tolerate the rule of a District Magistrate whose authority now I cannot wrench.

[1] Adapted from a report of the speech published in the *Hindu*, 15 November 1937.

44. Speech at Public Meeting, Royapettah, Madras, 23 November 1937[1]

The Congress Socialist Party has now become a powerful organization exercising considerable influence over the development of the national struggle in this country. In view of the great confusion and misunderstanding that appear to prevail as to the intentions of Congress Socialists, I want to point out that the Party grew out of the Congress movement, out of the very heart of the national struggle. Its main object is to reorganize the national struggle so that it may rise to higher levels and reach its goal and objective speedily.

There is a misconception that nationalism and Socialism are incompatible. The concept of nationalism varies from country to country and time to time. Indian nationalism has evolved through a very painful and torturous process. Today it is centred on complete independence.

The fundamental problems are hunger, poverty and unemployment and there is no getting away from Socialism as it is the only solution for these. That is the goal to which the national movement must progress in India. What else can be the trend of the Karachi resolution, if not in the direction of Socialism? Socialists feel that mere political Swaraj will not solve the problems of hunger, poverty and unemployment. In many countries which enjoy Swaraj, the problems remain unsolved. The Swaraj that Socialists visualize is a Swaraj of the people wherein, besides adult franchise and political power, they would also have the economic power transferred to them, and wherein the productive resources and wealth of the country would remain with the nation and not under the control of a small group of profit-makers. The concept of Purna Swaraj has, therefore, to be clarified so that people may know whither they are going. If the Congress wishes the masses to come to it, it must speak their language, present the national struggle in terms of their own daily life and immediate demands. Otherwise, the masses will not be attracted to the Congress to the extent to which it may desire. And if the people are to join the Congress and share in the fight, they must know what they are fighting for. It will not be fair to ask them to join the fight without telling them what the fight is for. Should they find that the fight would lead to their own emancipation their attitude towards the national struggle will change in its favour. Further, the upper classes are organized and conscious of what they want. Unless the masses are given the chance of sharing the struggle with eyes open, there will be grave danger of their interests being betrayed. Everybody now talks of a Constituent Assembly to decide India's future. As one who believes strongly in that idea, and who

[1] Adapted from a report of the speech published in the *Hindu*, 24 November 1937.

also believes that India will get independence in less than five years, considers it essential that Congressmen should have a clear idea as to what they want. Also, the average citizen should be enabled to know what sort of Government will be devised and what the different solutions for our problems are, if he is at all to be enabled to decide for one or other of these.

Some confusion has arisen as to the attitude of the Congress Socialists towards the present programme of the Congress. The Congress has launched upon a delicate experiment and Congress Socialists do not wish, in the least, to cause any embarrassment to Congress Governments in carrying it out. The only motive that Socialists are actuated by is that this experiment should succeed. The Congress having decided on a parliamentary programme and office acceptance, every Congressman was in duty bound to abide by the decision and help to work it. There seems, however, to be some attempt in some quarters to create the illusion that this constitutional method will enable the Congress to achieve its goal of independence. Such illusion, we must fight against. The Congress has launched on the present programme to wreck the constitution and develop strength among the people and strengthen the Congress so that, on some future occasion, they may be able to put up an effective fight. The programme means, if anything, preparation for a struggle. Wherever this objective is overlooked, it is the duty of Congressmen to point out the deviation. For discharging this duty, no one should be misunderstood. Of the Congress-governed provinces in India, Madras seems to be the one where there is most misunderstanding in the matter. It may be that there were certain instances where some persons belonging to the C.S.P. went beyond the bounds of propriety, but it is not right to judge the attitude of a whole party by such isolated instances. Criticism should not be taken for abuse. I have paid compliments and praise where these were due; for instance, the repeal of the Moplah Outrages Act was one of the boldest acts of the Congress Government of Madras. But a Congressman should not expect always praise from fellow Congressmen over carrying out a policy he is expected to. Where mistakes occur, Congressmen should offer, and those in office should accept, criticisms especially when they are friendly. Certain things had happened which disturbed me profoundly and if I had pointed this out it was because I felt it my duty to do so as a Congressman. Gandhiji has stated that criticism is the ozone of public life. Certain kinds of criticism can surely be embarrassing, but the criticism I stand for is that which will strengthen and not weaken the hands of the Congress Governments. But how can one help pointing out that Congressmen, who were pledged to the removal of all repressive laws, had no justification for resorting to the sedition law and the Criminal Law Amendment Act in dealing with political speeches and strikes? I had been followed by policemen and my speeches had been taken down by police shorthand writers everywhere.

A number of Congressmen are still being shadowed by policemen. I fail to understand how Congress Governments could sanction prosecutions under section 124-A, considering that the whole Congress is pledged to independence—sedition per se. The question of violence and non-violence is brought in and the matter has suddenly become a very vexed one, but I do not think that there has been any sudden burst of violence since the advent of the Congress to power. The tendency, on the other hand, seems to be towards non-violence, the latest instance being the statement of the 'terrorist' prisoners and detenus of Bengal. Some responsible people also seem to say that Socialists have no other work but that of fomenting conflicts and strikes. If there are more strikes today than before, the reason is not that the Socialists are actively engaged in fomenting trouble, but that conditions are such that these cannot be helped as labourers are anxious to secure early redress of their grievances and they have a feeling that now something can be done for them.

Congress Socialists only wish to see that the Congress programme succeeds. They want to strengthen the hands of the Congress and Congress Governments. If there is criticism, it is there because they feel that in carrying out the Congress programme, certain mistakes have been committed and when mistakes are committed, these have to be pointed out for being corrected. Mass agitations are intended to strengthen the hands of the Congress Ministers. Without such sanction, Congress Ministers may not be able to contend against the powerful influence of vested interests in carrying out the Congress programme. To sit quiet will be to devitalize the Congress programme and in the end the whole work would degenerate into nothing else than constitutionalism, which we have to avoid. The forces that Congress Ministries have to contend with in undertaking ameliorative measures in favour of the poor are illustrated in the case of the Tenancy Legislation proposals in Bihar and the Moratorium proposals in Madras. Such instances are bound to multiply unless the Ministers are enabled, by means of mass organization and agitation, to say to the vested interests that they will be playing with fire if they try to prevent such measures.

It was meaningless for any Congressman to say that the civil service and the police and other officers are friends of the people. Today they may be under Congress Ministers, but tomorrow, when Congressmen give up office, those very officers might arrest and convict them. Congressmen while in office should do their work bearing in mind that a struggle will surely ensue when they leave office, which will be not a long way off. They should take every opportunity while in office to destroy the hold of the steel frame over the lives of the people, to destroy its power to the extent possible and to weaken it. One of the methods I would suggest in this behalf is that the District Board should be made the highest authority in the district and the

District Magistrate reduced to the position of say the Chief Secretary of the District Board. Local bodies should be given control over the local police services. I want popular authority to be developed along with the authority of the administration, and that authority being given as much power as possible. Public servants should be brought under popular control not only exercised through the provincial government but also through local boards. This programme cannot be carried on without mass agitation.

Congress Socialists have not deviated from the path I have indicated. If they had done so, I would offer apologies and also give an assurance that they would not do so again. The feeling of Left and Right and the talk of purging the Congress of some men are all disturbing and painful; this is not the time for such talk. Should the time of testing come, there would be an automatic purge. In the meantime, let no unnecessary confusion and misunderstanding be created on the basis of isolated acts here and there.

There is nothing exotic in the idea of Socialism. I would contend that even if it was exotic, they need not reject it on that ground. Socialism came into existence along with the evils that followed Capitalism—unemployment and poverty. As far as I could understand, Socialism is not opposed to the genius of India. Hinduism and Islam encouraged the idea of co-operative and collective life.

45. Statement on the Ban by some District Congress Committees on Kisan activities of Swami Sahajanand Saraswati, 11 December 1937[1]

I returned here this morning after a long period of absence. I am surprised and pained to find that an unfortunate gulf has widened between the Congress and the Kisan movement. Since the birth of the Kisan Sabha, there has been no dearth of dismal prophets who made no secret of their misgivings. The facts, however, have invariably gone against these gentlemen. The Kisan Sabha, throughout the period of its existence, kept up an admirable united front with the Congress. A fine instance of this was the role of the Kisan Sabha during the last General Election.

In the past it was only the ostrich-politicians who refused to see what was going on around them and were in mortal fear of differences of opinion and who persisted in their prejudices against the Kisan Sabha. Fortunately for the province the main body of political workers behind those differences and clash of ideas are the very life-blood of any living organization and

[1] *Amrita Bazar Patrika*, 13 December 1937. Statement issued at Patna on his return from a long tour of Madras.

movement. Every time that the Congress took a forward step in the course of its history, it was due to such clash and conflict. Such were the cases when there was a conflict between extremists and liberals, direct actionists and constitutionalists, dominion-status-walas and those who stood for complete independence.

I understand certain Congress Committees in the province have placed a ban on the movements of Swami Sahajanand Saraswati. Swamijee, apart from being the very life of the Kisan movement, is one of the topmost Congress leaders of the Province and a member of the Executive Committee of the P.C.C. It is a most astounding procedure for any Congress Committee to forbid such a man from carrying on his activities. I am afraid such action is not likely to raise the prestige of the Congress, nor is it in consonance with its high ideals.

As far as the gulf between the Congress and the Kisan Sabha is concerned, I have not the least doubt that no time should be lost in bridging that gulf. The policy and attitude of the Kisan Sabha towards the Congress has been declared from time to time. Only a month ago the Council of the Kisan Sabha reiterated its attitude in a resolution[2] which was published in the press. The Sabha, I have no doubt, still stands by that resolution. I fail to understand what objection can any Congressman have to the policy as laid down in that resolution.

There has been a lot of criticism of the Government agrarian policy from the platform of the Kisan Sabha. I do not know what objection there can be to such criticism. I do not wish to uphold criticism that is hostile and destructive. I strongly believe however that friendly and constructive criticism is essential for the working of the Parliamentary programme of the Congress. The Congress President has upheld the right of criticism and Mahatma Gandhi has declared that criticism is the "ozone of public life". Criticism alone will enable the Government to keep in touch with public opinion and thus guide them in their work.

There has also been in Bihar a vigorous peasant agitation going on. There are some people to whom such agitation might appear as causing an embarrassment to the Government. This is the view of those who want to divorce parliamentary work from mass action and thus emasculate it. It is not appreciated, in spite of obvious facts to the contrary, that there are classes in the country which are inimical to the interest of the masses and who will place every obstacle in the way of the Government if it wishes to do anything for the masses. We have seen how in our province the big Zamindars went to the length of threatening Satyagraha against the Government. In face of

[2] Refers to the resolution passed by the All India Kisan Council at its meeting on 27-8 October 1937 at Calcutta reiterating its faith in the Congress.

these opposition and mobilization of the vested interests the Government would find itself helpless, if it wishes to give any real benefit to the masses unless there was a vigorous mass agitation in the province. It is peasant rallies like those which Patna has already witnessed that would strengthen the hands of the Congress Government. It is utter short-sightedness to decry or suppress agitation. This is not "agitation against ourselves" but agitation for ourselves. Mass agitation outside is a part of the constitutional programme. If there is a link maintained between the two, agitation will not weaken the Congress, it will only strengthen it.

I am aware that I am writing without concrete facts before me. I felt, however, that it was necessary to re-state those principles. It is possible that in applying them mistakes have been committed. But mistakes can be corrected by both sides. I wish only to issue a warning that it will be suicidal if we develop at this juncture a Hitlerite mentality or if we were too hasty or rash in our criticism and action. We cannot afford to disrupt our ranks at this or any stage. Wisdom requires that in spite of differences of opinion we march together. If any attempt is made to suppress criticism or difference of opinion or the struggle and agitation of the masses we are sure to lead to disruption. On the other hand I have not the least doubt that agitation and criticism should be such that they strengthen the freedom struggle and its organized expression—the Indian National Congress.

46. Statement regarding the Decision of Bihar P.C.C. on Kisan Sabha, 18 December 1937[1]

I consider the decision of the Working Committee of the Bihar Provincial Congress Committee on the Kisan Sabha[2] as one of the Himalayan blunders of the Congress. The decision is fraught with much mischief and it gives a handle to those in the Congress who do not approve of radical movements and ideas and who are today in a majority in this province, to disrupt the ranks of the Congress by preventing Congressmen from participating in the activities of the Kisan Sabha which has always been a bulwark of support to the Congress.

The action of the Working Committee in Bihar seems to be a part of a

[1] *Amrita Bazar Patrika*, 20 December 1937. Statement to Press at Patna.

[2] The Working Committee of the Bihar Provincial Congress Committee at its meeting at Patna on 14 December 1937 had endorsed the resolutions passed by the Champaran, Monghyr and Saran District Congress Committees, asking Congressmen not to participate in the meetings of the Bihar Provincial Kisan Sabha, keeping in view the fact that the propaganda carried by the Kisan Sabha, including attacks on the principle of non-violence, had created a 'poisonous atmosphere' in the province. See Appendix 6 for text of the resolution.

nation-wide offensive that the Right-wing leaders of the Congress have launched upon the growing Left. The Right-wing wants to divorce parliamentary activity from mass agitation and struggle. The Left is proving an obstacle. Hence this drive in the name of non-violence.

It is difficult to visualize the further development of this policy in Bihar. But the Kisan Sabha and the entire Left in the province is determinedly going to follow the policy of the united front. Even where outlawed, the Kisan Sabha has declared that it will continue to support the Congress. I have no doubt that this policy is bound to succeed and the disruptive tactics of the Right will fail in the end and will have to be given up. From bitter experience in other countries, notably in China, [we can see] how a conflict between these two sections essentially strengthens our Imperialist enemies and must be avoided at all cost.

The Bihar Kisan Sabha or for that matter the All India Kisan Committee and the various other Kisan Sabhas in general can safely claim some of the most responsible Congressmen among their workers and office-bearers whose devotion to the Congress and their contribution to the anti-Imperialist struggle is well known. Swami Sahajanand, apart from being a member of the All India Congress Committee, is an anti-Imperialist fighter of the first rank and it would be a tragedy if the Bihar Congress loses the sympathies of the Bihar Kisan Sabha. Who does not know that our Kisan Sabha workers have won the last general election for the Congress and are asking for nothing more than the fulfilment of the Congress Agrarian Programme? Under such circumstances Congressmen in every province should think twice before antagonizing the Kisan Sabha workers. If they do, the responsibility will be theirs. We on our part have decided to strengthen the cause of the Congress by building up strong and independent peasant organizations. Without Kisan Sabhas the Congress will collapse like so many other "National" organizations in face of the onslaughts of Imperialism or, worse still, compromise with our enemies.

47. Left Wing and Congress Elections: A Rejoinder to the *Searchlight*, 4 January 1938[1]

I am writing to protest against your unfair attack on the "left wing" and the Congress Socialists in your issues of December 31 and January 1. I have become used to violent and vulgar abuse from you and have reconciled myself to looking upon it as one of the inevitable experiences of public life in Bihar. I have never protested against it.

[1] *Searchlight*, 4 January 1938.

Your notes on "Left Wingers and Congress Elections" and "The Socialist Ways" are so shocking that I feel compelled to raise my voice in protest. You have hit upon the truth that rowdyism is the essence of left wing philosophy. I congratulate you upon this discovery, which I think will rank well with the best opinions on the subject of blue-blooded imperialists and diehard enemies of India and progress. I cannot, however, congratulate you on the regard you have shown for truth and fair dealing.

The way you have dealt with the Sheikhpura affair has taken my breath away. You make out as if the man who was beaten at Sheikhpura suffered his injuries because he protested against Babu Singheshwari Prasad being described as an agent of the Zamindars. There is just a contrary report of this published in some other local papers. The enquiries that I have been able to make into the incident also reveal a contrary state of affairs. It seems that the old man was beaten by Singheshwari Babu's voters because he insisted on voting for Shri Rambriksh Benipuri[2] and would not be intimidated into voting for his rival. The poor man was beaten rather badly. Soon after he was taken in a car to the Sadaquat Ashram[3] by Benipuriji and Mr. [S.H.] Razi. Mathura Babu,[4] on hearing the report of the disturbance and seeing the injuries, rightly postponed the election.

This, Sir, if I were inclined to use your phraseology and political logic, I would describe as right wing rowdyism. Yet nothing is farther from my mind than the thought that the right wing believes in rowdyism. I should also like to make it clear that I do not suggest that Babu Singheshwari Prasad was in the least responsible for this act of brutality. I have no doubt that he has already rebuked his over enthusiastic friends of Sheikhpura.

Regarding the incident at the Sadaquat Ashram it is true that Shri Mithilesh[5] broke the ballot boxes. But the circumstances in which he did it have been completely misrepresented. It has been made out that he found Benipuriji's position hopeless, so he calmly entered the booth and destroyed the boxes. These, however, do not seem to be the facts, as far as I have been able to get at them; and the thing did not happen, as indeed it could not in

[2] For biographical note on Ramvriksh Benipuri see *JPSW*, Volume One, p. 61.

[3] The Sadaquat Ashram was established by Mazhar-ul-Haque in 1920 at Digha near Patna with the help of students who had left school and college at the call of Mahatma Gandhi. The Ashram became the chief centre of Congress activities in Bihar. It also paved the way for the establishment in 1921 of the Bihar Vidyapith which was located on its campus.

[4] Mathura Prasad (1880-1947); lawyer; gave up practice to join the non-cooperation movement, 1921; participated in the civil disobedience movement and imprisoned; associated with Sadaquat Ashram; Assistant Secretary, Bihar P.C.C. for many years and also its General Secretary for some time; detained during the Quit India movement, 1942-5.

[5] Mithilesh Kumar Singh; labour leader; Secretary, Japla Labour Union; participated in the Quit India movement and arrested, 1942; detained in Hazaribagh Central Jail.

this cold-blooded fashion. What appears to have happened was that Mithileshji found, wrongly or rightly I cannot tell, that a large number of bogus voters were brought by the other party. He protested a number of times, but with no results. Finally, his patience gave way when a man of his own village was being passed off as another voter, and in a fit of anger he entered the booth and wrought his destruction. It was very wrong of him to have done so and he deserves punishment for it. I understand he himself is writing to the Congress authorities explaining his action and offering his apology.

I only wish to add that while we condemn Mithileshji's action we should not drag in the whole left wing or lose sight of the other side of the picture. For you, Sir, he is just a rowdy. But I cannot forget that he is one of those thousands of humble volunteers of the Congress whose silent labour and suffering have contributed not a little to make the Congress what it is.

I am unable to speak of the Samastipur affair, as I do not know anything about it. It is just likely, however, that Pandit Ramnandan Misra[6] has a different story to tell.

If you permit me, Sir, I should like to add a few words about the manner in which some right wingers have behaved in these elections. Persistent reports have reached me that responsible right wing men have been propagating the falsehood that Kisan Sabhaites have been expelled from the Congress. You will find an example of such propaganda in the report of a speech of Thakur Ramanand Singh[7] published in your columns on December 29, in which he is reported to have said that "henceforth (i.e. after the resolution of the Provincial Working Committee) no Congressman could be a Kisan Sabhaite nor a Kisan Sabhaite a Congressman". When his interpretation was challenged, Thakur Saheb is reported to have "asserted that his interpretation was the only correct interpretation as it had the authority of Babu Rajendra Prasad[8] behind it". Rajendra Babu's name has been utilized quite extensively in this manner.

There have been reports of influential men putting pressure on candidates

[6] Ramnandan Mishra (1905-89); member, Bihar P.C.C., 1927-34; participated in the salt satyagraha and imprisoned, 1930-1; member, C.S.P., 1934-47, and Socialist Party, 1947-52; arrested during anti-War propaganda, 1940; participated in the Quit India movement and arrested, 1942; escaped from Hazaribagh Central Jail along with J.P. and others, November 1942; rearrested, 1943, and released, 1946; General Secretary, Hind Kisan Panchayat, Bihar, 1949-52; member, National Executive, Socialist Party, 1949; left politics for spiritual pursuits, 1952; publications include *Jeevan Ke Char Adhyay*, *Socialism, Gandhism and Masani*, *Kisanon Ki Samasyayen*, and *Revolution: Method and Technique*.

[7] Thakur Ramnandan Singh; member, Bihar and Orissa Legislative Council, 1927-9; resigned in 1930; President, Sub-Divisional Congress Committee, Muzaffarpur, 1930; member, Bihar Legislative Assembly, 1937-45 and 1946-51; arrested during the Quit India movement and detained in Motihari Jail, 1942-5.

[8] For biographical note on Rajendra Prasad see *JPSW*, Volume One, p. 112.

to give written undertakings that they would always support Rajendra Babu in the P.C.C., and reports of promises of jobs and positions in the District and local boards and other institutions having been used widely. In Patna I understand a promise was made to voters of a certain locality that free land would be provided to them for their library building. In Patna I also know that the most common propaganda against the left wing candidates was that they had been expelled from the Congress and that they were standing against the Congress. The recent resolution of the Provincial Working Committee has been very skilfully utilized for this purpose. An advocate, who at least should have known better, asked a Congressman of the standing of Sri Manindra Narayan Roy [Manabendra Nath Roy?] if he was for or against the Congress.

A group of uniformed temperance volunteers greeted Benipuriji as an enemy of the Congress and of the country. Violent and vulgar slogans using such language as *gala ghont do* and *udhar deshdrohion ki bharmar hai*, etc., were used by the men of the right wing. And there has been this bogus voting. There was the case of that old man who went to vote for Sarangdhar Babu[9] (doubtless without his knowledge or approval) in Kadam Kuan. His age as entered in the register was 25 and he looked no less than 50. He insisted, however, on being the same person. But when he was asked to sign his name he was thrown off his guard and scribbled out his real name. At the Chaudharitola polling booth no less than half a dozen bogus voters were detected and rejected. Each one of them had gone to vote for the candidate whom you would describe as a right-winger.

I am giving these facts not to denounce the right wing. My purpose is only to show that undesirable things are done by the people on the other side too, and it is not fair play to overlook these facts and to drag the whole left wing through the mud just because some of its adherents have misbehaved.

Now, a few words about your note on socialist ways. I have no information of the expulsion of M. Mazdoor from the Allahabad branch of our Party and am not in a position to comment on it. Here I should only like to point out that the Allahabad branch is one of the best branches of our Party and has in it some of our most responsible members like Doctor Lohia, Ahmed[10]

[9] Sarangdhar Sinha (1901-82); advocate; Fellow, Patna University, 1925-30; participated in the national movement and suffered imprisonment; member, Bihar Legislative Assembly, 1936-51; Parliamentary Secretary for Education and Revenue, Bihar Government, 1937-9; Vice-Chancellor, Patna University, 1949-52; member, Lok Sabha, 1952-7.

[10] Dr. Z.A. Ahmad (1908-99); Secretary, Economic Information Department, A.I.C.C., 1936-7, and U.P.P.C.C., 1937-42; member, National Executive, C.S.P. 1937-40, and Secretariat of Communist Party, U.P., 1943-8; detained at Deoli Detention Camp, 1940-2; Secretary, U.P. Provincial Committee, C.P.I., 1951-6; member, Central Committee, C.P.I., 1951-8, and its Politbureau, 1953-8; General Secretary, All India Kisan Sabha, 1968; member, Rajya Sabha, 1958-62, 1966-78, and 1990-4.

and Ashraf[11] and Messrs. Sajjad Zaheer[12] and Mohanlal Gautam.[13] I cannot believe till I have facts to the contrary that these people will take any action without sufficient grounds.

There are two basic points involved in your note which I should, however, like to elucidate. The first is concerning our relation with Mr. M.N. Roy and his group. This is not the occasion to deal with this question in any detail. I shall touch on only one aspect of it. Mr. M.N. Roy, as you might be aware, holds the view that the Congress Socialist Party should not exist at all. He and his followers have done their best to disrupt and destroy the Party. We are, therefore, naturally careful not to allow any of his men in our Party. We cannot have people whose declared object is to destroy the Party. It is just as if the Congress were to harbour persons whose declared purpose was to break the Congress. I should like to make it clear, however, that once outside the Party we are always ready to work and co-operate with the Royists. If a Royist is expelled from the Party, it is not because we are carrying on a vendetta against Mr. Roy or that we do not allow criticism within our ranks. It only means that we cannot logically keep people in the Party who do not accept its very basis and necessity.

The other point concerns the difference between an organization like the Congress and a socialist party. You seem to believe that in point of discipline and freedom of opinion there should be no difference between them. I suppose you will readily agree that there is a difference in these respects between a body like the Gandhi Seva Sangh[14] and the Congress. The Sangh is a closed circle of persons who owe allegiance to a particular clear-cut ideology and there is no room in it for people who do not agree with it. It is the same with a Socialist Party.

The Congress, on the other hand, is a mass organization of the Indian people comprising all classes and sections of the people and a variety of opinions and views. The only basic agreement required is achievement of

[11] Kunwar Mohammad Ashraf (1903-62); participated in the freedom movement; member, C.S.P. and C.P.I.; in charge of Muslim Mass Contact Programme of the A.I.C.C., 1936; detained at Deoli Detention Camp, 1939-43; Head of the History Department, Kirori Mal College, Delhi, for some time; joined Humboldt University in Berlin as Guest-Professor, 1960; wrote *Life and Condition of the People of Hindustan (1200-1500 AD)*.

[12] S. Sajjad Zaheer (1905-73); joined the Communist Party of England in 1930 and started working among Indian students in England; elected General Secretary of the All India Progressive Writers' Association, 1936; member, National Executive, C.S.P., 1937-8; publications include *Angare, London Ki Ek Raat, Zikr-e-Hafiz, Roshnai,* and *Pighla Neelam*.

[13] For biographical note on Mohanlal Gautam see *JPSW*, Volume One, p. 88.

[14] The Gandhi Seva Sangh was founded by Jamnalal Bajaj at Wardha in 1923 by donating one lakh of rupees, with the purpose of providing maintenance to workers who had left their jobs for participating in the non-cooperation movement.

complete independence through peaceful and legitimate means. Within the limits of this ideal fullest freedom of opinion has been and is allowed. It seems to be very unreasonable to lose one's temper. . . . when there is criticism within the ranks of the Congress and a clash of ideas. Allow me to draw your attention to the history of the Congress and the stupendous ideological conflicts that have taken place within it. I might remind you of the conflict between the "moderates" and the "extremists", between those who stood for complete independence and those who clung to Dominion Status. I may also remind you that in the latter conflict Mahatma Gandhi himself and Rajendra Babu and Sardar Vallabhbhai[15] were for Dominion Status. But they were pushed ahead by the new forces that were at work. I may further remind you of the conflict between "no changers" and "pro changers", between "direct actionists" and "constitutionalists", between "Khaddarites" and "non-Khaddarites". I may also remind you that none of these conflicts ever weakened the Congress. Out of every one of them it emerged triumphant and more powerful than before. I assure you that out of the present conflict too it will emerge triumphant and more powerful than ever before.

Before I conclude, I should point out that if you compared the literature of the old conflicts with that of the present, you will find little reason to be angry with the nature and manner of our criticism. Or even if you compared the tenor of our criticism with your own far too frequent outbursts of abuse, you would, if you were inclined to be impartial, find far more fault with yourself than with us.

[15] For biographical note on Vallabhbhai Patel see *JPSW*, Volume One, p. 68.

48. Rejoinder to Rajendra Prasad, 17 January 1938[1]

Babu Rajendra Prasad has issued a long statement[2] justifying the action taken by his Working Committee against the Kisan Sabha. As one who is deeply concerned with the Kisan movement and its relation with the Congress, I feel compelled to examine that statement and place before the public the point of view of the Kisan Sabha. I have little taste for controversy and have no heart to enter into one with Babu Rajendra Prasad. I know that the official battery of abuse is sure to be let loose upon me for this

[1] *Searchlight*, 19 January 1938. Statement issued at Patna.

[2] Refers to the statement of Rajendra Prasad published in the *Searchlight*, 12 January 1938, regarding the activities of the Kisan Sabha in Bihar and the resolution of the Working Committee of the Bihar Provincial Congress Committee asking Congressmen not to participate in the meetings of the Provincial Kisan Sabha.

impertinence. But in the interest of truth as I see it I feel it to be my duty to say a few words in reply to Rajendra Babu.

In his statement Rajendra Babu has enumerated a formidable number of charges against the Kisan Sabha and its workers—charges that range from bazar-gossip on the one hand to the magnificent Kisan rallies on the other. The first thing to note about the statement is that we witness in it the unique procedure of a charge-sheet being published after the judgement has been pronounced. This is justice in accordance with non-violence and truth.

From the time that the symptoms of the disease which has gripped the Congress bosses of the Province became evident in Champaran, Saran and Monghyr, we have been shouting for facts, for definite charges and for time to be given to enquire and explain. But consistently the bosses have evaded the issue, and relying on the majority they have in the Congress organization taken partial and one-sided decisions. The accusers were the Judges. The result was a foregone conclusion.

Babu Rajendra Prasad says that "much capital is being made of its (the Working Committee's) omission to give detailed information of their (Kisan workers') activities". This may be a lawyer's way of putting things, but I am afraid it misses the whole argument of the opposite side. That argument has been that the action of the three D.C.C.s and the Working Committee of the P.C.C. was taken *ex parte*, that no opportunities were given to those who were being suddenly condemned to explain their position and defend themselves, that no enquiries were made, no explanations were asked. The so-called facts published by Rajendra Babu do not alter the situation and do not in the least weaken our argument. Babu Rajendra Prasad merely says that "the Provincial office has in its possession statements of hundreds of persons and reports from various District Congress Committees about these activities with the names of speakers and the places and the time where the speeches were delivered". It is on the basis of these "facts" that Rajendra Babu and his Committee took their terrible action. Nothing was done to enquire into these "facts", to verify the statements and reports, to find out the other side of the case, to sift the evidence. "Facts" do not become sacrosant truth merely because they are in the possession of the Provincial Congress office. Abyssinia did not become the aggressor merely because Mussolini declared it to be so. What reason had Babu Rajendra Prasad to believe that all the information received by the Provincial office was true? Does any fair-minded court in the world pass judgement without attempting to hear the other side of a case?

Take the case of the reports of speeches. Those of us who have some experience of public speaking know it too well how often speeches and statements are wrongly reported in the press. And this mis-reporting occurs in spite of trained reporters and the absence of a desire to misrepresent deliberately. In the case that we are considering, however, the reporters must often have been untrained and might often have been coloured by animus and bias. We have repeatedly pointed out that in every District there are factions in the Congress and it is not unnatural to expect that false or distorted information has been supplied to the P.C.C. In any case it should be obvious to any fair-minded person that in view of the extremely controversial and factious nature of the evidence, no action should have been taken on its basis without examining it and making a proper investigation.

In his statement Rajendra Babu mentions the fact that when complaints were made to him against the resolution of the Executive Committee of the Champaran D.C.C. prohibiting Swamiji[3] from entering Champaran, the matter was placed under investigation. We see thus when a complaint was made against the other party an investigation was immediately launched even though the case was one of such flagrant abuse of power. However no investigation was ever made into the hundreds of statements, etc. that were made against us. May we know why was this discrimination made?

Before I proceed to take up the charges detailed by Rajendra Babu, I should like to deal with another aspect of the decision of the Bihar Working Committee. Rajendra Babu says that consideration of the matter could not be postponed. He has not made it clear why it was thought to be so. What was the crisis that was impending on December 13 that could not have been averted except by a resolution of the Working Committee, such as was passed? It might not have struck Babu Rajendra Prasad, but I should like to point out that the crisis in all certainty was the Congress elections that were approaching. The resolution of the Working Committee was the Zinovieff letter[4] to quote Mr. Masani, which was to be used to suppress the inconvenient critics. Experience has amply borne out this interpretation.

One word about Swamiji's presence at the meeting of the Working Committee. In his letter of resignation Swamiji has made clear how on every other occasion when a critical matter was to be discussed he was particularly summoned and fetched and how in the present case notice of the meeting reached his Ashram on the very day of the meeting when he was out touring. Rajendra Babu mentions that members from distant places were able to attend the meeting. May I point out the likelihood of a telegraphic communication travelling faster than a postal one? Supposing,

[3] Swami Sahajanand Saraswati.

[4] Gregori Zinoviev, one of the leaders of the Third Communist International, sent a letter to the British Communists, urging them to promote communist revolution in England. This letter was published in the British Press on 25 October 1924, four days before the General Election and was assumed by some to have played an important role in the defeat of the labour Government.

however, that Swamiji was perverse enough not to attend the meeting what harm was there in postponing decision for a week or two in order to give him a chance to be consulted? There is no reason why a colleague, who was thought to be valuable enough during the Assembly elections to be retained on the Committee at the expense of so much persuasion and pleading, should have been dropped and disregarded in this fashion.

Let me take now the charges as they have been marshalled by Rajendra Babu. He says at the outset that on the basis of the information received in his office "it may be stated that very soon after the Congress Ministers came into office a section of Congress workers associated with the Kisan Sabha started an agitation regarding Kisan demands". This is an amazing statement for anyone in Bihar to make. Agitation regarding Kisan demands was not started "very soon after the Congress Ministers came into office" but very soon after the rebirth of the Kisan Sabha in 1933. Since then the Sabha has carried on ceaseless agitation for these demands. There were days and weeks observed, processions taken out, meetings and rallies held. There was the anti-salami, anti-certificate power agitation, there was the particularly sustained agitation for fifty per cent reduction in rents, for fixation of cane prices. There were local and spontaneous satyagrahas in Gaya and elsewhere. *Zamindari pratha nash ho, Kisan raj kaem ho* are slogans which have been reverberating in the Province for the last so many years. A comprehensive charter of Kisan demands was drawn up and popularized long before the last Assembly elections. All this went on during the days of the dyarchy and the "interim" Ministry; but neither of these ever made the sweeping charges against the Kisan Sabha and its workers as have been made now.

Rajendra Babu says that there would have been nothing wrong if they (Kisan Sabha people) had "confined themselves to putting their demands". Parenthetically I may add that it is a great consolation to find that putting forth of demands is not considered as an offence. However Rajendra Babu proceeds to say that an attempt was made to show that the "Congress Ministry could not be relied on to safeguard Kisan interests and it was therefore necessary to organize Kisans to force the hands of the Ministry". We do not know who made this attempt and here I would again repeat that cases in which this was done should have been brought to the notice of the Kisan Sabha which would have surely taken steps to mend matters. It never was the policy of the Kisan Sabha to preach that the Congress Ministry could not be relied on to help the peasants who should therefore organize themselves to force its hands. The question of organizing the peasantry did not arise after the Congress Ministries were formed. We were organizing it since a long time before and we were doing it not in the hope of forcing the hands of a likely Congress Ministry at a later time but in order to enable the peasants to gather strength for the much bigger struggle for freedom in order, in short, to strengthen the Congress movement itself. Just as some people hold that organization of Charkha Sanghs strengthens the Congress and the independence movement, so others hold that organization of the peasantry by Congressmen does the same and much more effectively.

In his charge-sheet Rajendra Babu mentions the peasant rallies that were held at Patna. It passes my comprehension how they have been found to be objectionable. To me they are the two high peaks of our movement. These peasant mobilizations were held not because we had no faith in the Congress Ministry, but because we wanted to utilize the freer atmosphere created to raise the agitation to a higher level (that agitation, be it remembered, is the motive force to the national movement itself) to link up mass agitation with the work done in the legislatures, to strengthen the hands of the Congress Ministry against the powerful interests in the Province which are opposed to the peasants, to create a mass sanction behind the measures that the Ministry might undertake, to bring pressure to bear upon such tendencies in the Ministry and the Congress party as might incline unduly towards the interests of the Zamindars. The rallies afforded the best background for an agrarian legislation. A revolutionary government, such as the Congress Governments are expected to be, should thrive on and derive strength from such rallies. Under the present circumstances when the Ministries are hedged in with so many limitations extra parliamentary action alone can strengthen their hands.

The next item on the charge-sheet is the memorandum of 61 Congress M.L.A.s. There are 96 Congress members in the Lower House, 61 of them make up roughly a two-thirds majority in the Congress party. We do not know what objection there can be to any member of the party or to any group of them presenting a memorandum to the Prime Minister as basis for legislation. Private members are not dummies. They have a certain amount of initiative. And if two-thirds of them combine their initiative becomes almost mandatory. It is a pity that even though such a majority was on the side of the memorandum it was not given any more importance than a scrap of paper. To my mind it is not the 61 members who are deserving of any censure but others. It is revealing that Babu Rajendra Prasad should in this manner discountenance and disapprove the initiative of private members. It is also revealing that this episode, which if anything is a commentary on the way opinion and initiative are disregarded and suppressed in this Province, should have been used as a stick to beat the Kisan Sabha with.

I might add here, though it may be none of my business to do so, that if the private members of the Congress party are alive to their responsibility, they should ever be alert, fight fearlessly for their point of view, canvass support for it and press it on the Ministry. I should think that the M.L.A.s who are associated with the Kisan Sabha should have many more occasions to prepare and submit memoranda. It would be interesting to see who prevents them from doing so.

Much has been made of the fact that the memorandum was published in the Press. I fail to see what offence there was in that. If I am keen on getting a certain thing done, I shall certainly seek the support of public opinion. I do not see why people should be so nervous of publicity or public opinion.

In the Congress there has been too much initiative from the top. It is time that initiative is allowed to grow from below. That at least was the intention of the Faizpur resolution on the Congress constitution.

The next charge we come to is that "on instructions from the Kisan Sabha, meetings began to be organized in constituencies of members who had refused to sign the demand (memorandum of the 61 members) and their conduct in not signing the demand was condemned. They were called upon to sign the demand or to resign". I do not know what copy of instructions is in the possession of the Provincial office (dreadful business for information to be in possession of that august body). I can state with authority, however, that no such grotesque instructions were given. The instructions were that meetings should be held in the constituencies to popularize those demands and that in the constituencies of those members who had failed to sign the memorandum their action should be criticized and the people should be asked to call upon them to support the demands set out in the memorandum. This is a thoroughly democratic procedure. This is the kind of relationship that should exist between constituents and their representatives. It should be remembered that the Congress had placed no ban on members of the Congress party signing that or any other memorandum. Two-thirds of the members had already signed it. The demands themselves did not go beyond Congress principles or even the broad outline of the Faizpur programme. Where was the harm if democratic pressure was put on the M.L.A.s to support a certain set of demands? If private members are dummies, are the people in the constituencies too nothing more than dummies? Surely they are entitled to place their demands before their representatives. Our High Command wants to have everything its own way and is therefore impatient of any democratic functioning of the Congress organization and its units. If, however this is allowed to continue, not only the leadership will isolate itself, but the whole organization will be stultified. It may even split.

I have stated above what the instructions of the Kisan Sabha were. I have reasons to believe that they were very largely followed. Very early in the campaign one or two cases were brought to the notice of the Sabha's executive in which speeches had been made demanding acceptance of the demands or resignation. Immediately instructions were sent out to stop that kind of foolish propaganda. The Provincial Secretary of the Sabha issued a public statement dated September 21 in which he disapproved of such action and restated the position of the Sabha. In view of this, I should think that Babu Rajendra Prasad should have been thankful to the Kisan Sabha for stopping the mischief rather than use the instance to discredit it.

Babu Rajendra Prasad goes on to detail various points which according to his information have been made in speeches by Kisan Sabha workers. It is difficult to say how far the reports of the speeches are accurate. It is often a slight variation in words that turns criticism into abuse and attack. However, granting that these reports are accurate, the Kisan Sabha cannot be held responsible for them. The Sabha indeed would have co-operated with Babu Rajendra Prasad in putting a stop to such talk. Or if it was considered infra dig to approach the Kisan Sabha, the Congress authorities themselves could have brought the offenders to book after proper enquiry. Rajendra Babu complains that in respect of the three cases that were brought to the notice of the Sabha, nothing was done except to submit a counter-statement. This is amazing indeed. What ground for complaints could there be in this? Is it expected that when complaints are made against Kisan Sabha workers, they must irrespective of what the facts are plead guilty and cringe for mercy before the powers that be? Surely if the complaints are false, they are entitled to state their position. It seems unfair to spurn their case as a mere counter-statement. The duty of a judge is to find the truth between statement and counter-statement and not to accept one at its face value and reject the other.

I have said above that among Rajendra Babu's charges are also included bazar-gossip. I was referring to the charge the people were talking about the Ministers and others having been bribed by the Zamindars. These are of course disgusting things and no organization is ever responsible for them. They just grow up—from filthy soil. All I wish to say is that if we began to take note of them in any serious political work we cannot get anywhere. Such talks somehow do arise when people in authority and power are not able to satisfy everyone as indeed they cannot. We all know, and Babu Rajendra Prasad too must be aware of it, how during the earthquake relief all sorts of baseless talks got current about responsible men in the organization. These things are never worth taking notice of. They must be treated with the contempt they deserve.

Much has been made of the *danda* business. Swamiji in his letter of resignation has thrown sufficient light on it. Babu Rajendra Prasad makes out that the tenants have been advised to use their sticks whenever the Zamindar or his Amla came to oppress them. If this were really the advice given, I can assure Babu Rajendra Prasad that the Kisan Sabha workers have sufficient influence over the peasantry to have caused a violent civil war in the Province. In fact, it has been the restraining influence of the Kisan workers that has been responsible, in spite of unprecedented peasant awakening and militancy, for preserving peace in the Province in face of grave provocation and dire suffering.

Mention has also been made of slogans like *malguzari loge kaise, danda hamara zindabad*. It is exasperating to find a person like Rajendra Babu seriously making such a charge. Surely, we must credit the masses with some sense of humour and inventiveness. We have not forgotten how during the last Assembly elections all kinds of slogans, songs and caricatures were abroad. They were all creations of the newly awakened mass mind. They were crude and rough-hewn, often far removed from Congress ideals and standards. However, they were, just the same, products of a great phase of our movement. The peasant movement likewise has produced genuine folk slogans and songs. And they may not always be in keeping with the fine and sophisticated standard of the Kisan Sabha.

Moreover, the particular slogan that Rajendra Babu has mentioned was certainly never widely current. Wherever it came to the notice of the Kisan workers it was discouraged. I even make bold to say that the slogan is hardly used in the Province now except perhaps by agent provocateurs.

Objection has also been taken to the old and well established slogans of the Kisan Sabha [such] as *zamindari pratha nash ho*, *punjivad nash ho*, and not *punjipatiyaon ka nash ho* as Rajendra Babu puts it. All I can say about this matter is that these slogans are of fundamental importance to the Kisan movement, and no amount of displeasure will make us drop them. And, if I may remind Rajendra Babu the first of these slogans has been adopted even by the highest Congress authority in the Province. Not long ago the Provincial Political Conference at Masrakh passed a resolution recommending abolition of the Zamindari system; and if I am not mistaken the decisions of the Conference are binding on the P.C.C. of Bihar unless they are inconsistent with Congress principles. It was thus the whole Bihar Congress which shouted at Masrakh *zamindari pratha nash ho*. It does not seem proper for the head of that body to condemn that slogan now.

Rajendra Babu further says: "Even the Congress programme of prohibition has not escaped criticism and on occasion national flags were not given due prominence in preference to red flags." I wonder what is there that is sacrosanct about the prohibition programme that it cannot even be criticised. I should make it clear, however, that no worker of the Kisan Sabha has ever opposed or condemned it. The only criticism that has been made is that it should not stand in the way of urgent relief to the people. As for the red flag, it is too common for this charge to be brought up of all places in Bihar. The Kisan workers in this Province are as good Congressmen as any one else, and nothing can be further from their mind than to show any kind of disrespect to the national flag.

It is too weary a task to deal with all the items on the charge-sheet. I have only this much to add that it is a pity that Rajendra Babu thought it fit to dig up dead issues and open up old sores. This serves no purpose except to create differences where none exist in reality.

I should like to say a few words about the manner in which Rajendra Babu has dealt with the action of the Saran, Champaran and Monghyr D.C.C.s. In the whole controversy that has raged in the past few weeks, nothing caused more resentment and bitterness as this and the manner in which it was taken. Many points had been raised concerning this matter. Rajendra Babu has not answered any of them. I should like very much to know what authority or justification has a Congress organization to prohibit any one from entering an area on the ground that it would lead to ideological conflict? Are Congress Committees now expected to perform duties of the police and the magistracy? Even a Magistrate never passes such an order except to prevent breach of peace. Ideological conflict never worried even the imperialist bureaucracy. And since when did the Congress become the monopoly of a single ideology?

Equally serious arguments have been advanced by us against actions of the Saran and Monghyr D.C.C.s. Rajendra Babu has justified the action without caring to reply to any of them.

After explaining the purport of the resolution of his Working Committee, Rajendra Babu asks how the civil liberty of any Congressman is jeopardized and how Kisan Sabhas have been banned and an order of the type of 144 been issued by the Congress. The answer should bot be as difficult as it is made out to be. Civil liberty of Congressmen is certainly jeopardized by such prohibitory orders as those of Saran and Champaran. If Congress Committees are encouraged to perform police functions surely civil liberty of Congressmen is in danger. As for section 144, what are the orders of Saran and Champaran D.C.C.s if not of the type of orders under section 144?—though only more drastic and lacking in justice. The action of the Monghyr D.C.C. amounts to banning the Kisan Sabha as far as Congressmen are concerned.

Just a few words about the influence of Zamindari interests over the Congress in Bihar. It is possible that while dealing with this point Kisan workers have spoken somewhat irresponsibly. It is necessary, however, that we understand the position properly. We know that there are various interests represented within the Congress and each one of them tries, if in an imperceptible manner, to dominate it. The influence of the upper classes has been so far largely predominant though recently the interests of the poorer people have been exerting themselves. In a period of struggle the influence of the latter grows. At Masrakh, coming as it did after the tremendous mass mobilization of the General Election in which economic issues played such a dominant role, the peasant interests almost ruled supreme. In safer times of constitutionalism particularly when the fruits of sacrifice have to be gathered, the Zamindari and other upper class interests grow stronger and begin to dominate the organization as we see happening at present. Nobody, no leader plans or directs all this. It is a social process which goes on automatically and inexorably.

The fact that ninety per cent of the Congress members in Bihar are peasants does not change the position. It is nothing new for the masses to be dominated by the upper classes. The millions of people who voted in England for the National Government were common people. Yet, we know and I hope even the Working Committee of our P.C.C. will agree, that the National Government is entirely a government of the British capitalist class.

There has been some apprehension on the score of the Kisan Sabha becoming a rival organization to the Congress. We have made it plain time without number that there is no question of rivalry at all. If that were the intention of the Kisan Sabha, it would never have given such undivided support to the Congress in the elections and would not have popularized and strengthened the Congress as the supreme political organization of the country.

This reply can be lengthened indefinitely but it has already become too long. I have attempted to elucidate the point of view of the Kisan Sabha on some of the issues raised by Rajendra Babu. I personally believe, however, that no good will come out of controversies though they become inevitable sometimes. The Kisan Sabha has repeatedly declared that it is prepared to co-operate with the Congress in stamping out anti-Congress and other objectionable activities. I repeat that assurance. The Kisan Sabha is as much opposed to preaching of violence and anti-Congress activities as the Congress itself is. It is prepared to take action against its workers who participate in such activities. But it is not prepared to condemn them on the basis of one-sided propaganda. I appeal to Rajendra Babu to approach this question with sympathy. The present attitude will only lead to further estrangement, bitterness and disruption. It is not too late even now to mend matters. For our part, our position is clear. We are Congressmen and will remain Congressmen. We shall continue to work for the Congress and spread our views. We shall continue to organize the peasants and workers and link up their struggle with the Congress. Only in that manner shall we be able to arrive at our goal of complete independence and to establish a people's Swaraj in this country.

49. Letter to Munshi Ahmed Din, 19 January 1938[1]

P.O. Bankipore
Patna
19 January 1938

My dear Munshiji,[2]

I hope you are doing well. I should like to know what reaction, if any, the publication of my verdict in the Mann case[3] produced. I should also like to impress on you the desirability of burying the issue. It should not be allowed any more to mar our political work in the Province and our relations with the other radical elements.

I also wish to draw your attention to certain things in your last news-letter. The first thing I wish to point is that these letters are not written dispassionately as reports should be. Will you please instruct the writer to avoid rhetoric and exaggeration. It should also be free from animus. Please look at these words "Reformists, opportunists, the self-styled communists, and sometimes, the hired agents of Imperialism, come to us in the garb of the socialist faith. That is why we have to purge our party, now and then. Karam Singh Mann[4] went after a trial and Sohan Singh[5] and his associates

[1] *Brahmanand Papers* (NMML).

[2] Munshi Ahmed Din (1906-67); associated with the Naujawan Bharat Sabha and Punjab Kirti Kisan Party; Founder-member, Punjab C.S.P., 1934; Chairman, Reception Committee, C.S.P. Conference, Lahore, 1938; elected to National Executive, C.S.P., 1938, and Socialist Party, 1948; arrested and imprisoned for anti-war activities, 1939-46; was in Deoli Detention Camp with J.P.

[3] The Mann Inquiry Tribunal was appointed by the Punjab C.S.P. in 1936 to inquire into the allegation against Karam Singh Mann that he was a C.I.D. agent who had got Baba Gurmukh Singh arrested in 1936 when the latter had gone to the General Post Office in Lahore to post his foreign mail. Tilak Raj Chaddha, Rachhpal Singh and Mangal Dass were members of the Tribunal. They gave their verdict against Karam Singh Mann. The matter was referred to J.P. who, after investigation, also found him guilty.

[4] Karam Singh Mann; Bar-at-Law; influenced by the Communist Party of England; associate of Shaukatullah; worked for the Ghadar Party; member, Provincial Anti-Imperialist League in the Punjab, 1934; arrested and detained at Deoli Detention Camp, later shifted to Gujarat Jail, 1940-2.

[5] Sohan Singh Josh (1898-1982); associated with the Ghadar Party; joined the Akali movement, 1921; Founder-member, Punjab Kirti Kisan Party, 1928; President, Punjab Naujawan Bharat Sabha, 1928, and All India Workers' and Peasants' Party Conference, Calcutta, 1928; arrested in connection with the Meerut Conspiracy Case, 1929, released, 1933; elected to the Punjab Legislative Assembly, 1937; detained at Deoli Detention Camp, later shifted to Gujarat Jail, 1940-2; publications include: *Tragedy of Komagata Maru*, *Hindustan Gadar Party: A Short History* (2 vols.), *The Great Attack: Meerut Conspiracy Case*, and *My Tryst with Secularism: An Autobiography* (published posthumously).

had to be turned out. Now it is Fazal Ilahi Qurban.[6] And with him goes Jai Gopal". Surely, this way of writing is not proper or fair. Mann was not a member of the Party who was driven out after a trial. Also the conclusions of the trial were under re-examination. Sohan Singh certainly is not an agent of Imperialism or a reformist or a self-styled communist. This is very unfortunate indeed if our Party in the Punjab continues to show such a spirit. Later on the letter refers to Jai Gopal as having been accused of being a spy. This spy business is really sickening. You must see that this sort of promiscuous stigmatization stops. No responsible Party should call anyone a spy unless the fact has been proved. It is necessary to be cautious, but let us not go on indiscriminately labelling people as spies—at least publicly.

I also do not approve of the description of the Party given in the letter. It says "The Congress Socialist Party is a mass organization. Its membership is not confined to a privileged few. Anyone who subscribes to the socialist faith can become its member. If it were not so, it would defeat its own purpose". The Party is certainly not a mass organization. It might become one in course of time if we are sufficiently active and our mass work increases. Nor are its doors open to anyone who belongs to the "Socialist faith". Any person who wishes to join the Party must not only be a Marxian socialist or oriented towards it, but he must also accept the Party's Thesis.

I hope that due attention will be paid to the points I have raised above.

Yours sincerely,
J.P.

[6] Fazal-i-Ilahi Qurban (1902-59); participated in the demonstration against Rowlatt Bills, Lahore, 1919; took part in the Khilafat movement; migrated to Afghanistan, 1920; stayed in Moscow, 1921-5; visited Europe, 1925-6; returned to India, 1926; arrested and imprisoned, 1927-9; associated with the Naujawan Bharat Sabha, Lahore, 1929; rearrested and imprisoned, 1930-4; arrested and detained at Deoli Detention Camp, later shifted to Gujarat Jail, 1940-2; President, A.I.T.U.C., 1945; migrated to Pakistan and edited *Mazdoor Duniya*.

50. Resolution Moved at the Bihar Provincial Kisan Conference, Bachwara, 23 January 1938[1]

This conference expresses its resentment and regret at the attitude shown in recent days by some Congress leaders and some Congress committees of Bihar to the Kisan Sabha and reminds the people of the province and the

[1] *Searchlight*, 26 January 1938. The resolution was moved by J.P., seconded by Ganga Sharan Sinha and adopted unanimously by the conference.

country at large as well as the Congress organizations that the Kisan Sabha has always co-operated wholeheartedly with the Congress in its pursuit of the national objective. This has been the policy of the Kisan Sabha towards the Congress and will continue to be so. The conference further declares that the Bihar Kisan Sabha has always followed the path of non-violence and will do the same in the future also.

'This conference is of opinion that the offensive, direct or indirect, that has been started and is being pursued by some Congress leaders and some Congress committees against the Kisan Sabha in the name of Truth and Non-violence in spite of this policy of the Sabha, is unjust and is calculated to impede the progress of the nation to the goal of independence. It is unjust because action has been taken *ex parte* on the basis of allegations without proper investigation and verification. It is detrimental to our struggle for freedom because it is certain to cause disruption in the Congress ranks and undermine the faith and regard hitherto shown by the peasants to the Congress. It is deplorable in the extreme because a campaign is being carried on in the Province, especially in Monghyr district, against the independent organization of the Kisans notwithstanding the recognition given by the Congress to the Kisan organizations since the Karachi Congress and notwithstanding the recent resolution of the Working Committee reaffirming the right of the Kisans to organize themselves into independent organization. This conference draws the attention of Congressmen and the public to this improper and unwarranted act and warns them that if the tendency is not checked yet, the energies of the nation will be dissipated in internecine quarrels and the responsibility for the unfortunate developments will rest on them alone.

This conference is of opinion that India being predominantly an agricultural country, the national movement can derive its strength mostly from the Kisans. The national movement will gain in strength and momentum from the organization and development of class consciousness among the Kisans.

51. Rejoinder to the *Searchlight*, 27 January 1938[1]

Once again your editorials[2] have dragged me into a controversy which I would much rather have left untouched. Duty, however, compels me to say just a few words.

Looking at your editorials, it appears amazing indeed that the language

[1] *The Searchlight*, 27 January 1938.

[2] Refers to the editorials in the *Searchlight* dated 19 and 23 January 1938. See Appendix 8.

of non-violence should be so replete with venom and vulgarity, hatred and abuse and that the non-violent armoury should be so full of poisoned arrows. However, let that be so.

In one of your editorials in which you denounced my rejoinder to Rajendra Babu, you tried to strengthen your case by suggesting that I was hostile to Rajendra Babu and was attempting to discredit and overthrow him.

It will ever remain a matter of regret for me that my rejoinder appeared in the press just when Rajendra Babu was stricken with illness. Had I known of his illness, the rejoinder would not have been published then.

I respect Rajendra Babu and have deep love and admiration for him. But I do not believe in making a show of my feeling for I covet no favours and no prizes. Politics to me are completely objective and impersonal. Respect and love do not and will not ever prevent me from pursuing resolutely what appears as truth to me. I differ seriously from Rajendra Babu on many questions and I deem it my duty to join issues even with him if occasion demands it. If it suits your purpose to denounce me as anti-Rajendra Babu, you may do so. I know what I am about, and abuse and slander will not deflect me from my path. It may sound like self-esteem, but I wish to tell you that I have better things to do than to intrigue and manoeuvre for power and position.

I do not wish to touch upon the other points raised in your denunciation. They are all so irrelevant and appear to be such deliberate misconstructions that no useful purpose is likely to be served by replying to them.

I wish, however, to say a few words about your more recent outburst occasioned by the presidential address of Pandit Jadunandan Sharma[3] delivered at the Provincial Kisan Conference. To pursue your meaning through the vicious tangle of invectives is no simple task. However, it seems that you have discovered violence in the address and anti-Congress propaganda. The mask has fallen, you say. And with some ado you ask me what I have to say now that the veil of hypocrisy and casuistry that I had woven through my statements has been torn asunder. Only this, Sir, that there never was any mask for me, nor is there any new revelation now. If there is violence in the address of Pt. Jadunandan Sharma then I too believe in violence. If it is anti-Congress I too am anti-Congress. I had read through

[3] Jadunandan Sharma; born in 1896; Kisan leader of Bihar; taught at Tekari High School, 1920; Manager, *Zamindar*, 1922; took part in the civil disobedience movement and jailed, 1930-1; led Kisan movement in Reora, 1936-9; Secretary and later President, Gaya D.C.C.; President, Bihar Provincial Kisan Conference, Bachwara, 1938; Chairman, Reception Committee, All India Kisan Sabha, Gaya, 1939, and elected member of the Central Kisan Council, 1939; went underground, 1940-2; President, Bihar Provincial Kisan Sabha, 1942; elected Treasurer of the Central Kisan Council, 1943, and one of its Joint Secretaries, 1944.

the manuscript of the address before it went to the press, and I stand by it. It is never possible for anyone to endorse every word of the address because people have different ways of expressing their ideas. But with the address as a whole I am in complete agreement. It is direct and forceful. It states the truth bluntly and truth is often unpleasant.

I might add here that it really is our good fortune that the courts of His Majesty in India have not been acting so far on the interpretation of violence and non-violence that you have given; otherwise, it is difficult to say where most of us would have been today. . . .

You have declared Pt. Jadunandan Sharma a charlatan, upstart, vulgar and many other things. I cannot believe that you are really ignorant of the stuff of which this man is made. Your vulgar charlatan is a remarkable man and I wish the Congress had more such men. He has grit and character and has shown extreme capacity for suffering. Went to school at the age of 18! Graduated. At the University worked as a blacksmith's assistant and did various other manual jobs to keep going. I know personally how as a Congress and Kisan worker he and his family have lived almost in accordance with the supreme Brahmanic ideal of *unchhvritti*. A man of stern virtues and stern life. Semi-naked, he looks uncouth and blunt, characteristics shared by those who come from the masses, but he has that inner fineness that comes out of devotion to a high cause. Forty miles on a bicycle a day through the roads and byways of rural Gaya is a normal practice with him. He lives with the peasants, he is their man. He has been to prison no less than four times during the Satyagraha movement. He has been Secretary of the Gaya District Congress Committee once, and twice its President—he is its present President. Such is your charlatan, Sir. Finally, if you will excuse me for it, I should like to warn you that the poison you are sowing through your editorials may one day blast the very plant you are anxious to nurture. You have done nothing in the past weeks but fan bitterness and hatred, stir up discord and trouble. That does not appear to me to be the role of a journal devoted to the cause of nationalism. Perhaps, you believe that the Congress in Bihar will be strengthened by a purge of the Leftists. Demand it plainly if you want it, but do not drive the iron too far into our souls. I am not afraid of a purge. I am confident of the future. Let them drive us out if they choose. But I doubt if that will be in the interest of the Congress. I doubt if history will approve of it.

Yours sincerely,
Jayaprakash Narayan

P.S. After the above was written, I saw your issue of Jan. 26. I was astounded to see what partisanship in journalism can do. Your headline shrieks: "No faith in Rajendra Babu's leadership".[4] I never said this. What I did was to analyse the well-known "constructive programme" of the Congress and to show that the ideology and the technique it represented were not likely to take us much further on the road to independence. Only in that sense did I refer to Rajendra Babu's leadership. I said nothing more than what we have been saying all these years, than what I said, for instance, four years ago in the first meeting of the Bihar P.C.C. (that was called after the Congress became legal again) in 1934.

[4] Refers to a report of the speech delivered by J.P. at the Bihar Provincial Kisan Conference at Bachwara on 23 January 1938 published in the *Searchlight* dated 26 January 1938.

52. Lecture on 'The Task Before Us', 30 January 1938[1]

There is a great deal of misunderstanding about the concept of Nationalism because people look at it as something static. Nationalism means different things to different people. To the British, it means the defence of their capitalist system; to the Germans, the glory of their Nazi Fatherland; to the Russians, the maintenance of the Soviet system. In our country the concept of Nationalism has been growing. In the days, when the Congress was formed, Nationalism was consistent with loyalty to the British throne. But through successive stages, during a period of fifty years, we resolved on complete independence. Even now the concept of Nationalism is in the process of evolution, social forces are still working, and when Nationalism ripens, our goal will be Socialism.

Socialism and Nationalism are not contradictory things. Already the Congress has moved a few steps in the new direction. The Karachi Congress declared for economic freedom and nationalization of the key industries under Swaraj. Some Provincial Congress Committees have adopted resolutions for the elimination of Zamindars and other middlemen. As the poor and the lower middle classes get increasingly drawn into the national struggle more and more power will pass out of the hands of the bourgeoisie and progressively the Congress will voice the demands and aspirations of the masses. In earlier years, for example, the national movement clamoured for the abolition of the excise duty on cotton, for fiscal autonomy, for introduction of the Permanent Settlement in the rest of India—all for the benefit of the upper classes. But now the problems of poverty and unemployment are coming to the fore and Swaraj is being thought of as a solution of these basic problems.

[1] Adapted from a report of the lecture at Socialist Study Centre, Patna, published in the *Searchlight*, 3 February 1938, and the *Congress Socialist*, 19 February 1938.

There is misunderstanding in the minds of some people, as to the meaning of Swaraj. By Swaraj is not meant the kind of democracy that exists in England and America today. True, in the eighteenth and nineteenth centuries this was the ideal and the revolutionary leaders fought for snatching power from the hands of the feudal oligarchy and transferring it to the hands of the people in general. But they were mistaken. It did not transfer power to the hands of the people in general, but to a new class—the capitalists—who have been ruling under the garb of democracy. Democracy has meant the dictatorship of the capitalists. The prosperity of the American or English people does not depend upon their form of government but upon the interests of this small class—consisting of mill-owners, financiers and bankers. England has been enjoying such "Swaraj" for several decades now, and the loot from many countries is collected there, yet over one and a half million people have remained permanently unemployed for the last ten years. Similarly in America, there is ostensibly a government of the people and for the people, and half the gold of the world lies deposited there, yet in a population of 150 million, ten to twelve million have been on the unemployed list. In contrast to this Russia has no unemployment. In India, where we have no show of democracy, little wealth, not much gold in our coffers, how are we going to solve these complex problems? For us, Swaraj must mean the power to solve these questions. Our Swaraj must mean Swaraj for the poor. Over and above political democracy, Swaraj must mean economic democracy. For this purpose, the capitalist oligarchy has got to be destroyed and economic power transferred to the people in general. It will take sometime after the establishment of Swaraj to establish Socialism. But the balance of power must immediately pass into the hands of the people so that it can work for the people and develop agriculture and industry.

If this is our objective, what must we do today? Our struggle for Swaraj has a definite purpose. We are not fighting for the restoration of the rule of the Nizam or any of the Rajas. We are fighting for an order of society where the masses will have the real power. For establishing contact with these classes, the Congress programme during the last fifteen years has been, with occasional spurts of constitutionalism, prohibition, Khadi and village industries. This programme has carried the people some way, but has not been able to create the momentum up to the requisite degree. The problem before us is to develop sufficient strength in the masses. Our basic problem being economic we have to organize ourselves on an economic basis. The final solution of this problem cannot be effected so long as the British rule continues to exist. But even before that we can take up on behalf of the masses the fight for the redress of their day-to-day grievances, explain to them the nature of their exploitation as well as the necessity for overthrowing not merely British rule but also capitalism. Now nobody is anti-British on sentimental grounds. Like the Charkha Sangh and the

Harijan Sevak Sangh[2] under the Congress, there can be an organization like a Peasant and Workers' Union. While establishing contact with the masses it will be affiliated to the Congress and its members will be also the members of the Congress organization. In this way a "link" will be established between the Congress, representing the anti-Imperialist struggle and the masses. The Kisan Sabhas should be otherwise independent bodies because there are some specific questions of the peasants which cannot be solved by the Congress.

What is the present role of Socialism? It is not only a body of principles providing for a certain order of society but also a science of society which explains certain questions of social organization and social change. It has a contribution to make to any country at any given time and at any stage of development. We cannot change the direction of social forces, but we can help them and facilitate their growth.

All movements must have some theory at their back. The Congress never adopted any theory consciously, but some how it has come to adopt Gandhism. So for a change in outlook, a change in theory is necessary. It is not correct to say that under the existing circumstances in the country there is no need for a party like the Congress Socialist Party. Socialism is a living theory and it cannot be put into cold-storage to be opened after a number of years. In order to influence the Congress ideology, the party must be correlated with the Congress through its members but the Party itself is independent.

[2] The All India Anti-Untouchability League was formed at a meeting of representatives of all sections of Hindus under the presidentship of Madan Mohan Malaviya at Bombay on 30 September 1932, to carry on propaganda for the abolition of untouchability. G.D. Birla was appointed its President, and A.V. Thakkar, its Secretary. It was renamed Harijan Sevak Sangh by Mahatma Gandhi in December 1932.

53. Letter to B. Rangasayi & K. Linga Raju, 3 February 1938[1]

Bankipore, Patna
3 February 1938

My dear Comrades Rangasayi[2] & Lingaraju,[3]
I have been getting rather disturbing reports about Andhra. I had hoped that

[1] *Brahmanand Papers* (NMML).

[2] Basavaraju Rangasayi (1902-45); belonged to Ellore, West Godavari District, Andhra Pradesh; participated in the civil disobedience movement and imprisoned, 1932; first Organizing Secretary, Andhra C.S.P., 1934, and later its Joint Secretary, 1936.

[3] K. Linga Raju (1904-84); journalist; Assistant Editor, 1923-9, and Editor, 1929-31, *Congress*, a Telugu weekly; Founder-member, Gautami Satyagraha Ashram, Sitanagaram;

you would keep me informed of the developments there and of your own opinion about them. I expected full co-operation from you both. After I returned from Andhra I saw a copy of the *Independent India* in which a very malicious report on the re-organization of the Andhra party and my part in it was published. I expected that Comrade Rangasayi would reply to that letter which was written by someone from Bhimavaram. But I was disappointed that the lies remained unrefuted. Subsequently, as points of difference arose between you and the Andhra Executive, I hoped I would be informed of them from time to time. In this too, I was disappointed. And now I suddenly find from Sundarayya's[4] letter that the breach has widened so much that your group had threatened to resign from the party. I request you to send me a full report of your differences and also not to precipitate things till we have had the opportunity to discuss them at Haripura.

With regards,

Yours sincerely,
Jayaprakash Narayan

---

participated in the civil disobedience movement, individual satyagraha, and Quit India movement; imprisoned, 1930, 1931, 1941, and detained, 1942-5; Secretary, Andhra C.S.P.; member, Madras Legislative Assembly, 1946-52.

[4] P. Sundarayya (1913-85); organized Communist movement in south India; became member of Central Committee, C.P.I., 1934; Secretary, Andhra C.S.P., 1937; member, Rajya Sabha, 1952-5, and Andhra Legislative Assembly, 1955-67; General Secretary, C.P.I. (M), 1968-76.

54. Interview to Press on Congress Working Committee Resolution on Hunger-Strike in Hazaribagh Central Jail, 4 February 1938[1]

The resolution of the Working Committee[2] is shockingly disappointing. One might call it an essay in irrelevance. Here is a basic programme of the Congress to be fulfilled and here are first rate patriots at death's door and yet the Working Committee finds time to expatiate sublimely on the ethics of hunger-strike. Instead of giving a bold lead to the Congress Governments it marks time and hopes against hope that the hunger-strikers will be persuaded to desist from their evil course. It is difficult to imagine how

[1] *Searchlight*, 6 February 1938. Interview to Press at Patna.

[2] Refers to the resolution of the Congress Working Committee asking the prisoners to desist from hunger-strike passed at its meeting at Wardha, 3-6 February 1938.

many of these brave men will have to follow Harendra Nath Munshi's[3] path before our leaders are compelled to appreciate the gravity of the situation. It seems to be clear that the provincial Governors are the real villains of the piece. It was necessary at this stage to tell these agents of the foreign Government to keep their proper place and let the popular will function through the elected Governments or to carry on the administration without the fiction of provincial autonomy. This was the time to give a supreme battle to the new constitution. The Governors have no power under the Act to interfere with the normal administration of law and order and if they were found to be perverse enough to do so, the Working Committee should have given them no quarter. However, the public agitation must go on and be further intensified till the prisoners are released.

I should like to add a word about the report of certain messages sent by me to Wardha, published in the press this morning. The report was not sent by me and is utterly unauthorized. It is regrettable that any responsible journalist should make use of gossip and unauthorized news.

[3] Harendra Nath Munshi (1914-38); participated in the freedom movement; convicted in Titagurh Arms Case and sentenced to five years' imprisonment, 1937; began hunger-strike in Dacca Central Jail on 21 January 1938 in protest against the system of classification and treatment of prisoners; died in jail while fasting on 30 January 1938.

55. Lessons of Haripura: Article in the *Congress Socialist*, 26 February 1938[1]

The deserted banks of the Tapti were alight for a few momentous days. The banks must already be once again enveloped in darkness. But the rays of light that went forth from there will penetrate every home in India and shine upon our path till we gather again a year hence to light another lamp on our darkened road.

Fifty thousand visitors everyday. A three-mile city sprung from the jungle. An army of disciplined workers—saffron-saried girls and uniformed boys. Thousands of them. Parks, roads, a fortressed pandal with magnificent feudal gates of bamboo. Vithalnagar will remain a proud memory, a reminder of the power that is the Congress.

Gandhiji's conception of a village Congress took shape for the first time at Faizpur. No one will deny that Faizpur pales in comparison with Haripura. Yet, Faizpur was much nearer the village and the soil. The village Congress is yet to come into its own. In fact, it is doubtful if we can ever have a real village Congress. The Congress represents rural India as much as urban

[1] *Congress Socialist*, 26 February 1938.

India and its sessions must symbolize both. Haripura seemed to emphasize this fact. Its village exterior had the soul of commerce.

When the first batches of delegates began to arrive, the political horizon was rather clear and the session promised to be occupied with no new and exciting issues. The only issue of importance was that of Federation. The resolution of the Working Committee, however, that had already been published was not expected to arouse much controversy. Then came on the very eve of the A.I.C.C. meeting news of resignation of the U.P. and Behar Ministries. The situation in those provinces was causing anxiety, but the delegates present were frankly not prepared for this sudden development.

The universal reaction was one of vigorous indignation at the interference of the Viceroy, attended with a certain amount of bitterness against the 'leftists', for forcing the pace. Due to the suddenness of the crisis, there was a general feeling of unpreparedness, but no lack of enthusiasm to face it with determination. This was the chief note of the Haripura session. There was fight in the speech of Sardar Vallabhbhai, when he moved the resolution on the ministerial crisis. There was spontaneous closing of ranks. Differences were pushed into the background and the whole Congress spoke with one voice. Behind that mildly worded resolution of the Working Committee lined up socialists and non-socialists, Gandhites, ex-terrorists. The importance and significance of Haripura lie in this great demonstration of national unity. Well may the enemies of the country ponder over it.

Haripura's chief contribution to my mind would be in the direction of opening a new chapter in the relations between the 'right' and 'left' wings of the Congress. Haripura is a grave warning to us and a pointer. We have talked of united front and of solidarity in the ranks of the Congress. Yet in spite of these talks, we found and were shocked to find how wide the gulf has become and how threatening for our cherished solidarity. We saw that even while we pledged our undivided support in the moment of crisis and action, there was suspicion, bitterness, hostility. Sardar Vallabhbhai's attack, Mr. Jairamdas's[2] and Mr. Bhulabhai's[3] remarks about 'left' and 'right',

[2] Jairamdas Doulatram (1892-1979); lawyer; participated in the national movement and suffered imprisonment; member, Bombay Legislative Council, 1927-9, and Congress Working Committee, 1929-41; General Secretary, Indian National Congress, 1931-4; member, Constituent Assembly, 1946-7, 1948-50, and Rajya Sabha, 1959-76; Governor, Bihar, 1947-8, and Assam, 1950-6; Minister of Food and Agriculture, Government of India, 1948-50.

[3] Bhulabhai Jivanji Desai (1877-1946); advocate, Bombay High Court; appeared on behalf of the peasants before the Broomfield Committee appointed as a result of the Bardoli satyagraha, 1928; participated in the civil disobedience movement and imprisoned, 1932; member, Congress Working Committee, 1934-5, and Indian Legislative Assembly, 1935-46; took part in the individual satyagraha, 1940; defended I.N.A. prisoners, 1945.

Mr. Kripalani's[4] veiled threats, all pointed to a much deeper estrangement than was expected and signalled a bitter and determined fight that is bound to prove ruinous for the Congress. I think all of us who were at Haripura realized that with such a background of suspicion and hostility, it was not possible to work together. It is clear that no effort should be spared to bridge the gulf if the strength of the Congress and even of the 'left' are to be developed.

It would be a considerable gain even if we did no more than recognize this problem. We have been rather complacent in the past and have seldom paused to consider what results our activities were producing. We must change this mentality. The prime consideration before us should be not what progress we as a sectarian group are making in the Congress, but what progress the Congress as a whole is making as a result of our efforts; our programmes and activities should not be for ourselves alone but intended to attract the whole Congress mass.

Suspicion and hostility have always been there and to a certain extent they are natural. However, we seem to have arrived at a stage where they are threatening to make work impossible by putting internecine quarrel before everything else. There are, doubtless, many reasons for this development. The objective causes, such as the attempt of the vested interests to drive a wedge between the two wings of the Congress and to increase their hold over it by alienating the 'left' from the 'right', we cannot remove. There are many other factors of a subjective nature which it is in our power to remove or control. The estrangement between the new and old ranks of the Congress has deepened very markedly since the formation of Congress ministries. There are many factors responsible for this. But the one single factor that is more responsible than the others is that somehow it has come to be believed that we who were opposed to acceptance of office wish to discredit the Congress ministries and engineer their downfall in any manner possible. This I understand is the honest belief of many of our leaders and colleagues.

It should be clear to us that we must do everything possible to remove such fatal misunderstandings. First, let me restate our attitude towards the Congress ministries. We were opposed to their formation. But after they came into existence we want them to fulfil the Congress programme; and

[4] J.B. Kripalani (1888-1982); began his political life with participation in the Champaran satyagraha, 1917; General Secretary, Indian National Congress, 1934-46, its President, 1946-7; member, Constituent Assembly, 1946-50, and Provisional Parliament, 1950-2; resigned from the Congress and formed the Kisan Mazdoor Praja Party, 1951; member, Lok Sabha, 1953-62, and 1963-70; publications include *The Gandhian Way*, *The Non-Violent Revolution*, *The Indian National Congress*, and *The Politics of Charkha*.

as Congressmen we want to assist them in their task. Above all, we want them to be instruments for strengthening the Congress and the national movement. We do not want them to concentrate on constitutionalism, but to combat the constitution and to fulfil their share of the task of preparing the country for the struggle that is inevitable on the issue of Federation. This we believe is the desire of the majority of Congressmen.

It is a fact nevertheless that our intentions and policies have been misunderstood. We have therefore to seriously set about clearing up this misunderstanding and so modifying our activities that no cause is given for misunderstandings to arise. It is my personal view that some of us have been hyper-critical of the Congress ministries and have emphasized shortcomings and overlooked achievements. I think a helpful course for us would be to reexamine our practical approach—I think the theoretical approach has always been sound—to this problem and mould our activities accordingly.

Another aspect of criticism which we have overemphasized is the distinction between 'right' and 'left'. This has irritated many of our leaders and co-workers. Apart from causing irritation, this distinction if emphasized too often is likely to obscure the fundamental unity of all ranks within the Congress and introduce an element of sectarianism in our thought and action that is bound to prove harmful in the end. I do not mean to suggest that there are no 'right' and 'left' wings in the Congress. But in the words of Professor [Harold] Laski by insisting too much and too often on the wings, we run the risk of forgetting the flight of the bird. It is that flight—progress of the organization as a whole—that we should keep before our eyes.

There is also another aspect of this problem which we are apt to ignore. Taking the Congress as a whole, it is, to my mind, more 'left' than 'right' in its resolutions and manifestos. This ought to have been of distinct advantage to us. But we have failed to make use of it. Our failure has been due largely to the fact that we have sought to emphasize group differences and have identified in our thinking the dominant group within the Congress. Here also is a definite problem before us. Instead of giving the impression of advocating group policies we should so act as to further the Congress programme itself. Finally, in our characterization of rightism, we should remember that the term rightist as applied to Congressmen means only those whose activities repudiate independence and the struggle for independence. One whom we might call a rightist in the socio-economic sense may be as staunch a fighter for independence as any socialist. If he has a political philosophy and technique which we believe might prove an obstacle in the achievement of independence after a certain stage, he does not on that account deserve to be called names but rather requires to be convinced through experience and understanding. Causing irritation is surely not the proper way to carry conviction.

There are some comrades who believe that Gandhism and Socialism are so fundamentally contradictory that it is impossible for their adherents to work together. It is true that there are fundamental contradictions between the two ideologies and I myself have so frequently drawn attention towards them. But as far as I am concerned there was and is no doubt in my mind that apart from power politics there is no reason why both groups cannot work in the closest cooperation possible. I believe further that both groups can march shoulder to shoulder as far as the final goal of independence. On the way adjustments will have to be made, clashes will have to be reconciled. But the companionship can and must remain unbroken.

There are many other things which one should write about the Haripura Congress. I have deliberately picked out [this] problem . . . because I was deeply impressed by it and because I felt there was need for us to take stock and indicate if necessary a new approach. I feel certain that the situation demands the sort of approach which I have described above. It is not concrete and definite perhaps. But then it cannot be so because it purports to be nothing more than an approach, a new start. I hope comrades will carefully consider it and adopt it.

56. Message to the *National Front*, 13 March 1938[1]

All glory to the *National Front*.[2] But please don't forget to work for the merger with the *Congress Socialist*.

Jayaprakash Narayan,
General Secretary
Congress Socialist Party

[1] *National Front*, 13 March 1938.

[2] An English weekly started from Bombay in 1938 as an organ of the Communist Party of India under the editorship of P.C. Joshi.

57. Speech at the Congress Socialist Party Conference, Lahore, 12 April 1938[1]

The Socialists are second to none in showing their respect for the Tricolour and even though we have a red flag which represents the will of the exploited

[1] *Tribune*, 13 April 1938. The speech was delivered after unfurling both the Red Flag and the National Flag at the site of the Conference.

masses of the whole world yet we honour the Tricolour as being the flag of the brave fighters for India's freedom.

The unfurling of the two flags together is a unique event so far as the Punjab is concerned and the event which took place today on the occasion of the All India Congress Socialist Party's fourth annual conference marks the dawn of a new era and beginning of a new understanding between the Socialists and the Congress ranks in this Province where the question of the importance of either of the two flags had been the cause of vital differences between the Socialist and the Congress workers.

The Red Flag which is an international flag represents the will of the exploited masses to be free politically and economically. That flag represents the unity of the oppressed masses of the world.

There is no quarrel between the Socialists and the Congressites over the Red Flag and the Tricolour. Those who stand under the Red Flag to fight the battle of the poor Kisans and the oppressed Mazdoors take pride in standing under the national flag of India to fight the battle of her freedom. The Socialists firmly believe in strengthening the Congress which body represents the will of the nation to be free. The differences which exist in the Punjab between the Socialists and the more progressive section of youth in the Congress are on the question of the importance to be given to the two flags at public functions.

The Congress Socialist Party has after due consideration come to the conclusion that they must respect the Tricolour as much as the Red Flag. Under the National Flag we have to fight the battle of India's freedom and under the Red Flag we have to carry the message of Socialism and trade unionism to the poor and the exploited classes and tell them that the Swaraj which India is striving to achieve will be Swaraj not of the capitalists but of the poor Mazdoors and Kisans.

58. Resolution on Socialist Unity at the Congress Socialist Party Conference, Lahore, 13 April 1938[1]

This Conference reiterates the need that the Party has always felt for the integration of all socialist forces in the country and reaffirms its burning desire to bring into existence a single united socialist party in India.

The Conference realizes that there are many obstacles at present in the way of such unity, the most notable being the inability so far of socialists with diverse groups and party attachments to work together smoothly and

[1] *Congress Socialist*, 23 April 1938.

in a spirit of co-operation and comradeship. It therefore appeals to all socialists to co-operate with the Party in removing these obstacles and in developing this most essential and urgently needed unity-in-action.

This Conference while it endorses the statement and the decision of the National Executive* made at its Patna meeting [9 August 1937] strongly feels that the most essential condition for the birth of a united party in India is unity between the C.S.P. and the "Red" Group, which are the two main Marxist Socialist parties in the country and that therefore particular care should be taken to bring these parties together.

Finally, the Conference calls upon all members of the Party to realize that their primary task is to strengthen the Party itself as a Marxian socialist party and to develop that independent initiative through which it has been able to make such a notable contribution not only to the socialist but also to the national movement.

*(Barring the admission into the Party of members of the Communist Party and those adhering to its Statement).

59. Speech while Moving the Resolution on Socialist Unity at the Congress Socialist Party Conference, Lahore, 13 April 1938[1]

The C.S.P. has strived from its inception for unity in socialist ranks. It has done more in that direction than any other group. From the beginning, it scrupulously refrained from arrogating monopolist and exclusive claims. It recognized the socialist character of other parties—the Communist Party was legal when the C.S.P. was formed.

A review of the various measures taken by the Party to realize socialist unity in India will convince even the most sceptic that the C.S.P.'s record in that direction has been the proudest and the best.

The group nearest to us was the Roy Group. The members of the group participated in our Patna conference and after and most of them were soon absorbed in the Party. The Party made every effort to accelerate this process of absorption.

The Communist Party was then not close to us. It was opposed to our programme, approach and tactics. It had characterized the Party as a Left manoeuvre of the bourgeoisie. This was not a stray remark of some individuals but the considered opinion of the Party voiced by the leaders

[1] *Congress Socialist*, 23 April 1938.

and in the Party pronouncements. It went to the extent of denouncing us as social-fascists. There could be no question of unity with them then. The "reds" were out to break the Party which they considered to be a spurious one.

We did not hit back. We did not point out their degrading of Marxism, their counter-revolutionary role. They persistently disturbed our meetings, ever demanding: "Why within the Congress?" We patiently kept on explaining our position, clarifying the situation. There was no participation in the recrimination from our side.

The concepts of united front and popular front, as we understand them today, were yet undiscovered. The Party was the pioneer in popularizing these concepts and in evolving the tactics necessary for realising them.

The Communist Party was by then declared illegal—it then functioned through the Red T.C.—a product of the communist sectarianism in the Trade Union movement. The Party had appointed a united front committee. That committee entered into agreements with the A.I.T.U.C., N.T.U.F. [National Trade Union Federation] and the R.T.U.C. [Red Trade Union Congress]. We co-operated in meetings and demonstrations and thrashed out the united front tactics.

We not only sought contact with the C.P. leaders who were free but took every opportunity to meet those who were in internment. While emphasizing the correctness of our approach and tactics we missed no occasion to express our desire for unity in socialist ranks. We worked for mutual association and co-operation.

In 1935 the Comintern met at Moscow. By the end of 1935 the attitude of the C.P. members towards the Party began to change. Some of them recognized our bonafides and genuineness. This clearer appreciation of the Party resulted not from any discussions between the two Parties but from personal talks and private exchange of views.

While from the beginning we had freely admitted Royists to the Party we had refused to take members of the "Red" group into the Party because of their hostility to the Party. Things began to change by 1936. The "reds" realized that the C.S.P. was a revolutionary party destined to play an important role in the national movement.

In our eagerness to realize socialist unity we took the unprecedented step of taking members of another group, e.g., the Roy group, in the Party. At Meerut in 1936 I recommended the extension of this concession to the "Red" group also, a suggestion unanimously agreed to by our Executive Committee.

We were so anxious for unity that we even agreed not to "boost the Congress" from the united front (with the C.P.) platform. The Royists were in complete agreement with the Party on the characterization of the Congress—the absorption of the members of the group was therefore greatly facilitated.

When Roy was released from jail, I met him and had many friendly talks with him. He told me that he approved of what we had been doing so far though he disapproved of the name of the Party. He said: "I want you to consider me as one of you" and even evinced his willingness to join the Party. To join the Party or not was, I told him, a choice that he alone could make. This was at Allahabad [1936].

In Bombay [1936] in some of his public pronouncements a different note was struck. When I went and saw him about it he said reassuringly that he stood by every word he had said at Allahabad. His followers in the Party, he assured, would loyally abide by the Party discipline.

But at the time of the National Convention at Delhi, the Roy group decided to smash up the C.S.P. and the procedure decided upon was that of mass resignations. These mass resignations were soon carried out and furious attempts were made to discredit the Party. The unity realized by the Party was thus partially shattered by Roy.

There were a number of local and provincial socialist parties. The C.S.P. has absorbed most of them. The Socialist Party of the Punjab at first refused to accept our approach to the Congress but was soon convinced about the correctness of our line and soon fell in step with the all India movement. In Andhra, the Labour Protection League was persuaded to drop its sectarianism and was absorbed in the Party. A Co-ordination Committee was appointed between the Bengal C.S.P. and the Labour Party. Our Party has thus ceaselessly strived for unity.

At Lucknow, after the Congress [1936], we arrived at a closer agreement with the "Red" group. As a result of the agreement a number of "reds" came and were taken into the Party.

At the Delhi meeting of the Executive Committee [1937] it was found that fraction-work, including from the C.P., was being carried on inside the Party. The Executive circularized the provincial parties to be more vigilant.

At the Patna meeting of the National Executive [1937], we received a statement on the C.S.P. from the C.P. The statement characterized the C.S.P. as a party of Left unity and denied it any claims to be a Marxist socialist party. This statement shook up the united front relations that had been developing between the two parties. As a wide difference in the conception of the C.S.P. [on the part] of the C.P. and the C.S.P. has now discovered it was no longer possible to admit the "reds" in the Party. This decision was unanimously reached by the Executive at Patna.

The refusal of admission to "reds" into the Party did not mean breaking off of friendly relations with the C.P. Our reply to its statement reiterates in no uncertain terms our continued desire for united front between the two parties.

The jolt to growing socialist unity had thus come from the C.P. I had several talks with the C.P. members on the statement of their Party on the C.S.P.

At the Calcutta meeting of the Executive [1937] a second statement was sent by the C.P. wherein it was suggested that we had misunderstood their first statement. But the clarification they offered was far from satisfactory. The Patna decision was therefore endorsed.

A third statement has just come wherein the "reds" recognize their mistake and accept the Marxist socialist character of the Party. At the same time the slogan is raised "all socialists inside the C.S.P.".

It is sometimes made out that by refusing admission to the "reds" to the Party we are balking socialist unity. That is hardly a correct perspective.

Today the C.S.P. and the C.P. cadres are not working in unity and harmony. So long as this unity is not achieved the admission of the "reds" into the Party will only make the Party an additional forum for disunity.

Even if all socialists are taken into the C.S.P. a number of important issues remain unresolved. What is to be the character and development of the C.S.P.? Will the C.S.P. be dissolved or not? With the realization of socialist unity the question of international affiliation assumes increasing importance. It is no unity where an independent party exists even after the united party is formed. It is sometimes suggested that under colonial conditions illegal work is necessary. But that does not mean sanctioning two parties—it only indicates the need for an illegal apparatus. The question of unity is thus more complex than the raising of the facile slogan of "all socialists inside the C.S.P." suggests.

There are a number of difficulties in the way of unity—the most important and obvious is the absence of unity in action between the cadres of the two parties. That unity must first be realized and the other difficulties must be discussed by the two parties through their executives.

Until a united party is created it is the primary duty of our members to strengthen the C.S.P. and develop its independent initiative. Confining the question of socialist unity to "all socialists within the C.S.P." is to put it in a wrong perspective. Emphasizing that aspect and ignoring the others and maligning those who refuse to be stampeded by this one-sided emphasis is hardly furthering the cause of socialist unity.

The C.S.P. has worked hardest for socialist unity and it will continue its endeavours in that direction in a spirit of realism.

60. Circular to Members of National Executive, Congress Socialist Party, 3 May 1938[1]

Bombay
3 May 1938

Circular Letter No. 1

To Members of the Executive Committee.

Dear Comrade,
You will have seen the statement[2] issued by me along with P.C. Joshi[3] in the press.

The question arises what is to be done if neither the Congress Working Committee nor the States' People's Conference take up the organization of volunteers from other Provinces to participate in the Flag Satyagraha in Mysore.

I feel that we should, in such an event, take the initiative in such organization and set up an *ad hoc* Committee including other Left groups and also individuals from the Congress and the States' People's Conference. Such a Committee would organize the sending of volunteers to Mysore from various provinces. [M.R.] Masani agrees with this.

I would like to know whether you are agreeable to the Party taking such a course of action.

As a decision may have to be taken immediately after the Working Committee and before our Executive meets, I am asking for your opinion by circular.

Will you please indicate what response can be expected from your province to such an appeal for volunteers for Mysore?

I would also suggest preparing the ground in your province for such action as is indicated above.

Please reply to Masani at Bombay immediately.

Yours sincerely,
Jayaprakash Narayan

[1] *AICC Papers* (NMML).

[2] See Appendix 11 for joint appeal issued by J.P. and P.C. Joshi to observe Mysore Day.

[3] P.C. Joshi (1907-80); organized the U.P. branch of the C.P.I., 1928; arrested in connection with the Meerut Conspiracy Case, 1929, and released, 1933; General Secretary, C.P.I., 1935-48, expelled, 1948, readmitted, 1951, and elected to its Central Committee, 1956.

61. Letter to Rammanohar Lohia [before 17 May 1938][1]

[Before 17 May 1938]

Dear Rammanohar,

I wrote to you sometime ago[2] to request you to lecture at our Summer School of Politics. Owing to the All India Kisan Conference the dates of the school have been shifted to 17th May to 18th June. The main subjects in which instructions will be given are Economics, Politics, History, Socialism, Volunteering, Congress, Peasant and Labour work, etc. Each one of the subjects will be divided into a number of topics to be covered in one or more lectures. I indicate below the topics which I desire you to take up. The lectures will be of an elementary but informative kind. It will be necessary to have notes prepared on them. Copies of your notes may be duplicated and distributed among the students. We may even try to prepare some pamphlets on the basis of the lectures delivered at the school. I therefore request you to prepare your topics with some care.

Please let me know when it will be possible for you to come to the school. We have decided that instructors must remain at the school at least for a week. I shall be obliged for an early reply.

The school will be held at Sonepur, B.N.W.Ry. If you come by the E.I.Ry., you have first to come to Patna and from there to cross the Ganges to Sonepur.

Let met know the time of your arrival so that somebody can meet you at the Patna Junction Station.

Yours fraternally,
Jayaprakash Narayan

P.S.
Your subjects are:

(1) World Politics
(2) Development of Capitalism & Imperialism
(3) Indians Overseas
(4) Decline of the British Empire

[1] *AICC Papers* (NMML).
[2] Not available.

62. Letter to Leonard M. Schiff, 24 May 1938[1]

Shri Jayaprakash Nagar
Summer School of Politics
P.O. Sonepur (Saran)
24 May 1938

Dear Schiff,[2]

Lots of thanks for your letter. I think we have been much at cross purposes in our correspondence. The point of view from which you write, and your friend too (for I have now received his letter), and the problems you raise are not common to my mental make-up though they have set me thinking along new lines. My attitude to Russia and my reactions to Lyons[3] are of a very different character—much simpler and far less psychological. Though not a member of the C.P., I have always been orthodox—even my slight unorthodoxies have [been] or are considered to be more orthodox than the misguided orthodoxies of the orthodox set (that is the way of all orthodoxies). How much Russia means to me it would be impossible for me to fully describe. The achievements of Russia are the stock-in-trade of people like myself. The history of Russia in the last two decades is to us not of academic interest but of great practical value. We who in our humble way are trying to mould Indian history (it is not out of immodesty that I write this) must take a serious note of everything that is happening in Russia and modify our practice here if necessary.

If I gave you any impression that I accepted all that Lyons says the fault must have been mine. But the impression is wrong. I have obvious differences with Lyons. But as I wrote in my last letter there are things happening in Russia which are no part of Marxism and do not fall under the category of mistakes. While the cruelties that attended collectivization might have been necessary, or might in parts have been caused by errors of leadership, things like the valuta chambers (if one does not doubt their historicity) can never be justified or excused. Absence of civil liberties under conditions of proletarian dictatorship is hypothetical with us; but there cannot be any excuse for absence of democracy within the Party.

I see what is happening within the Congress since the formation of

[1] *JP Papers* (NMML).

[2] Leonard M. Schiff; Christian missionary; visited India, 1929-32, and 1937-8; stayed for some time at Allahabad and worked in the Congress office; author of *The Present Condition of India: A Study in Social Relationships* (London, 1939) with an Introduction by Jawaharlal Nehru.

[3] Eugene Lyons; an American Communist of Russian origin; spent many years in the Soviet Union; returned to the U.S.A. disillusioned with the Soviet experiment; author of *Assignment in Utopia* (1937).

Congress ministries. Men of ideas, but with a certain amount of independence of thought and initiative (not necessarily socialists) are becoming suspect. And those who are prepared to be yes-men are being pushed up despite the fact that they might lack capacity and character and that some of them might have been even enemies of the Congress and the national revolution. Something akin to this seems to have happened in Russia. I might be mistaken. But if it is so, we cannot treat it lightly.

A word about the C.S.P. and C.P. affair. It is a pity that in spite of all that the C.S.P. has done from the very beginning for unity and the counter fact that the C.P. for a long time had been hostile to the C.S.P., the latter has been misunderstood in its recent attitude towards the problem of unity. I cannot tell you all about it in this letter. There may be a little of what you apprehend at the bottom of our recent decision. But the question of unity (if it is real unity) is more serious than merely the question whether C.P. members should be allowed within the C.S.P. My view is and has been that the C.P. of India has yet to arise. The present C.P., C.S.P., etc., are its nuclei and represent the largest Marxist tendencies in the country. These tendencies have come together largely due to C.S.P.'s efforts. . . . There must also be a movement in the other direction. True fusion and one party can only arise when the two leaderships have also fused (excluding the fringe of impossibles on both sides). But more of this when we meet—which we might before long.

Thanking you again for your letter and assuring you that I have not felt any annoyance at all at your writing and that I have very much appreciated that you have taken so much trouble to do so. I shall write to your friend in a few days. I am rather busy with my school.

With regards,

Yours sincerely,
(Jayaprakash Narayan)

63. Letter to Sri Krishna Sinha, 11 July 1938[1]

C/O *Janata*
Bankipore, Patna
11 July 1938

My dear Shree Babu,[2]
I wish to bring just a fact or two to your notice in the hope that they will receive due consideration from you.

[1] *JP Papers* (NMML).

[2] Sri Krishna Sinha (1887-1961); joined the Bar, 1915; gave up practice to join the non-

I do not know if you are aware that it has become common in Darbhanga for Congress workers to be proceeded against *en masse* after Congress elections for rioting, violence, theft, etc. It is regrettable that a quarrel between two groups of Congressmen should be taken so far and that the police should feel encouraged under a Congress ministry to behave in this manner. I have heard it freely alleged that the Party in office in Darbhanga Congress taking advantage of the confidence it enjoys of the ministers encourages the police and magistracy to use means to harass and suppress the workers of the other group—I cannot vouch for this, but the allegations, the *en masse* prosecutions at any rate, are worthy of your notice.

An evidence, perhaps, of the truth of these allegations, is that in the case of Pandit Dhanraj Sharma,[3] about whom I wished to write to you, the Crown has engaged the Public Prosecutor. Now, I understand that in cases under such sections as 379,323,147, etc., it is not customary for the Public Prosecutor to appear; and that if he does so, it means that the Government is particularly interested in the case and is keen about the punishment of the accused. This naturally weighs with the trying magistrate. In the case in question, there is another circumstance that might well influence the magistrate: I mean the fact that at one stage you had stayed proceedings in Court and had called for papers and later had allowed the case to proceed. That circumstance too would mean to the Magistrate that the Government is keen about the prosecution.

Returning to the question of the Public Prosecutor, I fail to understand why Government should be so keen about the conviction of Pandit Dhanraj Sharma. It is inconceivable that you desire it. I therefore request you to order the District Magistrate to withdraw the public prosecutor from the case.

Another case which I request you to look into—the case of Suraj Narayan Singh[4] of Darbhanga. He was convicted for six months in an Arms Act case by the S.D.O. Madhubani. The Additional District Judge confirmed the sentence which was reduced by the High Court to three months.

---

cooperation movement, 1921; imprisoned, 1922-3; member, Bihar Legislative Council, 1927-9, Indian Legislative Assembly, 1935-7, and Constituent Assembly, 1946; Secretary, Bihar Provincial Kisan Sabha, 1929; jailed during the civil disobedience movement, 1930, and 1932-3; Chairman, Monghyr District Board, 1934-7; Premier, Bihar, 1937-9, and 1946-52; arrested for taking part in the individual satyagraha, 1940, and released, 1941; detained for participating in the Quit India movement, 1942-5; Chief Minister, Bihar, 1952-61.

[3] Dhanraj Sharma (1899-1981); left studies to join the non-cooperation movement, 1921; participated in the Kisan movement in Bihar; imprisoned for 14 years with breaks during the national movement; President, Forward Bloc, Bihar, for some time; member, Bihar Legislative Assembly, 1946-51, and 1952-6.

[4] Suraj Narain Singh (1908-73); participated in the non-cooperation movement, 1921, and civil disobedience movement; jailed, 1930; joined the Hindustan Socialist Republican

Sir Manmath Mukherji[5] who defended the accused in the High Court held the view (I have it on the authority of Phulan Babu[6] who was his junior in the case) that the charges were false and fabricated. The High Court too in its judgement failed to take into consideration certain important points which have been set out in the memorial already sent to Government and to which you may be good enough to refer.

There are only a month and 27 days left of the sentence and I would therefore request you to look into this matter at your earliest convenience. You may secure the opinion of Sir Manmath Nath on this question if you desire.

Hoping to be excused for this trouble and with regards,

Yours sincerely,
Jayaprakash Narayan

Association, 1931; imprisoned, 1932; associated with revolutionary activities in Bihar; joined the C.S.P., 1936; associated with the Kisan and Trade Union movements; arrested in December 1940 and detained at Deoli Detention Camp, later sent to Hazaribagh Central Jail; escaped along with J.P. from Hazaribagh Central Jail, 9 November 1942; organized Azad Dasta in Nepal; arrested, November 1944, released, 1947; member, Bihar Legislative Assembly, 1962-7; Chairman, Bihar P.S.P., 1963.

[5] Sir Manmatha Nath Mukherji (1874-1942); practised at Calcutta High Court, 1898-1923; Judge, Calcutta High Court, 1924-35; Acting Chief Justice of Bengal, 1934, and 1935; Acting Law Member, Viceroy's Executive Council, 1938; President, Bengal Provincial Hindu Mahasabha, 1939, and Bihar Provincial Hindu Mahasabha, 1939, and 1940; associated with various educational and social organizations; publications include *Civil Procedure Code*, *Evidence Act*, *Bengal Tenancy Act*, and *Partnership Act*.

[6] For biographical note on Phulan Prasad Verma see *JPSW*, Volume One, p. 62.

64. Letter to Bepin Behary Varma, 11 July 1938[1]

c/o *Janata*
Bankipore
Patna
11 July 1938

My dear Bepin Babu,[2]

As one who has so far remained a silent spectator of all that is going on within the Congress organization of the Province and as one who has been appalled at what is being done in the name of Gandhiji and of truth and

---

[1] *JP Papers* (NMML).

[2] Bepin Behary Varma (1892-1974); participated in the Champaran satyagraha, 1917, non-cooperation movement, 1920, and civil disobedience movement, 1930; imprisoned, 1930-1; member, Indian Legislative Assembly, 1934-9, and 1946-7; General Secretary, Bihar P.C.C., 1937-9; member, A.I.C.C. for thirty years; General Manager, Bettiah Estate, 1939-42, and 1947-50; member, Provisional Parliament, 1950-2, Lok Sabha, 1952-61, and Rajya Sabha, 1962-8.

non-violence, I wish to bring to your notice a few facts in the hope that they will receive at your hands due consideration and that proper steps will be taken. I wish to add that I am writing to you merely as a friend and in my personal capacity entirely.

The facts I wish to bring to your notice are in themselves of no particular significance in the context of the great task before us, but are symptomatic of the disease that threatens to overpower the Congress. I hope those to whom are entrusted the fate and future of the Congress will soon take steps to check this malady.

I have been convinced in the past few months that dishonesty and self-seeking are on the ascendant in the Congress today, helped by the programme of power politics inaugurated from above. In my opinion these are developments which irrespective of who is responsible for them must be put down with an iron hand if the fair name of the Congress is to survive.

However, to come to my point. The first fact that I wish to place before you is that in the case that is proceeding against Pandit Dhanraj Sharma under sections 379, 323 and 147 at Darbhanga there is a statement which the Court has called for as an exhibit from the prosecution which purports to be the original report of the presiding officer (in a Congress election), Sjt. Harendra Kishore Chaudhary, to the returning officer Sjt. Jadunandan Sahay.[3] It has been brought to my notice that the report exhibited is not the original report but has been amended at several places so that it might tally with the evidence given before the Court by Sjt. Harendra Kishore Chaudhary. The original report was in the possession of the P.C.C. which had forwarded it to the Violence Enquiry Committee and was later taken away, I understand, by Babu Satyanarayan Sinha[4] (who took it as immaterial, however) for the purpose of exhibiting it before the Court. The point may appear unimportant but it seems very regrettable to me that such forgery should be committed in a Congress document. May I hope that you will make enquiries into this matter and take the trouble of satisfying me regarding it? The Violence Enquiry Committee has in its possession another copy of the said report and Pandit Dhanraj Sharma too has a copy which bears the initials of the returning officer, Sjt. Jadunandan Sahay. These

[3] Jadunandan Sahay; elected delegate to Haripura Congress from Darbhanga, 1938.

[4] Satya Narayan Sinha (1900-83); joined the national movement, 1920; member, Bihar Legislative Council, 1926-30, Indian Legislative Assembly, 1934-46, Constituent Assembly, 1946-50, Provisional Parliament, 1950-2, and Lok Sabha, 1952-70; President, Darbhanga D.C.C., 1930-47; General Secretary, Bihar P.C.C., 1942-7; Minister of Parliamentary Affairs, 1952-63, of Parliamentary Affairs, Information and Broadcasting, 1963-4, of Parliamentary Affairs and Communication, 1964-7, of Health, 1967-9, and of Information, Broadcasting and Communication, 1969-71, Government of India; Governor, Madhya Pradesh, 1971-7.

copies tally completely but there are material differences with the copy exhibited before the Court. The question is, has the Violence Enquiry Committee forged the report or has Pandit Dhanraj Sharma done so, and also forged the initials of Sjt. Jadunandan Sahay, or has the forgery been committed by the complainant or the prosecution? Sjt. Harendra Kishore Chaudhary deposed before the Magistrate that the report exhibited was the report that he submitted to the returning officer. In view of the atmosphere of utter demoralization prevailing, it would be quite worthwhile to look into the question carefully. At any rate I would request you as a friend and comrade to give me satisfaction on this point. If you find after enquiry that the report exhibited is not the original one, I would request you to write to the Magistrate about it and send him a true copy of the true report.

The second fact which I wish to place before you is concerning a D.C.C. election and its aftermath at Bisanpur polling station in Darbhanga Sadar Thana. The candidates were Bachnu Chaudhary and Harbans Misra, the first supported by the party in office and the second by the rival group.

There are two noteworthy things about the elections. While polling was in progress, there was some disturbance and the ballot-boxes were removed from the booth. The presiding officer reported to the returning officer that the ballot-boxes had been taken away by the supporters of Harbans Misra. On the basis of this report, the returning officer declared Bachnu Chaudhary elected.

Now, it transpires that this Bachnu Chaudhary had filed a complaint on instruction from the R.O., as the complaint itself admits, after polling had been suspended, to the Sub-Inspector, Sadar, charging Harbans Misra with arson in which he stated that the presiding officer himself had given him the ballot-boxes in question.

Here is an amazing case of dishonesty. The presiding officer reports—the report perhaps is now in possession of Pt. Prajapati Misra[5]—that the ballot-boxes were taken away by Harbans Misra's supporters and on that basis the latter loses the election. On the other hand, we have a statement of the candidate who was declared elected that the ballot-boxes were actually with him and were given to him by the presiding officer himself. I request you to look into the matter and take such steps as may have a deterrent effect on such dishonest practices.

[5] Prajapati Mishra (1898-1953); President, Bettiah Sub-Division Congress Committee, and later Champaran D.C.C.; participated in the non-cooperation movement, 1920-1, and civil disobedience movement, 1930-1; presided over Bihar Youth Conference, 1929; Chief Organizer, Champaran Earthquake Relief Committee, 1934; Chairman, Champaran District Board and Bettiah Municipal Board, 1934-35; offered individual satyagraha and arrested, 1940; detained for participating in the Quit India movement, 1942-5; member, Bihar Legislative Assembly, 1946-53; President, Bihar P.C.C., 1948, and 1952.

The other noteworthy thing in this case is the sorry fact that a false charge of arson, as I have already mentioned above, was lodged against his rival by Bachnu Chaudhary. That recourse should be taken to such despicable tactics in the course of an election quarrel, I, at least, could not have imagined. I might remind you again that the complaint was lodged by Bachnu Chaudhary on instructions from the returning officer! The police on enquiry found that the charge was "false and concocted" and dropped the matter. The complainant, however, pursued it and filed a cross petition before the S.D.O. who rejected the petition.

Such are the circumstances attending this election. Both indicate a deplorable state of affairs. Will you be good enough to make your own enquiries and take necessary steps. Those who are found guilty of dishonest practice should receive a severe punishment.

The last point is concerning the Madhubani Municipal election. Fortunately or unfortunately, the Madhubani Town Congress Committee is in the hands of people belonging to the group of Pt. Dhanraj Sharma and Pt. Ramnandan Misra. This T.C.C. [Town Congress Committee] has, I understand, nominated twelve persons for the twelve elective seats of the Municipality. The official party has raised objections to these nominations and has asked the P.C.C. through the D.C.C. to interfere, and revise the nominations. I also understand that your Working Committee is going to interfere in this matter. I do not question the right or desirability of the P.C.C. reviewing and revising nominations made by subordinate bodies, but I do desire to draw your attention to a few facts in this connection.

Sometime ago elections of the Darbhanga Municipality were held. Nominations were made by the Darbhanga T.C.C. At that time there was a vigorous protest lodged by a large number of members of the D.C.C., against some of the nominations. Wires and letters were sent to the Provincial office. But the latter saw no reason to interfere. The office did not even reply to the letter of protest. Forty-five members of the D.C.C. requisitioned a meeting of the D.C.C., but the office-bearers refused to call it.

To me this strikes as a case of partiality. The P.C.C. should take a non-partisan view in local disputes and equal weight should be attached to complaints received from different Congressmen irrespective of party considerations.

However, as I have said I do not question the right of the P.C.C. to interfere in such matters. But I should like to suggest that unless the individuals nominated do not satisfy the test we have for such positions, the P.C.C. should refuse to interfere with the decisions of a properly constituted Congress Committee. Care should be taken that no one who has an anti-Congress record, at least in the recent past, is given the Congress ticket. I do not know if you agree with me on this view. I should nevertheless urge it upon you in the hope that you will give it due consideration.

I have presumed much upon your time for which I ask to be excused. These facts were concretely brought to my notice and I felt I should write to you about them. I shall feel obliged for a reply.

With regards,

Yours affectionately,
Jayaprakash Narayan

P.S.
I am going to Gaya tomorrow and will stay in the District for a week. I shall send you my report when I return.

J.P.

65. Message to the *Congress Socialist*, 30 July 1938[1]

I should have sent you my congratulations on the new aspect of the *Congress Socialist*. It is in its changed shape and size really very attractive. I believe it is more attractive than the other weekly journals.

Jayaprakash Narayan

[1] *Congress Socialist*, 30 July 1938.

66. Letter to Z.A. Ahmad, 17 August 1938[1]

Bankipore
Patna
17 August 1938

Dear Zain,
You must have received my last letter.[2] Since then I have received Jawaharlal's letter from Houlgate.[3] The letter is depressing and full of irrelevant scepticism. The upshot is that he does not want to associate himself with new ventures till he is sure about its (*sic*) future—or, at least, its (*sic*) business aspect. I have sent him a letter of thanks. He seems to have been

[1] *JP Papers* (NMML).

[2] Not available.

[3] See Appendix 13 for text of Nehru's letter to J.P. dated 2 August 1938. Nehru wrote this letter in reply to J.P.'s cable inviting him to become a foundation member of the Socialist Book Club which was started to create a solid intellectual foundation for the socialist movement. Foundation Members were: Subhas Chandra Bose, Narendra Deva, J.P., M.R. Masani, P.C. Joshi, Rammanohar Lohia, Mulk Raj Anand and Z.A. Ahmad. The Board of Directors consisted of Narendra Deva, J.P. and Z.A. Ahmad. The club, however, proved a non-starter.

much depressed by the failure of the National Publications and he has made some disparaging remarks about the *National Herald*[4] too.

Well, that's that. Subhas has not replied yet. I am writing to him again. Perhaps we will have to go without both of these gentlemen.

Have you assigned any work yet out of those we discussed here. I should like to do the Labour Manual myself. If you have written to Adhikari[5] already, please write him again not to worry about it. I have a conception of the thing & should like to execute it myself.

I am definitely leaving Patna for Calcutta en route to Malabar on the 24th August. I shall take the Calcutta Mail from here at about 9.30 p.m. reaching Calcutta the next morning. You should also so arrange your programme that we either travel together or meet in Calcutta on the 25th. I shall give two or three days to collection work and then proceed down South. I expect to bring with me two or three pamphlets for you from Malabar.

Expecting to hear from you soon with greetings.

Yours affectionately,
Jayaprakash Narayan

[4] *National Herald*, an English daily, started from Lucknow by Jawaharlal Nehru along with Purushottam Das Tandon, Narendra Deva and others in September 1938. K. Rama Rao was its first Editor. Jawaharlal Nehru was Chairman of its Board of Directors from 1938 to 1946.

[5] Gangadhar Adhikari (1898-1981); one of the prominent leaders of the C.P.I.; accused in the Meerut Conspiracy Case and imprisoned, 1929-33; like other Communist leaders, associated with the C.S.P. in the late thirties.

67. Comment on M.R. Masani's Speech [after 5 September 1938][1]

For the time being I do not however contemplate that the Congress including both its Right and Left wings will compromise in the smallest measure on this fundamental issue about which there never has been any ambiguity regarding Congress policy.

While I cannot say definitely what course will be adopted by us and other radical elements in the Congress if the latter comes to a compromise on the Federation issue, there is no doubt that the situation would be more serious than any that has occurred in the recent history of the Congress.

[1] *Amrita Bazar Patrika*, 8 September 1938. Statement issued at Calcutta. M.R. Masani in a speech at public meeting at Ahmedabad on 5 September 1938 had threatened to offer satyagraha if the Congress accepted Federation.

68. Letter to Subhas Chandra Bose [before 22 November 1938][1]

[Before 22 November 1938]

My dear Subhas Babu,[2]

Sometime back I wrote to you about the Socialist Book Club which we wish to organize. I also sent you a copy of the Memorandum and Rules of the Club.[3] We would like to know if you would agree to be a Foundation Member of the Club and also a member of its Advisory Council. We would be obliged for an early reply, because we wish to advertise the scheme and enrol members. Your association with the Club would be of tremendous value to us.

The day I wrote to you I also cabled to Jawaharlal for his consent to the Foundation Membership. I regret to say that he has declined our request because he says he does not know well what the scheme is like. I have sent him a copy of the [Memorandum and Rules of the Club] by air mail, but I don't know what he will decide. I hope his decision will in no way influence your own and you will agree to our earnest proposal.

I shall be in Calcutta on the 25th and will stay for a few days to raise funds for the Club. We are counting on your active help in this.

With regards,

Yours affectionately,
Jayaprakash

[1] *JP Papers* (NMML).
[2] For biographical note on Subhas Chandra Bose see *JPSW*, Volume One, p. 114.
[3] See Appendix 14.

69. Letter to Jawaharlal Nehru, 23 November 1938[1]

Calicut
23 November 1938

Dear Bhai,

I hasten to add my welcome to that of the Nation to you on your homecoming. I wish it were possible for me to rush up to Allahabad to meet you and talk to you about the tragic events you have witnessed in Europe and about things that have happened here since you left. I may be able to fulfil this desire in a couple of weeks if you are not immediately caught up in a whirlwind programme. I have been vegetating here in Malabar

[1] *Jawaharlal Nehru Papers* (NMML).

undergoing a special Ayurvedic treatment for my sciatica. I feel improved though not cured. Prabhavati[2] is with me. It gave us great pleasure to read in the papers that you are much improved in health as a result of your European tour.

I hope that having been in the midst of tremendous happenings you have not forgotten the small affair of the Socialist Book Club of which I wrote to you. We have been able to make some progress with our scheme, and with the help of Subhas Babu we were able to raise about Rs. 3,000/- for it at Calcutta. The office of the Club is at Allahabad and Z.A. [Ahmad] is in charge as Managing Director. The Club is a non-party affair. In the letter[3] you wrote from Europe you expressed your inability to join the Club as a Foundation Member till you had occasion to know more about it. You had also expressed your reluctance to identify yourself with any group. As I have said, the Club is not a group affair and has no allegiance to anything except to Socialist literature. As for the other thing, if you have time, Ahmed will discuss with you our scheme, and I need hardly say that we shall only be too glad to accept any suggestions you might make. Subhas Babu is already a Foundation Member of the Club. Your refusal to join it would be a great blow to us. I admit that the Club would work on a small scale, but I think it would be unreasonable to expect from the Socialist movement in India results that are beyond its resources. And, if you will excuse me for saying so, it would be unfair of you, who are naturally used to doing things on a grand scale, to non-cooperate with the efforts of Socialists in India just because they are puny as compared with those of older and wider organizations. We are, I think, not unjustified in expecting that, if you will not fully identify yourself with us, you will, as a Socialist, at least help us in doing well the little we may undertake to do.

In your letter you had said that politics in India had fallen into a rut. In your absence they have only gone deeper into it. I feel that away from the louder (*sic*) stage of politics things are slowly happening which are converting the Congress from a democratic organization of the millions of the down-trodden people into a hand-maid of Indian vested interests. A vulgarization of Gandhism makes this transition easy and gives this new Congress the requisite demagogic armour. It seems to me that the need has arisen of examining closely the trend of Congress policy, particularly in the Congress provinces and of redefining the socio-economic goal of the Congress. The attitude of Congress Governments towards the Labour Movement as represented by the Trade Union Congress should be an eye-opener to those who do not wish that the Ministries should be utilized to

[2] For biographical note on Prabhavati Devi see *JPSW*, Volume One, p. 41.

[3] Not available.

bind the workers' organization hand and foot and deliver them to the employers. We are faced today with the real danger of Indian industry being made a synonym for Indian nationalism. Then there is the working of the Congress organizations. These are largely defunct and where they are working they have either been reduced to election machines or work with no appreciation of their tasks and of the preparations they should make to face them. I think you will have to answer the question, not so much in words as in action, whether you will have the Congress depend for the achievement of its goal entirely on its so-called constructive programme. When the Gandhian is faced with the question whether the Congress is adequately being prepared for its tasks his answer is clear and honest that only by carrying out the constructive programme shall we reach our goal. You should tell the country if there is anything more that needs be done and show it how it should be done. The Socialist movement, as you know, has placed in the foreground the programme of labour and peasant organization to which may be added volunteer, youth and student organization. Labour and peasant organizations have been conceived as supporting limbs of the Congress and not as rival bodies. You have on innumerable occasions made your position clear on this programme. But I feel the time has come when you should go further and take a hand in moulding and developing it. It is necessary for you to consider what must be done to give shape and firmness to that undoubted urge towards social freedom that exists among the overwhelming majority of the people of this country and also, I believe, of the Congress members. This urge has not found any wider expression yet than that represented by the incipient Socialist movement in the country. I believe that basic work has to be done for this purpose and that you alone can do it if you only spared a little time and thought for it.

So much for giving a fresh direction and push to the social aims of the national movement. There remains the immediately more important question of the next offensive (will it be the last?) against the enemy. Have we any clear conception of it? What are we doing to prepare ourselves for it? When shall we launch it? Are we to wait till the British chose a time for us which will naturally be more favourable to them? I suppose the technique of Satyagraha does not permit one to prepare plans of offensive in advance. The only plan we may conceive of is that we must spin more and do other soul-stirring things like that. But will you be satisfied with it? Practically all that you added to the Congress programme after such strenuous fights in the Working Committee have been shelved—the democratization of the Congress committees, mass contacts, Muslim contacts, combating the slave constitution. Of course, there is a silver lining too—the awakening in the States and it is heartening that you intend devoting some attention to it. But the other things need your attention much more.

I expect to leave Calicut on November 23 and reach Bihar in the first week of December.

With regards,

Yours affectionately,
Jayaprakash

70. Letter to District Magistrate, Gaya, 15 January 1939[1]

Rajendra Ashram
Gaya
15 January 1939

To
The District Magistrate,
Gaya.

Dear Sir,
I thank you for your letter of Jan. 14 asking me to meet you and the Superintendent of Police to discuss the demonstration that has been announced for tomorrow in connection with the trial of Pandit Jadunandan Sharma. I appreciate very much your desire to seek our cooperation in this matter. The District Congress Committee is always prepared to lend its co-operation to you and the other officers in the district whenever it is required in public interest. In this matter of demonstration also we are prepared to cooperate with you and I assure you that there is no desire on our part, or on the part of the District Kisan Sabha, about which too I may speak with knowledge, to interrupt or cause any disturbance to the proceedings in Court. I should have gladly accepted your invitation to see you, but I have just (10 a.m.) returned from Nawada and have to leave immediately by the afternoon train for Patna. I shall, however, be returning tomorrow morning and shall be present when the demonstration takes place. If necessary I may meet you tomorrow. In the meanwhile, Babu Jamuna Prasad Singh,[2] whom you must know, and the Secretary of the District Congress Committee, Pandit Ramchandra Sharma,[3] will see you today whenever you desire. It would be desirable to have the meeting as soon as possible so that there

[1] *JP Papers* (NMML).

[2] Jamuna Prasad Singh; one of the prominent leaders of the Kisan movement in Gaya; member, Bihar Legislative Assembly, 1937-50.

[3] Ramchandra Sharma; Secretary, Gaya D.C.C., 1939; arrested for participating in the individual satyagraha, 1941, and Quit India movement, 1942; Secretary, Patna District Forward Bloc; member, Provincial Kisan Council in the 1940s.

may be time left for notices to be printed giving instructions to the public on the lines as may be agreed upon between them and you.

Thanking you again for your letter.

Yours sincerely,
Jayaprakash Narayan

71. Statement on Causes of Rioting at Gaya, 29 January 1939[1]

I came here from Gaya for a few hours to acquaint Babu Rajendra Prasad with the situation there. I have not much to say at this stage except this that the incidents at Gaya[2] were such that no sensible Hindu or Musalman would fail to be ashamed of. The riot was communal only in name because there was no communal issue involved. It would be well if the leaders of both communities took serious note of this. We never lacked grounds for fighting among ourselves to afford to invent fresh ones. There is little doubt that the insignificant flag incident at the school, which had been settled amicably between the parties concerned, would never have led to such a serious situation, had not feelings been aroused and hatred and enmity deliberately been spread around. There seem to be difficult times ahead for all those who have the interests of the nation, and therefore of all communities, at heart if this kind of poisonous atmosphere is allowed to persist. It is possible that the Muslim community has been persuaded for the time being to remain out of the Congress, but no one can believe that it is ever possible for people to persuade the Hindu and Muslim communities to seek their undoubted destruction by fighting each other without any rhyme or reason. As far as we Congressmen are concerned, this is a time for the utmost forbearance. We must avoid in the national interest all such issues which offend our Muslim countrymen. For instance, I have no doubt that the national flag should not be made a matter for controversy and bad blood and that it should not be flown over public institutions without the approval of the members of the minority communities that may be connected with it. To do otherwise is not only a disservice to the national flag but also to the entire national cause which we hold so dear.

As far as the situation in Gaya is concerned I am glad to say that it has

[1] *Searchlight*, 31 January 1939. Statement issued at Patna.

[2] Refers to the incidents of rioting at Gaya over the question of hoisting the national flag on the City School on 26 January 1939. Muslim students wanted either to bring down the national flag or to hoist the Muslim League Flag. As a result of stray assaults, violence and panic spread in the city and curfew was imposed and police patrols were posted. J.P. and other leaders intervened to pacify the agitated students.

improved considerably since the outbreak of the riot and is now completely under control. Feelings have not yet subsided to the normal, though neighbourly relations are being steadily restored. A very hopeful sign is that leaders of all communities are co-operating in re-establishing peace, order and neighbourliness. So we hope for the best.

72. Statement on Resignation of Congress Working Committee Members, 25 February 1939[1]

The developments that have taken place at Wardha and the decision of the 13 members[2] of the Working Committee to resign from it and not to join it under Subhas Babu's presidentship have come to us, as I am sure they have come to many others, as a great shock. The statement[3] of Pandit Jawaharlal Nehru, a believer as he has been all these years in the policy of 'united front' has made that shock more painful. I do not think that the situation as it has been created demands that it should be allowed to deteriorate further by raising a public controversy over it. I for one have no intention to wish it so. But as Secretary of the All India Congress Socialist Party, I do represent a considerable section of Congressmen in the country as also the views of a Party which for good or for evil has been functioning these five years in the country and has stood consistently for definite policies and programmes. Therefore, the Wardha developments call for at least a bare statement of the Party's position.

It was as if in the shadow of these coming developments that the National Executive of our Party met at Allahabad.[4] Its decisions have already appeared in the press. The Executive emphasized the need for maintaining the unity of the Congress and offered the cooperation of the Party to both Mahatma Gandhi and Mr. Bose in this task. The twelve members of the Working

[1] *Searchlight*, 28 February 1939. Statement issued at Patna.

[2] Twelve members of the Congress Working Committee namely—Vallabhbhai Patel, Abul Kalam Azad, Rajendra Prasad, Sarojini Naidu, Bhulabhai Desai, Pattabhi Sitaramayya, Shankarrao Deo, Harekrushna Mahtab, J.B. Kripalani, Abdul Ghaffar Khan, Jairamdas Doulatram and Jamnalal Bajaj resigned from the Committee on 22 February 1939 due to their differences with Subhas Chandra Bose. Jawaharlal Nehru sent his resignation separately.

[3] Jawaharlal Nehru issued a statement to Press at Wardha on 22 February 1939 (published in the *Bombay Chronicle*, 23 February 1939) explaining reasons for his resignation from the Congress Working Committee and indicating that he would not be prepared to cooperate with the new Committee. See also *Selected Works of Jawaharlal Nehru*, Volume 9, pp. 485-7.

[4] The National Executive of the Congress Socialist Party met at Allahabad on 18-20 February 1939. Its resolutions were published in the *Searchlight*, 22 February 1939.

Committee, who have resigned in a group, have, however sought to knock the bottom out of this unity by raising the question of incompatibility of groups within the Congress. It is clear from their letter of resignation that, whatever might have been the issue of the Presidential contest, the breach that has been made at Wardha would have occurred nevertheless, because the time has come to quote their words, when the country should have a clear-cut policy not based on compromise between different incompatible groups. In my humble opinion, there are no incompatible groups within the Congress, because every group accepts its aim and creed. If the Congress is conceived of as an ideological party, it would be necessary to change the qualifications for membership and demand that only those who accepted certain theories should sign the Congress membership pledge and be admitted into its organization. It seems unreasonable first to admit everyone who accepts the aim of independence and peaceful and legitimate methods and then to demand that only one group of these members should shape the policy of the organization. Never in the long history of the Congress has this been so. Its policies ever have represented the largest common measure of agreement between the various groups that have constituted it. Only for that reason, the policies of the Congress were able to attain the status of national policies and only on that condition can they continue to be so.

It is the height of illogic to contend, on the one hand, that the Congress represents all sections, classes, communities and interests and, on the other, to demand that only one group of Congressmen should decide its policies. It is natural that the decisions of such a wide national organization should represent a compromise between all the multifarious interests which make it. Taking only the recent history of the Congress, it should not be difficult to see how every important decision that was reached was in the nature of a compromise between the ideas of its various groups. The decision of the Lahore Congress, and before it of the Calcutta Congress, the decision of the Karachi Congress, all represented such a compromise. When Mahatma Gandhi called off civil disobedience at Patna in 1934, and initiated the legislative programme, he compromised, as he said then, with the parliamentary mentality which according to him had come to stay. When Sardar Vallabhbhai Patel blessed office acceptance at the Delhi A.I.C.C., in spite of the fact as he was careful to explain, that he still stood firmly by the policies of the "no change" days he did it to compromise with Mr. Satyamurthi's mentality because otherwise as he said a thousand Satyamurthis would arise where now there was only one. Thus every vital decision of the Congress has represented a compromise.

The need for such compromise is greatest when the time approaches for a big step forward irrespective of who gives the lead and who symbolizes the big forward step; it is foolish to expect that the Congress or the country can advance very far if only one group takes into its head to march forward leaving the rest behind. If the country is today, as it undoubtedly seems to be, on the threshold of another big step forward, the need is not for disunity and non-cooperation but for their very opposite. I would go further and say that not only must the whole Congress act together in that case but that some compromise and some understanding should be reached even with organizations outside it, which may have objectives in common with the Congress.

If, therefore, this theory of incompatibility which has been trotted out is the only reason for the non-cooperation of the twelve members of the Working Committee, it seems to me to be a very slender reason for plunging the country into confusion and deliberately causing such injury to the organization as is bound to result from such a policy.

The 12 leaders have also talked of leaving Mr. Subhas Bose free to frame his policies. This is a gift that is forcibly thrust into unwilling hands. I do not think that Subhas Babu has demanded dictatorial powers so as to be able to formulate his policy. Indeed, neither he nor the other twelve can assume that power for themselves. It is the delegates who shall assemble at Tripuri, who will ultimately determine Congress policy for the coming year.

The utmost the President and his Cabinet are expected to do is to recommend their considered proposals to the delegates. It would have been appropriate for these members who have resigned to first discover what their differences were and whether they were unbridgeable. Only after that if it was found that an agreement was not possible, they could have resigned, though it should be added that such has not been the practice heretofore. However, even after their resigning, the proper course to my mind would be for both the President and the 12 members of the Working Committee to place their respective proposals before the delegates at Tripuri and leave it to them to decide. Only after their verdict the question of the new Working Committee and the question of cooperation and non-cooperation would arise. This seems to me to be the straightforward conduct to adopt in a democratic political organization. I, therefore, cannot help feeling that the resignations in these circumstances of the 12 members has been a great blunder and has been prompted by other than political considerations.

Coming to the statement of Pandit Jawaharlal Nehru it has come to me and I am sure to many others who have looked to him for a bold and farseeing lead, unaffected by the subjective factors that are inevitable in political life, but that should have no bearing on political decisions, as a great blow. I confess to a sense of having been deceived, unwillingly, no doubt, because during this crisis I have been much in touch with him. It was my own denseness undoubtedly that had led me to expect otherwise and to believe that Jawaharlalji, while disapproving of much that had happened, would yet take a hand in guiding the destinies of the Congress and would not like the others to adopt an attitude of non-cooperation unless he found that he was not in agreement with what Subhas Babu was wanting to do.

I have reasons to believe that it was easily possible for Panditji and Subhas Babu to evolve an agreed policy to be laid before Tripuri. Our regret is keener, therefore, that Panditji has taken such a step. There is only one cause for satisfaction in the stand that he has taken, namely, that he has not accepted the theory of incompatibility and homogeneity and that he still stands on the ground of united front. But, for that very reason his action becomes incomprehensible. Nor are the reasons he has given convincing. He refers to his disagreements with Subhas Babu regarding national and international questions. But has he had no disagreements regarding these questions with his colleagues in the past and with Gandhiji? And did he on that ground non-cooperate with them or did he try to evolve a common formula and act up to it? Can the same not be done today? He further refers to the atmosphere of suspicion and lack of mutual faith at the very top. Surely, such [a] condition is deplorable, but one doubts whether the method adopted is the remedy for it. I am sure Jawaharlalji, of all the leaders, is the last person whom we have to remind of this atmosphere. He himself has not forgotten it when he refers to his repeated desire during his Presidentship to resign his office.

As for the specific complaint that Subhas Babu made certain statements about his colleagues during the election which he has not cleared up yet, I confess that I was among those who did not like those statements when they were made and I too feel that Subhas Babu should clear up his position about them. I understand that his remarks were not aimed at the members of the Working Committee, but he alone can say it authoritatively. Again, Panditji mentions the tendency for local disputes to be dealt with from the top and deprecates it. By all means let us deprecate such tendencies. But, firstly, Panditji does not know the extent to which this tendency had spread in the past, though in his report to the Haripura Congress, he seemed to be vaguely conscious of it, and secondly, he fails to place such a matter in its right perspective when he tries, instead of preventing it in a direct and simple manner, to make it a ground for the disastrous and far-going step that he has taken. He also talks of chaos and ordered and disciplined progress as if these were the alternatives between which he had to choose. I do not know what has given him the impression that Subhas Babu and those who may be with him are working for chaos. I can only say that the chaos is elsewhere.

Jawaharlalji might answer by saying that he has functioned as an individual to escape the responsibility that surely weighed heaviest on him at the present moment, but he has not justified his action. It is insupportable for a Socialist to contend that he functions as an individual. A Socialist is nothing if he does not stand for a definite policy at all times, normal or critical.

Finally, much as we regret the decision of Wardha, we consider it ill-advised and unfair both to the Congress and Subhas Babu. I can only conclude with the following words from the resolution of the National Executive of the Party:

In view of the Party's share of responsibility in the issue of the Presidential contest and of its adherence to democratic principles, it cannot free itself from the responsibility that may be consequent upon that contest except when it may have to be answerable for policies with which it may not be in agreement.

73. Amendment to G.B. Pant's Resolution at Subjects Committee Meeting, Tripuri, 9 March 1939[1]

The amendment sought to make the last paragraph read as follows:

In view of the critical situation that may develop during the coming year, and, for which we have to prepare the country, and in view of the fact that the cooperation of Mahatma Gandhi is essential in order to lead the Congress and the country to victory during such a crisis, the Committee regards it as imperative that the Congress Executive should command his implicit confidence, and requests the President to nominate the Working Committee in accordance with the wishes of Gandhiji.

[1] *Hindustan Times*, 10 March 1939. J.P.'s amendment was lost by 210 votes to 128. G.B. Pant in his resolution moved at the Subjects Committee meeting at Tripuri on 9 March 1939 emphasized the need to reaffirm faith in Gandhi's leadership, expressed confidence in the old Working Committee and urged the President to nominate the new Working Committee according to Gandhi's wishes. See Appendix 16 for text of the resolution. See item 78 for biographical note on G.B. Pant.

74. Speech while Moving the Amendment to G.B. Pant's Resolution at Subjects Committee Meeting, Tripuri, 9 March 1939[1]

The Party had its differences with Mahatma Gandhi. We have not made that a secret from him. Whenever it became necessary, we have expressed our differences. In spite of it, we have stated in this amendment that the leadership and guidance of Gandhiji are necessary. Some may express surprise as to why we who have differences with Gandhiji should have

[1] *Hindustan Times*, 10 March 1939.

moved this amendment. But differences should not mean that we should be far away from Mahatma Gandhi. We Congress Socialists, have always worked for, and convinced the Congress and Mahatma Gandhi of the efficacy of our programme and policy, and Gandhiji has always taken into account the views of different groups within the Congress. The Congress Socialist Party is as anxious as ever to maintain a united front in the country, and Mahatma Gandhi has approved of it. We are sure that a crisis will develop very soon. This fact is admitted even in the resolutions moved. A crisis may come possibly within a year. We should, therefore, prepare the country to face the coming crisis.

75. Speech while Moving the Resolution on National Demand, Tripuri Congress, 11 March 1939[1]

Hon'ble Chairman[2] and friends, I would like to move this resolution before you:

I would like to make it clear to you that not I, but Pandit Jawaharlal, was to move this resolution.[3] But now that this responsibility has been passed on to me, I would move the resolution quite briefly. Among all the resolutions moved at the Tripuri Congress, this is the most important. This matter is being discussed afresh in the country for the last few months and the masses are struggling in various ways at many places. A great crisis is spreading in native states as well as in other parts of India and also in other countries. Everywhere some sort of turmoil has been raging, and conflicts and revolutionary movements are dominating the scene. The Congress had firmly resolved in Lahore (1929) that it aimed for Swaraj—Purna Swaraj. We are still far from that goal but internal and external circumstances have made it clear to us that the struggle is imminent in India too. We have evolved

[1] *Report of the 52nd Indian National Congress, Tripuri (Dt. Jubbulpore) Mahakoshal, 1939*. Original in Hindi.

[2] Maulana Abul Kalam Azad (1888-1958); one of the most prominent leaders of the Congress and its President, 1923, and 1940-6; participated in all the movements started by the Congress between 1920 and 1945, and suffered imprisonment on several occasions; member, Constituent Assembly, 1946-50, Provisional Parliament, 1950-2, and Lok Sabha, 1952-8; Minister of Education, 1947-58, and of Natural Resources and Scientific Research, 1952-7, Government of India; publications include: *Tarjuman-ul-Quran*, *Ghubar-i-Khatir*, and *India Wins Freedom*.

[3] The resolution on national demand had been moved by Jawaharlal Nehru on behalf of the Congress Working Committee at the meeting of the Subjects Committee on 11 March 1939. It declared afresh the solemn resolve of the Indian people to achieve independence and called upon Congressmen at all levels to prepare the country for a nationwide struggle to achieve it. See Appendix 17 for text of the resolution.

much since the struggle of 1930-1, but the goal is still far away. It was only after that struggle that the British Government conspired to introduce the Government of India Act (1935) which is working as a hurdle to our move forward. When the Congress looked into that conspiracy, it found that it also contained some provisions that might help us move to our goal. This was why the Congress decided that it would make use of Provincial Autonomy and form Ministries. The idea was that by forming Ministries, the Congress would make the country better prepared to move towards Independence. But there was not much scope in Provincial Autonomy, and, as mentioned in the resolution, whatever scope there was is now exhausted. On the one hand, the Congress has reached the conclusion that the federal part of the Government of India Act does not confer any power on us. On the other hand, the British regime is bent upon thrusting it upon us. The Viceroy[4] and the Secretary of State[5] have been reiterating again and again that it would be imposed upon us. Now when the scope of Provincial Autonomy is over and Federation is being forced upon us, we have no option but struggle and immediate struggle, and we must quickly get ready for it.

There is also a mention of the masses of native states in this Resolution. The awakening of these people has made us confident that this one third population of ours would work shoulder to shoulder in the ensuing struggle. Now Mahatma Gandhi has involved himself in their cause. Therefore, the masses of these states must rise to the occasion immediately. Responsible leaders, as well as provincial and other Committees, must gear themselves up for more and more direct support to the movement in native states. Sardar Patel is helping this movement and other Congress leaders are also associated with it. Therefore, it has become the duty of the Prajamandals to get fully prepared for the ensuing struggle.

Simultaneously, we should support and facilitate the peasants' and workers' movements and provide momentum to their struggles so that these peasants and workers get organized and be fully prepared for the struggle. The time has come when all these organizations should march towards Swarajya under the banner of the Congress, regardless whether they are workers, peasants, urban masses, clerks, or landlords, or belong to any other category. All these forces should be integrated. But you must beware of the fact that the more the Congress gains in strength, the more and more will different types of persons join it to serve their selfish interests. They will

[4] Victor Alexander John Hope, 2nd Marquis of Linlithgow (1887-1952); Chairman, Royal Commission on Indian Agriculture, 1926-8, and Joint Select Committee on Indian Constitutional Reforms, 1933; Viceroy of India, 1936-43.

[5] Marquis of Zetland. For biographical note see *JPSW*, Volume One, p. 151.

pose to be our representatives, or representatives of the masses, and come up to solve important matters. The destiny of India will depend upon such representatives. Therefore they should be elected with utmost care. This is the main weakness of the Congress at present, and we must get rid of it by whatever means possible. Today's happenings[6] are the outcome of just this weakness.

These handful of persons did not even bother that representatives of Egypt's Wafdist Party[7] have come here with a message of freedom for our country. What impression would they carry back about India and how would they describe the happenings of the Congress session? My head goes down with shame and I apologize, on behalf of Pandit Jawaharlalji, Maulana Azad, my party and myself for this demonstration.

We have to solve the communal problem right now. We have to solve the problem of the native states. We have to organize peasants and workers. We have to eradicate poverty from the country. We have to organize the full force of the country. These are not minor issues. But what will happen if our party is infested with these (undesirable) elements? Our struggle for independence would then become a farce only. The Congress has to get rid of such elements. Only then can we move towards our goal.

I place this resolution before you, so that you may firmly resolve to fight for independence, for Purna Swaraj, and take measured steps towards this goal.

[6] This refers to a noisy demonstration by some supporters of the Congress President Subhas Chandra Bose against the old leadership of the Congress, at that time embroiled in a serious controversy with the former.

[7] The Wafd (al-Wafd al-Misri), Egypt's main nationalist party, was founded in 1923 by Zaghlul Pasha to work for freedom from British rule.

76. Reply to Debate on the Resolution on National Demand, Tripuri Congress, 11 March 1939[1]

Hon'ble Chairman and Friends, there was nothing left for me to say after Pandit Jawaharlal's speech,[2] but still there are one or two points which Panditji was not aware of. Hence, I have to say something. I was surprised

[1] *Report of the 52nd Indian National Congress, Tripuri (Dt. Jubbulpore) Mahakoshal, 1939*. Original in Hindi.

[2] Jawaharlal Nehru, speaking just before J.P. rose to reply to the debate on the resolution, had explained that nothing would be gained by issuing empty threats and using strong words like 'ultimatum' in the resolution.

to hear that Sarat Babu[3] is opposing this resolution.[4] I felt as if I have been stabbed. I never thought that a leader like Sarat Babu would oppose it.

When we came here to Tripuri, the issue of drafting a plan of action came up. We wanted to draft such a plan of action as could put an end to communal strife and take us towards our goal of independence. We thought that unless we put an end to our internal strife, nothing could be achieved. Hence, I and other socialist leaders met Sarat Babu and he agreed to drop that issue of ultimatum. So I was all the more surprised to see him raising this question again here.

As Pandit Jawaharlal has said, you should not expect that by creating a deadlock in the ministry or talking big we can make the enemy kneel down. In our last battle, only around one lakh workers were sent to jail, but crores of persons will have to enter jail this time. Whatever differences may be there so far as our socialist thinking is concerned, we would adopt a united strategy against the enemy and struggle along with the Congress.

Sarat Babu is free to oppose it. We believe that only those who do not want total independence would oppose this resolution. Only those would oppose it who do not want our strength to increase so that we can shape our own destiny and work alongside with the Congress in this nationwide struggle. This amendment has been defeated in the Subjects Committee and I hope that you would also reject it and pass the resolution unanimously.

[3] Sarat Chandra Bose (1889-1950); elder brother of Subhas Chandra Bose; joined the non-cooperation movement, 1921; member, Bengal Legislative Council, 1924-9; participated in the civil disobedience movement and arrested, 1932; elected to the Indian Legislative Assembly (1934) while in detention, released, 1935; arrested and detained without trial, 1941-5; member, Constituent Assembly, 1946, and Congress Working Committee, 1946-7; formed the Socialist Republican Party after resigning from the Congress, 1947; founded *Nation*, 1948; elected to the Bengal Legislative Assembly, 1949.

[4] After J.P. had finished his speech Sarat Chandra Bose explained that he was opposed to the resolution as it did not include the idea of issuing an ultimatum, with a fixed time limit, to the British Government. This had been suggested in the presidential address of Subhas Chandra Bose.

77. Speech on G.B. Pant's Resolution, Tripuri Congress, 12 March 1939[1]

Today's debate on this resolution has created such a situation inside the Congress that I, with the permission of the Chair, would like to make a statement on behalf of myself and my comrades (in the C.S.P.). The

[1] *Report of the 52nd Indian National Congress, Tripuri (Dt. Jubbulpore) Mahakoshal, 1939.* Original in Hindi.

(Congress) Socialist Party helped Subhas Babu in this year's presidential election, but we had made it clear that this election was not between the Leftists and the Rightists, and we do not want to create a rift by starting such a debate now. We elected Subhas Babu as he was the better candidate of the two. At that time, we did not expect that the situation would take this turn. There are so many factors behind the curtain, which you all know. Our Party has made it clear that it has no intention of taking sides in this tug of war. We thought that the conflict could be resolved and we tried also, but it could not be resolved.

Both the sides disappointed us. I mention both sides because when many statements were issued before and during the elections, we came to know that the Working Committee members were unhappy over a statement of our President. They did not like the mention of the formation of a Congress Ministry under a federal government. When I met Sri Bose, he promised to me he would issue a statement that he did not intend to blame the members of the Working Committee, but his statement did not clear up the situation. Then we contacted leaders from the other side at Tripuri and extended our help for a compromise but they also disappointed us and did not like our initiative. We put forward an amendment[2] which would have settled many issues, had it been approved. Then, there was a debate in the Subjects Committee. Even after that, a number of deliberations took place. Considering all these facts, we have decided that for maintaining the unity of the Congress, it is imperative that the Working Committee should be formed and should function as per the wishes and directions of Mahatmaji. Therefore, we were prepared to accept this resolution. Had our amendment been accepted, our hurdle for supporting this resolution would have been removed. But this could not happen, so our party will neither support nor oppose this resolution and will remain neutral.

[2] See item no. 73.

78. Statement on the Congress Socialist Party's Neutrality on G.B. Pant's Resolution, 17 March 1939[1]

The question why the Congress Socialist Party remained neutral when Pandit Govind Ballabh Pant's[2] resolution was voted upon in the private session of the delegates is exercising the minds of many people and a variety of misunderstandings seem to be current. It has been suggested in some

[1] *Searchlight*, 18 March 1939. Statement issued at Patna.

[2] Govind Ballabh Pant (1887-1961); one of the most prominent leaders of the Congress who went to prison several times during the freedom struggle; member, Indian Legislative

quarters, to which such thoughts have never been foreign, that the leaders of the Socialist Party merely wanted to play the good boy in order to please the powers that be. To such quarters I find it needless to reply.

To the question why we remained neutral I have a brief answer to make. We did not oppose the resolution because we did not want to be a party to driving Mahatma Gandhi and his followers out of the Congress, for that and nothing short of it would have been the consequence if that resolution had been defeated. What that would have meant to the cause of the country I need hardly point out. Particularly would such a consequence have been disastrous at the present juncture when a crisis is impending and we are thinking in terms of a nationwide struggle. The need and importance of unity in our ranks in such circumstances become far greater. We did, incidentally I should add here that it is a matter for rejoicing that Pantji's resolution, unacceptable as it was to us on certain grounds, at least gave the go by to the theories of incompatibility and homogeneity which we had so strongly criticised and which had threatened at one time to bring disunity in the ranks of the Congress.

We, further, did not oppose the resolution because it was made clear that it did not imply in any manner a vote of censure on the President. Lastly, we did not oppose it because we firmly believed, after considering the various forces that were at work and that had manifested themselves in various undesirable forms, that it was in the interest of the Congress and the national movement as a whole that the Working Committee should command Gandhiji's implicit confidence and be appointed in accordance with his wishes.

On the other hand, we did not support the resolution because we were unable to accept all its ideological implications. For instance, we were not prepared to admit that Gandhiji "alone" could lead the country to victory in the event of a crisis.

The above considerations taken together left no option to us but to adopt an attitude of neutrality. Only those who are labouring under a misapprehension or who are acting upon hostile motives can lay the charge against us that we sold Socialism to Gandhism. This charge might have had some justification if we had supported the resolution. But it can have no basis at all when we made it clear in an authoritative statement that we had ideological differences with the resolution and that it was due to them that we were unable to support it. The action we took was prompted entirely by considerations of unity and I am firmly of the opinion that it was the best course to follow in the national interest. Any other decision would

---

Assembly, 1934-6; Premier, 1937-9, 1946-52, and Chief Minister, 1952-5, U.P.; member, Rajya Sabha, 1955-61; Minister of Home Affairs, Government of India, 1955-61; awarded Bharat Ratna, 1957.

have been factional and sectarian. The issue involved was not whether the Congress should accept Gandhism or Socialism, but whether it should be split up or hold together, giving scope to all sections in it to work, subject to the acceptance of the fundamental policies of the Congress with which there was to be no break. Such a break has never been contemplated by us nor have we ever demanded it. Our final verdict was clear.

A question may be asked, why, if such were our views, did we oppose the same resolution in the Subjects Committee. This is an important question which demands a straightforward answer. In view of the considerations given above we should have remained neutral in the Subjects Committee also. But we did not. Why? Because till then we were rolling along enmeshed in the logic of our action in supporting Subhas Babu at the elections and were functioning in a block with others of his supporters. Much as we disliked to divide the Congress into two rival groups which were intent upon measuring their strength on unreal issues, we were caught up in the stream and were running with it. There was also irritation in our minds at the leaders' refusal to agree to make any change in the resolution. So considering the pros and cons and striking a balance, we had decided to oppose the resolution. After the Subjects Committee, however, certain things happened, which forced upon us the conclusion that in the circumstances it would be ruinous if we took the responsibility of defeating the resolution in the delegate's session. Clearly forces were at work in the Congress which were working for chaos in the name of "leftism" and these would have been strengthened if we yet opposed the resolution. We felt more strongly the need for unity and the necessity of Gandhiji in playing his due and unique role in the Congress. This decision was strengthened by Sarat Babu's opposition to my resolution on National Demand, exposing lack of a serious political purpose in one of the topmost leaders of the so-called left wing and later on by his denial—that the draft of a certain resolution had been agreed upon between him and us. Due to the shortage of time and our faulty organization at Tripuri for which I take the entire blame, it was not possible for us to consult our delegates and this led to a certain amount of confusion in our ranks. Outside too misgivings and discontent seem to be prevalent, part of them due to faulty press reports.

For instance, it has been generally believed that the Party moved only one amendment and that that was mine. There were, however three party or rather joint amendments, one moved by Shri Patwardhan,[3] another by me and the third by Shri Bharadwaj.[4] I feel that these misgivings and

[3] Achyut Patwardhan.

[4] R.D. Bharadwaj (1909-48); worked with Bombay Mill workers, 1931-4; imprisoned for involvement in Bombay Mill strike, 1934-6; worked in Kanpur, 1936-40; member, A.I.C.C., 1939; arrested for anti-war activities and detained at Deoli Detention Camp, 1940-1.

misunderstandings it would be soon possible for us to remove. I appeal to those who have both the interests of the national and socialist movements at heart not to carry on controversy over this issue in a manner that can only disrupt the Socialist movement.

The question has been asked if the price we paid for unity was not incommensurate with the results. I do not think that we have paid any such price at all. By remaining neutral and by making it clear as I did on behalf of the Party, that we had ideological differences with the resolution we have taken no responsibility for certain views expressed therein. Furthermore, the resolution leaves affairs in the Congress exactly where they were before it was passed and therefore it places no new obstacles in our work. The Congress has been functioning on the basis of certain fundamental policies and we have been working within their framework. These fundamental policies have so far been accepted by us and therefore they create no new fetters for us.

Before concluding, I wish to draw the attention of the public from this fruitless controversy to some of the positive and very far-going gains and achievements of the Tripuri Congress which should guide our nation in the coming year.

For those who are interested in the Socialist movement it should be a matter for gratification that throughout the session of the Congress but for one exception the Socialists and Communists acted together, thus establishing for the first time Socialist unity in practice. Even on the one occasion when there was difference among them on the vote on Pantji's resolution, there was agreement to begin with. The difference arose only later. But I should like to state that the policy agreed upon between our Party and the Communists is not to utilize this difference for the sake of disrupting the Socialist movement. In my humble opinion those who are trying to exploit this difference are not doing any service to the movement and are only creating confusion and disruption in it.

From the larger national point of view Tripuri has marked a great advance and I am sure it shall be a landmark in our movement just as the Lahore Congress. In its resolution on the National Demand, the Tripuri Congress took a clear and definite step forward. The resolution first of all declared that the time had now come to apply immediately the principle of self-determination to India. Secondly, it declared that the capacity of the Provincial Autonomy to be of use in strengthening the country was being rapidly exhausted, thus indicating the near termination of constitutionalism.

Lastly, the resolution called upon the Congress organizations and the country generally to prepare for a "nationwide" struggle.

I particularly wish to emphasize the phrase "nationwide". To my mind it is [to] this last call that we have to turn our attention and seriously prepare to give effect to. Tripuri sounded the bugle of war. Let us commence the march instead of wasting time over fruitless controversy.

79. Speech in Support of Jawaharlal Nehru's Resolution at A.I.C.C. Meeting, Calcutta, 29 April 1939[1]

We had thought after Tripuri that we would prepare for the fight for which we had made a declaration. But it is regrettable that the Working Committee had not yet been formed. In this connection, the statements and speeches which have been made at the meeting are not at all convincing. It is difficult to understand what is the real obstacle. The old leaders have not been able to make any decision and have left the matter to be decided by the A.I.C.C. This is not proper. The best thing would have been to form the Working Committee according to Mahatmaji's wishes, but I do not know what the difficulties are in Sri Subhas Bose's way. Another solution would have been to come to a mutual agreement, but even that has not been possible.

We must think what the result of the acceptance of resignation would be. Socialists have always stressed the need for unity in the Congress. I know there are some old leaders who do not care for the Socialists and think that they can run the Congress organization without the help of the latter. But I belong to that group which believes that the strength of the Congress lies in unity and want to maintain it.

If Sri Bose resigns, the repercussions will be serious. Forces of disruption will be let loose and the struggle for independence will recede in the background. Therefore, I suggest that the Congress President should withdraw his resignation.

Regarding the formation of the Working Committee, I do not agree with the proposal of Pandit Jawaharlal, but since this is the only way out of the difficulty, it has to be accepted. It is a relief to hear that the need for taking fresh blood in the Working Committee is being realized. It is an additional relief to hear that two old members of the Working Committee will make place for others. I also hear that Pandit Jawaharlal is being requested to accept the General Secretaryship of the Congress. I shall be glad if it happened. It is painful that the old leaders have not agreed to the formation of a composite committee. Still since there is no other way, I support the ideas underlying the resolution, feeling at the same time that the difficulty should have been solved in a better manner.

[1] Adapted from a report of the speech published in the *Amrita Bazar Patrika*, 30 April 1939. Subhas Chandra Bose submitted his resignation to the A.I.C.C. at Calcutta on 29 April 1939. Jawaharlal Nehru moved a resolution requesting Bose to withdraw his resignation and renominate members of the old Working Committee for the next year.

80. Interview on Policy of the Congress Socialist Party towards the Forward Bloc, 12 May 1939[1]

I do not have much to say about the Forward Bloc[2] at this stage. My Party has always been against any organizational crystallization of the Left Wing which would only check its growth and lead to a struggle for power within the Congress. The perusal of the statement of the policy of the Forward Bloc made by Subhas Babu makes it clear that it has no policies other than those of the Congress as a whole, except opposition to what has become the common fashion to call 'High Command'. Such opposition can hardly be the policy of the Congress Socialist Party. The only things the Party is opposed to at present are imperialism and its Indian allies. If the purpose is to get the policies of the Congress implemented, the Party would much rather appeal to all Congressmen than only to those who choose to form Blocs and Leagues.

The Party thinks it is not wise to divide Congressmen as Congressmen into groups. This might sound queer coming from the C.S.P. But the Party by bringing socialist Congressmen together has not divided Congressmen as such. The Congress Socialists have objectives that go beyond those of the Congress and, as such, they have formed a party for their achievement. Inasmuch as their objectives are common with the Congress they work within it and with other Congressmen. For the achievements of their objectives, they do not wish to divide Congressmen any further. Their policy has always been to press forward with the Congress as a whole. This they can do not by forming 'Blocs', but by their political initiative and action. The C.S.P., as already reported, has therefore decided not to join the Forward Bloc. It would not, however, oppose the latter and cooperate with it to the extent it agrees with its policies.[3]

[1] Adapted from J.P.'s interview to the United Press of India at Patna published in the *Bombay Chronicle*, 13 May 1939, *Hindustan Times*, 14 May 1939, and *Congress Socialist*, 21 May 1939. Later in an interview to the *Searchlight* on 19 May 1939 he clarified that his observations in the interview not only represented his personal opinion, but also reflected a decision taken by the National Executive of the C.S.P. at Calcutta on 29 April 1939. See the *Searchlight*, 20 May 1939.

[2] Forward Bloc, a Leftist party founded within the Congress by Subhas Chandra Bose in 1939 after his resignation from the Congress presidentship. The object of the Party was to rally all radical and anti-imperialist progressive elements in the country on the basis of a minimum programme, representing the greatest common measure of agreement among radicals of all shades of opinion.

[3] See also the joint statement by J.P. and P.C. Joshi, 7 June 1939 (Appendix 21).

81. Reply to Government's Communiques on Rahul Sankrityayan, 17-19 May 1939[1]

A few days ago the Government of Bihar issued two communiques[2] on Pandit Rahul Sankrityayan,[3] one on his fast and the other on his being handcuffed. As one who has been deeply hurt by the Government's attitude towards such an eminent scholar, I have read the communiques with care and compared them with facts as are known to me. It gives me no pleasure to say that the communiques are full of mis-statements, half-truths and even full-blown lies. It is possible to believe, if one wishes to be generous, that for these the lower officers of the Government are responsible and that they have misled the Minister in charge. But what cannot be excused and for which no explanation whatever is possible is the spirit of meanness that the communiques show. Meanness is a strong word and, though I do not believe in strong language, I am using it deliberately and advisedly because I cannot find a better or more truthful word to describe the spirit of the communiques. The whole purpose of the latter is not to explain or justify the action of the Government but to decry Rahulji's conduct, impute mean motives to him, and to show him up as an individual who is petty, self-seeking and vain. Even such a serious thing as staking life has been attempted to be shown as arising from a mean desire for comfort and luxury. Even where ground exist for the Government to entertain such pleas, one expects dignity and fairplay. But where, as in the present one, not only no ground exists but the entire blame is with the Government, such behaviour as the communiques represent can only point to the complete moral bankruptcy of the Government or at least of those members of it who have been dealing with this affair.

[1] *Searchlight*, 17 May 1939 and 19 May 1939.

[2] The two communiques issued by the Bihar Government on 11 May 1939 (published in the *Searchlight*, 13 May 1939) explained its difficulty in arriving at a suitable definition of political prisoners which was the main ground for the hunger-strike by Rahul Sankrityayan convicted in connection with Amwari agrarian agitation, and contradicted the statements appearing in the Press that he was ill-treated after his conviction at Siwan.

[3] Rahul Sankrityayan, original name Kedarnath Pandey (1893-1963); Hindi writer and Buddhist scholar; took part in the non-cooperation movement, 1921; imprisoned for six months, 1922; participated in the civil disobedience movement; associated with the Communist Party of Bihar, 1939-40; President, Kisan Sammelan, Motihari, 1940; imprisoned, 1940-2; Professor, Leningrad University, U.S.S.R., 1944-7; President, All India Hindi Sahitya Sammelan, Bombay, 1947; Professor of Philosophy, Vidyalankara University, Sri Lanka, 1959-61; publications include: *Baisvin Sadi, Volga Se Ganga, Meri Jivan Yatra* (5 vols.), *Stalin*, and *Lenin*.

In passing I may draw the attention of the public to the fact that the communiques have not hesitated to use and distort even private conversations and remarks made in confidence. Such use, even without the distortion, is highly objectionable, with the distortion it is mean and vulgar.

I shall briefly deal with the communiques. First, there is the short one about the handcuffing affair. The points made out in it are:

1. Rahulji himself insisted on being handcuffed; 2. Rahulji himself insisted on being tied with the leading rope; 3. He did all this so that he may have his photograph taken and thus discredit the Government; 4. He insisted on walking in the "scorching sun" and refused the *ekka* that was provided for him in addition to the one provided for another accused who was ill.

The facts about these points are as below:

Rahulji was handcuffed not twice as one of the communiques says, but four times, i.e. on March 31 when he was escorted with his co-accused from Chapra jail to Siwan for trial; on April 2 when he was escorted back to Chapra; on April 14 (after full two weeks of public protest) when he was again taken to Siwan; and lastly on April 16 when after conviction he was brought back to Chapra.

On the first three occasions the escorting party handcuffed Rahulji in the normal manner and on their own initiative completely. The public should take note of the fact that he was handcuffed on the third occasion, i.e. on April 14 after full two weeks of public protest and agitation. The Government by distorting facts have given the impression that the escort was compelled by Rahulji's insistence on handcuffing him. There was no such insistence on these three occasions. Why was he handcuffed then? Why was he handcuffed even after the expression of strong public feeling and when the matter had been pressed to the Government's attention ceaselessly for two weeks? Even supposing, though the supposition is not justifiable, that on the first two occasions due to lack of alertness on the part of the Government the local officials followed the usual practice and handcuffed Rahulji on the first occasion, the question remains why was he handcuffed on the two subsequent occasions. Instead of answering this straight question and admitting its mistake and negligence, the Government have tried to take cover under half-truths and falsehood.

I have said that the supposition that local officials in the absence of instructions from above follow the usual practice is not justifiable. I have reasons for saying so. Rahulji is not the first Congress worker arrested in the course of the Kisan movement by the present Government. There was Pandit Jadunandan Sharma. At no time was he handcuffed or roped and I have reasons to believe that this was not because of any instructions of the Provincial Government. More examples can be given. I shall explain later why Rahulji was treated so shabbily by the local officials of Saran and how the Government allowed itself to be misled in this matter by them.

Coming to the last occasion, i.e. April 16, on which Rahulji was handcuffed, the fact is that the escort party on taking charge of the prisoners handcuffed all except Rahulji. Upon that Rahulji quite naturally suggested that if the others must be handcuffed it were better that he too was treated in the same manner. His suggestion was accepted. There was no insistence and no scene.

The Government have utilized this one fact to cover up all their sins and have tried to paint this natural conduct of Rahulji in the worst colour possible. I leave the public to draw their own conclusion from it. The questions to ask the Government are: 1. Why was Rahulji handcuffed at all? 2. Why were not the Government alert enough and why did they not issue instructions immediately after his arrest for superior treatment being given to him as an undertrial including his not being handcuffed? 3. Why, after the first instance, was he handcuffed twice?

About the escort rope being tied around him. The communique says that Rahulji refused to move unless this was done. This is a pure concoction. On all the four occasions the escort party without any ado tied, or passed the rope around him and the other prisoners as is done with common felons. Not once did any occasion arise when Rahulji had to remonstrate for the rope being tied round him. This is one of the full-blown lies of the communiques.

The photographic account is the most vulgar part of the whole sordid communique. It is a pity that the Government should [believe] falsehood and concoctions of its subordinates, who in Saran have reasons to be hostile to Rahulji, to deliberately malign an Indian whose reputation is not confined to the borders of India. The Government by this action have not enhanced their prestige nor the prestige of Indians. The suggestion of the communique is that Rahulji had himself handcuffed and tied only to be photographed and that a photographer was kept ready at the station for this purpose. The communique goes into details to show how instead of facing the compartment as he would when boarding the train he faced the station building, the suggestion being that he did this especially to pose for the camera. The writer of the communique has again been careless with his facts, thus again been exposing his real intentions. The facts are these. The photograph in question was not taken at Siwan where Rahulji would be boarding the train and so should have his back towards the station building, but at Chapra where he was alighting and should naturally face the building. If the direction of Rahulji's face and back were of such importance as to find elaborate description in a Government communique, the bungling with facts have knocked the bottom out of the Government's insinuations.

Though, on my part, having some experience with the photographers, I do not see if it is "malafide" to pose for a picture leaving the direction of the face and other parts of the body to the cameraman's convenience.

There is another point about this photograph affair which should be before the public. Rahulji was handcuffed thrice before the last time when he is suggested to have play-acted for the sake of being photographed. He could thus have arranged to be photographed on any one of those occasions. Did he do so and did the Government carry out researches into the directions in which his face and back were turned? I suggest that the Government should pursue this fruitful enquiry.

The last point in the communique is about Rahulji refusing to use the *ekka* so kindly provided by a considerate Government so that his friends outside, who are the enemies of the Government, might shout about forcing a reverend gentleman to walk long distances on foot "in the scorching sun". Surely, the Government is giving us more credit for brains than we deserve. How clever really are all of us who deliberately create grievances so that we may exploit them later against the Government. I know that the Government has long been suffering from the illusion that the Kisan Sabhaites exist only to embarrass them. I thought Reora Satyagraha[4] would cure the Government of this illusion but apparently I was being too optimistic. What better understanding of the Kisan movement can we expect from a Government which after nearly two years of office still thinks, as its communique says, that there is no principle involved in the Bakasht struggle that the Kisan Sabha is conducting. Whatever be the feelings of the Government in this matter, I shall repeat a statement that I have often made, that it is only out of a desire not to queer the pitch for the Congress to carry on with its experiment of office acceptance that the Kisan Sabha exercises such restraint and endeavours to limit direct action to only such cases where no other channels remain open. Let me assure the Government that if the desire were really present to embarass them, there would literally be thousands of peasants knocking at their jail gates.

Turning to the *ekka* business Rahulji had to walk simply because no *ekka* was provided for him. In all he was moved five times between Siwan and Chapra. Even the Government communique mentions *ekkas* on only one of those occasions. Should not the writer of the communique, who seems to be so fond of details, have enquired whether *ekkas* were provided on the other occasions? The fact is that one *ekka*, not two, was provided

[4] Jadunandan Sharma started Kisan satyagraha at Reora in Gaya district on 23 December 1938 by cutting the crops in the disputed lands. Swami Sahajanand Saraswati continued the struggle after the arrest of Sharma and organized Kisan demonstrations at Gaya.

upon the recommendation of the jail Doctor on the last two occasions not for Rahulji but for another prisoner who was ill. The story about the second *ekka* for Rahulji is another concoction.

II

I shall take up now the other communique that deals with the demands of Rahulji and his fast. In this the same motive is at work and the same disregard for facts is shown.

Take the statement in the communique that Rahulji gave only four days' notice to the Government when he first presented his demands. He wrote to the Jailor on March 11, intimating that he would begin his fast on the 18th if his demands were not satisfied. Elementary arithmetic would show that the notice was not four days' but a week's.

Take another "fact" from the communique. It says that after Rahulji had started his fast the "I.G. of Prisons saw him and other prisoners and allowed them concessions upon which Sjt. Rahul Sankrityayan gave up the hunger-strike saying that as the Government had been busy with the work of the Assembly he postponed hunger-strike till the 30th April, 1939". The facts are: (1) The I.G. did not see Rahulji at this time. (2) He did not break his fast because Government were busy with the Assembly work but because on the third or fourth day of his fast he was informed that as an interim arrangement the Government had sanctioned Div. II treatment to all the Amwari prisoners and that they were considering his demands and also because the authorities had complained of the shortness of the time allowed to them; (3) He did not postpone his fast till April 30 but till April 23. That is, he gave a full month's time to the Government to consider his demands.

I shall have occasion to point out other similar distortion and falsification of facts in the course of this statement.

The communique tries to give the impression that the Government have been very anxious to settle the questions raised by Rahulji and that they have used commendable despatch dealing with them for which the public should pat them on the back. My impression is quite the contrary and I hope to show that this is well-founded. I feel that it is not possible to condemn the Government too much for their dilatoriness and irresponsibility in this matter.

Rahulji gives notice of his demands and fast on March 11. He begins his fast on March 18. During the week the Government does nothing. Three days later an interim action is taken. Rahulji postpones his fast till April 23, thus giving a month's time to the Government. The Government in its turn again does nothing during the whole month. On the last day, the day the fast was to begin, Babu Krishnaballabh Sahay[5] interviews Rahulji. Is this not sheer irresponsibility? Does it not show that the Government refused to take the matter seriously? Why should anyone in Rahulji's position have shown any further consideration to the Government's pleas for time? And yet this "unreasonable" man gave the Government a further seven days' respite. The Government's veiled justification in the communique for its failure to use the month allowed by Rahulji is that they were busy with the Assembly work. The communique says that "as soon as the Government were free from the work of the Assembly, they deputed the Parliamentary Secretary, Mr. Krishnaballabh Sahay" etc. It is difficult to understand what this statement means. The Assembly was not in session between April 15 and 24. Surely some representative of the Government could have seen Rahulji between these days. I suggest that Babu Krishnaballabh Sahay was sent to interview Rahulji on the 23rd not because the Government were free from the Assembly work, because the Assembly was really to sit from the next day, but because that was the zero hour and no further delay was possible as the fast was to begin on that day.

However, Rahulji, anxious not to create unnecessary difficulties, agreed again to postpone his fast for a week, i.e. till May, 1. The communique feigns surprise and states that "contrary to their (i.e. Government's) expectation, Sjt. Rahul Sankrityayan went on hunger-strike on the 1st May, 1939". There should have been no ground at all for surprise. We had all been given to understand that Rahulji would resume his fast on May 1 if no final settlement was reached between him and the Government before then. This was clearly that Rahulji had told the Government representative. Actually no attempt at settlement with him was made by the Government before that date. Naturally Rahulji started his fast as announced. It is true that the Government published another interim arrangement on April 28, but Rahulji was no party to it, nor did it give any satisfaction on the principal questions in dispute. Rahulji would not have been true to himself, nor to the cause he had taken up, if he did not begin his fast on May 1. Any honourable man would have done the same.

When Rahulji's fast began, the Government took no notice of it for several days. It was on the 5th day of the fast that Babu Krishnaballabh Sahay was sent to see him! Could there be anything more callous? And yet, our Government expects a pat on the back from the public. For what? For insulting a great Indian, for showing utter disregard for his suffering and for his life, for its exemplary sense of responsibility and fairplay.

[5] Krishna Ballabh Sahay (1898-1974); joined the non-cooperation movement, 1920; imprisoned for participating in the civil disobedience movement, 1930-3; Parliamentary Secretary, Bihar Government, 1937-9; took part in the individual satyagraha, 1940, and Quit India movement, 1942; Minister for Land Revenue, 1946-57, and for Cooperation and Planning, 1962-3, Bihar Government; Chief Minister, Bihar, 1963-7.

Let me turn now to Rahulji's demands. The communique deliberately and on purpose has mixed up his demands with the suggestions he had made for jail reform. It is the latter which have been exploited by a section of the Press for decrying Rahulji's attempt to create a prison-paradise.

Radio, electric fans and lights, septic tanks, filtered tube-well water, carrom, ping pong, chess, badminton, these have been used to ridicule Rahulji's fast. But it is not for these that he fasted. These, indeed not even all of these, were no more than suggestions made to the Government. He did not demand a radio for himself, but suggested that it would be useful if every jail were provided with it. The suggestion to my mind is well worth considering. Cost may not prove to be much of a difficulty. Can the Science College not be asked to assemble and construct radio sets in its laboratories? Rahulji never even suggested electric fans; they are an invention. He did suggest that as the electric supply line passed by the jail wall at Chapra Government might use electricity instead of oil and might even find it cheaper. He did not demand tube-well water. In the jails there is often an inadequate supply of water. He merely suggested that provision for adequate supply of pure water may be made and that electric pumps, etc., might prove useful. Septic tanks too did not form a part of his demands. As for the games, Rahulji never insisted that unless badminton was allowed or carrom or ping-pong, he would fast unto death. I do not think he himself plays any game. Writing seems to be his chief sport. He has utilized his time in the Chapra Jail to write 500 pages of fiction! Regarding games, all he meant to do was to draw the attention of the Government to the necessity of allowing some indoor and outdoor games in the prisons, and he named some games. When names of inexpensive Indian games were suggested to him he readily agreed that they could take the place of those he had named. I do not think the suggestion of allowing games in the jails is as ridiculous as it may appear to those whose conception of justice is a tooth for a tooth and an eye for an eye. Those who have been to jail know that where games are not allowed various kinds of games are improvised and materials for them smuggled. Even Satyagrahi prisoners were not free from this vice!

As for the actual demands, I understand there was not much of very serious difference left between Rahulji and Babu Krishnaballabh Sahay as far as they concerned food, books, periodicals, interviews, etc. The main difficulty was about the general definition of a political prisoner so as to include Kisans and workers arrested in the course of the peasant and labour movements. The communique again indulges in a falsehood when it says that Rahulji was at one time prepared to exclude the Amwari Kisans from the political class and only later "developed his ideas". It was never so.

I might point out here that Rahulji's demand about political prisoners should not have appeared as anything new to the Government. It is a demand that the Kisan Sabha has been placing before them for at least two years past. The Government therefore had ample time to consider it.

The communique has referred to my part in the discussions regarding the definition of political prisoners. I should like to clear up one or two points. Every time I had occasion to discuss the matter with the Government's representative I made it absolutely clear that there was no likelihood of any difficulty arising about the details of Rahulji's demands if the problem of the definition of political prisoners was satisfactorily solved. I can say the same thing for Swami Sahajanandji also. I should therefore like to tell the public clearly that the reason why no agreement was reached between Rahulji and the Government was not that he insisted on a prison paradise but because he wanted that all Kisans arrested in the course of the Kisan movement should be classed as political prisoners. I do not say that there were no other disputed points, but they were such as could have been easily settled.

It is wearisome to be pointing out the communique's distortions. There is an important one, however, which should not go unnoticed. The communique suggests that Rahulji was anxious for classification of political prisoners and wanted himself to be placed in Division I. The facts, again are quite to the contrary. When Rahulji first presented his demands there was no mention of classes. It was Babu Mathura Prasad who persuaded him to agree to the existing classification. Even then Rahulji made it clear that his demands were mainly for the Division III Class.

A reply to the communique can be endless. What is important for the public is to remember that the Government from the beginning have bungled this affair and shown an inexcusable lack of responsibility. Instead of expressing their regret for the conduct of their officials towards Rahulji they have tried to apply a veneer to them through these communiques. The landlord of Amwari against whom the Satyagraha was started is a man of some local notoriety. His intimate connection with the C.I.D. and his unrepentant past and present anti-Congress conduct are public knowledge. The ill-treatment of Rahulji and the bungling of his case is largely due to the influence of this man with the local officials. The public may not have forgotten that one of the employees of this landlord had assaulted Rahulji in the presence of the police and while he was in their custody. Yet the assailant was let at large and orders for his prosecution were passed by Government only after considerable public excitement.

I do not know what purpose the Government wanted to serve by releasing Rahulji.[6] I hope this much is clear to them that none of the questions that were raised by Rahulji's fast has thereby been solved. The Amwari struggle[7] continues and there is no doubt that Rahulji shall again soon be in prison.

[6] Rahul Sankrityayan was released on 10 May 1939.

[7] Refers to Kisan satyagraha led by Rahul Sankrityayan at Amwari in Shahabad district of Bihar in February 1939.

He will doubtless renew his demand and resume the fast. Even if something untoward prevents him from doing so, these questions are bound to be raised by other Kisan Sabha prisoners. May we hope that the Government realizes that nasty communiques cannot solve difficult problems?

82. Strike in Bihariji Mill (Patna): Issues at Stake, 18 June 1939[1]

The strike in Bihariji Mill[2] has been going on for some days past. Now news comes that a settlement has been reached.

Labour strikes even in our province have become the order of the day. The Bihariji Mill strike was after all a small one. It was a struggle of 400 workers only. As I have already stated, a settlement has also been reached. There is nothing so particular or important in this struggle which calls for any special discussion. Workers fought for their demands and they won. There is nothing extraordinary about it. They would have been defeated; but they won because of their determination and solidarity and the public sympathy they received from the people of the town. Class struggle has taken a step forward. Workers will march forward. They deserve our congratulations on their success.

I have not much to say about this strike. But certain regrettable things have happened in this connection and I consider it my duty to invite public attention, particularly the attention of Congressmen, to these.

The reins of administration in the province are in the hands of the popular Congress Ministers. A small strike takes place in the capital of the Province. It is conducted in an organized manner by the Labour Union. The president of the Union and the leader of the strike is Shri Ramvriksh Benipuri, who is a prominent Congressman in the province and who had been a president of this Town Congress Committee. Among his comrades are efficient organizers like Shri Yogendra Shukla.[3] There is no violence in the conduct of the strike, no rioting, nor any kind of damage to the mill. There is perfect non-violence. The District officials proclaim Section 144 in area covering 500 yards around the mill. It becomes difficult for people to reach the banks

[1] *Congress Socialist*, 18 June 1939.

[2] About four hundred workers of Bihariji Mills at Patna went on strike on 22 May 1939 as a protest against the dismissal of seven workers by the Management.

[3] Yogendra Shukla (1896-1966); one of the revolutionary leaders of Bihar; participated in the non-cooperation movement and imprisoned; convicted in several conspiracy cases and served prison terms for many years; joined the C.S.P., 1938, arrested soon after in connection with the Madras Bomb Case, detained at Deoli Detention Camp, and later shifted to Hazaribagh Central Jail; escaped from jail along with J.P. in 1942; re-arrested and imprisoned, 1942-6; member, Bihar Legislative Council, 1958-9.

of Ganges or walk the roads. Police charge innocent onlookers with lathis. Dr. Ayodhya Prasad, an old worker of the town, is severely beaten, is dragged on the streets and even after falling down, given lathi blows. The next day he is called to the Malsalami Thana where the Police officer abuses him and slaps him. Forty-one workers, women and children, are put in a lorry and left in the scorching midday heat miles away from the town. Those women who refuse to get down from the lorry and demand to be sent to the prison are forcibly dragged out by the hair and legs. Children were thrown down on the road. Shri Benipuri is charged under the *goonda* Section 107. Notice under Section 144 is served on Shuklaji. In all seventy arrests are made. Benipuriji himself is arrested under Sections 107 and 114.

This happens not in an obscure village, but in the capital of the Province in front of the Sadaquat Ashram, before the eyes of the Ministers as if on the laps of the Town Congress Committee. What does it all mean? And what is the lesson for us?

Have these the sanction of the Ministry? It is possible that the lathi charge was ordered by some misguided officer. To take people in a lorry and leave them in unknown places might be the work of some police officer. But application of Section 144, the arrest of Shri Benipuri and 70 others—how can these happen in Patna City without the authority of the Ministry or the Minister for Law and Order? If that can happen then the conclusion will be that our Ministers are not governing, they are just killing time.

Be that as it may, the fact remains that such things have happened and the responsibility for them is on our Ministry. For every act of repression by the police the responsibility is its [own], especially when it is again and again said that the honour of the police is the honour of the Ministry. It is not known, whose it is,—the self-respect of the people, of our mothers and sisters, of the old Comrades in the Congress. Does anyone care for them in these days of the Congress Ministries?

These regrettable incidents of Patna have a deep relation to our national problem. They point to the danger ahead and if we ignore it we will fall into such a ditch from which it will be well nigh impossible to come up. Congress accepted Ministries in order to strengthen Congress, to bring the bureaucracy under the control of the people, and restore civil liberties. The Patna events seem to indicate that we are going in the opposite direction. Today Congressmen in Patna will have to hang down their heads, the honour of the Congress has been brought to the dust. There it is the rule of the police and Magistrates. We have not even the freedom to conduct an ordinary strike. The Ministry is turning its face against one of the fundamental objects of the Congress. No Congressman can be proud of the record of two years of the Congress Ministry. If the Congress had not accepted office and if the province was under any other Ministry, I am convinced that things would not [have] gone to the pass they did during the recent strike. I do not remember a single instance in any part of the country where the government had acted with such violence in a small strike like this when the Congress was not in Ministry. What is the reason? Non-Congress Ministries are afraid of popular opinion. But unfortunately, our Ministry thinks that it is the people, like Louis XIV. What do they care for our shouts? Why should they respond? They were elected by the people. So they do not care.

It is unfortunate that Congressmen in the province, Congress committees and the Provincial Congress Committees having got enmeshed in election activities, and having developed false notions of discipline, they are today far removed from their post of duty. In my humble judgement the time has come for each responsible Congressman, each Congress committee to wake up, examine the work of the Ministry. Condemn where it has gone wrong and put it on the right path. It is the duty of the Congress Legislative Party to discuss the work of the Ministry from time to time and keep suitable control over it. I believe that the Provincial Congress Committee and its Working Committee have been thoroughly indifferent in this matter. This has resulted in great harm to the Congress. I have had enough opportunities of meeting those Congressmen who are neither Socialists nor have any connection with peasant and labour organizations. I know how much discontent there is with the work of the Congress Ministry. Though often such displeasure is due to personal considerations, still I do also find criticism based on fundamental principles. What is, however, regrettable is that even those who valiantly fought the British Raj with bared chests, do not show that moral courage for a frank and open criticism of the work of the Ministry. Such weakness in the leadership will lead to our fall. I have no doubt that if Congressmen do not come out fearlessly to defend basic things, we will be going down and down into the ditch.

The situation is deteriorating daily. Arrests have become the order of the day, if our Ministers cannot implement the election of Pandit Jadunandan Sharma, Rahulji is taken away next and Benipuri also. The prison doors are kept open for the tallest among us. This has happened in Dehri, Gaya, Harinagar and Patna. And now in the Capital, before our very eyes in daylight, police excesses are perpetrated. At Tripuri the Congress declared that whatever hopes there were of strengthening the country through acceptance of office are rapidly being exhausted. Capacity of doing good may be exhausted but not that of doing bad. I have absolutely no doubt and I say this with a full sense of responsibility that if our Ministers cannot carry out the election Manifesto without throwing us in jail, as we experienced in Patna, then let them resign their posts. In a situation like that for them to hold on to their position is harmful to the country.

A few words about what has happened in Patna. A settlement, of course, has been reached between the workers and their employers. The strike has ended. Benipuriji has been released. But even now about 70 workers are in jail. They must immediately be released. If this is not done there is no particular gain from the settlement.

Then there is the question of police excesses. Their conduct has been intolerable. Let the Government institute a non-official inquiry and punish those officers and other Government officials who may be found guilty. Specially deserving of punishment are those who ordered the lathi charge, who ordered workers to be taken in the lorry and left in a desolate place, who abused and slapped Dr. Ayodhya Prasad in the Police Station. For the promulgation of Section 144 without reason for the arrest of 70 workers for charging Benipuri under Section 107 and Shuklaji under Section 144, the responsibility is that of the Government. It must express regret for these.

In conclusion I would appeal to my colleagues in the Congress committees, the Provincial Committee and its Working Committee to watch the activities of the Ministry and give it suitable directions. I would [like] that special pressure is exerted to deal with the matters I have drawn attention to here. If such incidents cannot arouse them, the future of the Congress is dark indeed.

83. Speech at Public Meeting, Lahore, 11 July 1939[1]

Though in view of the present international situation it is a very opportune moment to launch a fresh struggle for independence, I confess that the country, or at any rate the brave Province of the Punjab, is not prepared for the struggle. There is no doubt about a general awakening in the country but that is not enough. I am clear in my mind that the struggle to be started now will be a final struggle and we shall have no truce or pact with the British Government. I have no hesitation in saying that the necessary preparation for that struggle has not yet been made. Even the Socialists have organized neither the peasants nor the labourers properly. In fact we have no influence or control over the peasant and labour organizations. I, therefore, suggested that instead of giving any ultimatums we shall be well advised to organize the peasantry and the labourers in the country, more especially the labourers in the Railways, on the docks and other concerns under Governmental control. After we have organized the peasants and labourers they will be having the power and the strength to launch a struggle even without Gandhiji. It is no use criticising Gandhiji and other leaders for not launching a struggle at the present moment. The best course for us is to do active work in all the spheres and create strength to fight our last battle under the Congress.

[1] Adapted from a report of the speech published in the *Tribune*, 12 July 1939.

We must condemn all attempts at creating a split in the Congress on minor matters and trying to organize groups for the main purpose of fighting or overthrowing the present Congress leadership. Such an approach virtually amounts to treachery. Unity in the Congress and unity in its leadership are most essential for the Congress to continue to wield the influence it has hitherto done. There is no question of any member of the Congress Working Committee or the Congress entering into a compromise with the British on the issue of Federation. So no split should be created on that issue. So far as the attitude of the Congress Socialist Party towards the Congress leadership is concerned the Party has never acted as a party in opposition to the present leadership but always acted with a view to influencing the Congress policy and it has had a lot of success in that mission.

84. Letter to Mian Muhammad Iftikharuddin, 23 July 1939[1]

Kadamkuan (New Area)
Patna
23 July 1939

My dear Mian Saheb,[2]
I expect you would be back in Lahore by the time this reaches you. And I hope Mussoorie had done you lots of good.

Well, I returned to Lahore not quite according to schedule, but on the same day as I had intended. Your Munshi and Khalil were at the station. It was very good of them to have taken the trouble of attending all the trains. You see I was stupid enough not to send them a wire about the change in my programme. However, I was very grateful to them and very sorry that they were put to so much trouble. At your house they made everything as comfortable as possible. I stayed there for the night and left the next afternoon for Amritsar. I cannot help expressing my gratitude for your hospitality and kindness which I shall always cherish.

The job that you had entrusted to Sant Prakash (is that the way to spell it?) was not quite a success. He was able to collect only Rs. 150/-, fifty

[1] *JP Papers* (NMML).

[2] Mian Muhammad Iftikharuddin (1907-62); member, Punjab Legislative Assembly, 1937-46; Secretary, Congress Parliamentary Party; President, Punjab P.C.C., 1940-5; joined the Muslim League, 1946; member, Constituent Assembly, 1946; migrated to Pakistan after Partition and became Minister of Rehabilitation; President, Punjab Muslim League, 1950; expelled from the Muslim League; founded the Azad Pakistan Party, 1950.

from Santanam[3] and a hundred from [Sardul Singh] Caveeshar. The latter gave a cheque for "the *Congress Socialist*, Bombay", which I have not still been able to cash! The barrister gentleman who was to scrape up a hundred from the High Court pleaded lack of time, your friend the aviator, Lala Rupchand, I suppose, went away to Kashmir, Sampuran Singh also melted away for his bulk! I hope you will be able to get at these chaps soon enough and send me the money.

Since my return I have hardly been for twenty-four hours in Patna. What with peasant satyagrah and what with the strike at Tatanagar my time has entirely been taken up with running about. The strike situation is rather disquieting.

I hope things at your end are not too bad.

With kindest regards,

Yours affectionately,
Jayaprakash Narayan

P.S. Do not forget to reply. Please.

[3] K. Santanam (1885-1949); Barrister; practised at Lahore, 1911; Defence Counsel, 1919; General Secretary, Punjab Congress, 1921-2, and the Indian National Congress, 1926.

85. Letter to Munshi Ahmed Din, 23 July 1939[1]

Kadamkuan (New Area)
Patna
23 July 1939

My dear Munshiji,

I am sorry I did not write earlier. At Lucknow I spoke to Narendradevaji about publications scheme. He said the matter was present to his mind and that he would do what was possible when the Sub Committee met. He also said that he would inform you when the Committee's meeting was announced so that you could be personally present at Lucknow. As for the Bihar Government, the ministers are all at Ranchi at present. When Dr. Mahmud[2] returns to Patna, I shall speak to him about it.

Kindly keep informed of political developments there and particularly about Party work.

With greetings,

Yours sincerely,
Jayaprakash Narayan

[1] *JP Papers* (NMML).

[2] For biographical note on Syed Mahmud see *JPSW*, Volume One, p. 69.

86. Letter to Ram Chandra and Mangal Dass, 27 July 1939[1]

Kadam Kuan (New Area)
Patna
27 July 1939

My dear Comrades Ramchandra[2] & Mangaldas,[3]
I owe you an explanation for running away from Lahore without keeping my appointment with you. I should have written earlier, but I hope you will excuse me for it.

That morning when we had gone to Bradlaugh Hall I was detained there longer than I had expected. I therefore went straight back to Baghhanpura intending to return and see you at the Lakshmi Insurance before I took my train from Amritsar. I had intended to leave after 4 p.m. While I was at Baghhanpura I received a telephone call that a messenger had come from Amritsar and that I must leave by the 3.30 train. There was no time after that for me to go to the city again. When I left Lahore I thought I would write and explain to you how I could not keep my appointment.

Now, as to the solution of the difficulty[4] which was before us. After my talks with the comrades at Bradlaugh Hall there was no particular conclusion which we came to and we were left exactly where we had started from. Under the circumstances, I had no definite proposal to place before you except this: that we should give some more time to the matter and tackle it again later. I shall request you therefore to leave matters as they are for the time being and, if possible, co-operate with the party to the extent you can. If co-operation be not possible you may carry on with your activities without coming in any conflict with the Party. That might pave the way for a future settlement. I should like to make it clear that I do not wish to exert any pressure on you at all. You are free to follow or reject my advice. . . .[5]

I shall be glad to have a word from you.

With regards,
Yours sincerely,
Jayaprakash Narayan

[1] *Brahmanand Papers* (NMML).

[2] Ram Chandra (1903-97); a prominent revolutionary leader; General Secretary, Punjab Press Employees' Union, Lahore, 1924; Founder-President, Naujawan Bharat Sabha, 1926; Labour Secretary, Punjab Congress, 1926; President, Punjab Sweepers' Union, Lahore, 1924-7, and East Punjab Railway Staff Union, Delhi, 1947-9; member, Punjab University Senate, 1924-7; General Secretary, Hindustan Majdoor Sevak Sangh, Delhi, 1948-9.

[3] Mangal Dass (1907-80); a prominent revolutionary leader; member, Naujawan Bharat Sabha, Punjab P.C.C., and Karam Singh Mann Inquiry Tribunal; imprisoned for participating in the salt satyagraha, 1930 and 1932; joined the C.S.P., 1934; arrested for anti-war propaganda, 1940; participated in the Quit India movement and detained, 1942-5.

[4] This apparently refers to some point of difference or dispute between Ram Chandra and the C.S.P. leadership.

[5] Paper damaged.

87. Comment on Disciplinary Action taken by Congress Working Committee against Subhas Chandra Bose, 12 August 1939[1]

It is a very shocking and drastic decision.[2] Instead of narrowing it would further the gulf in the Congress organization, although unity is the supreme necessity at the present juncture. No amount of disciplinary action can cement the rift. Basically the conflict arose because one wing was advising caution and constructive programme while another wing was insisting on immediate struggle, rightly or wrongly. I have no doubt that both the wings could be united and satisfied only if a struggle was launched. The Congress has become today a tremendous mass organization, and millions of people are ready to jump into the struggle when the call from the fifteen persons who constitute the Working Committee comes, if they would give such a call.

[1] Adapted from a report of the speech at Ravenshaw College, Cuttack, published in the *Bombay Chronicle*, 14 August 1939.

[2] The Congress Working Committee at its meeting at Wardha (9-12 August 1939) disqualified Subhas Chandra Bose from the presidentship of the Bengal P.C.C. and debarred him from membership of any elective Congress body for three years in response to his organizing a day of protest on 9 July against the two resolutions on 'Satyagraha in Provinces' and 'Congress Ministries and the P.C.C. s' adopted by the A.I.C.C. at its meeting at Bombay (24-7 June 1939).

APPENDICES

APPENDIX 1

Meerut Thesis, 1936[1]

STATEMENT ON PARTY'S NATURE, TASK AND PROGRAMME

(Adopted by the Second Annual Conference of the Party at Meerut on 20 January 1936.)

ORIGIN OF THE PARTY:

The Congress Socialist Party grew out of the experiences of the last two national struggles. It was formed at the end of the last Civil Disobedience movement by such Congressmen as came to believe that a new orientation of the national movement had become necessary: a redefinition of its objectives and a revision of its methods. The initiative in this direction could be taken only by those who had a theoretical grasp of the forces of our present society. These naturally were those Congressmen who had come under the influence of, and had accepted, Marxian Socialism. It was natural, therefore, that the organization that sprang up to meet the needs of the situation took the description "Socialist". The word "Congress" prefixed to "Socialist" only signified the organic relationship—past, present and future—of the organization with the national movement.

The Socialist forces that were already in existence in the country were completely out of touch with the Congress and had no influence on the national movement. Therefore, there did not take place, as otherwise there would have, a fusion of the emerging Congress Socialist Party with the groups previously existing. Given the adoption of correct and sensible tactics by all the parties concerned, there is every likelihood of such a fusion taking place at a later stage.

PARTY'S TASK:

The immediate task before us is to develop the national movement into a real anti-imperialist movement—a movement aiming at freedom from the foreign power and the native system of exploitation. For this it is necessary to wean the anti-imperialist elements in the Congress away from its present bourgeois leadership and to bring them under the leadership of revolutionary

[1] *All India Congress Socialist Party. Constitution & Programme, Resolutions of the Third Conference of the Party, Thesis, Report of the General Secretary, 1937.*

Socialism. This task can be accomplished only if there is within the Congress an organized body of Marxian Socialists. In other words, *our* Party alone can, in the present conditions, perform this task. The strengthening and clarification of anti-imperialist forces in the Congress depends largely on the strength and activity of our Party. For fulfilling the Party's task it will also be necessary to co-ordinate all the other anti-imperialist forces in the country.

WORK WITHIN THE CONGRESS:

Consistent with its task, the party should take only an anti-imperialist stand on Congress platforms. We should not in this connection make the mistake of placing a full Socialist programme before the Congress. An anti-imperialist programme should be evolved for this purpose suiting the needs of workers, peasants and the lower middle classes.

It being the task of the party to bring the anti-imperialist elements under its ideological influence, it is necessary for us to be as tactful as possible. We should on no account alienate these elements by intolerance and impatience. The Congress constructive programme should not be obstructed or interfered with. It should, however, be scientifically criticised and exposed.

In Congress elections, we should not show keenness to "capture" committees and offices nor should we form alliances with politically undesirable groups for the purpose.

PARTY'S PROGRAMME:

This does not mean that the Party shall not carry on Socialist propaganda from its own platform. It must continue to do so—and do it more systematically and vigorously.

It follows that the Party's own programme must be a Marxist one, otherwise the Party will fail to fulfil its task and leadership. Marxism alone can guide the anti-imperialist forces to their ultimate destiny. Party members must therefore fully understand the technic of revolution, the theory and practice of the class struggle, the nature of the state and the processes leading to the Socialist society.

APPENDIX 2

Faizpur Thesis, 1936[1]

THESIS

(Adopted by the Third Annual Conference of the Party at Faizpur on 23 and 24 December 1936.)

THE MEERUT STATEMENT:

The present Thesis is an extension of the Meerut Thesis adopted by the Conference of the Party at its last session. While it reiterates the earlier thesis, it seeks to incorporate the experiences of the past year and to take into account the development of the anti-imperialist movement that has taken place in the intervening period.

THE UNITED NATIONAL FRONT AGAINST IMPERIALISM:

The chief task facing us and all other anti-imperialists is the creation of a powerful National Front against Imperialism. This is not a task that has to be begun anew. The struggle against Imperialism is on and has been on for many years past. It has now to be widened, integrated and raised to a higher stage of intensity.

While the working class and the peasantry has led in the past and is leading today important militant struggles against Imperialism, the main organized expression of the anti-imperialist movement has been the Indian National Congress. But as is evident it has not yet become an adequately consistent and effective anti-imperialist force. It does not yet embrace the broadest possible sector of the masses, whether organized or unorganized, and still stands aloof from their day-to-day struggle for the satisfaction of their pressing immediate needs.

It is the task of all anti-imperialists in the country to bring together and unite all anti-imperialist sectors and to build up a mighty front against Imperialism, made up of the broadest possible sector of the masses. It is clear that in our attempt to do so it is the Congress that we must take as the basis and starting point, and we must attempt to make it an all-embracing united front against Imperialism. The Congress has already succeeded to a

[1] *All India Congress Socialist Party. Constitution & Programme, Resolutions of the Third Conference of the Party, Thesis, Report of the General Secretary, 1937.*

large extent in uniting wide forces of the Indian people for the national struggle and remains today the principal existing mass organization of diverse elements seeking national liberation. It is for us now to find means to assist and extend that unity to a still wider front. This task, though being a single whole, can be divided, for the purpose of elucidation, into three main parts: our work within the Congress; our work among the masses outside the Congress; the task of integrating the anti-imperialist struggle outside and inside the Congress and consolidating the leadership of the anti-imperialist and Left forces.

This thesis is mainly concerned with the elaboration of this triple task.

OUR WORK WITHIN THE CONGRESS:

The Congress is organized at present on the basis of individual membership. Its members come mainly from the peasantry and the middle class. Most of these members do not take any active part in the anti-imperialist movement and simply meet once a year to elect their delegates and representatives. The Congress Committees too do not have any day-to-day programme of work. They have usually no contacts with the organizations of peasants and workers and do not take any appreciable part in their day-to-day struggles. The only contact they could have had with the masses, apart from the fact that it was not calculated to develop mass struggle, was through the "constructive programme". But this programme too is not in the hands of the Congress Committees but of autonomous associations like the A.I.S.A., A.I.V.I.A., etc. The form of open struggle—disobedience of specific laws—that the Congress has so far used does not give the masses wide scope for participation. It is not in fact a form of mass struggle which can develop only out of the day-to-day struggle against exploitation and oppression.

The reason for this is that while the Congress is a mass organization, its leadership is predominantly bourgeois. This leadership is unable within the framework of its conceptions and interests to develop the struggle of the masses to a higher level. But it should be kept in view that the Congress leadership is no longer undivided. Recently a conscious Left has been forming within the Congress and this development is reflecting itself in the leadership also, in which a sharp division is taking place. But as yet the Left is largely ineffective and the effective leadership is in the hands of the Right. This should not be understood to mean that the class composition of the Right is itself bourgeois. A part of it is undoubtedly so. On the whole it is petty-bourgeois, but it is under the dominance of bourgeois interests and bound by the limitations of the Indian bourgeoisie.

This analysis of the character of the Congress defines our task within it.

In the words of the Meerut Thesis it is to "wean the anti-imperialist elements in the Congress away from its present bourgeois leadership and to bring them under the influence of revolutionary socialism". The present thesis must further elucidate this.

The Meerut Thesis conceives of the task in too narrow a manner. Our task within the Congress is not only to wean away the anti-imperialist elements from the bourgeois leadership but so to develop and broaden the Congress itself as to transform it into a powerful anti-imperialist front. The problem is not only one of change of leadership. It requires a complete reorganization of the Congress—a building up of the Congress from the bottom upwards. As it has already been pointed out, this cannot be done by confining our activities to the Congress alone. Here, however, let us see what we have to do within the Congress. Taking the organizational aspect first, we should work for the democratization of its constitution so as to give more initiative to the primary members and committees and should endeavour to enlarge the membership and extend the organizations of the Congress further and make them active and alive. We should further try to bring the masses into the Congress by securing their representation in the Committees of the latter. Till this is done we should build up a close link between such organizations and Congress Committees for the purpose of joint work.

OUR ALTERNATIVE PROGRAMME:

As for the programme of the Congress, we should so shape it that it comes actively to develop the struggle of the masses taking their immediate demands as a basis. The formation of peasants' and workers' unions and active support to the struggle conducted by them should be kept in the forefront of this programme. In all other possible ways also, working on the principles laid down above, we should endeavour to provide Congress Committees with a programme of day-to-day work among the masses.

We should try to rally the rank and file of the Congress workers around this alternative programme. The political backwardness of the rank and file is due to their lack of contact with the economic struggle of the masses. Propaganda alone will not radicalise them. They must be drawn into the peasant and labour movement so that they may realize that our programme is a more dynamic one and will raise the anti-imperialist struggle to a higher pitch.

The Meerut Thesis declared that we have to bring the anti-imperialist movement under the leadership of revolutionary socialism. It is necessary to further elucidate this. The anti-imperialist struggle in India is a multi-class struggle of the peasantry and the working and middle classes. The working class in India, though organizationally weak and politically not sufficiently conscious of its role, is nonetheless potentially the most revolutionary class. The struggle of the Indian masses for freedom will not reach its objective unless the working class is in the vanguard of that struggle. Therefore, it is our task as Socialists to see that it assumes its historic role in the national movement. The leadership of revolutionary Socialism can mean nothing else.

OUR WORK OUTSIDE THE CONGRESS:

The anti-imperialist struggle cannot be separated from the day-to-day struggle of the masses. The development of the latter is the basis for a successful fight against imperialism. Therefore, our foremost task outside the Congress is to develop independent organizations of the peasants and workers and of other exploited sections of the people.

Besides these class organizations we should also attempt to organize the youth of the country so as to mobilize the most active elements of the lower middle class.

We should not be content with the formation of these separate organizations. We should try to harness them in the anti-imperialist front. These organizations while functioning independently and carrying on their own programme should be linked up with the Congress Committees and there should be joint action as often as possible. This should ultimately lead as already pointed out to the masses mobilized in these organizations entering the Congress through collective representation. Thus will the Congress become a wide national front against imperialism. This transformation is bound to change the entire structure and leadership of the Congress which will be composed of the strongly welded alliance of the various anti-imperialist classes, organized and unorganized.

CONSOLIDATION OF SOCIALIST FORCES:

In the conditions of India, the conscious leadership of the anti-imperialist movement falls on the Socialist forces. These forces are unfortunately still divided. The Party from the beginning has stood for unity in the Socialist ranks.

It is of the utmost importance that in the Congress, in the mass movement outside, in all spheres of anti-imperialist activity, a united lead is given. If Socialists speak with a divided voice there will be utter confusion and it will only retard the national struggle.

Till such unity is arrived at, the minimum that is necessary is agreement on the immediate tasks and line of action. On the basis of this agreement the various Socialist groups should work together till the time we are in a position to form a united Party.

Apart from unity or agreement among Socialist ranks, it is necessary that the forces of the Left are also consolidated and an understanding developed within its leadership. The Party should continue its efforts in this direction.

ORGANIZATION OF THE PARTY:

Our Party has generally grown in the last year. In certain provinces there has been a set-back and the growth has not been uniform everywhere. While there are parties with a membership of hundreds, certain other parties, also quite active, have not enlarged their organization beyond a few scores of members. It is obvious that the line of development and the scope of organization have not clearly been laid down. Without prejudice to the Marxist basis of our party, it is necessary to enlarge the membership of the Party so as to include a wider section of Congress workers and conscious elements active in the labour, peasant and other movements.

APPENDIX 3

A.I.C.C. Resolution on Office Acceptance, 17-18 March 1937[1]

The All India Congress Committee records its high appreciation of the magnificent response of the country to the call of the Congress during the recent elections and the approval by the electorate of the Congress policy and programme. The Congress entered these elections with its objective of independence and its total rejection of the New Constitution, and the demand for a Constituent Assembly to frame India's constitution. The declared Congress policy was to combat the New Act and end it. The electorate has, in overwhelming measure, set its seal on this policy and programme and the New Act therefore stands condemned and utterly rejected by the people through the self-same democratic process which had been invoked by the British Government, and the people have further declared that they desire to frame their own constitution, based on national independence, through the medium of a Constituent Assembly elected by adult franchise. This Committee therefore demands, on behalf of the people of India, that the New Constitution be withdrawn.

In the event of the British Government still persisting with the New Constitution, in defiance of the declared will of the people, the All India Congress Committee desires to impress upon all Congress members of the legislatures that their work inside and outside the legislatures must be based on the fundamental Congress policy of combating the New Constitution and seeking to end it, a policy on the basis of which they sought the suffrage of the electorate and won their overwhelming victory in the elections. That policy must inevitably lead to deadlocks with the British Government and bring out still further the inherent antagonism between British Imperialism and Indian Nationalism, and expose the autocratic and undemocratic nature of the New Constitution.

1. The All India Congress Committee endorses and confirms the resolutions of the Working Committee passed at Wardha on February 27 and 28, 1937 on the extra-parliamentary activities of Congress members of legislatures, mass contacts, and the Congress policy in the legislatures, and call upon all Congressmen in the legislatures and outside to work in accordance with the directions contained in them.

[1] *Indian National Congress, 1936-7. Being the resolutions passed by the Congress, The All India Congress Committee and the Working Committee during the period between April 1936 to January 1938.*

And on the pending question of office acceptance, and in pursuance of the policy summed up in the foregoing paragraphs, the All India Congress Committee authorises and permits the acceptance of office in provinces where the Congress commands a majority in the Legislatures, provided the ministerships shall not be accepted unless the leader of the Congress party in the legislature is satisfied and is able to state publicly that the Governor will not use his special powers of interference or set aside the advice of ministers in regard to constitutional activities.

APPENDIX 4

Statement of National Executive of the C.S.P. on Acceptance of Offices by the Congress, 22 March 1937[1]

The Congress has, though not without stiff opposition, finally decided to accept offices under the New Constitution. The Congress Socialist Party has from the very beginning opposed this policy. To this end it helped in organizing the Anti-Ministry Committee of Congressmen and conducted an unceasing campaign for a revolutionary parliamentary programme and the rejection of ministerial offices.

It would be wrong to think that the decision of the A.I.C.C. shows that the Party's work in this connection has yielded no fruits. In fact, that work went a long way to stiffen the parliamentary programme of the Congress and to prevent it from being dragged further towards Constitutionalism. It helped to create a new understanding of the nature of our national struggle and its relation to imperialist legislatures, and provided slogans which are today accepted by the entire Congress.

There is no doubt that the decision to form Congress cabinets has strengthened the Constitutionalist tendency in the country and is fraught with other dangerous tendencies. It may act as a brake upon the growth of the freedom struggle by suggesting to the people that power, at least partially, has been won. Further, the decision to stipulate for assurances, from Governors threatens a reversal to the policy of attempting to arrive at "understandings" with the British Government. The Party will therefore have to exercise greater vigilance and see that the country does not drift into reformism and the power mobilized in the last few months does not get dissipated.

The Party will always act in such a way as will convince the masses of the futility of Constitutional action and will prepare them increasingly for direct action, even though localized.

While unable to mobilize enough strength to enable the A.I.C.C. to take a correct decision, the Party's campaign has shown the utility of the organized Party like the Congress Socialist Party working within the Congress with a definite policy. Its defeat on this issue does not in any way affect its policy or basis of work.

Though it continues to be opposed to this decision on the office issue the Party will not withdraw its co-operation from the Congress. It will adopt an attitude of critical co-operation in the parliamentary work of the Congress

[1] *Congress Socialist*, 27 March 1937.

and its main anxiety is to see that the Congress carries out its declared programme and policy of combating and ending the slave Constitution. The Party lays special emphasis on the agrarian and other demands of the masses and its chief task now will be to agitate and organize them on the basis of these demands. In this manner the mass of the people will be able to exercise a continual pressure from below on the Congress cabinets.

We are confident that soon this phase in our national movement will come to an end and we shall be launched upon a mighty and triumphant struggle for freedom.

APPENDIX 5

Ratification of Congress Working Committee Resolution on Office Acceptance, 29 October 1937[1]

By a resolution dated the 18th March 1937 passed by the A.I.C.C. at Delhi, it was resolved that permission be given for Congressmen to accept office in provinces where the Congress commanded a majority in the legislature if the Leader of the Congress Party was satisfied and could state publicly that the Governor would not use his special powers of interference or set aside the advice of ministers in regard to their constitutional activities.

Since the said resolution, statements and declarations were made on this issue on behalf of the British Government.

After examining those declarations and the situation created as a result of circumstances and events which occurred after the A.I.C.C. resolution of March last, the Working Committee was of opinion that it would not be easy for Governors to use their special powers.

Having considered the views of the Congress members of the Legislatures and Congressmen generally, the Working Committee at Wardha at its meeting held in July 1937 came to the conclusion and resolved that Congressmen be permitted to accept office wherever they were invited thereto.

Had circumstances permitted, the Working Committee was anxious to obtain the sanction of the All India Congress Committee in the matter but the Committee felt that delay in taking a decision at that stage would have been injurious to the country's interests and that the matter demanded a prompt and immediate decision.

It is therefore resolved that the action of the Working Committee in taking the said decision be ratified.

[1] *Indian National Congress, 1936-7. Being the resolutions passed by the Congress, the All India Congress Committee and the Working Committee during the period between April 1936 to January 1938.*

APPENDIX 6

Resolution of Bihar Provincial Congress Committee, Patna, 14 December 1937[1]

The Working Committee of the Bihar Provincial Congress Committee considered at length the situation arising out of the resolutions passed by the Champaran, Monghyr and Saran District Congress Committees, asking Congressmen not to participate in the meetings of the Provincial Kisan Sabha and adopted the following resolution:

Resolved that in the opinion of this Committee Champaran, Saran and Monghyr District Congress Committees had the right to adopt the resolutions which they did, keeping in view the situation obtaining in their districts and the province, and this Committee does not consider it proper to interfere in any way with their action. In the opinion of this Committee the kind of propaganda that is being carried on in this province, has been responsible for producing a poisonous atmosphere and attacks are being made on the principle of Ahimsa which is the cherished creed of the Congress. An atmosphere is developing in certain parts of the province which it is apprehended is likely to do much harm to the country and to put obstacles in the way of country's march towards freedom. The Committee, therefore, considers it necessary and proper to enjoin upon all Congress workers and those sympathising with it, to keep themselves aloof from such activities and in accordance with the Congress policy to fight those who may be found indulging in them. In view of the fact that the Committee has before it enough material to prove that many workers of the Kisan Sabha are engaged in such activities and that in public meetings organized under the auspices of the Kisan Sabha, statements are being made as a result whereof the situation is going from bad to worse and there is the likelihood of the work of the Congress being hampered this Committee impresses upon such Congress members as are working in the Kisan Sabha that not only their active co-operation in such activities but also their passive association with them is improper and it directs District Congress Committees to keep an eye on these activities of its workers and to report them to Provincial Congress Office.

[1] *Amrita Bazar Patrika*, 15 December 1937.

APPENDIX 7

Joint Statement on the Resolution of Bihar P.C.C., 25 December 1937[1]

We, the members of the A.I.C.C. and members of the Congress Party in the Legislatures who have been associated with the Kisan Sabha, have felt extremely aggrieved by the resolution of the Working Committee of the B.P.C.C. It assumes that those of us, who are working in the Kisan Sabha are anti-Congress in our attitude or activities. We most indignantly repudiate the charge. We would regard it as a colossal folly to weaken the Congress in any way. It is our firm conviction that the Indian National Congress is the only organization that can lead the struggle for Independence by co-ordinating the revolutionary efforts of peasants and workers. By working also in the Kisan Sabha we want to provide the inevitable link between the Congress and the peasant movement.

We do not certainly expect the Ministers to perform miracles. We do want to strengthen their hands by mass pressure. And the mass struggle that the Kisan Sabha is developing is intended not only to enable the Ministers to enforce the demands of the Election Manifesto, to combat the Act and to end it, but to help the Congress in forging sanctions for the attainment of independence. In this effort the Kisan Sabha undoubtedly expects the Ministers to encourage such development of the mass struggle from the strategic position they occupy and not to stifle the expression of mass discontent by lulling it into inaction or into a false sense of security. It is no good raising irrelevant issues. It may be that some Kisan Sabha workers may have made speeches that may constitute incitement to violence.

The proper procedure in such cases would have been to confront the workers with their speeches, and in the absence of a satisfactory explanation from them, to have taken disciplinary action against them.

In its resolution dated November 22, 1937 the Kisan Sabha emphasized the need of a peaceful mass action and warned the Kisans that any act of violence or its encouragement would hurt their cause irretrievably. It will be remembered that the last demonstration in Patna of thousands of peasants was peaceful, organized and disciplined. It is likely that in spite of resolutions and warnings there may have been lapses. There have been lapses on the

[1] *Hindustan Times*, 26 December 1937. The joint statement was issued by Sahajanand Saraswati, J.P., Ganga Sharan Sinha, Ramvriksh Benipuri, Ramnandan Mishra, Dhanraj Sharma, Awadheshwar Prasad Sinha, Kishori Prasanna Singh, Jamuna Karjee and others.

part of even Congress workers who are not Kisan Sabhaites.

It will be remembered that during the last election there was a spontaneous outburst of rural literature in the shape of songs, plays, and caricatures which were very effective, but some of which were as far removed from non-violence and truth as Mahatma Gandhi is from violence and untruth. It would be entirely wrong to attribute all these to Congress inspiration or influence. Similarly the peasant movement brings in at times elements that have to be controlled. But there is no doubt that neither the Congress nor the Kisan Sabha can permit its workers to attack the basic policy of the Congress and if any [one] does so, action should be taken against him. But it would be terribly wrong to generalize and damn the Kisan Sabha.

We can safely assert that the sum total of the activities of the Kisan Sabha has been to create a revolutionary spirit and a mass consciousness which should be welcomed by the Congress as great assets to the movement for freedom. But instead we are stigmatised as people encouraging anti-Congress activities.

The effect of the resolution will be to hand over the Kisan Sabhas to the reactionary elements to fight with the moral support of the Congress. And supposing the Congress Government goes out and a reactionary government comes in, not a very unlikely thing, it will find sufficient moral justification to declare the Kisan Sabha as illegal and no one can blame it for that. We, therefore, feel that the resolution was ill-conceived and it has also by justifying the resolution of the Monghyr D.C.C. done irreparable injustice to the Kisan Sabhas.

We do not want to comment so much upon the Constitutional impropriety of the resolution of the Monghyr D.C.C. as upon its justification by the Working Committee. In view of the unusual and grave character of the resolution it was not too much to expect that the Working Committee would come to enquire what materials were before the Monghyr D.C.C. before it passed the resolution, whether any warnings had been given to local Kisan Sabha workers that they were indulging in anti-Congress activities and whether those warnings had gone unheeded. It is incomprehensible why Kisan Sabha workers would suddenly start an anti-Congress campaign in the district and it is equally incomprehensible that the District Congress Committee would suddenly discover it and without giving a warning, ban the Kisan Sabha.

Not a single instance of objectionable activities of any Kisan Sabha worker was brought to the notice of the District Kisan Sabha, and still such a drastic action was taken. In the Working Committee of the Monghyr D.C.C. consisting of fifteen members, nearly half are Kisan Sabha workers—an unmistakable proof that the Kisan Sabha was so far enjoying the confidence of the local Congress Committee.

We feel pained that the Working Committee without caring to appreciate the psychological reactions that the resolution was likely to have, justified it. It would affect the prestige of an organization that was co-operating with the Congress in intensifying its activities, and will so co-operate in future in spite of the gravest shock it has got from quarters from which it expected a little consideration.

We think it was not dignified for the Working Committee to have justified the action of Saran and Champaran D.C.Cs against one of its members. It is shocking that Congress Committees should try to interfere with the elementary right of freedom of movement on the ground that it would lead to ideological conflict, particularly against one who is a member of the Working Committee and occupies a very important position in public life. We can only explain these things on the hypothesis that the tendencies towards reformism in the Congress are trying to stifle mass agitation.

We, however, want to make it abundantly clear that nothing can affect our allegiance to the Congress and we will go on working for it. We appeal to the Working Committee to reconsider its decision and to repair the injustice it has done to Kisan Sabha and to the Congressmen working in the Sabha.

APPENDIX 8

Editorials in the *Searchlight*, 19 and 23 January 1938[1]

MR. JAYAPRAKASH NARAYAN'S APOLOGIA—I

Mr. Jayaprakash Narayan's lengthy apologia for his proteges of the Kisan Sabha furnishes an eloquent illustration of *suppressio veri* and *suggestio falsi*. We have no heart in a controversy with him because we recognize his worth and appreciate his possibilities. Nor is it necessary for us to emphasize that Babu Rajendra Prasad is Babu Rajendra Prasad however much Mr. Narayan and his friends may choose to forget it. It is hardly necessary to do so. For if the worst that could be said against Babu Rajendra Prasad and the Congress Working Committee can be so poor at the best, we see no prospect of any of the two losing in the estimation of the public at large as a result of the determined onslaught of Mr. Jayaprakash Narayan. The statement is, however, an interesting study in left-wing bumptiousness. One would almost think from the reason advanced by him for the Congress decision that the Congress High Command under Babu Rajendra Prasad were on the run and that some stunt had to be staged which was the desperate gamble of a dying leadership. With that cool *sang-froid* so characteristic of left-wing audacity, which however turns into a whine when they are hit back, he has likened the Congress decision to the now notorious episode of the Zinovieff letter, manufactured and manipulated by the then desperate British Conservatives to seal the fate of the Labour Party in the impending elections and turn the latter's possible triumph at the polls into a victory for themselves. As if Swami Sahajanand and Company were so thoroughly entrenched in strength that Babu Rajendra Prasad had no choice but to stoop to a low and dirty manoeuvring to discredit them in order to be able to retain his tottering supremacy in the Congress? As if Babu Rajendra Prasad, of all persons, is capable of what, according to Mr. Jayaprakash Narayan, was an act of pure political manipulation? He says experience has amply borne out this interpretation. Has it? Does Mr. Narayan seriously expect the public to believe with him that his motley crew of the disgruntled and the dissatisfied, who swell the Kisan Sabha official hordes, would have, in any event, secured a majority in the Congress elections? It may be folly to be wise at times. But Mr. Jayaprakash Narayan would do well to at least try to realize that the action of the Champaran, Monghyr and Saran Committees were at least pointers indicating the way the Congress wind

[1] *Searchlight*, 19 January 1938 and 23 January 1938.

was blowing consequent upon the revulsion of feeling against the ways of the Kisan Sabha stalwarts. It may please vanity and flatter conceit to visualize possible triumphs which the Congress decision was intended to prevent and frustrate. But Mr. Narayan knows that even in the district of Patna, which is Swamiji's and Kisan Sabha's stronghold and where the official Congress machinery has been in their hands for years, they have failed to secure a majority in the elections.

Mr. Jayaprakash Narayan does not do justice to his intelligence much less to his common sense, by asking over and over again what reason had Babu Rajendra Prasad to believe that all the information received by the Provincial office was true and by peeling out such commonplace apologetics as that misreporting often occurs, that factitious reports are possible and that a slight variation in words often turns criticism into abuse and attack. Unfortunately for Mr. Narayan and his friends, Babu Rajendra Prasad knows who's who and what's what and does not choose to pawn his judgement in the safe custody of partisan prejudice. For Mr. Jayaprakash Narayan to attempt to plead injured innocence is to outrage ordinary obligations of truth and fair play. Mere denials do not become sacrosanct because their author is Mr. Jayaprakash Narayan. Kisan Sabhaite antics were public property long before the Congress Committee took action. We are assured that it never was the policy of the Kisan Sabha to preach that the Congress Ministry could not be relied upon to help the peasants who should, therefore, organize themselves to force its hands. This is, however, exactly what was done within the knowledge of the entire province pace a handful to whom the admission is inconvenient. Throughout his lengthy rigmarole Mr. Jayaprakash Narayan naturally does not choose to refer to the fact that almost as soon as Swamiji returned from his sojourn in Kashmir he, a member of the Congress Working Committee, proceeded to pronounce his anathema on the Congress Ministry at Gaya without having done them the ordinary courtesy of previous consultation. What followed is well known. It is no use, story-telling that speeches are misreported, misrepresented and distorted. Mr. Narayan may tell these to the marines. Ordinarily, Kisan rallies would be helpful as emphasizing mass sanction. But Mr. Jayaprakash Narayan gives the show away by acknowledging, almost against his inclinations, that the rallies were intended, among other things, to bring pressure to bear upon "such tendencies in the Ministry and the Congress party as might incline unduly towards the interests of the Zamindars". That was it.

Our Kisan Sabha friends had satisfied themselves that the Congress leaders and the Congress Ministers were likely to betray the Kisans out of their loving solicitude for the Zamindars and they set about trying to distinguish between mere Congressmen and Kisan Sabhaites in order to drive home that the latter alone were the saviours of the Kisans. The Kisan rallies were a part of the game. They were also intended to measure and assert the influence and the prestige of the Kisan leaders. So were the ultimatum hurled on the Ministers by the 61 M.L.A.s and the campaign of repudiation—Mr. Narayan himself calls it "foolish propaganda" inaugurated in the constituencies of those who refused to sign this curious document. All these were a part of a systematic whole, to impress upon the Kisans that the Ministry were much too solicitous of the Zamindars but that the Kisan Sabhaites were there to keep them up to the mark. They lacked therefore, the agitational bonafides harped upon by Mr. Jayaprakash Narayan who deliberately blinds himself to the sharp and obvious contrast in human material between his Kisan Sabha friends on the one hand, and Babu Rajendra Prasad and his co-workers, on the other. The campaign that followed is, as we have said, well known. Swamiji's attention was repeatedly drawn to the speeches that were being made and the language that was being employed but, as Babu Rajendra Prasad pointed out in his statement the other day, they but whetted his desire to secure counter statements. Now, these counter statements may impress Mr. Jayaprakash Narayan, labouring under the pitful constitutional malady of being willing to believe everything of Babu Rajendra Prasad and nothing against such paragons of virtue as Swami Sahajanand and his lieutenants, but they would be nothing short of all rout in the eyes of those who know their authors.

The Working Committee had, therefore, no choice. It is sheer nonsense, utter unmitigated twaddle, even for Mr. Jayaprakash Narayan to talk of accusers being the judges. For a Congressman the Working Committee is the highest and the final forum of authority. The Committee has the privilege of having at its head Babu Rajendra Prasad whose honour is supposed to be above reproach except by the all-knowing wiseacres of the self-constituted saviours of the Kisans. The Committee was surely entitled to say that Congressmen shall not indulge in certain kinds and forms of activities—activities so well known that people will prefer to respect their own knowledge about them rather than accept the tutored *ipse dixits* of Mr. Jayaprakash Narayan to whom every Kisan Sabhaite is a swan and every opponent of theirs a goose. He asks, what is sacrosanct about the prohibition programme that it cannot even be criticized? Only this, that it is an integral part of the Congress programme and therefore, not open to a Congressman not only to make fun of it but hold up the Ministry's proposed effort to give effect to it, slowly and by stages, as an illustration of a design on the interests and the well-being of the Kisans. For a Congressman to go about exalting drink and toddy as compared with tea is bad enough but when it is stated that the Ministry was so hopeless that it proposed to take away even the poor man's toddy it is positively nauseating. And yet Mr. Jayaprakash Narayan asks, what is sacrosanct about prohibition that it cannot even be criticised?

Mr. Narayan's psychology is thoroughly understandable. Between him and the Kisan Sabhaites there has been, as it were, a sort of an unwritten alliance, offensive and defensive. He does not believe in the Gandhian philosophy of political action that dominates the Congress today. He believes in no private property. Outside the Congress he will be a fish out of water. His communism will wither and perish. The Congress, therefore, is a convenient garb, however out of tune its programme may be. But Gandhism must be sapped and undermined. Doing so involves the discrediting of the Congress leadership. On the other hand, the Swami and the members of his General Staff, men whose career is an open book, have their own reasons to do all they can to displace the present Congress leadership. The two naturally drew, thrived and flourished together and would have continued to do so but for the fact that they overdid the chapter. They missed their footing. They were found out a little too soon and, what is more, even Rajendra Babu's patience was exhausted. The Socialist Kisan Sabha's apple-cart was thus overturned and the very interesting game of using the Congress for ulterior purposes was upset. Who will not appreciate the resulting disappointment and the consequent bitterness? Even Pandit Jawaharlal Nehru's endorsement of the Bihar Congress decision is not conclusive. So be it, for aught we care. Only we wish they behaved like men and not like naughty school boys caught in the act of pilfering.

THE MASK REMOVED—II

Our hearty congratulations to the eminent Socialists now gathered at Bachhwara for the so-called Bihar Provincial Kisan Conference, on their latest acquisition in left-wing leadership. We wish them the joy of Pandit Jadunandan Sharma's wise, sagacious and superb counsel. It must have been a privilege for them to have listened to the masterly performance to which Pandit Sharma treated them, a veritable feast for their intelligence and common sense. So far as Pandit Jadunandan Sharma is concerned, he can honestly claim that the hypocritical humbug that has characterized the recent protestations on behalf of the Kisan Sabha do not hold water with him. He is not adept in concealing his purpose under a cloak of fine words. A tub-thumper by nature and long practice—he glories in being one. He makes no attempt to impose upon intelligence by recourse to specious reasoning and a whole catalogue of sophistry and casuistry. He lays his cards on the table and makes no bones about stating what he thinks of Congress leadership and Congress organization. He is frankly anti-Congress and lays bare the ideology of the Kisan Sabhaite wiseacres in no uncertain terms. He is, indeed, entitled to gratitude for having authoritatively given the quietus to much unnecessary speculation and controversy over the objective and the purpose of Swami Sahajanand and Company. Terminological inexactitudes, half-truths and even deliberate misstatements do not worry him. Hardihood and truculence are the badge of his tribe and the address shows that he flourishes on them. To him Congress leaders, from Mahatma Gandhi and Pandit Jawaharlal Nehru down to Babu Rajendra Prasad, Babu Srikrishna Sinha and Babu Anugrah Narayan Sinha, are either fools or knaves. He and his patrons are many beacon lights in the long and dreary march that lies ahead before the suffering millions where they can come into their own. His explanation of the genesis of the Kisan Sabha is simple. The Congress persisted in its folly of trying to reconcile irreconciliable interests in its attempt to keep intact its national character, or in other words, in maintaining a united anti-Imperialist front. And it would not even allow freedom to the masses to ventilate their genuine grievances against their exploitation by Indian feudalism and rising capitalism. Hence the necessity of the Kisan Sabha. It matters little to this pinchbeck exponent of Leninism run riot, that an anti-Imperialist united front, which he has the ignorance to laugh at has been declared by the greatest Indian socialists as the *sine qua non* of the social revolution that must follow and not precede the disappearance of British Imperialism from India. Far from suppressing expression of genuine grievances, the Congress has had the sense to bend more and more towards an economic orientation of its programme consistent with the paramount consideration of maintaining intact the anti-Imperialist front. That economic programme is being given effect to, to the extent possible, under the circumscribing limitations of the new constitution by the Congress Ministers in at least seven provinces of India.

Pandit Jadunandan Sharma does not lack in candour. On the contrary with the characteristic ruthlessness of the vulgar upstart, he has torn the mask of the faces of those who have been rending the working with the cries of "help, murder" ever since the Congress Committee considered it necessary to twist their tales. We will not dwell on his dissertation on the ethics of non-violence for to even the dullest of man it amounts to an incitement of violence. If violence is the law of nature and destruction is as natural as creation, why have the cowardice to parade non-violence as the creed of the Sabha? If the indispensability of violence has to be emphasized *ad nauseum* before ignorant and excited audiences, why can't the Swami and his satellites drop all pretence of non-violence? Profession of non-violence is, however, their safety valve, the instrument to save their skin if and when the thousands of their dupes have to suffer and pay for the cowardly ministrations of their leaders? This is, however, a minor matter though, we hope, it will engage the attention of the Congress authorities who cannot permit charlatans, who have little to lose, to expose the innocent Kisans to the dire consequences of ill-concealed incitement to violence and yet occupy a place in the Congress organization.

According to the great Pandit Jadunandan Sharma, the Congress leaders are the dupes and the tools of the Zamindars, the members of the All India Congress Working Committee but so many witless nincompoops easily scared and outwitted and the Congress itself dominated by the upper classes, determined to perpetuate the social order in which they live and, therefore, naturally resolute in suppressing the aspirations of the exploited classes. The attempt to effect a compromise between the landlords and the tenants is an absurdity; it is the height of cruelty to legislate for the easy realization of rent; it is against all canons of justice to sacrifice the millions for adding to the comforts of a comfortable few. The leaders of the Congress, we are told, continue to have a tender solicitude for the artificially created proprietors of the land and it is therefore, nothing but mockery to talk of doing good to the peasants. Indeed, the Kisans were assured that the vested interests who now control the machinery of the Congress have already started their offensive against them. Unfortunately for him, we cannot imagine the Kisan millions trooping under the banners of Pandit Jadunandan Sharma, their self-appointed saviour and the self-advertised hero of the hour. To examine his half-baked, ill-digested shibboleths is to admit his credentials, to invest him with a sense of understanding and responsibility. In a word, the proclamation has gone forth that the Congress leaders and the Congress Ministers are in the service of the Zamindars and, therefore, determined to suppress the aspirations of the Kisans and that their offensive has already begun. Hence the Kisans must organize and strengthen the Kisan Sabha and with the determination to stake their all, and their victory is certain.

Now, Pandit Jadunandan Sharma by himself is small fry. But he speaks for Kisan Sabhaites like Swami Sahajanand Saraswati and Mr. Jayaprakash Narayan. The latter was laboriously at pains the other day in trying to demonstrate the falsity of Babu Rajendra Prasad's charge against the Kisan Sabha. We wonder if his obsession will permit him to realize, even after Pandit Sharma's speech, that what the provinces confronted with is an open, brazen faced and impudent campaign against the Congress in the name of the Kisans. We will not refer to the indecency and deceit of men sitting and listening without protest to insolent reflections on the motives, indeed, the honour of men who are assets to the national movement by persons about whom the less said the better. If Mr. Jayaprakash Narayaṇ and his friends enjoy such crudities, they are welcome to do so. But the Congress in Bihar is not yet on the run and is strong enough to deal with men who use the

Congress cloak to sap the foundations and the fundamentals of the Congress and undermine its prestige and position. That such a campaign is, in fact, being carried on is borne out as never before by Pandit Jadunandan Sharma's address. Gone is the veneer of hypocrisy. Congress leaders should be able to know how to deal with the situation.

APPENDIX 9

Joint Petition for Release of Political Prisoners, 3 February 1938[1]

You are our Prime Minister, we have therefore come to tell you what we feel about the continued imprisonment of some of the bravest sons of the Motherland, the twenty-seven political prisoners who are still languishing in your prisons and half of whom are already on the threshold of death.

The names of these comrades are:

(1) Messrs Jogendra Shukla, (2) Kedarmani Shukla, (3) Ram Pratap Singh, (4) Chandrika Singh, (5) Shyam Krishna Agarwal, (6) Kanhailal Mishra, (7) Lekh Narayan Das, (8) Shivakant Misra, (9) Mahanth Ramraman Das, (10) Panna Lal, (11) Rajendra Prasad, (12) Brahmadeva Thakur, (13) Ramprasad Singh, (14) Dayanand Jha, (15) Ragho Prasad, (16) Rambabu Shiva Prasad, (17) Suryanath Chaubey, (18) Chandrama Singh, (19) Satyanarayan Misra, (20) Sant Sevak, (21) Murlidhar, (22) Surya Narayan Jha, (23) Jogeshwar Prasad, (24) Shivashankar Bharathi, (25) Shekaldeep Raut, (26) Shyamdeva Narayan.

Of these the first eight have been on hunger strike since Jan. 17. Today is the 17th day of their supreme sacrifice. We have already heard alarming reports of their condition. The life of many of them now hangs only by a slender thread. Every hour that passes brings them nearer death.

Other five of them, namely, Sarvashree Pannalal, Rajendra Prasad, Brahmdeva Thakur, Ragho Prasad Singh and Shiva Shankar Bharathi have been fasting since Jan. 25 and one of them Mahanth Ramraman Das, since January 21. From reports we gather that four or five more were to join the strike yesterday. Thus, of the twenty-seven, eight have already been on strike for 17 days, one for 13 days and five for 9 days. Others are reported to be joining the strike.

We feel, Sir, that all the political prisoners in this Province should have been released immediately after you took the reins of Provincial Government. It was mistake to have initiated a policy of piecemeal release. That has strengthened the hands of those who are possibly standing in your way

[1] *Searchlight*, 4 February 1938. The joint petition was submitted to Srikrishna Sinha, the Premier of Bihar. The deputation was headed by J.P. and consisted of Phulan Prasad Verma, Kishori Prasanna Sinha, Kesho Prasad, representatives of the Students Union, Youth League, Socialist Party, Kisan Sabha, Press Workers Union, Coachman's Union Sabha, and Bihar Political Prisoners' Release Committee. It also included Bishwanath Prasad Mathur and other ex-Andaman prisoners and ex-detenues.

today. The delay that has already occurred has caused us intolerable pain. But now, the situation has become too desperate and calls for bold action. Everyday, nay, every hour that passes is like a nail driven into the coffin of Swaraj.

We are aware of your anxiety to release the prisoners. We also do not forget that you have often hinted at the limitations which the slave constitution imposes on the elected Governments. But these limitations, whatever they may be cannot be allowed to stand in the way of your carrying out fundamental policies. They cannot force you, the head of a peoples' Government to share the responsibility of the death of martyrs. For imperialism and its agents these brave men are their impeccable enemies. But for us, they are our comrades. They are your comrades. They are soldiers of freedom. It is natural for the agents of Imperialism to seek their ruination. But how can a peoples' Government be a party to it? No fraud of provincial autonomy can induce such a Government to do so. The Congress Government cannot have the blood of martyrs on its head.

Therefore, Sir, we have come to ask you to release forthwith all the political prisoners who are imprisoned in the jails of the province. If you cannot, then you and your cabinet must resign.

We know that the question of resignation is in the hands of the Congress Working Committee. We have, however, sought this opportunity of meeting you so that you may be acquainted with the intensity of feelings in this Province on this question, and may be in a position to advise the Working Committee accordingly. The Congress is pledged to combat the new Act and its limitations. It must do so. But if it cannot overcome the limitations, it must never give in. That would be suicide.

We finally assure you Sir, that in event of the resignation of your Cabinet, we shall be behind you. The whole province will be behind you. Once again the soldiers of freedom will rally under the flag of the Congress and they shall march on till victory is theirs.

APPENDIX 10

Joint Appeal by Jayaprakash Narayan and P.C. Joshi for Legalizing the Communist Party, 10 March 1938[1]

On 20 March 1929 British Imperialism arrested 32 militant Trade Unionists and national workers and launched the famous Meerut Communist Conspiracy Case. The Meerut Case was a part of the imperialist terror to suppress the communist movement in India and to outlaw the Communist Party.

After the conclusion of the Meerut Case the Communist Party of India was declared illegal by a notification of the Government of India in July 1934, and a further campaign of repression of the communists began.

Today under the Congress Ministries the civil liberties of the people are being extended. The demand for the enjoyment of democratic rights is growing.

Communist parties are legal in all civilized countries. There is no reason why the Communist Party should not be legal in India.

20th March, the anniversary of the Meerut arrests, is fast approaching. There can be no more opportune day for making a nationwide demand for the legalization of the Communist Party. We therefore appeal in the name of the elementary liberties of the people and of the right of association and expression of opinion to the public, particularly to the Congress, labour, peasant and other organizations throughout the country to hold meetings and demonstrations on March 20 in order to voice the demand for legalizing the Communist Party of India. We hope that irrespective of political differences and only in defence of the civil liberties of the people every public organization and every liberty loving individual in the country will rally behind this demand.

[1] *Searchlight*, 12 March 1938.

APPENDIX 11

Joint Appeal by Jayaprakash Narayan and P.C. Joshi to observe Mysore Day [before 3 May 1938][1]

For nearly a year the people of Mysore have been waging a heroic struggle for democratic liberties and responsible Government.

The battle has been fought under our National Tricolour which became in Mysore, as elsewhere, the banner of people's struggle and the emblem of their aspirations. The State Government banned the use of the flag. The people of Mysore launched Satyagraha in honour of the Flag. Thirty-six martyrs have been mowed down by police bullets, newspapers have been closed down, indiscriminate mass arrests are taking place, a reign of terror prevails.

The people of Mysore are our own kith & kin, their struggle is our struggle, we must solidly stand behind them and actively support their cause—our own cause.

The National Congress and States' People's Conference must immediately organize a Solidarity Campaign to which we pledge the fullest support of all Socialists and Communists in the country. Volunteers must be poured into Mysore to fight shoulder to shoulder with the brave Mysoreans for the honour of the National Flag. A non-official public enquiry committee must be appointed. The demands of the Mysore State Congress must be unequivocally supported. An All-India Day must be fixed to inaugurate the campaign to assist the victory of the Mysore States' People and bring about the retreat of the autocratic Government. We suggest May 8 as such a Day and we request Congress Committees, Congress Socialist Parties, Trade Unions, Kisan Sabhas, Students' Unions and every progressive organization to join hands together in every locality and hold mass meetings throughout the country on 8 May to voice popular indignation against the black deeds of the Mysore Government and demand the inauguration of an All-India Mysore Campaign. The Working Committee is meeting on 12 May. The people must speak on 8 May.

[1] *Congress Socialist*, 7 May 1938.

APPENDIX 12

Joint Circular by Jayaprakash Narayan and M.R. Masani, 3 May 1938[1]

60A, Hughes Road
Bombay, 7
3 May 1938

Dear Friend,

We are sure you are feeling horrified at the massacre of about 36 persons at Viduraswatham in Mysore State as a consequence of the ban on the National Flag. You must also be perplexed as to how most effectively we in British India can express our strong feelings in the matter and help the people of Mysore to win the right of flying the National Flag. In our view, what is called for is action such as was taken in connection with the Nagpur Flag Satyagraha when volunteers from all over the country went to Nagpur and participated in defiance of a similar ban.

We take the liberty of forwarding a draft letter[2] addressed to the President of the Congress and of requesting you as a Member of the A.I.C.C. to join the many other members of the A.I.C.C. who are sending such letters.

If, as we hope, you agree with the suggestion, may we request you to sign the letter and send it to the above address so that all such letters may be forwarded together to Subhas Chandra Bose on the eve of the meeting of the Congress Working Committee in Bombay? In view of the little time left before that meeting, we shall appreciate an immediate response.

Yours fraternally,
Jayaprakash Narayan
M.R. Masani

[1] *AICC Papers.*
[2] Not available.

APPENDIX 13

Letter from Jawaharlal Nehru to Jayaprakash Narayan, 2 August 1938[1]

Houlgate (France)
2 August 1938

My dear Jayaprakash,

Your cable has been forwarded to me here but it does not say where you are at present. I am sending a reply to Patna suggesting that you (sic) might wait. I do not think it will be desirable for you to include my name among the foundation members of the proposed Socialist Book Club. I do not know what the idea is, except of course generally. It seems to me that any book club venture must be very carefully organised, especially on the business side. I have been going into this matter with (Victor) Gollancz and others and I have found that without this preparation such ventures are likely to fail. It seems to me that we are too eager to start ventures without thinking out how they will get on. We are always in difficulties and a succession of failures cling to us. We started this Nationalist Publications Society with Shah and Narendra Dev and others and it is in a dormant state. There is the proposal to start a daily from Lucknow and this is also in a bad way. I would much rather concentrate on something we have already begun than start a new venture.

The Left Book Club has succeeded because of Gollancz's business ability and a certain wide appeal that he made outside socialist circles. I do not see any comparable ability on our side.

Besides I feel that all our politics are getting far too much in the ruts and we must get them going on the right lines. What I shall do on my return to India I do not know but I want to keep myself detached at present so far as I can. We must see the whole problem and not lose ourselves in minor aspects of it. Therefore I would rather not associate myself with a new venture.

I have come here for a week for some rest and writing work. I hope before returning to India to visit Russia and Turkey but I am not sure yet.

I hope you are well.

Yours affectionately,
Jawaharlal

[1] *JP Papers* (NMML).

APPENDIX 14

Socialist Book Club[1]

Scheme for a Socialist Book Club

NAME OF THE CLUB

The Club will be called 'The Socialist Book Club'.

OBJECT OF THE CLUB

The object of the Club will be to undertake, promote and direct the production and publication of literature on various aspects of socialism, particularly with a view to

(1) explain the basic principles of socialism.
(2) explain and analyse the application of socialist theory to Indian conditions.
(3) remove popular misunderstandings about socialism.
(4) present Indian problems in their correct international setting.
(5) acquaint the Indian public with the history of social and national struggles of other countries.
(6) supply correct information about the socialist reconstruction of society in the U.S.S.R.

PUBLICATIONS OF THE CLUB

The Club will issue its publications in English, Hindi, Urdu and in as many other Indian languages as facilities for translation and publication permit.

The Club will as far as possible bring out at least one publication every month.

Since the Club aims at bringing Socialist literature within the reach of the widest section of people, its publications will be available to members at popular prices, generally below Re. 1/- per copy.

MEMBERSHIP OF THE CLUB

The Club will have the following categories of members:

[1] *AICC Papers* (NMML).

Foundation Members

The following will constitute the Foundation Members of the Club:

Subhas Chandra Bose.
Acharya Narendra Deva.
Jayaprakash Narayan.
M.R. Masani.
P.C. Joshi.
Rammanohar Lohia.
Mulkraj Anand.
Z.A. Ahmad.

Life Members

Any person can become a Life member on payment of Rs. 100/ as admission fee to the Club.

Ordinary Membership

Any person can become an Ordinary member on payment of Re. 1/- as admission fee to the Club.

PRIVILEGES OF MEMBERSHIP

Foundation and Life members will receive all the publications of the Club free of charge.

Ordinary members will be entitled to receive all the publications of the Club at half price (excluding postage).

The membership of an Ordinary member will lapse if he does not buy publications worth at least half the total price (for members) of the literature issued by the Club in any one year.

BOARD OF DIRECTORS

The following will constitute the Board of Directors of the Club:

Acharya Narendra Deva.
Jayaprakash Narayan.
Z.A. Ahmad.

The Board of Directors will be responsible for the general management of the Club. They will also act as editors of the literature produced by the Club.

In the event of any vacancies arising on the Board of Directors, the

Foundation Members will be empowered to elect suitable persons to fill the vacancies.

ADVISORY COUNCIL

The Club will have an Advisory Council consisting of not more than 25 members. The functions of the Council will be to advise the Board of Directors in all matters relating to the publications of the Club.

The Foundation Members will be empowered to elect suitable persons to constitute the Advisory Council.

FUNDS OF THE CLUB

The Club will be registered under Societies' Registration Act and the accounts of the Club will be audited and published every year.

All Subscriptions and letters should be sent to Dr. Z.A. Ahmad, 9 Muir Road, Allahabad.

WHY YOU SHOULD BECOME A MEMBER OF THE SOCIALIST BOOK CLUB

Because:

The Socialist Book Club will provide you with a cheap and handy Socialist Library in English and the chief Indian languages.

It will bring you the works of Marx, Engels, Lenin, and the other founders of Socialism, especially edited for Indian readers.

It will explain all aspects of the contemporary socialist movement in the world.

It will reveal the special significance and role of Socialism in India today.

It will enable you to understand the meaning of socialist construction in the Soviet Union.

It will help to convince you that Socialism alone provides the key to a solution of the Social, Economic and Political problems that face mankind today.

APPENDIX 15

Joint Statement by Jayaprakash Narayan and Swami Sahajanand Saraswati regarding the Congress Presidential Election, 27 January 1939[1]

We regret very much that there should have arisen this year such a controversy regarding the presidentship of the Congress, particularly when Mr. Subhas Chandra Bose has been persuaded to carry on his onerous duties for another year. It seems to us that rather than being made a matter for controversy, this should have been heartily welcomed by all concerned.

Mr. Bose's youth, his breadth of vision, his grasp of the world situation, his firm attitude towards the question of federation, all fit him so eminently for the high office which so many of us want him to continue to hold for another year.

We do not think that even those who do not agree with his views believe that Mr. Bose would not be an asset to the Congress presidentship at the present junction, or that Dr. Pattabhi Sitaramayya would do his job better than him. Therefore, this organized move on the part of some influential members of the Working Committee, in fact of all of those who constitute the leadership of the right wing of the Congress to shunt out in this unfortunate manner the present chief and bolster up against him the candidature of a gentleman whose name without any doubt was never before the public mind in connection with the presidentship, cannot be considered as anything less than regrettable in the extreme.

It is these leaders, who are in this manner responsible for emphasizing the difference within the Congress and not Mr. Bose who indeed has done his best to carry every section in the Congress with him. It has been suggested that there has been no controversy heretofore about the Congress presidentship. We are amazed at this statement. We have not forgotten, for instance, to give only one example, that it was Dr. Pattabhi Sitaramayya himself who only a few years back contested Pandit Jawaharlal Nehru who had nearly been coerced into standing a second time for the Faizpur presidentship.

We unhesitatingly request all delegates to the Congress to give their votes to Mr. Bose whom it would be a mistake to consider only as a candidate of the left wing and who is undoubtedly the most eminently fitted person for this high office.

[1] *Amrita Bazar Patrika*, 28 January 1939.

APPENDIX 16

G.B. Pant's Resolution at Subjects Committee Meeting, Tripuri, 9 March 1939[1]

In view of various misunderstandings that have arisen in the Congress and the country on account of the controversies in connection with the Presidential election and after, it is desirable that the Congress should clarify the position and declare its general policy. This Congress declares its firm adherence to the fundamental policies which have governed its programme in the past years under the guidance of Mahatma Gandhi, and is definitely of opinion that there should be no break in these policies and that they should continue to govern the Congress programme in future.

This Congress expresses its confidence in the work of the Working Committee, which functioned during the last year, and regrets that any aspersions should have been cast against any of its members.

In view of the critical situation that may develop during the coming year, and in view of the fact that Mahatma Gandhi alone can lead the Congress and the country to victory during such crisis, the Committee regards it as imperative that its executive should command his implicit confidence and requests the President to appoint the Working Committee in accordance with the wishes of Gandhiji.

[1] *Report of the 52nd Indian National Congress, Tripuri (Dt. Jubbulpore) Mahakoshal, 1939.*

APPENDIX 17

Resolution on National Demand, Tripuri Congress, 11 March 1939[1]

The Congress has for more than half a century striven for the advancement of the people of India and has represented the urge of the Indian people towards freedom and self-expression. During the past twenty years it has engaged itself on behalf of the masses of the country in struggle against British Imperialism, and through the suffering and disciplined sacrifice of the people, it has carried the nation a long way to the independence that is its objective. With the growing strength of the people, it has adapted itself to a changing and developing situation, and while pursuing various programmes, has ever worked for the independence of India and the establishment of a democratic state in the country. Rejecting the Government of India Act and with the full determination to end it, it decided to take advantage of the measure of provincial autonomy that the Act provided, restricted and circumscribed as it was, in order to strengthen the national movement and to give such relief to the masses as was possible under the circumstances. To the Federal part of the Act the Congress declared its uncompromising opposition and its determination to resist its imposition.

The Congress declares afresh its solemn resolve to achieve independence for the nation and to have a constitution framed for a free India through a Constituent Assembly, elected by the people on the basis of adult franchise and without any interference by a foreign authority. No other constitutions or attempted solutions of the problem can be accepted by the Indian people.

The Congress is of the opinion that in view of the situation in India, the organized strength of the national movement, the remarkable growth of consciousness of the masses, the new awakening among the people of the states, as well as the rapid development of the world situation, the principle of self-determination must now be applied to the fullest extent to India so that the people of India might establish an independent democratic state by means of a Constituent Assembly. Not only do the inherent right and dignity of the people demand this full freedom, but also the economic and other problems which press insistently on the masses, cannot find solution nor can India get rid of her poverty and keep pace with modern progress, unless her people have full opportunities of self-development and growth which independence alone can give. Provincial autonomy affords no such scope for development and its capacity for good is being rapidly exhausted; the

[1] *Report of the 52nd Indian National Congress, Tripuri (Dt. Jubbulpore) Mahakoshal, 1939.*

proposed Federation strangles India still further and will not be accepted. This Congress is therefore firmly of opinion that this whole Government of India Act must give place to a constitution of a free India made by the people themselves.

An independent and democratic India will face the solution of her great problems rapidly and effectively and will line herself with the progressive peoples of the world and thus aid the cause of democracy and freedom.

With a view to speedy realization of the Congress objective and in order to face effectively the national and international crisis that loom ahead and prepare the country for a nationwide struggle, this Congress calls upon all parts of the Congress organization, the Congress Provincial Governments and the people generally, to work to this end by promoting unity and seeking to eliminate disruptive forces and conditions which lead to communal conflicts and national disunity, by co-ordinating the activities of the Provincial Governments with the work outside the legislatures, and strengthening the organization so as to make it a still more effective organ of the people's will.

APPENDIX 18

Joint Appeal by Jayaprakash Narayan and P.C. Joshi to celebrate Communist Party Day [before 19 March 1939][1]

20th March last year saw nationwide demonstrations demanding the legalization of the Communist Party of India and calling upon the Congress Ministries to raise the matter with the Central Government which imposed the ban, and themselves declare legal the provincial organizations of the Party. We call upon our countrymen to once more celebrate the day. Every citizen must support the demand, for it is a vital matter of Civil Liberties—the right of organization. Every Congressman must be in the forefront of the agitation for a legal Communist Party would be an asset to the anti-imperialist movement. The Communist Party brings to our national movement the rich heritage of the world revolutionary movement.

Ten years ago, on 20th March, there took place countrywide arrests for the Meerut Conspiracy Case, to create the legal basis for declaring the Communist Party illegal. This year, as in the last, we must make this day the occasion to demand its legality. Every democratic organization, Congress Committee, Kisan Sabha, Trade Union, Students Federation, etc., must be drawn in. To every Indian who cares for freedom of opinion and association we appeal for support.

[1] *National Front*, 19 March 1939.

APPENDIX 19

Joint Statement by Jayaprakash Narayan and P.C. Joshi on the formation of Congress Working Committee, 17 April 1939[1]

With the meeting of the A.I.C.C. fast approaching, the fact that the Working Committee of the Congress has not yet been formed is causing great concern to all Congressmen and the country in general. We feel certain that if the A.I.C.C. meets without the Working Committee, there would be utter confusion and renewed bitterness and conflict. It is imperative, therefore, that the Working Committee is to be formed before the A.I.C.C. Delay whatever its causes may be, and certainly the President's illness and Gandhiji's pre-occupation with the Rajkot affairs are, among the main, already been regrettable particularly, in view of the critical state of affairs in Europe.

Discussions regarding the formation of the Committee had been proceeding some time now between the President and Gandhi. We feel strongly that this is a matter that cannot be settled satisfactorily through correspondence. In our humble opinion, it is necessary that the President and Mahatmaji should meet. If due to the Rajkot tangle such a meeting is not possible before the 28th, the A.I.C.C. should be postponed for a week or two as found necessary. An issue of such a momentous character should not be left to hazardous chances of correspondence.

We further feel that in the formation of the Working Committee, no irrelevant considerations should be allowed to intrude. Questions such as that raised by *ultra vires* issue and of programme for the year, etc., should not be allowed to cloud the issue.

We are glad that the *ultra vires* matter has been cleared up and as we understand, settled to Gandhiji's satisfaction. As for the programme for the year, the issue is irrelevant to the formation of the Committee. The latter cannot lay down new programme; it can only execute those laid down by the annual session of the Congress and the A.I.C.C.

Regarding the constitution of the Working Committee, while according to the Congress resolution, the latter must be formed in accordance with Gandhiji's wishes and while it must consist of men of proved integrity, ability and standing, it should in our opinion be a composite committee symbolizing the united leadership. In view of the national and international situation, this becomes doubly imperative. We hope, Gandhiji will not overlook the necessity.

[1] *Amrita Bazar Patrika*, 18 April 1939.

Finally, we hope that nothing will be allowed to happen that may put any obstacle in the way of Gandhiji's giving his advice in this matter and of the Tripuri Resolution being implemented. Any such eventuality would recreate a crisis at the A.I.C.C. which can only damage further the unity and prestige of the Congress and deflect the country's attention from the main tasks and problems facing it.

These problems clearly are how Congress and the country are to meet the war crisis that is fast overtaking Europe and Asia and that already extends from Shanghai to Gibraltar, and how to prepare in accordance with the resolve of the Tripuri Congress to strike at the root of Imperialism in India and to prepare for a nationwide struggle. The nation looks to the forthcoming sitting of the A.I.C.C. to give a concrete lead in this regard and to devise means of strengthening the Congress and maintaining and extending that national unity that it already represents and expresses. Let us endeavour so that the A.I.C.C. may fulfil the hopes of the nation.

APPENDIX 20

Joint Statement by Jayaprakash Narayan and P.C. Joshi on May Day [before 30 April 1939][1]

This year's May Day finds the Indian working class on the threshold of a new and decisive struggle. It will have to prepare itself for meeting the new offensive of wage cuts which the textile and railway bosses are preparing to launch. It will have to play its part in the nationwide attack for which the Indian people and the National Congress are preparing to assert their right to independence and self-determination.

A year of widespread economic struggles is behind it. These fights embraced an ever broadening strata of workers in backward parts and industries. For the first time workers in Bihar, Malabar, Tamilnad and in Andhra have entered into the fray. Workers in backward industries are lining up.

Unity of the central Trade Union Organization achieved a year back has given a new impetus to the struggle and organization of industrial workers throughout India. New unions are springing up in backward industries. Rival unions are closing their ranks. Unitedly the workers are beginning to fight for labour legislation and for their democratic rights.

Last year the Indian working class scored significant victories in the political arena. It showed that it was able to rally the sympathy and active cooperation of the people in general in the defence of its conditions of life and labour. The glorious building of the Congress-Labour Unity in Cawnpore, Chalisgaon, and the growing association between labour and Congress in the struggles of the jute workers in Bengal are significant landmarks.

In the gigantic upsurge of the people of the states, the workers have wholeheartedly thrown in their lot with the democratic struggles of the entire people against the brutal rule of these princely autocracies. The textile workers of Rajnandgaon and Rajkot and the railway workers of Kathiawar, 40,000 coir factory workers of Travancore have by their initiative and struggle identified themselves with the popular struggle of the 80 million people of the states for democratic rights.

These gains have to be carried forward. The base of trade union unity has to be widened and made more stable organizationally, greater political initiative and action especially in building Congress-Labour Unity, greater efforts in participating in all national political demonstrations under the Congress is the need of the hour. Only if the working class develops greater

[1] *Congress Socialist*, 30 April 1939.

political activity, and achieves Congress-Labour Unity will it be able to play its right role as the builder and initiator of the united front of the people in the coming struggle against imperialism.

The Indian working class has joined its powerful forces to the forces of democracy and freedom precisely at a moment when the people of the world are menaced by the dangers of fascist enslavement and the peace of the world is threatened by the catastrophe of a new imperialist world war.

In the words of Stalin the second imperialist war has begun. Already 500 millions of people have been drawn into its orbit from Shanghai to Gibraltar. The pro-fascist agents, henchmen of the finance capitalists in Great Britain and France are driving the fascist madmen to a war against the Soviet Union. Under the guise of the policy of "non-intervention" as in Austria, Abyssinia, Spain, Czechoslovakia, China so in the Balkan today, the Chamberlain and Daladier agents of fascism are preparing the small nations to further betray democracy and in the cause of peace and to divert the fascists of the so-called anti-comintern block against the Soviet Union.

Thus they hope to save themselves, to crush their own people at home and to destroy the Soviet Union—the Socialist Fatherland of the workers and toiling people of the whole world.

On this May Day . . . the workers of India greet and confirm their undying support to the land of completely victorious socialism, of freedom and prosperity and greatest peace. The working class of India and the whole people this day pledge their honour to defeat any imperialist-fascist war plans against the U.S.S.R.

The workers and people of India greet and confirm their undying support to the heroic people of Spain, the unconquerable people of China. The united national struggle of the people of China serves as the truest source of inspiration, as the surest guide to the whole people of India in the tactic of united national front. In the successes of Chinese people the people of India see a vindication of their own historic struggle.

War clouds are gathering fast, British imperialism is preparing to snatch the resources of Indian people once again, for its murderous war designs. Consistent with its support to the fascists abroad, British imperialism inspires the reactionary forces of princely autocracy to disrupt the struggle of the people of the states, goads the police and bureaucracy in the Congress provinces to shoot, lathi charge and break up workers, peasants and democratic movements to prevent the unification of the parliamentary and extra-parliamentary mass struggles. Black reaction inspires communal programmes to cut across national unity and harmony.

Within the National Front disruption grows apace. The ever increasing national unity in the years since Lucknow is being vitally threatened. The remarkable unity in the ranks of the Left displayed at Tripuri is in danger.

For some time past disruption from the Right in the form of catch word and in the tread towards constitutionalism, in the form of drift and avoidance of nationwide mass struggle leading eventually to capitulation has endangered the common front. Now we are face to face with the threat of disruption from a section of left in the form of the slogan of "alternative leadership".

The Tripuri resolution gave the slogan for nationwide struggle against imperialism and for the enforcement of National Demand for Independence. To implement that resolution we require all round unity—above all Socialist-Communist Unity—the bedrock of Left unity and the main lever of the United National Front.

May Day 1939 places the heaviest responsibility on the shoulders of the working class and of the entire Left to maintain trade union and political unity in its own ranks, to consolidate its own gain and those of the entire nation to be able to function more effectively, in the coming battle, to come forward as the unifier of the people. To fulfil these tasks first necessity is Socialist unity. The entire experience of the working class of the world which is our own experience inescapably lead us to this single conclusion:

MAINTAIN TRADE UNION AND KISAN UNITY;
ALL INTO THE MAZDOOR AND KISAN SABHA;
FOR A MINIMUM LIVING WAGE;
LEAVE WITH PAY;
RECOGNITION OF UNIONS;
IMPLEMENT FAIZPUR PROGRAMME FOR KISANS;
SAVE NATIONAL UNITY—CONGRESS ABOVE ALL;
NO QUARTER TO DISRUPTION FROM THE RIGHT OR THE LEFT;
BUILD SOCIALIST COMMUNIST UNITY & FORWARD TO LEFT UNITY;
FOR UNITED NATIONWIDE STRUGGLE;
LONG LIVE THE CONGRESS.

APPENDIX 21

Joint Statement by Jayaprakash Narayan and P.C. Joshi on the Forward Bloc and Left Unity, 7 June 1939[1]

A stalemate continues in our struggle for freedom since Tripuri. Calcutta has only worsened the situation. The crisis in the national leadership has deepened. The Tripuri resolution which gave the call for a nationwide struggle remains a dead letter. Rajkot has cast a gloom over the states' people's struggle. On the other hand, imperialism and the forces of reaction are on the offensive. Witness for instance the recent amendment of the Government of India Act, the war preparations of imperialism in India, the Indo-British Pact forced upon the country in the teeth of unanimous national opposition and the all too frequent communal riots. This is where the policy of drift unfortunately persisted in by the old leadership and the tragic events of the past few months have led us. The task of every Congressman, irrespective of labels, and of every Congress organization is clear. We make bold to say so in spite of the utter confusion that prevails. Congress policy itself is definite and unambiguous. In view of this definite policy it is the task of every Congressman and every Congress organization to undertake immediately active resistance to all war plans and activities in India and to prepare the Congress and the country for the impending struggle. The Tripuri resolution on the national demand must be converted from a dead letter into a powerful lever for moving the whole nation onward to its declared goal. The present stalemate must be ended. All Congressmen who agree with this view must join hands, not in opposition to the others, but in order to give effect to this policy.

The important question is how may all such Congressmen join hands and be able to co-ordinate their activities. Clearly, among them will be people who hold different political views, who belong to different political groupings and parties. All these come together on the platform of the Congress. They may not be willing to do so on any other platform. Yet, it is essential, if the next step forward has to be taken, for them all to pool their efforts and unify their policies.

Attempts are being made to accomplish this task in exclusive and sectarian ways. That, to our mind, would only result in an end just the contrary of what we desire. While such a consolidation of what, for want of a better word, may be termed the Left forces in the Congress is an urgent need of

[1] *Searchlight*, 9 June 1939.

the hour, we must be careful that an ill-conceived attempt at it does not result in creating new barriers within these forces or lead to a factional conflict between them and the other forces in the national movement.

We feel constrained to say that the present move for the formation of a Forward Bloc would not lead to such a consolidation as we desire. This consolidation cannot be conceived of as an opposition party to those in power. The Congress is not a parliament where opposing parties must try to oust one another from power. It is a front the unity of which must not be impaired. In our opinion a consolidation of the Left forces must be based on the voluntary co-operation and co-ordination of all the Left groups, parties and individuals and on a common and united programme and policy, jointly discussed and evolved. Further, the policies of such a consolidation should aim at embracing and drawing together as wide section of the Congress as possible, and ultimately of moving the whole Congress onward to a struggle. The Forward Bloc does not fulfil these conditions, nor the manner in which it is being organized conduces to the kind of consolidation we have in mind.

We, therefore, suggest that as a first step towards such a consolidation a consultative conference should be called at the time of the forthcoming meeting of the A.I.C.C. in Bombay of representatives of all the existing Left groups and all such Congressmen as agree with the two-fold aim of preparing for a nationwide struggle and resisting the war measures of imperialism. The purpose of this conference shall be to devise a machinery for Left consolidation and to arrive at a common policy and programme of work.

Two questions remain: First, what should be the machinery of consolidation and, second, what should its policy and programme be?

Regarding the latter, we believe that the policy must be non-sectarian and non-factional. That is to say, it must aim at maintaining the unity of the Congress and at achieving a united leadership that would move the entire forces of the nation against imperialism. It should make it clear that what is aimed at is not an anti-Right bloc but united working of all the forces within the Congress which are opposed to constitutionalism and the policy of drift and which stand for concrete and immediate preparation for struggle and resistance to war in a manner that would succeed ultimately in moving the entire Congress. The programme of the consolidation should include the implementing of the National Demand and anti-War and anti-fascist resolutions of the Congress, development of the States' people's struggle as part of the fight against Federation, pressure to secure the implementing of the Congress election programme, cooperation with the struggle and organization of the workers and peasants, fight against communal reaction. Finally, the programme must include as one of its most important items and the democratization of the Congress, elimination of corruption and opportunism from it and the counteracting of the tendency in certain quarters to disrupt it by driving out the socialists and communists.

As for the machinery or the organizational form of the Left consolidation, it must be such that it does not result in the formation of a rigid organization or a new party. It should make possible effective and expeditious co-operation of all the Left forces without in any way preventing their independent functioning and curtailing their initiative. Its decisions must be based on agreement and not on counting of votes. We, therefore, suggest that at the conference which we have proposed an All India Left Co-ordination Committee should be formed with representatives from each of the existing Left groups and parties and a certain number of prominent Congressmen who agree with the objects of the consolidation. The Committee shall enrol no members and shall have no provincial and district branches.

In the end we appeal to all those who agree with our aims to co-operate in preventing split and disruption and in laying a foundation for the largest possible mobilization of the pro-struggle forces inside the Congress and ultimately for leading the whole Congress to struggle. Only positive political initiation and action can succeed in achieving this end. Let us therefore, concentrate our energies on it in a co-ordinated and united manner.

Onward to struggle, comrades.

INDEX